Natsume's BOOK of FRIENDS

Shojo Beat

Natsume's BOOK of FRIENDS

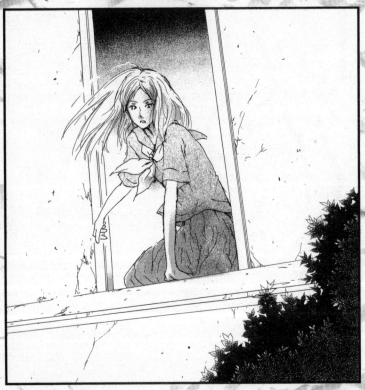

STORY *and* **ART** *by*
Yuki Midorikawa

VOLUME **16**

Natsume's BOOK of FRIENDS

VOLUME 16 CONTENTS

Chapter 64 —— 5

Chapter 65 —— 36

Chapter 66 —— 77

Chapter 67 —— 109

Special Episode 14
Out of Season Blossoms
—— 141

Afterword —— 181

End Notes —— 185

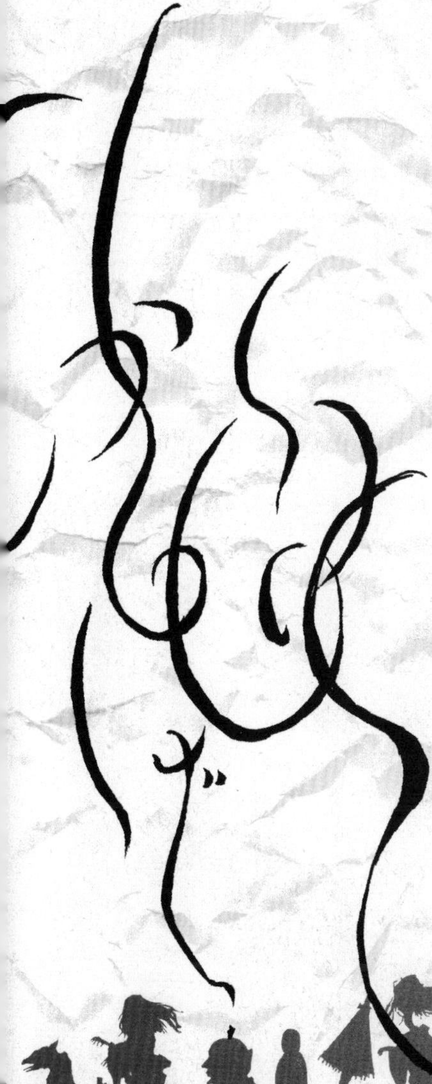

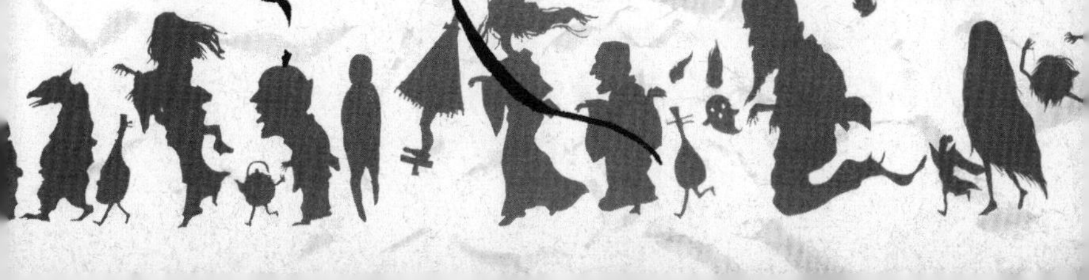

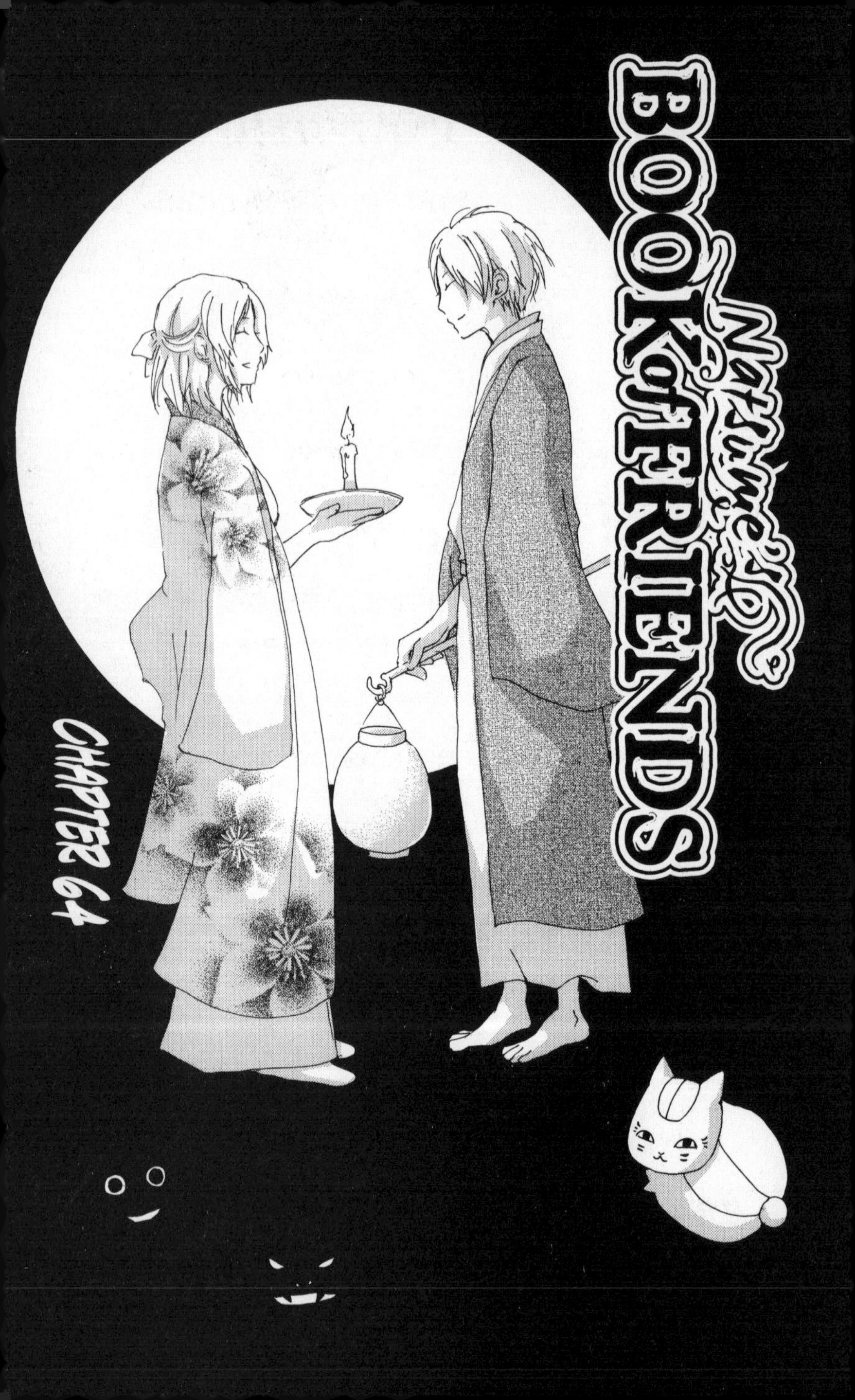
Natsume's BOOK of FRIENDS
CHAPTER 64

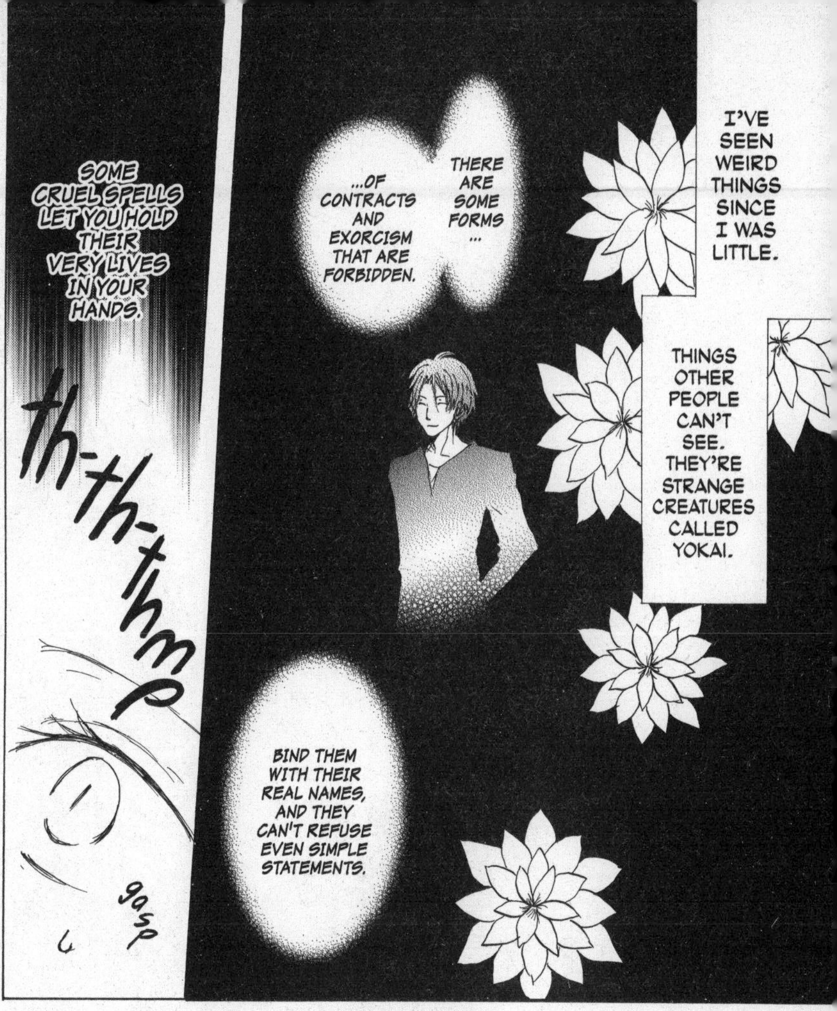
I'VE SEEN WEIRD THINGS SINCE I WAS LITTLE.
THINGS OTHER PEOPLE CAN'T SEE. THEY'RE STRANGE CREATURES CALLED YOKAI.
THERE ARE SOME FORMS ...
...OF CONTRACTS AND EXORCISM THAT ARE FORBIDDEN.
BIND THEM WITH THEIR REAL NAMES, AND THEY CAN'T REFUSE EVEN SIMPLE STATEMENTS.
SOME CRUEL SPELLS LET YOU HOLD THEIR VERY LIVES IN YOUR HANDS.
th-th-thump
gasp

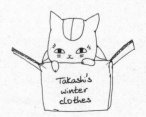

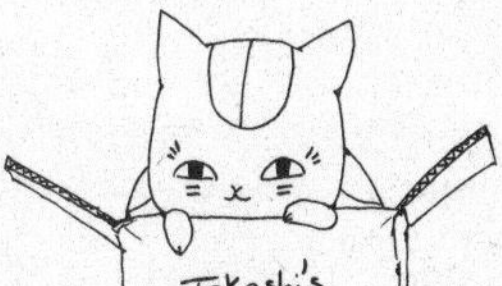
Takashi's winter clothes

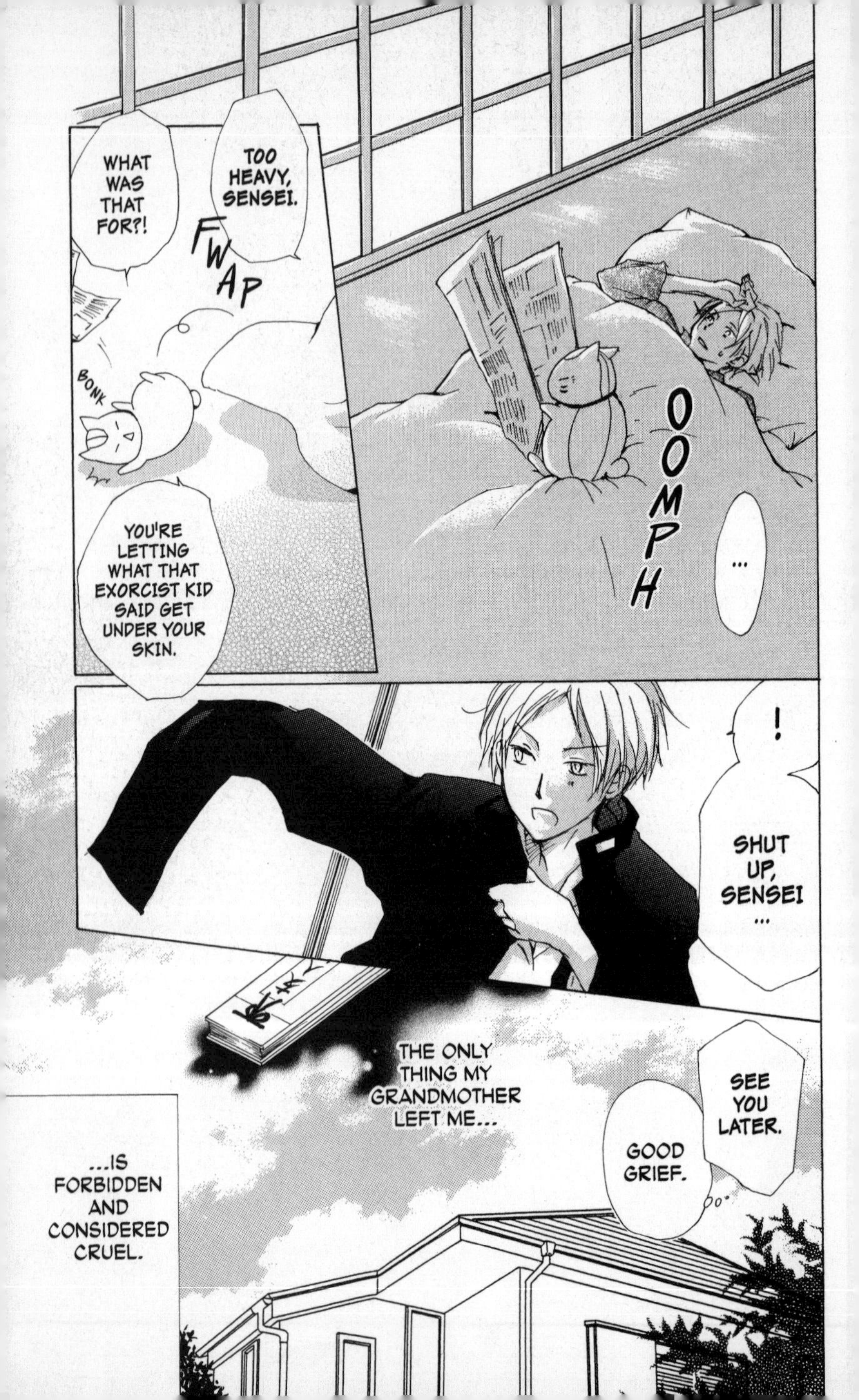
...
OOMPH
TOO HEAVY, SENSEI.
WHAT WAS THAT FOR?!
FWAP
BONK
YOU'RE LETTING WHAT THAT EXORCIST KID SAID GET UNDER YOUR SKIN.
!
SHUT UP, SENSEI ...
SEE YOU LATER.
GOOD GRIEF.
THE ONLY THING MY GRANDMOTHER LEFT ME...
...IS FORBIDDEN AND CONSIDERED CRUEL.

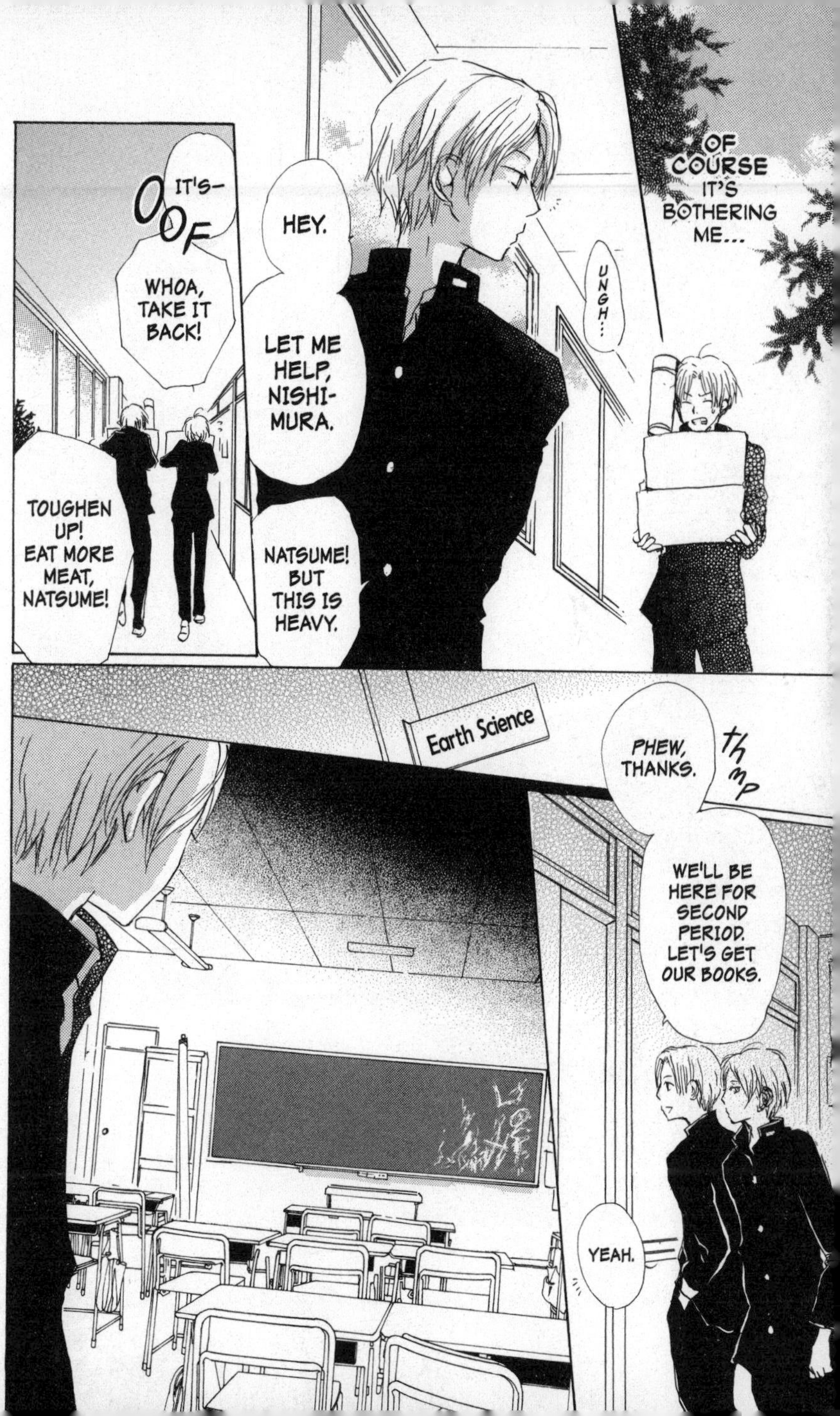
OF COURSE IT'S BOTHERING ME...
UNGH...
HEY.
LET ME HELP, NISHIMURA.
NATSUME! BUT THIS IS HEAVY.
IT'S—
OOF
WHOA, TAKE IT BACK!
TOUGHEN UP! EAT MORE MEAT, NATSUME!
Earth Science
PHEW, THANKS.
thmp
WE'LL BE HERE FOR SECOND PERIOD. LET'S GET OUR BOOKS.
YEAH.

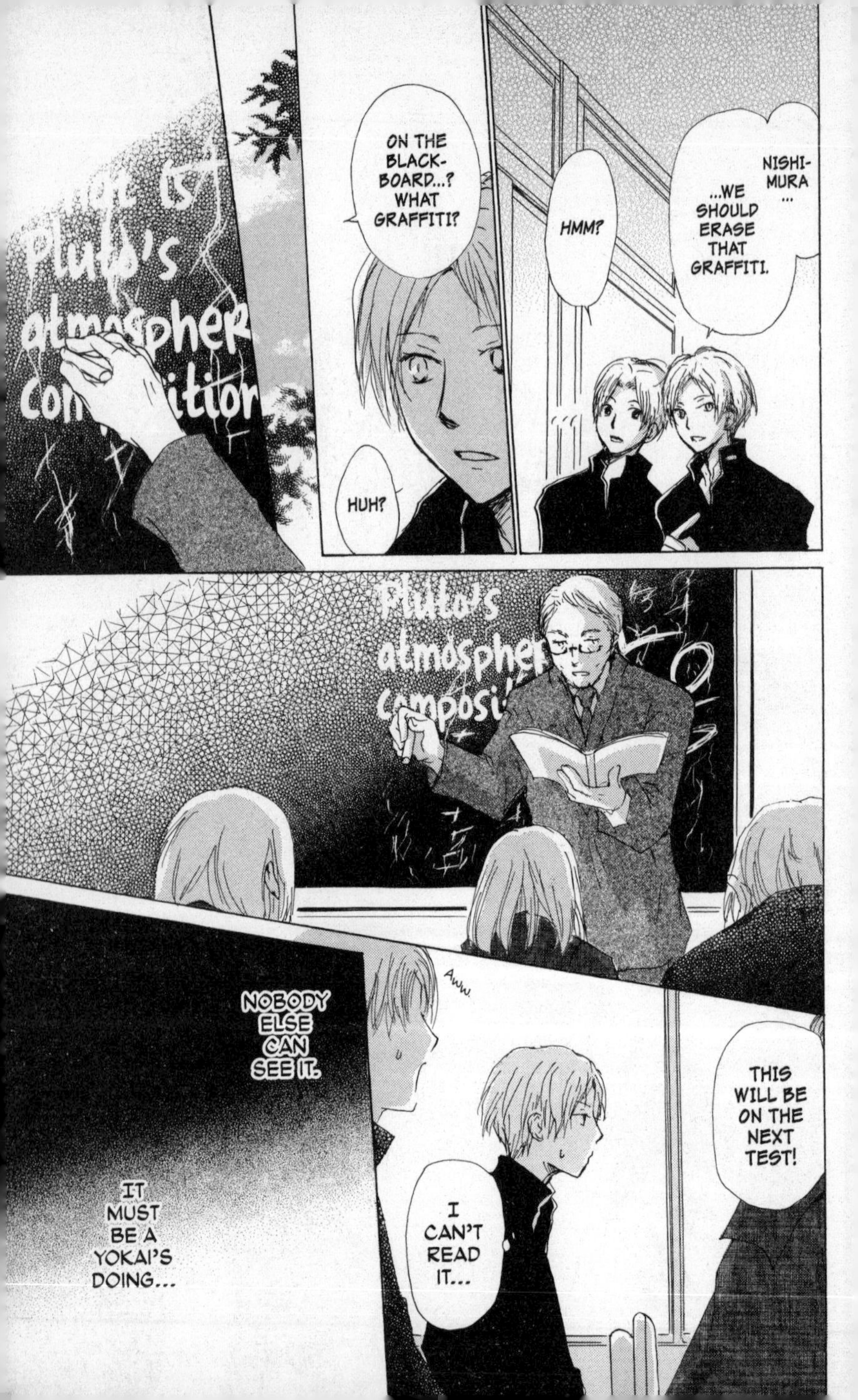
NISHIMURA...
...WE SHOULD ERASE THAT GRAFFITI.
HMM?
ON THE BLACKBOARD...? WHAT GRAFFITI?
HUH?
AWW.
THIS WILL BE ON THE NEXT TEST!
I CAN'T READ IT...
NOBODY ELSE CAN SEE IT.
IT MUST BE A YOKAI'S DOING...

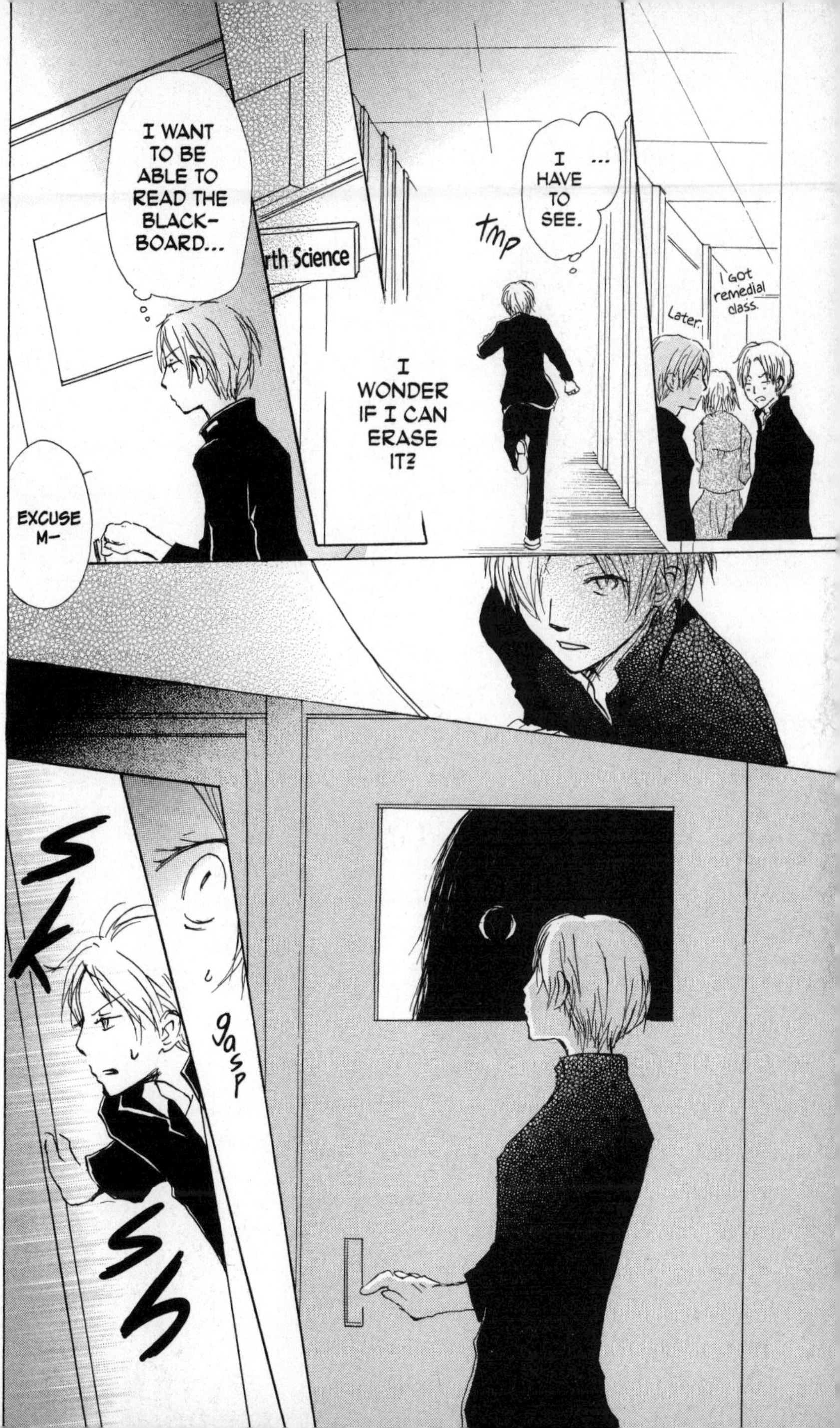
I got remedial class.
Later.
I ... have to see.
xmp
I wonder if I can erase it?
I want to be able to read the blackboard...
rth Science
Excuse m-
gasp
SK
SSS

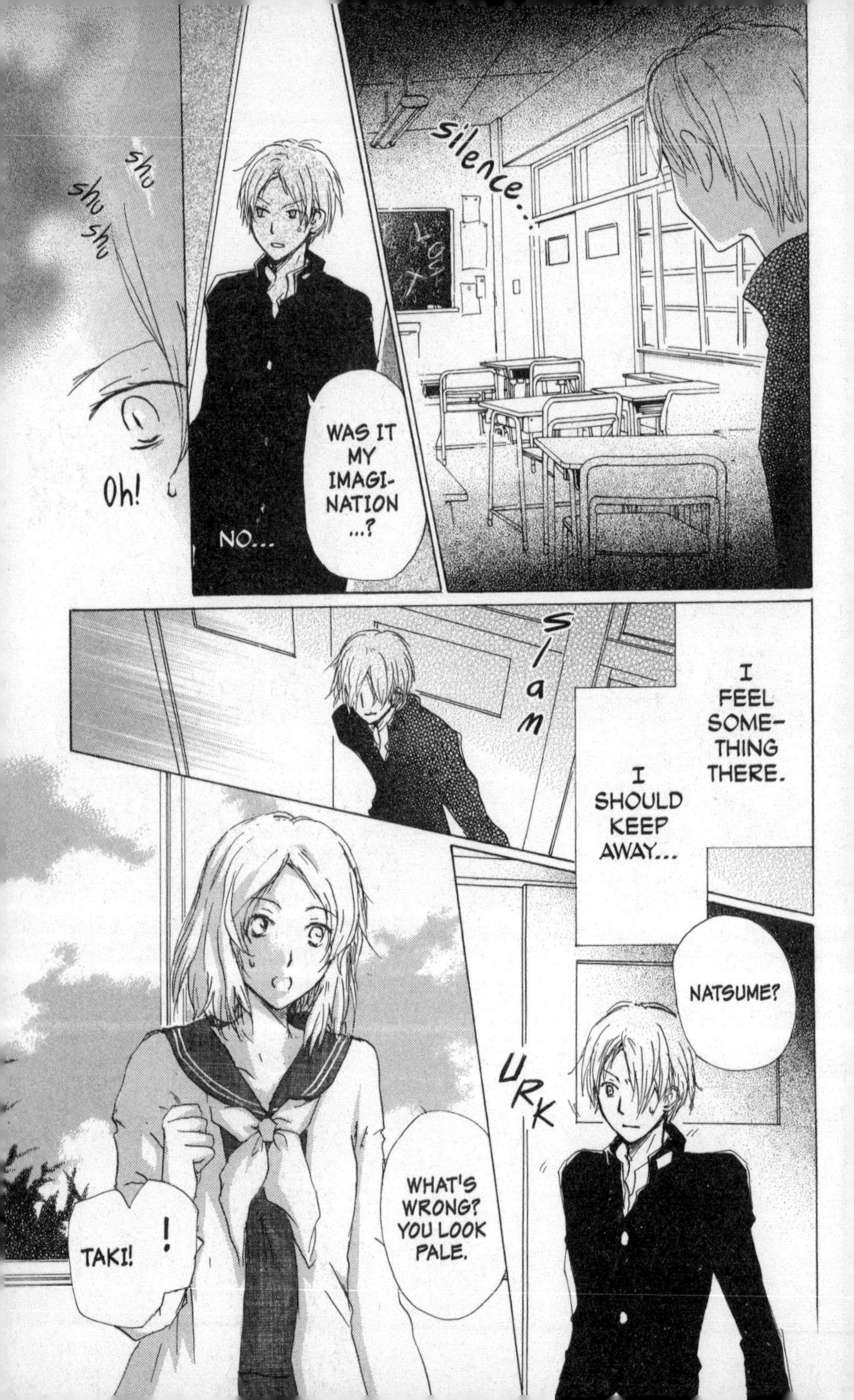
silence...
WAS IT MY IMAGINATION ...?
NO...
shu shu shu
Oh!
slam
I FEEL SOMETHING THERE.
I SHOULD KEEP AWAY...
NATSUME?
URK
WHAT'S WRONG? YOU LOOK PALE.
!
TAKI!

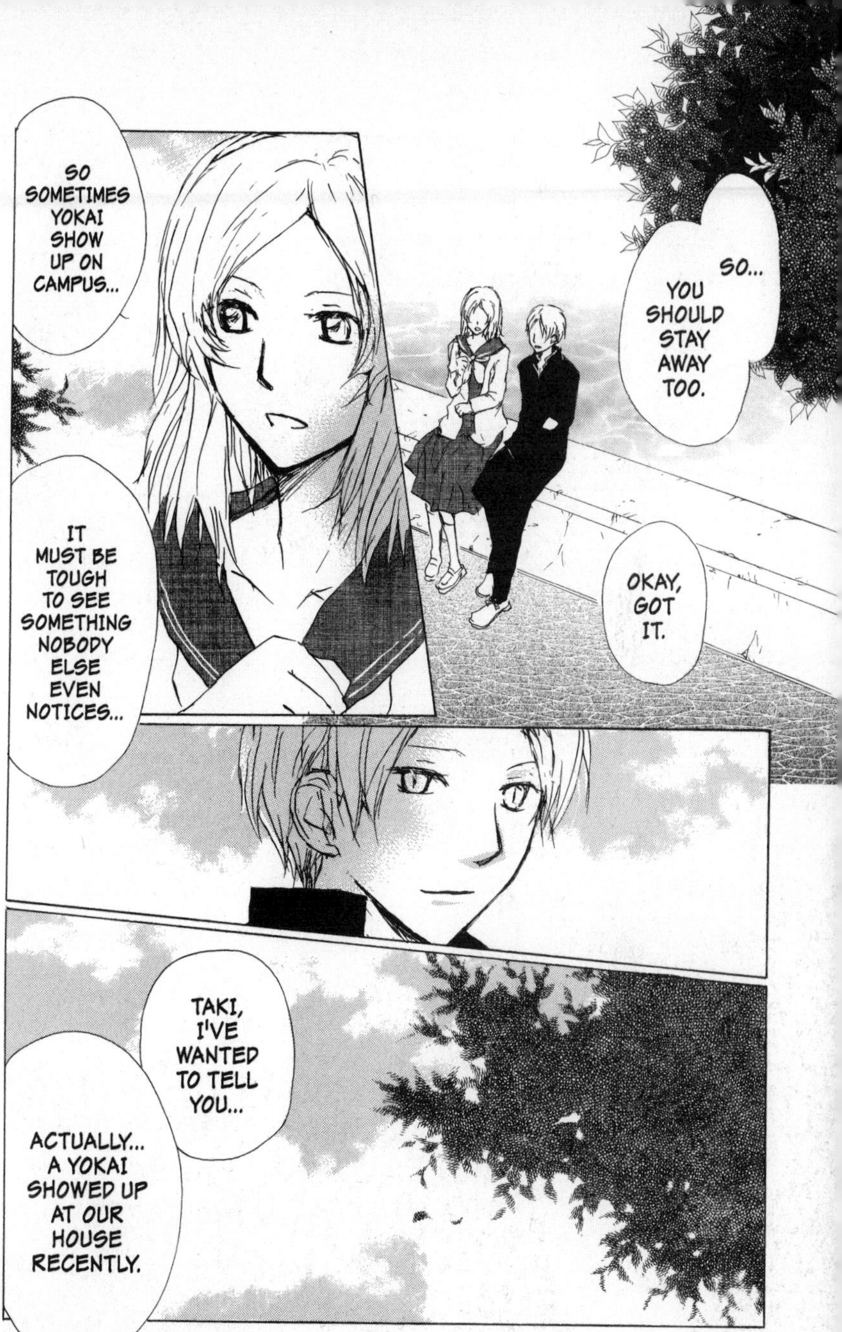
SO... YOU SHOULD STAY AWAY TOO.
OKAY, GOT IT.
SO SOMETIMES YOKAI SHOW UP ON CAMPUS...
IT MUST BE TOUGH TO SEE SOMETHING NOBODY ELSE EVEN NOTICES...
TAKI, I'VE WANTED TO TELL YOU...
ACTUALLY... A YOKAI SHOWED UP AT OUR HOUSE RECENTLY.

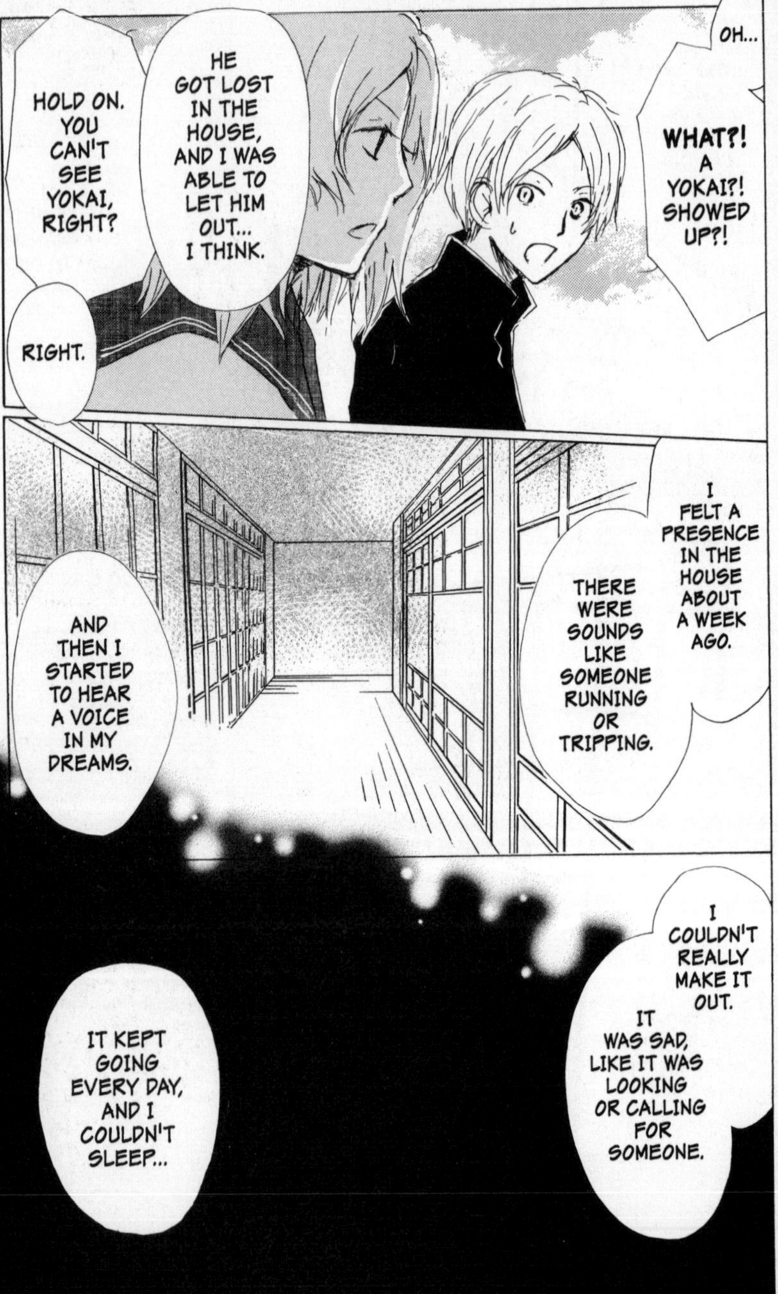
OH...
WHAT?! A YOKAI?! SHOWED UP?!
HE GOT LOST IN THE HOUSE, AND I WAS ABLE TO LET HIM OUT... I THINK.
HOLD ON. YOU CAN'T SEE YOKAI, RIGHT?
RIGHT.
I FELT A PRESENCE IN THE HOUSE ABOUT A WEEK AGO.
THERE WERE SOUNDS LIKE SOMEONE RUNNING OR TRIPPING.
AND THEN I STARTED TO HEAR A VOICE IN MY DREAMS.
I COULDN'T REALLY MAKE IT OUT.
IT WAS SAD, LIKE IT WAS LOOKING OR CALLING FOR SOMEONE.
IT KEPT GOING EVERY DAY, AND I COULDN'T SLEEP...

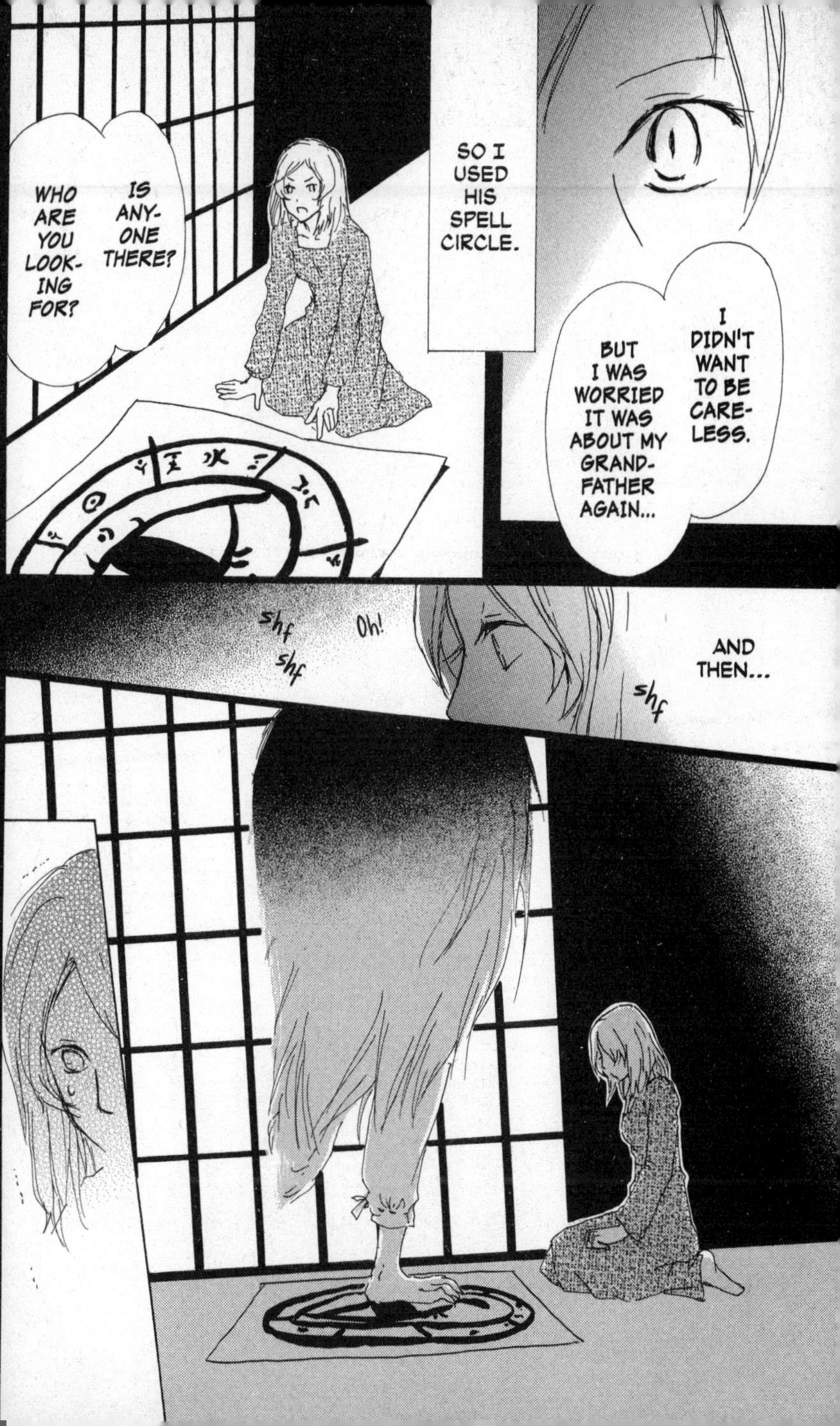
I DIDN'T WANT TO BE CARELESS.
BUT I WAS WORRIED IT WAS ABOUT MY GRANDFATHER AGAIN...
SO I USED HIS SPELL CIRCLE.
IS ANYONE THERE?
WHO ARE YOU LOOKING FOR?
AND THEN...
shf
Oh!
shf
shf
...

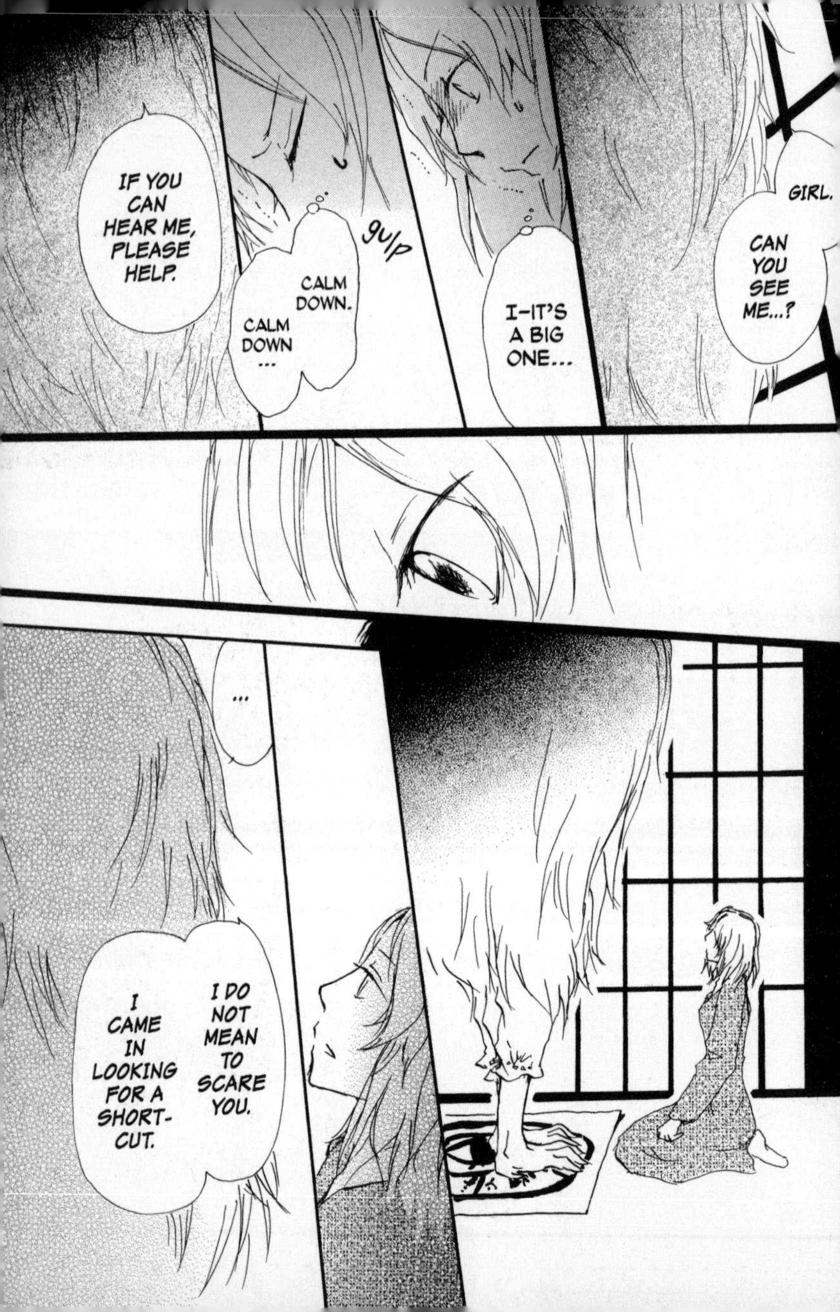
GIRL.
CAN YOU SEE ME...?
I-IT'S A BIG ONE...
gulp
CALM DOWN.
CALM DOWN...
IF YOU CAN HEAR ME, PLEASE HELP.
...
I DO NOT MEAN TO SCARE YOU.
I CAME IN LOOKING FOR A SHORT-CUT.

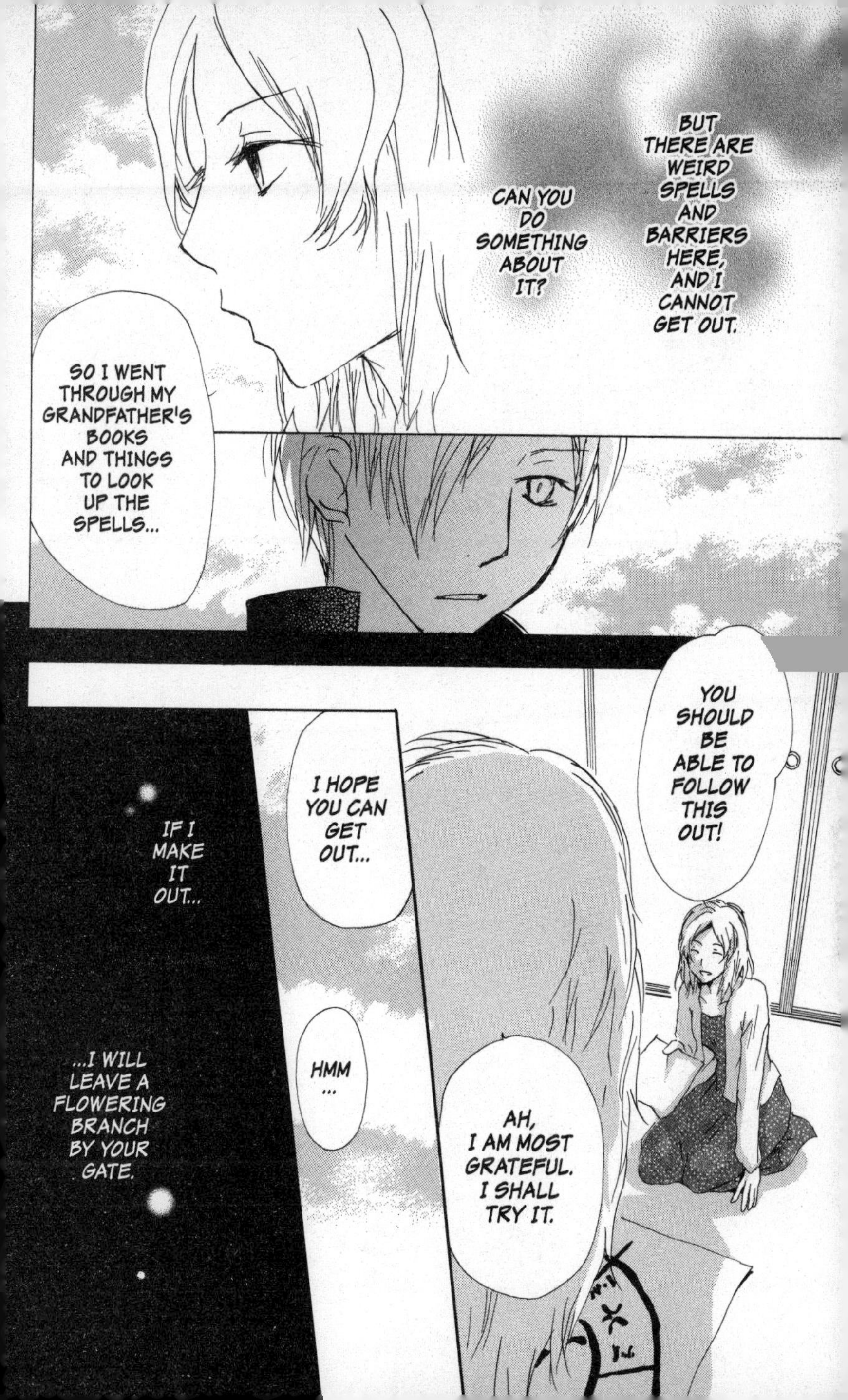
BUT THERE ARE WEIRD SPELLS AND BARRIERS HERE, AND I CANNOT GET OUT.
CAN YOU DO SOMETHING ABOUT IT?
SO I WENT THROUGH MY GRANDFATHER'S BOOKS AND THINGS TO LOOK UP THE SPELLS...
YOU SHOULD BE ABLE TO FOLLOW THIS OUT!
I HOPE YOU CAN GET OUT...
AH, I AM MOST GRATEFUL. I SHALL TRY IT.
HMM...
IF I MAKE IT OUT...
...I WILL LEAVE A FLOWERING BRANCH BY YOUR GATE.

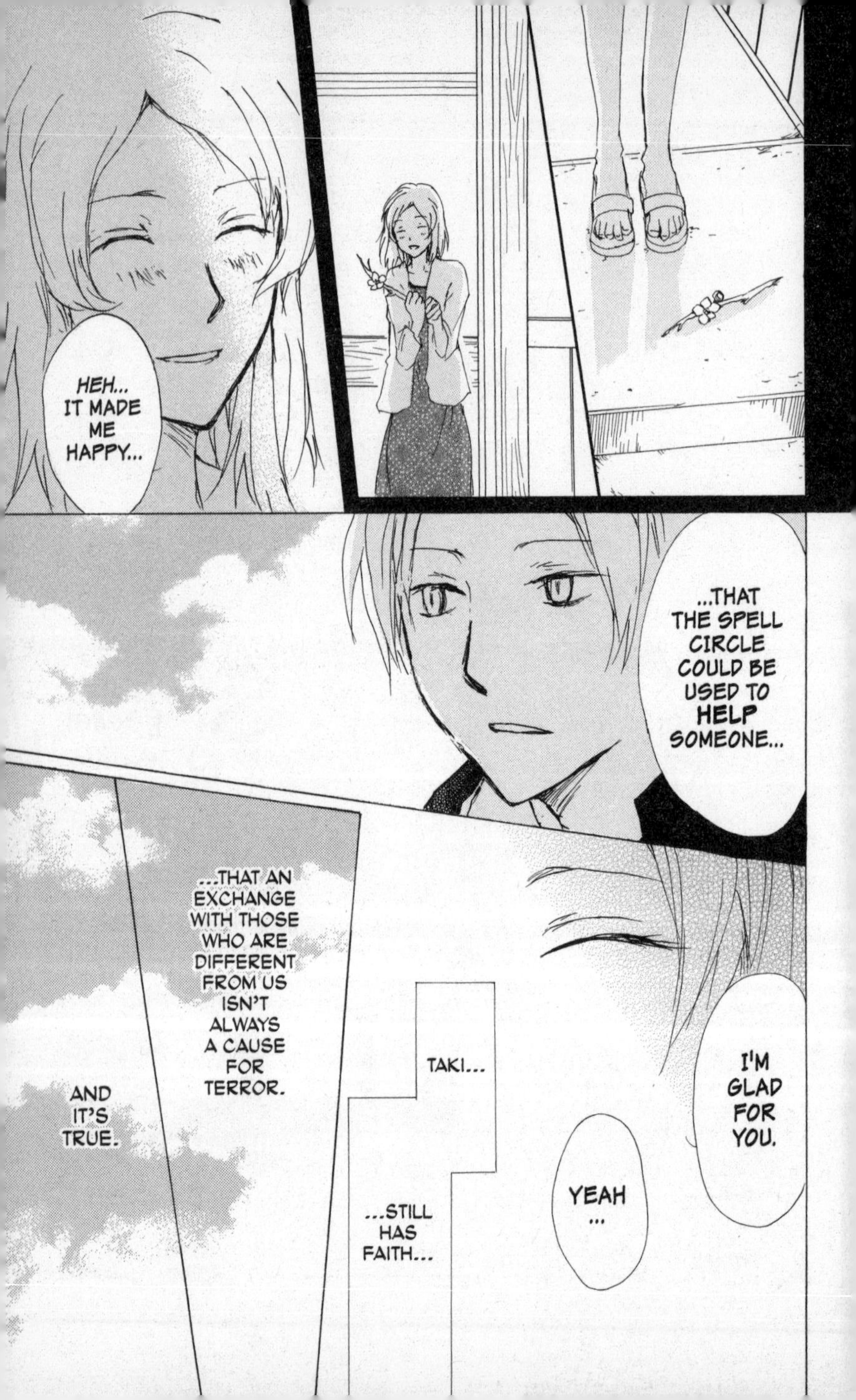
HEH... IT MADE ME HAPPY...
...THAT THE SPELL CIRCLE COULD BE USED TO HELP SOMEONE...
I'M GLAD FOR YOU.
YEAH ...
TAKI...
...STILL HAS FAITH...
...THAT AN EXCHANGE WITH THOSE WHO ARE DIFFERENT FROM US ISN'T ALWAYS A CAUSE FOR TERROR.
AND IT'S TRUE.

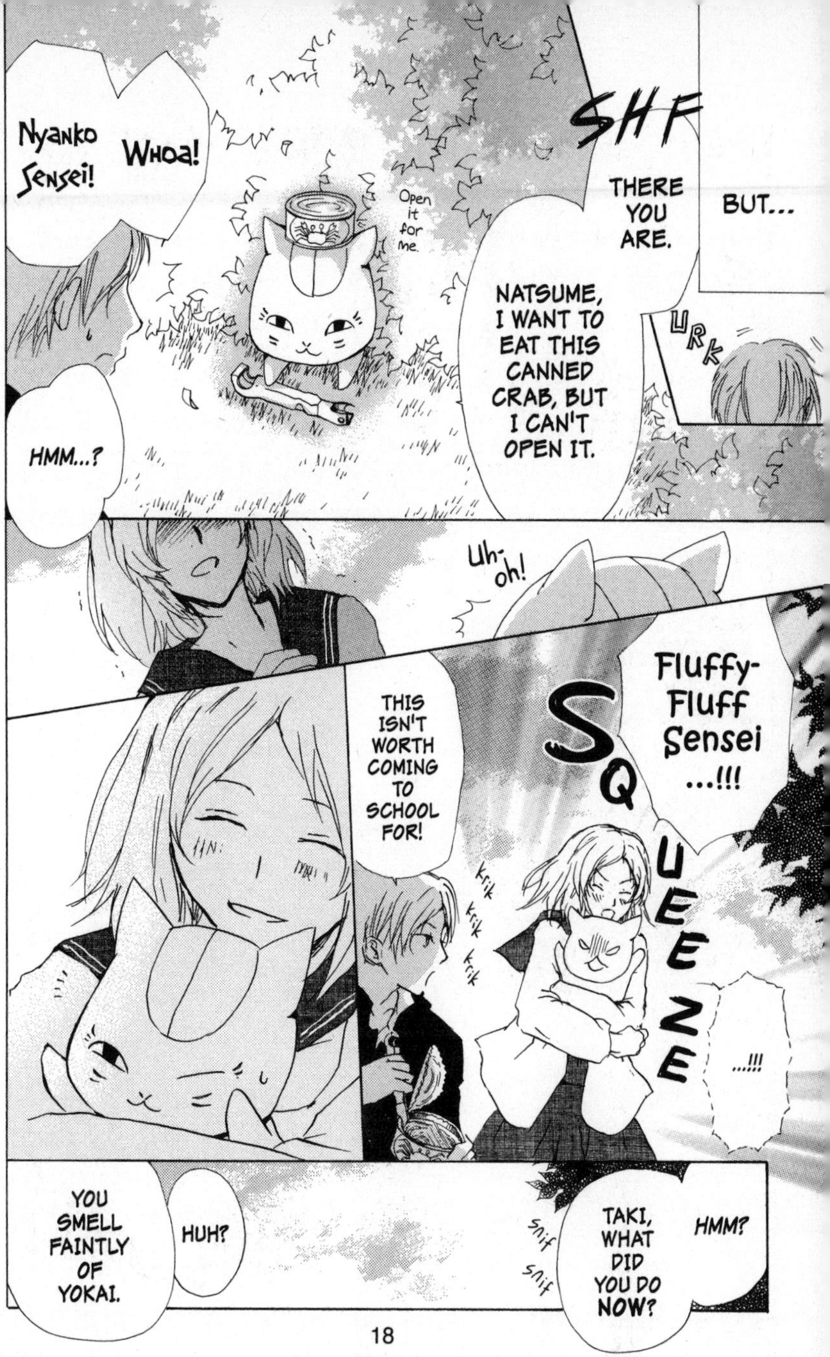
BUT...
URK
SHF
THERE YOU ARE.
NATSUME, I WANT TO EAT THIS CANNED CRAB, BUT I CAN'T OPEN IT.
Open it for me.
Whoa!
Nyanko Sensei!
HMM...?
Uh-oh!
Fluffy-Fluff Sensei ...!!!
SQUEEZE
...!!!
krik krik krik
THIS ISN'T WORTH COMING TO SCHOOL FOR!
HMM?
TAKI, WHAT DID YOU DO NOW?
Snif Snif
HUH?
YOU SMELL FAINTLY OF YOKAI.

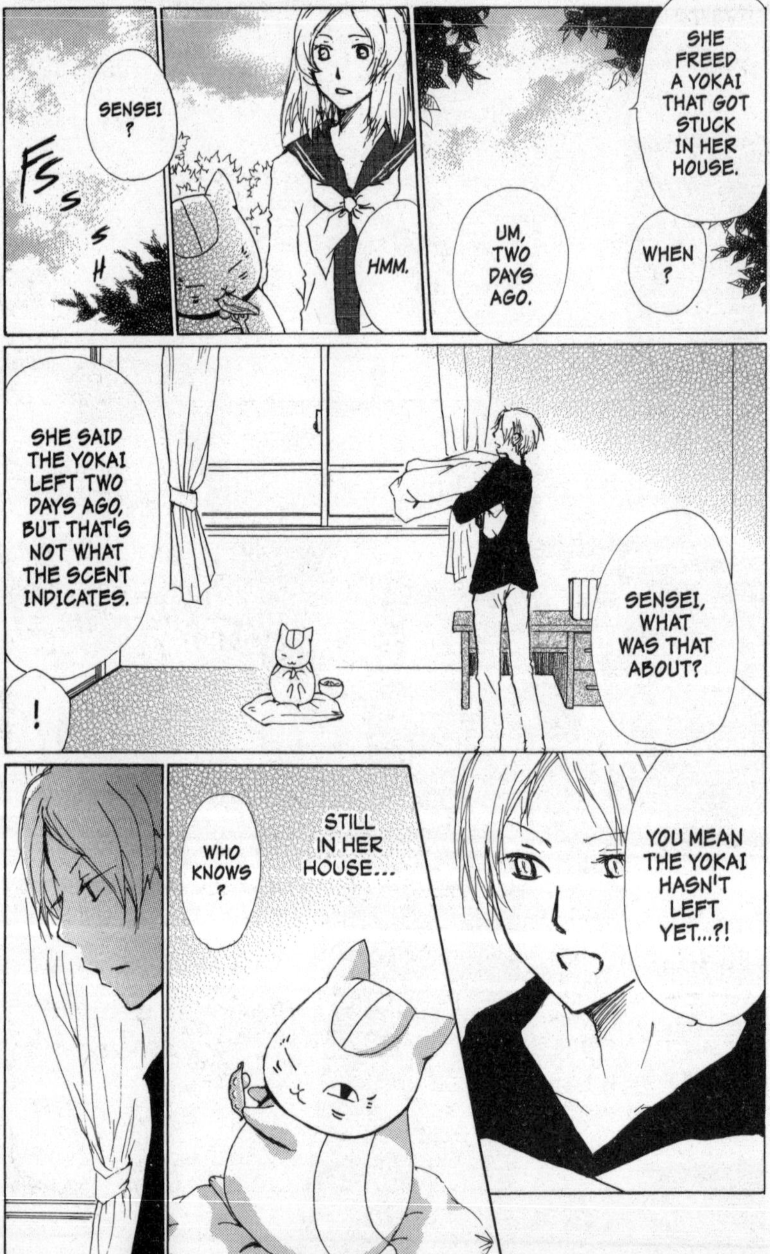
SHE FREED A YOKAI THAT GOT STUCK IN HER HOUSE.
WHEN?
UM, TWO DAYS AGO.
HMM.
SENSEI?
FSSSH
SENSEI, WHAT WAS THAT ABOUT?
SHE SAID THE YOKAI LEFT TWO DAYS AGO, BUT THAT'S NOT WHAT THE SCENT INDICATES.
!
YOU MEAN THE YOKAI HASN'T LEFT YET...?!
STILL IN HER HOUSE...
WHO KNOWS?

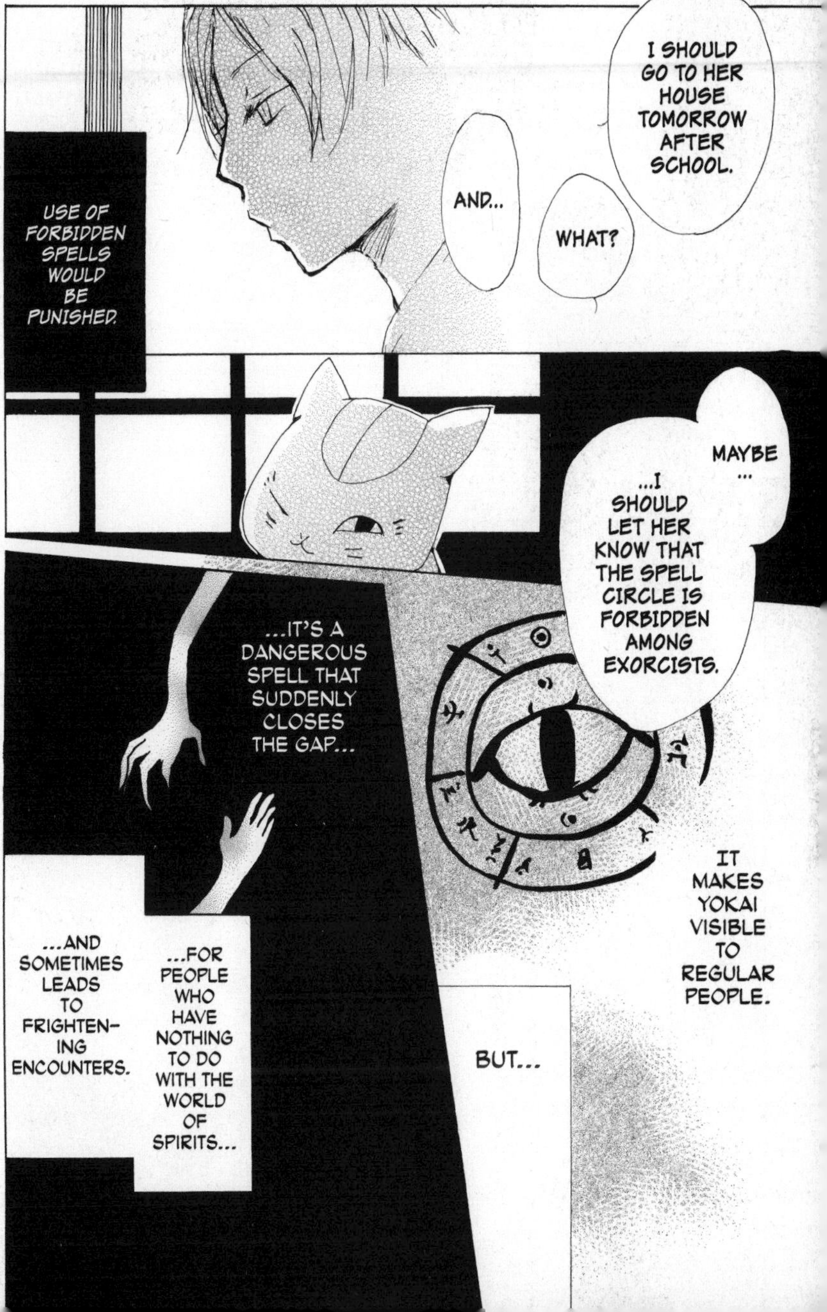
I SHOULD GO TO HER HOUSE TOMORROW AFTER SCHOOL.
AND...
WHAT?
MAYBE...
...I SHOULD LET HER KNOW THAT THE SPELL CIRCLE IS FORBIDDEN AMONG EXORCISTS.
USE OF FORBIDDEN SPELLS WOULD BE PUNISHED.
IT MAKES YOKAI VISIBLE TO REGULAR PEOPLE.
BUT...
...IT'S A DANGEROUS SPELL THAT SUDDENLY CLOSES THE GAP...
...FOR PEOPLE WHO HAVE NOTHING TO DO WITH THE WORLD OF SPIRITS...
...AND SOMETIMES LEADS TO FRIGHTENING ENCOUNTERS.

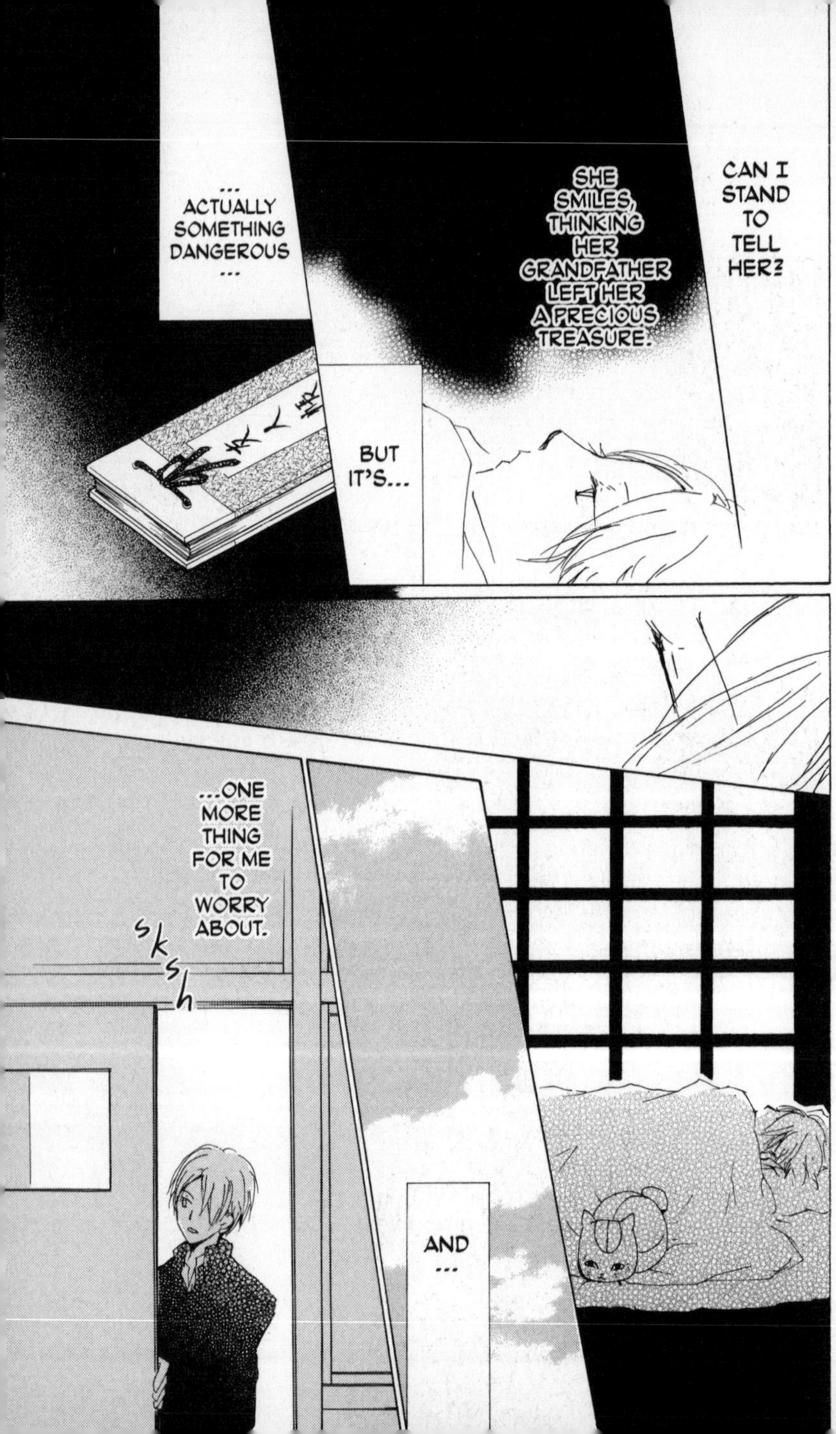
CAN I STAND TO TELL HER?
SHE SMILES, THINKING HER GRANDFATHER LEFT HER A PRECIOUS TREASURE.
BUT IT'S...
...ACTUALLY SOMETHING DANGEROUS...
AND...
...ONE MORE THING FOR ME TO WORRY ABOUT.
sksh

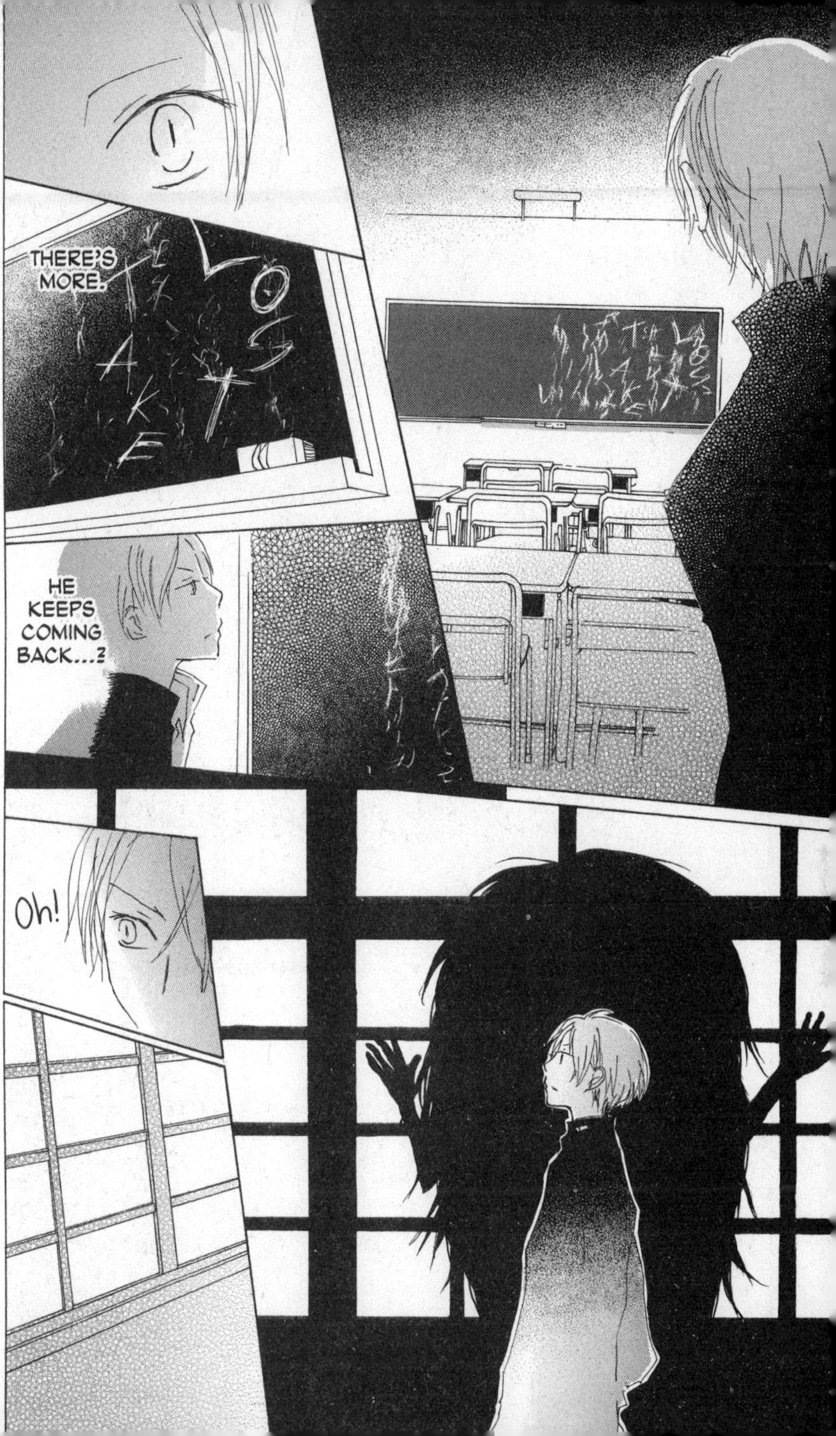
THERE'S MORE.
HE KEEPS COMING BACK...?
Oh!

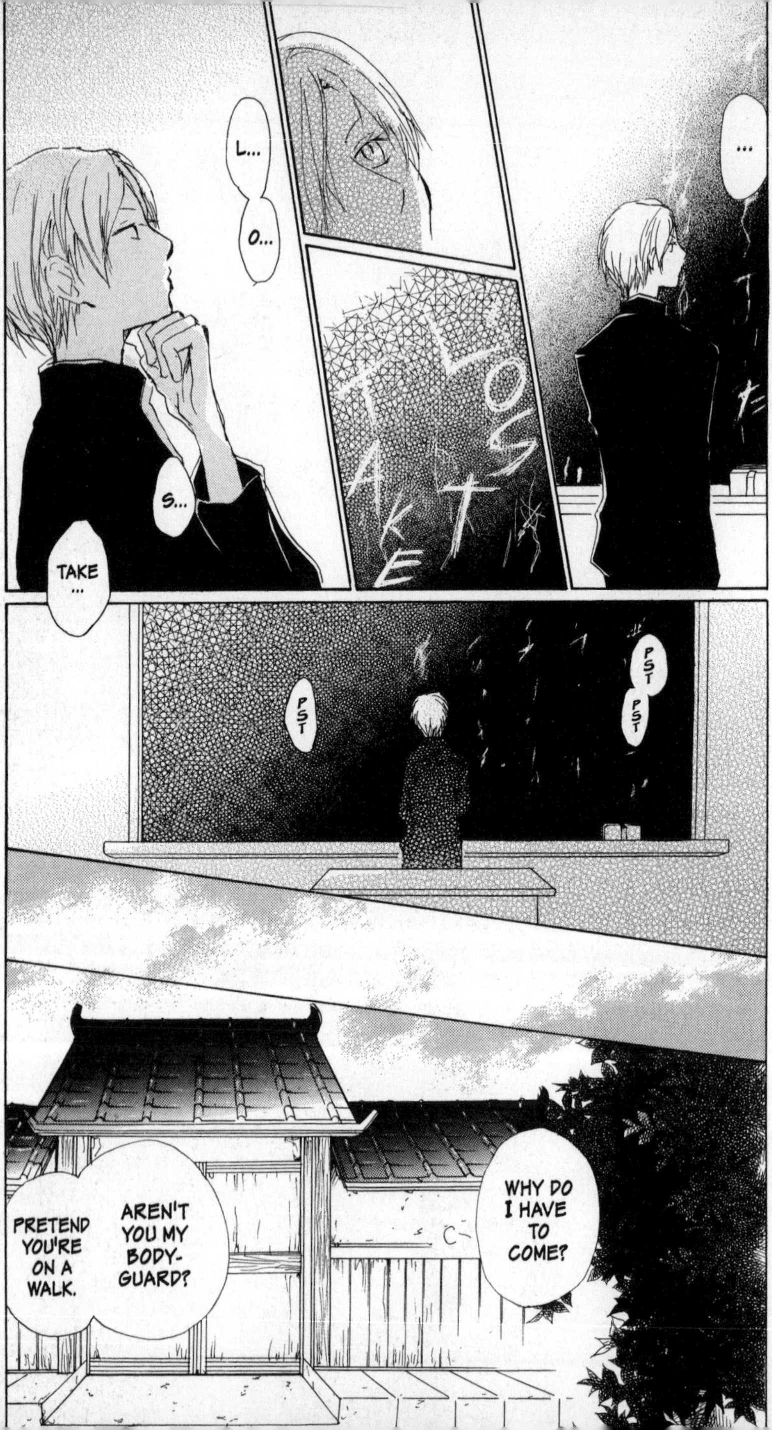
...
L...
O...
LOST
TAKE
S...
TAKE ...
PST
PST
PST
WHY DO I HAVE TO COME?
AREN'T YOU MY BODY-GUARD?
PRETEND YOU'RE ON A WALK.

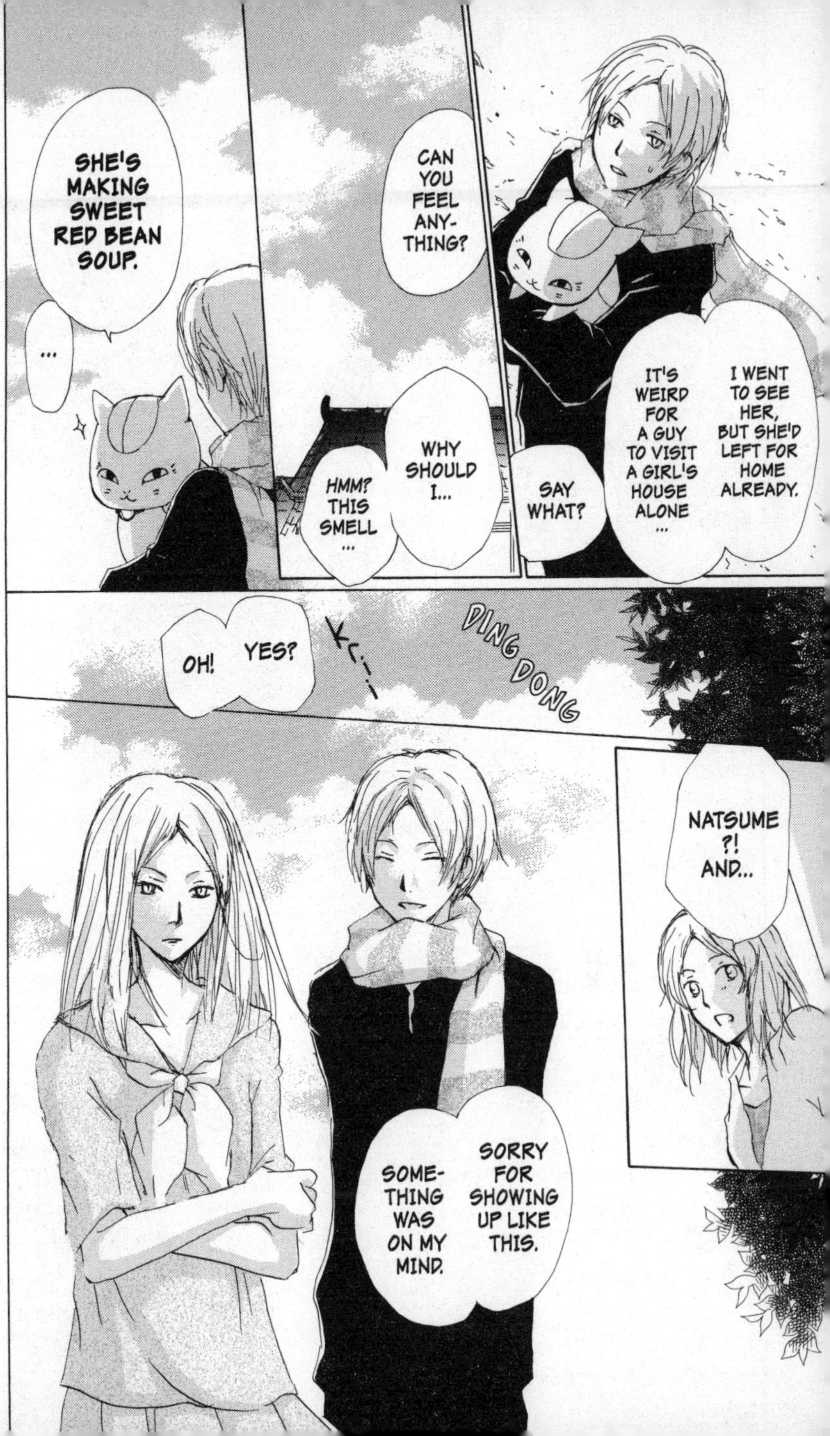
I WENT TO SEE HER, BUT SHE'D LEFT FOR HOME ALREADY.
IT'S WEIRD FOR A GUY TO VISIT A GIRL'S HOUSE ALONE...
SAY WHAT?
CAN YOU FEEL ANY-THING?
WHY SHOULD I...
HMM? THIS SMELL...
SHE'S MAKING SWEET RED BEAN SOUP.
...
DING DONG
YES?
OH!
NATSUME ?! AND...
SORRY FOR SHOWING UP LIKE THIS.
SOME-THING WAS ON MY MIND.

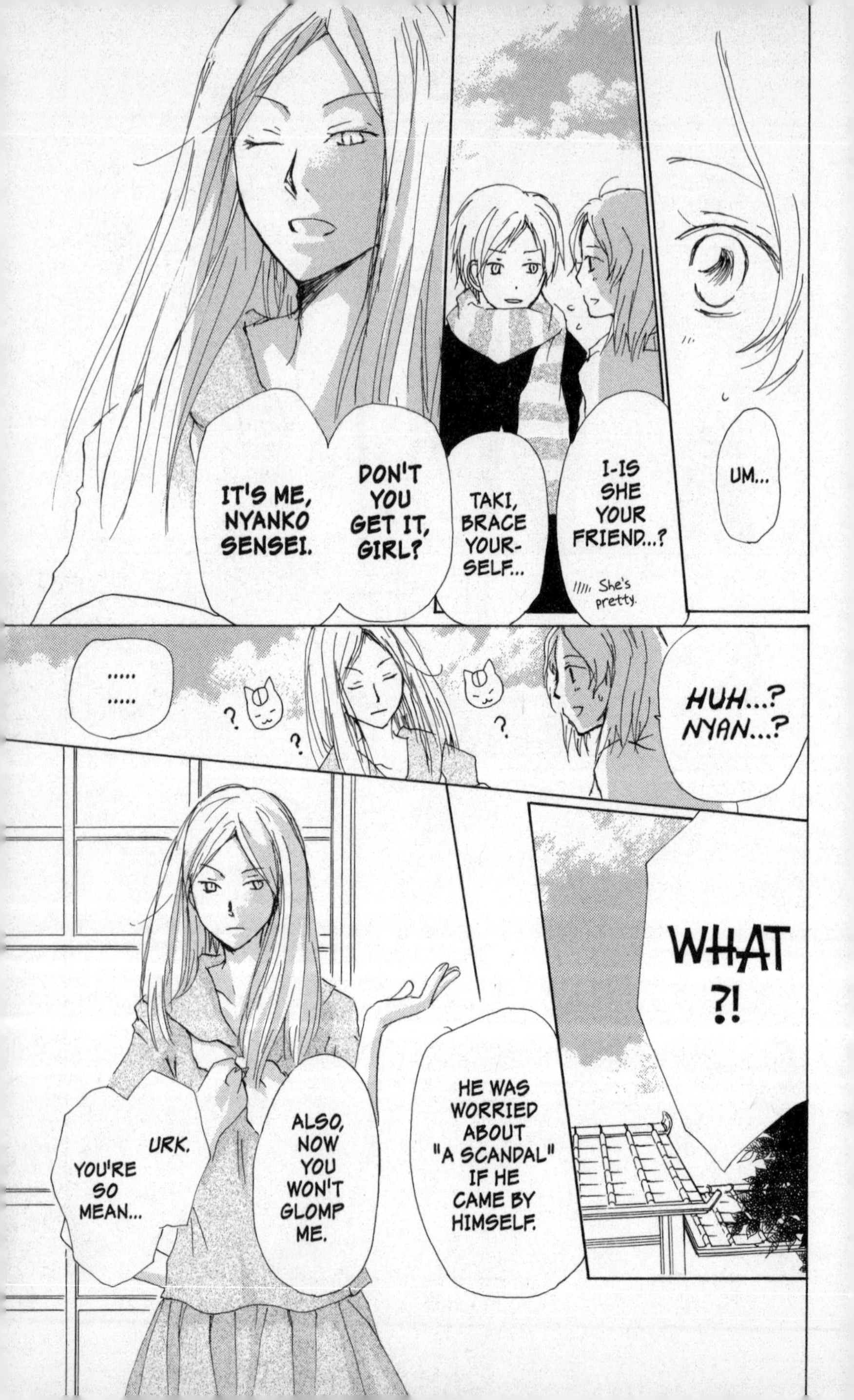
UM...
I-IS SHE YOUR FRIEND...?
She's pretty.
TAKI, BRACE YOUR-SELF...
DON'T YOU GET IT, GIRL?
IT'S ME, NYANKO SENSEI.
HUH...? NYAN...?
.....
.....
WHAT ?!
HE WAS WORRIED ABOUT "A SCANDAL" IF HE CAME BY HIMSELF.
ALSO, NOW YOU WON'T GLOMP ME.
URK.
YOU'RE SO MEAN...

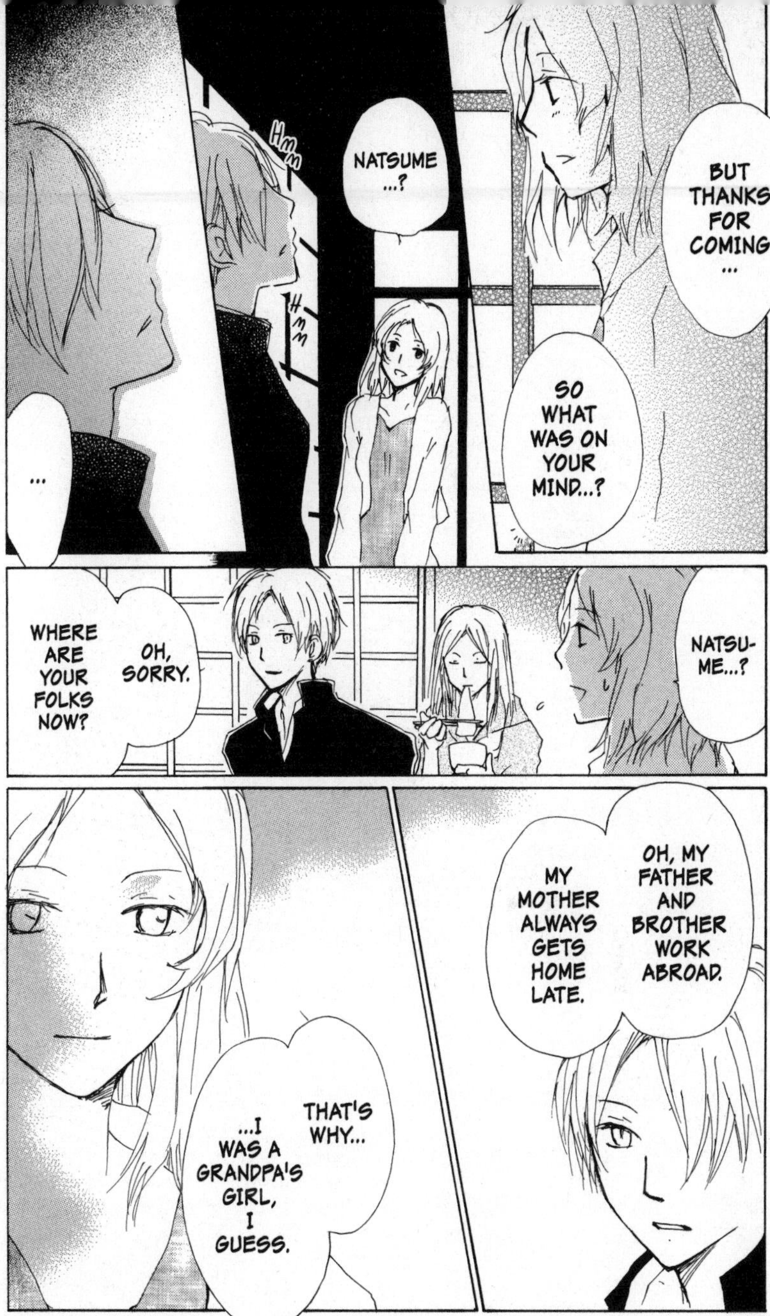
BUT THANKS FOR COMING...
SO WHAT WAS ON YOUR MIND...?
NATSUME...?
Hmm
Hmm
...
NATSU-ME...?
OH, SORRY.
WHERE ARE YOUR FOLKS NOW?
OH, MY FATHER AND BROTHER WORK ABROAD.
MY MOTHER ALWAYS GETS HOME LATE.
THAT'S WHY...
...I WAS A GRANDPA'S GIRL, I GUESS.

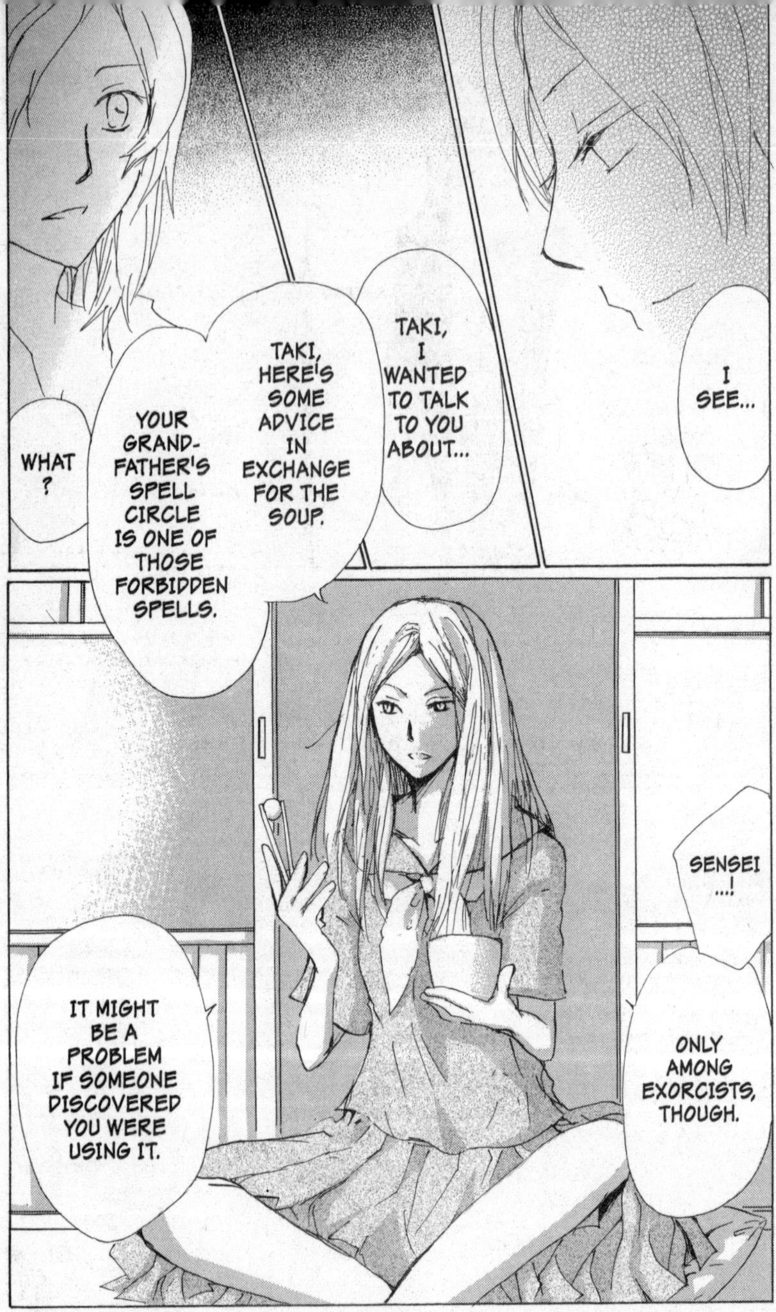
I SEE...
TAKI, I WANTED TO TALK TO YOU ABOUT...
WHAT?
SENSEI ...!
TAKI, HERE'S SOME ADVICE IN EXCHANGE FOR THE SOUP.
YOUR GRAND-FATHER'S SPELL CIRCLE IS ONE OF THOSE FORBIDDEN SPELLS.
ONLY AMONG EXORCISTS, THOUGH.
IT MIGHT BE A PROBLEM IF SOMEONE DISCOVERED YOU WERE USING IT.

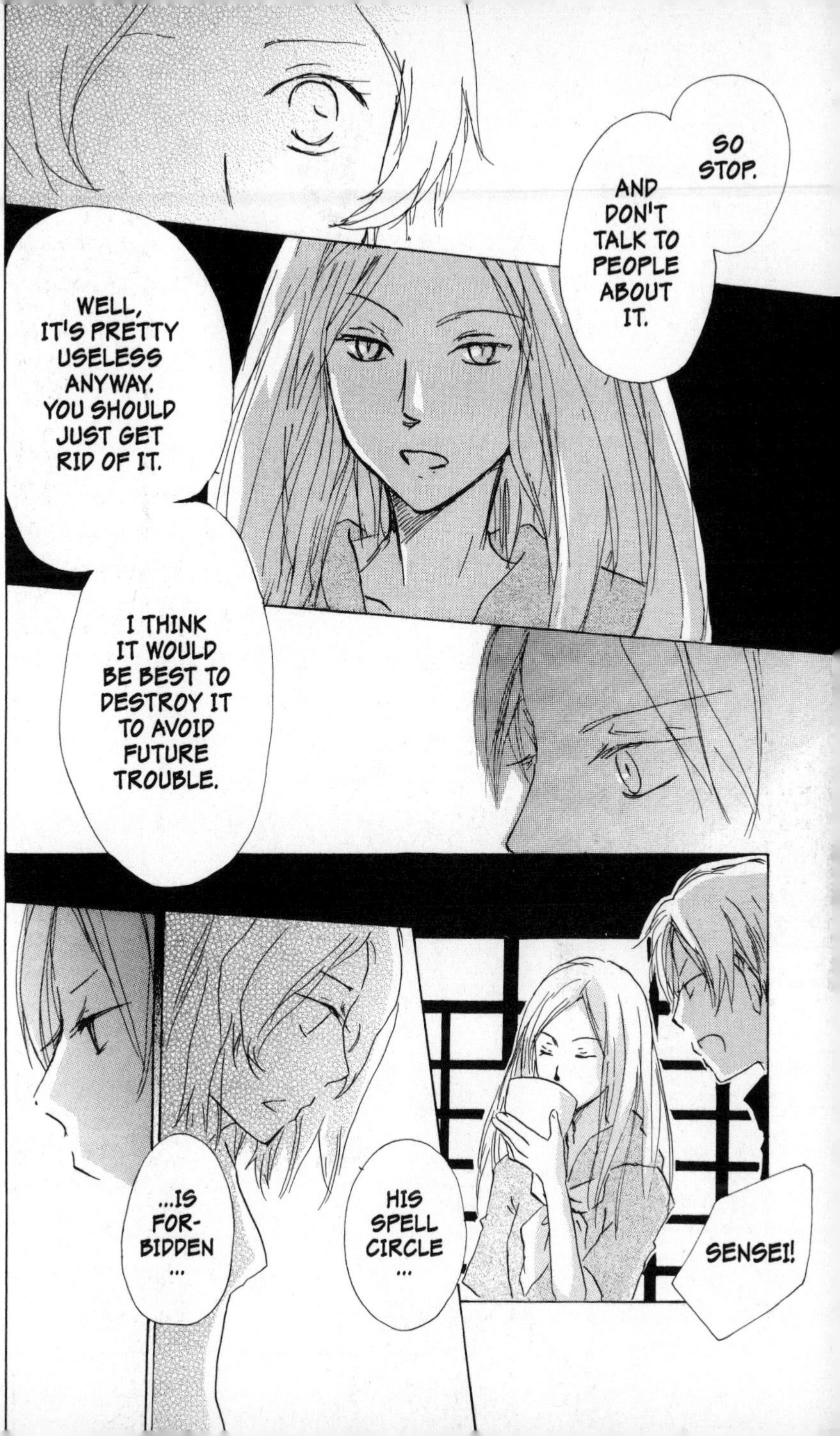
SO STOP.
AND DON'T TALK TO PEOPLE ABOUT IT.
WELL, IT'S PRETTY USELESS ANYWAY. YOU SHOULD JUST GET RID OF IT.
I THINK IT WOULD BE BEST TO DESTROY IT TO AVOID FUTURE TROUBLE.
SENSEI!
HIS SPELL CIRCLE ...
...IS FORBIDDEN ...

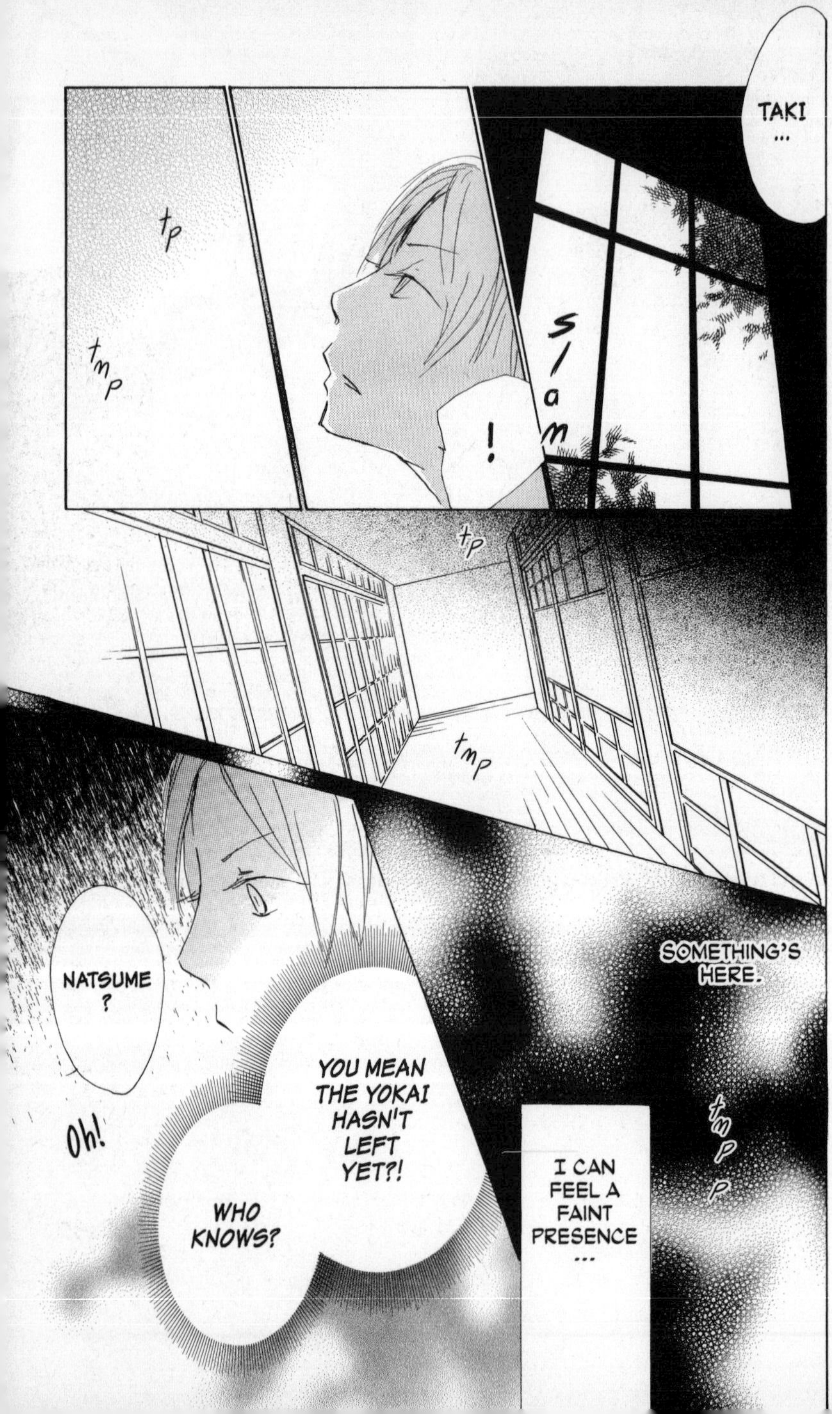
TAKI ...
slam
!
tp
tmp
tp
tmp
SOMETHING'S HERE.
tmp p
I CAN FEEL A FAINT PRESENCE ...
YOU MEAN THE YOKAI HASN'T LEFT YET?!
WHO KNOWS?
NATSUME ?
Oh!

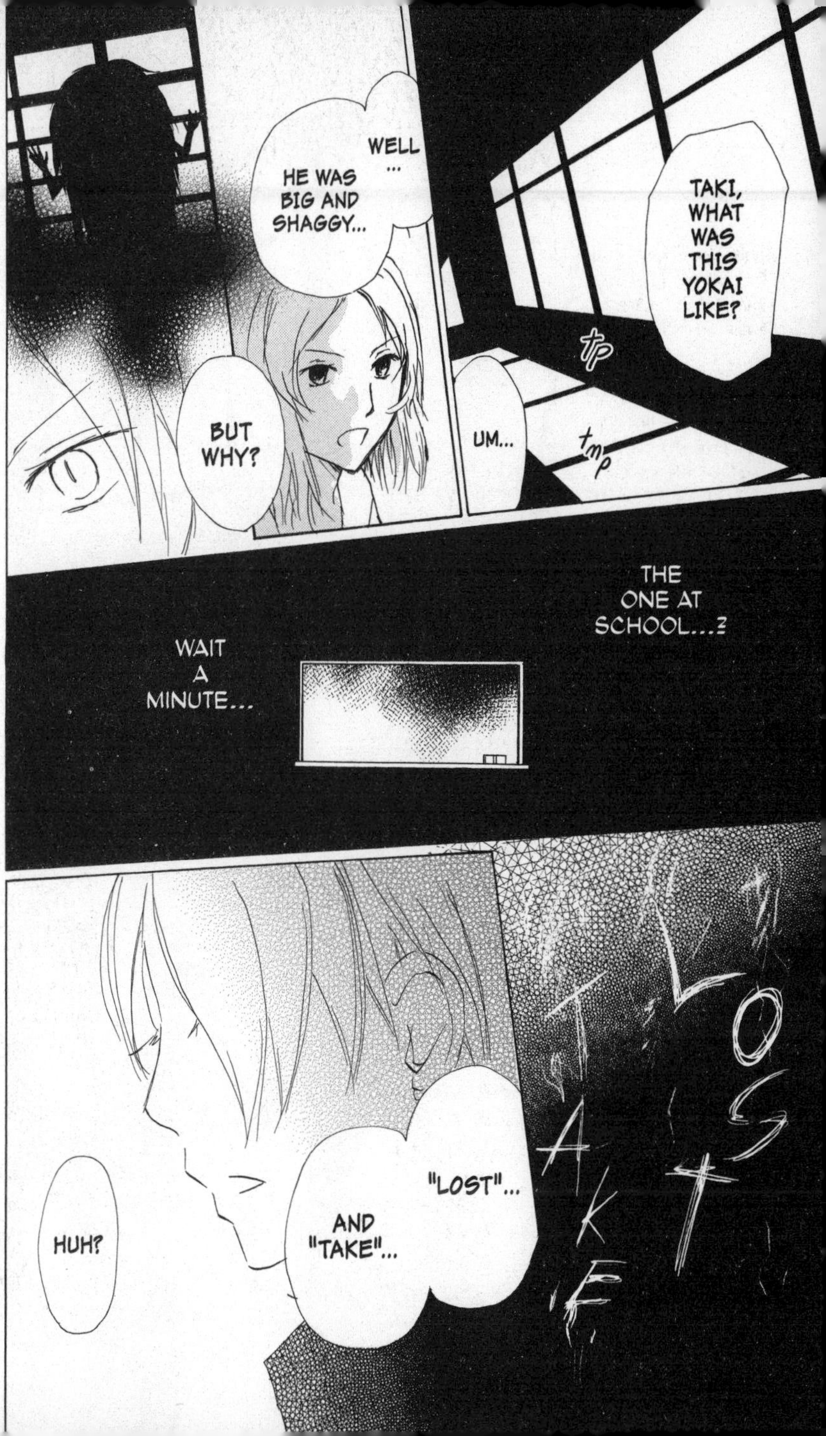
TAKI, WHAT WAS THIS YOKAI LIKE?
tp
tmp
UM...
WELL ...
HE WAS BIG AND SHAGGY...
BUT WHY?
THE ONE AT SCHOOL...?
WAIT A MINUTE...
LOST
TAKE
"LOST"...
AND "TAKE"...
HUH?

01

Hello, I'm Midorikawa. This is the 16th volume of Natsume's Book of Friends.

The years went by so fast working on it. I still feel like I'm not used to it, and I get anxious and nervous, but I enjoy it a lot.

I really appreciate being able to draw manga, and that there are readers who read my work.

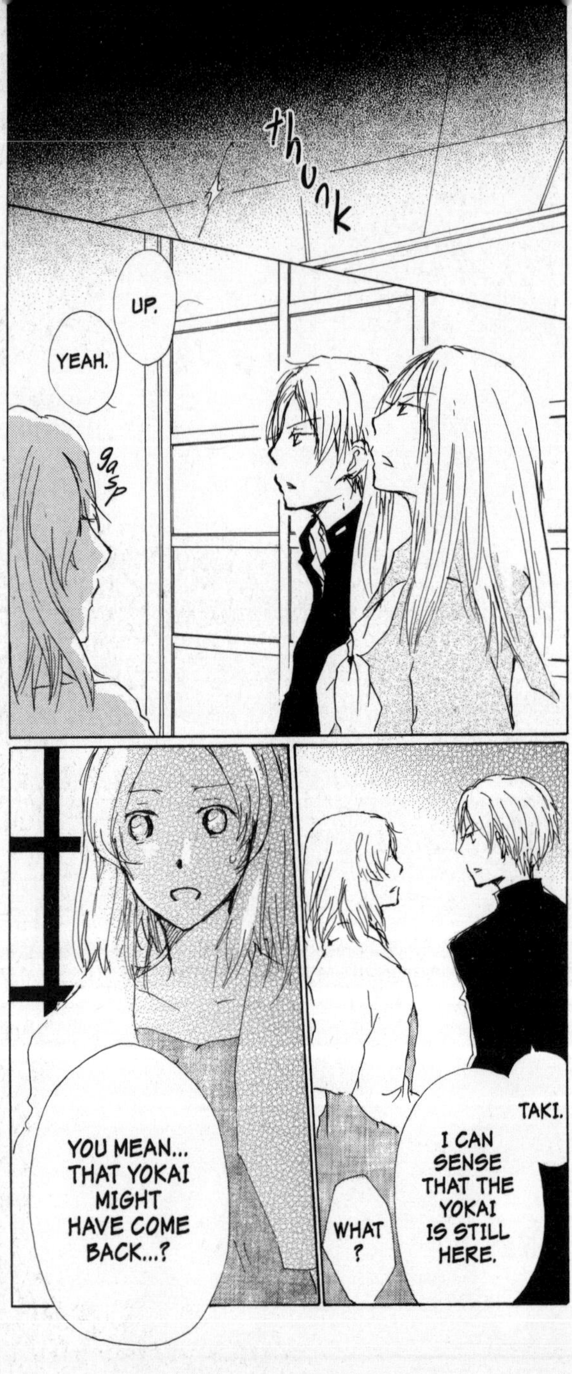
thunk
UP.
YEAH.
gasp
TAKI.
I CAN SENSE THAT THE YOKAI IS STILL HERE.
WHAT?
YOU MEAN... THAT YOKAI MIGHT HAVE COME BACK...?

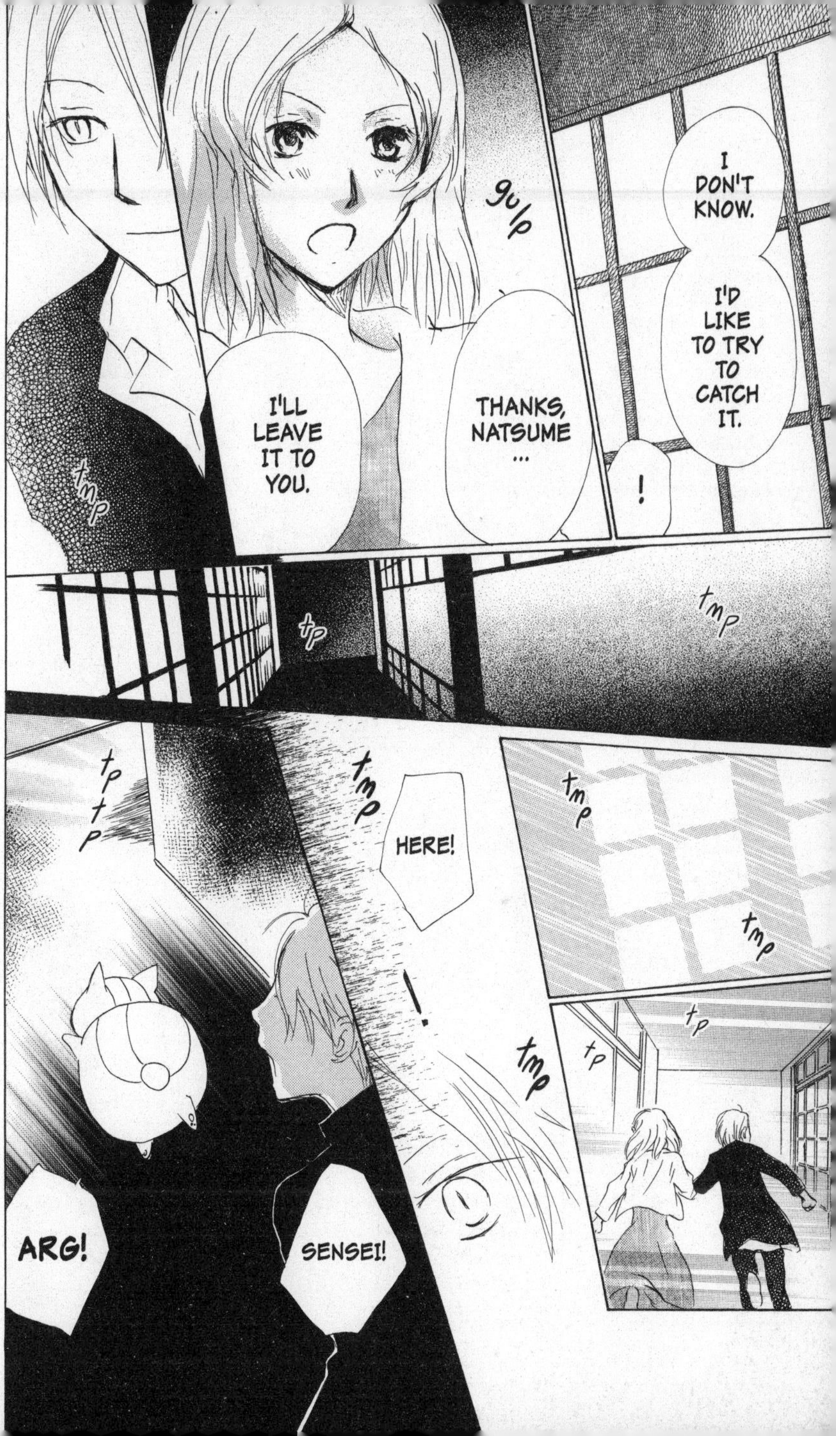
I DON'T KNOW.
I'D LIKE TO TRY TO CATCH IT.
!
gulp
THANKS, NATSUME ...
I'LL LEAVE IT TO YOU.
tmp
tmp
tp
tmp
tmp
tp
tp
tmp
tmp
HERE!
tp tp
!
SENSEI!
ARG!

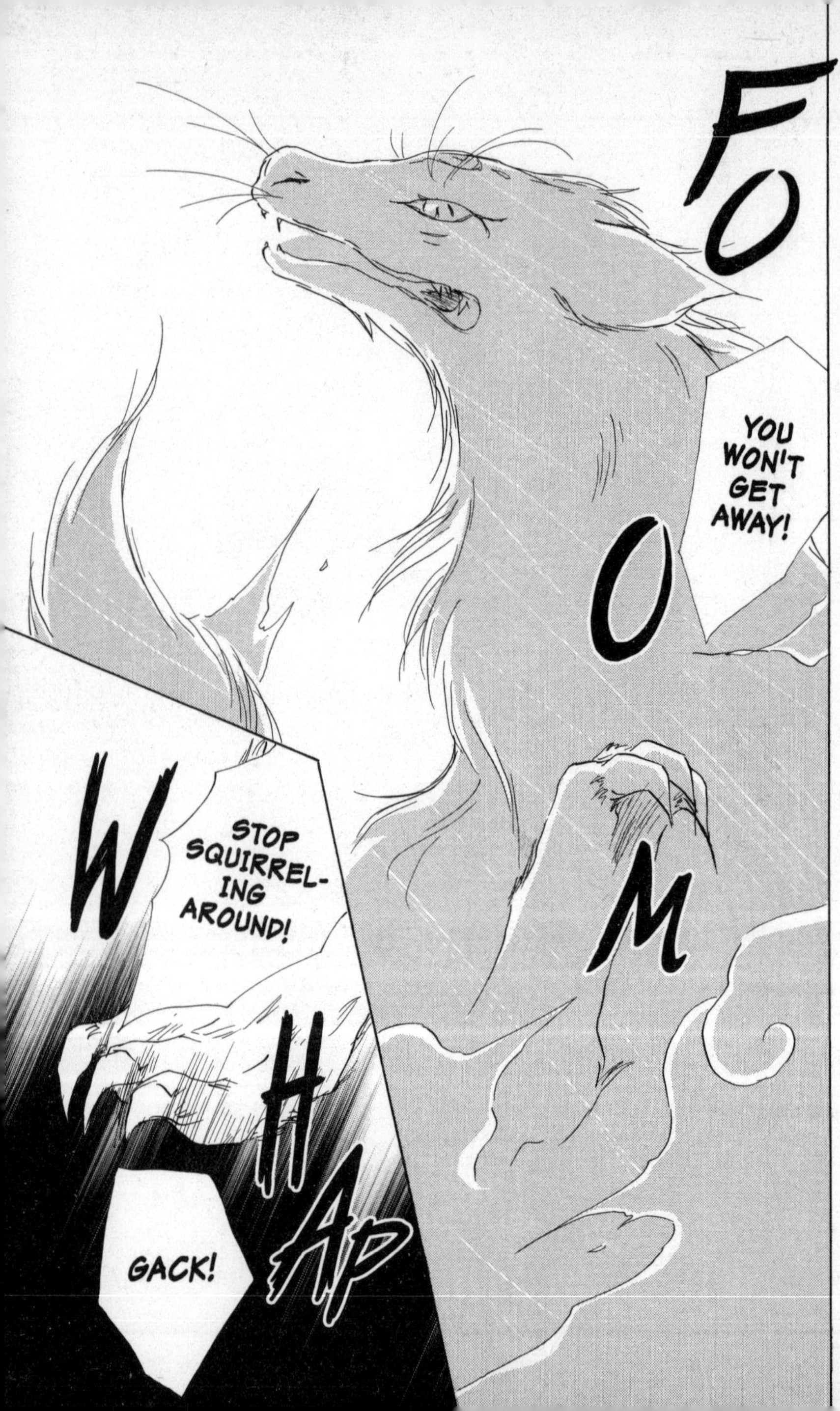
FOOOM
YOU WON'T GET AWAY!
STOP SQUIRREL-ING AROUND!
WHHAP
GACK!

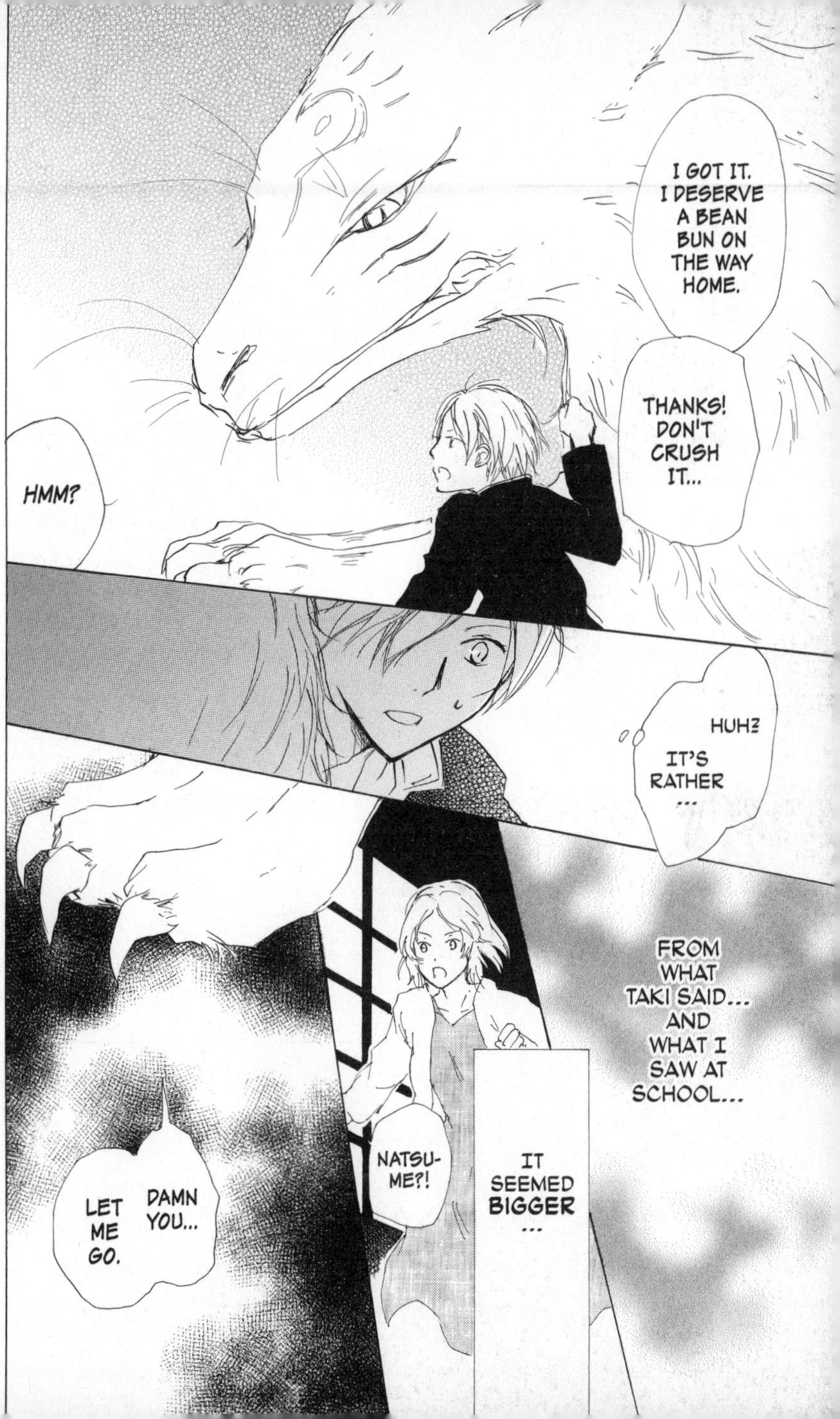
I GOT IT. I DESERVE A BEAN BUN ON THE WAY HOME.
THANKS! DON'T CRUSH IT...
HMM?
HUH?
IT'S RATHER...
FROM WHAT TAKI SAID... AND WHAT I SAW AT SCHOOL...
IT SEEMED BIGGER...
NATSUME?!
DAMN YOU...
LET ME GO.

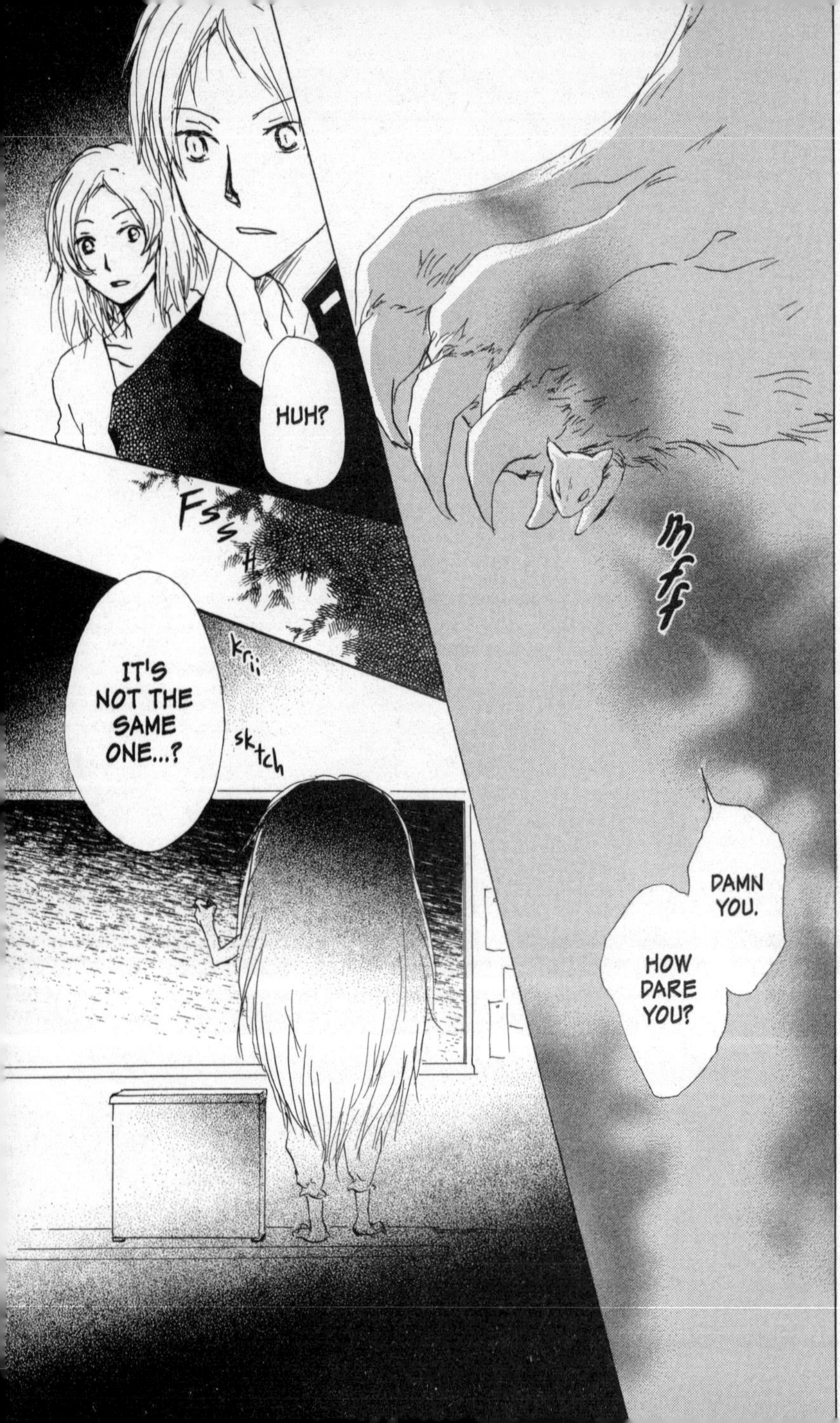
mff
DAMN YOU.
HOW DARE YOU?
HUH?
Fsssh
IT'S NOT THE SAME ONE...?
krii
sktch

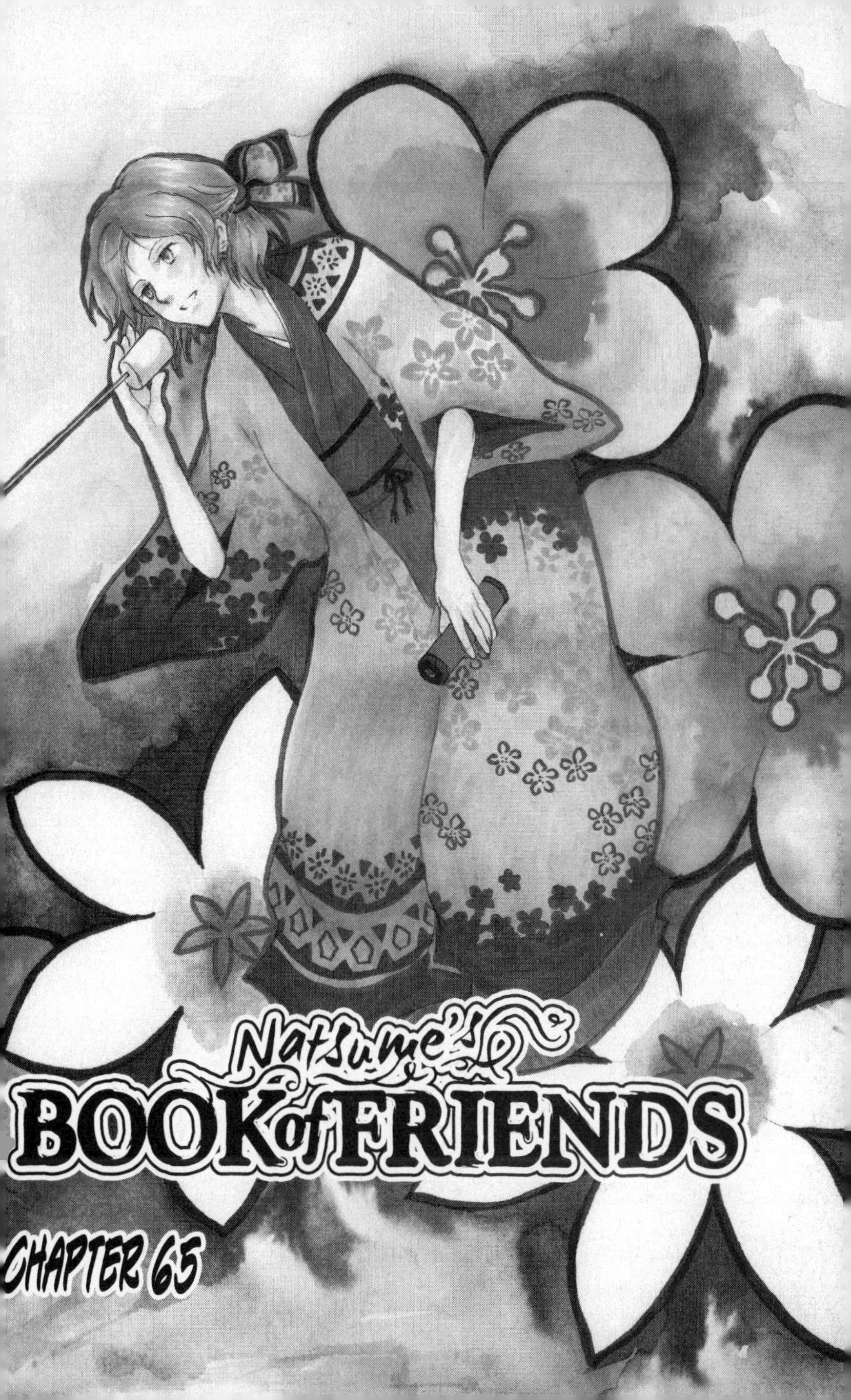
Natsume's
BOOK of FRIENDS
CHAPTER 65

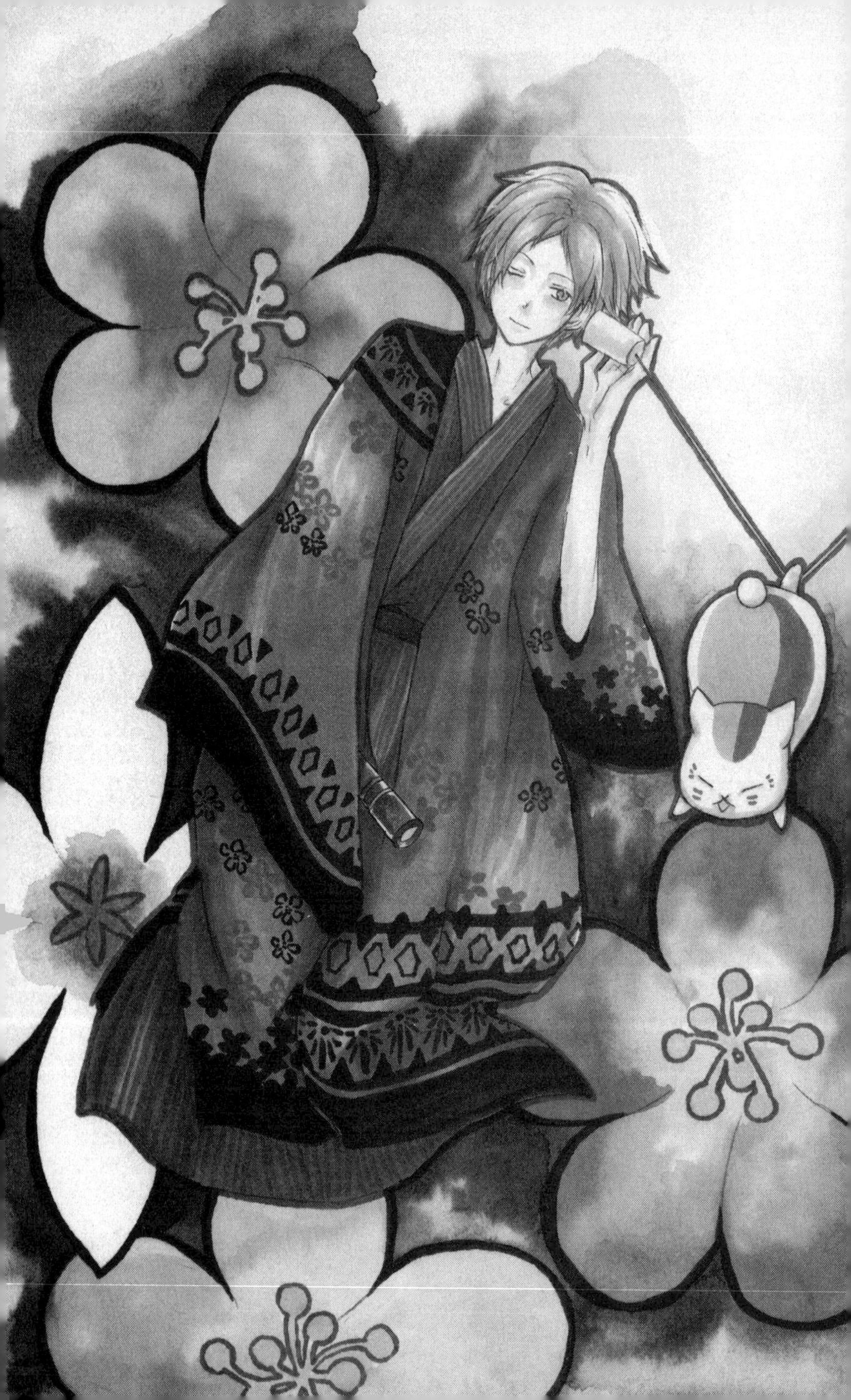

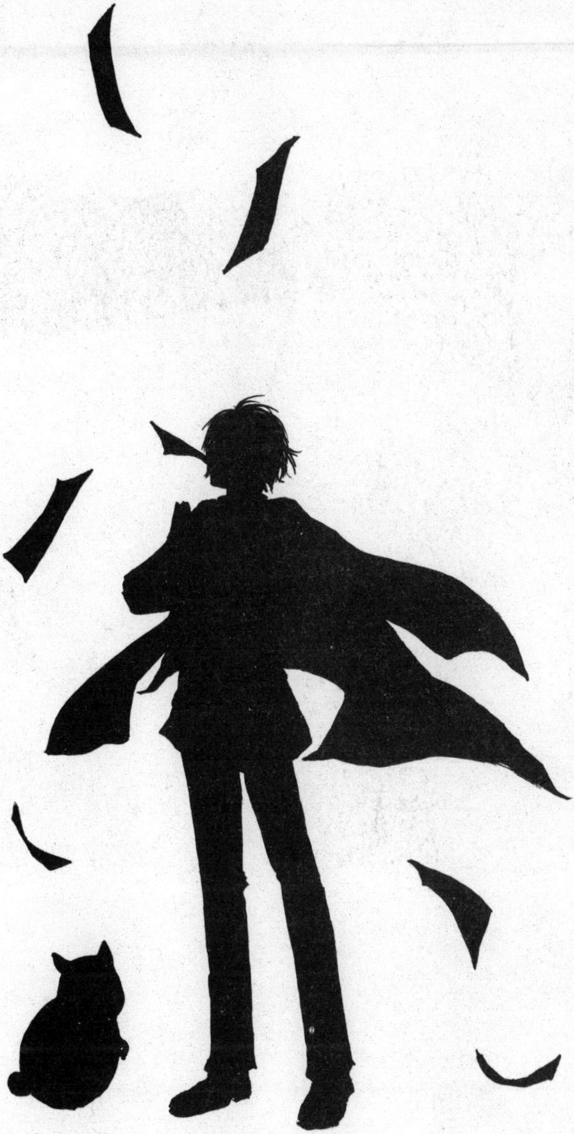

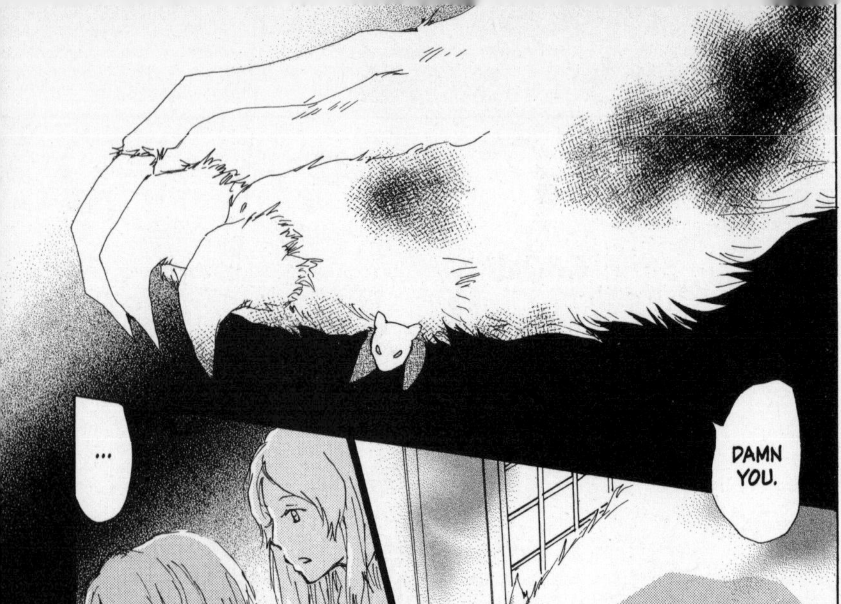
DAMN YOU.
HOW DARE YOU?
...
NATSUME ...?

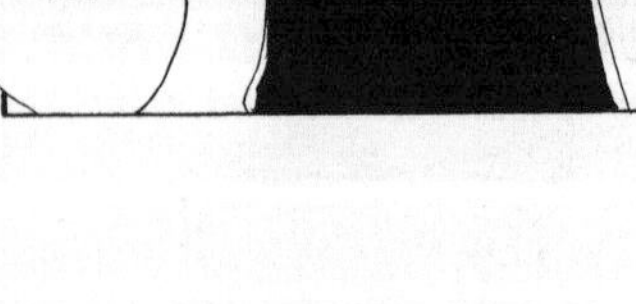

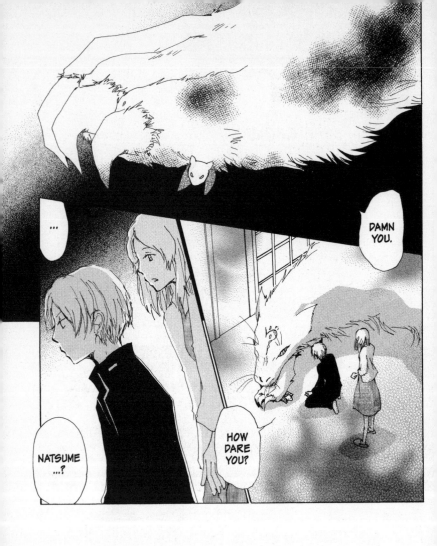

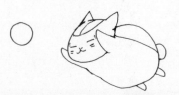

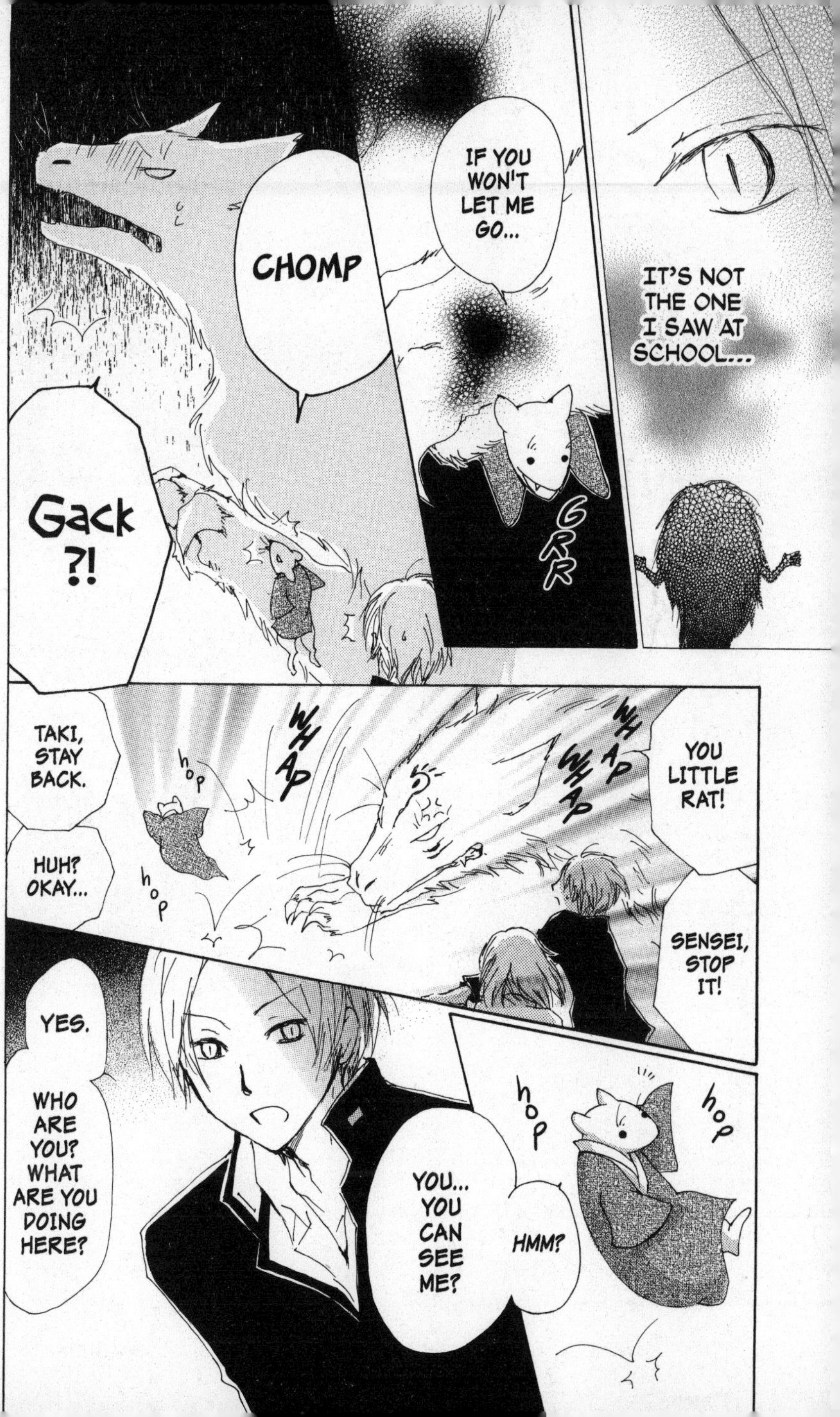
IT'S NOT THE ONE I SAW AT SCHOOL...
IF YOU WON'T LET ME GO...
GRR
CHOMP
Gack ?!
YOU LITTLE RAT!
WHAP
WHAP
WHAP
TAKI, STAY BACK.
hop
HUH? OKAY...
hop
SENSEI, STOP IT!
hop
hop
HMM?
YOU... YOU CAN SEE ME?
YES.
WHO ARE YOU? WHAT ARE YOU DOING HERE?

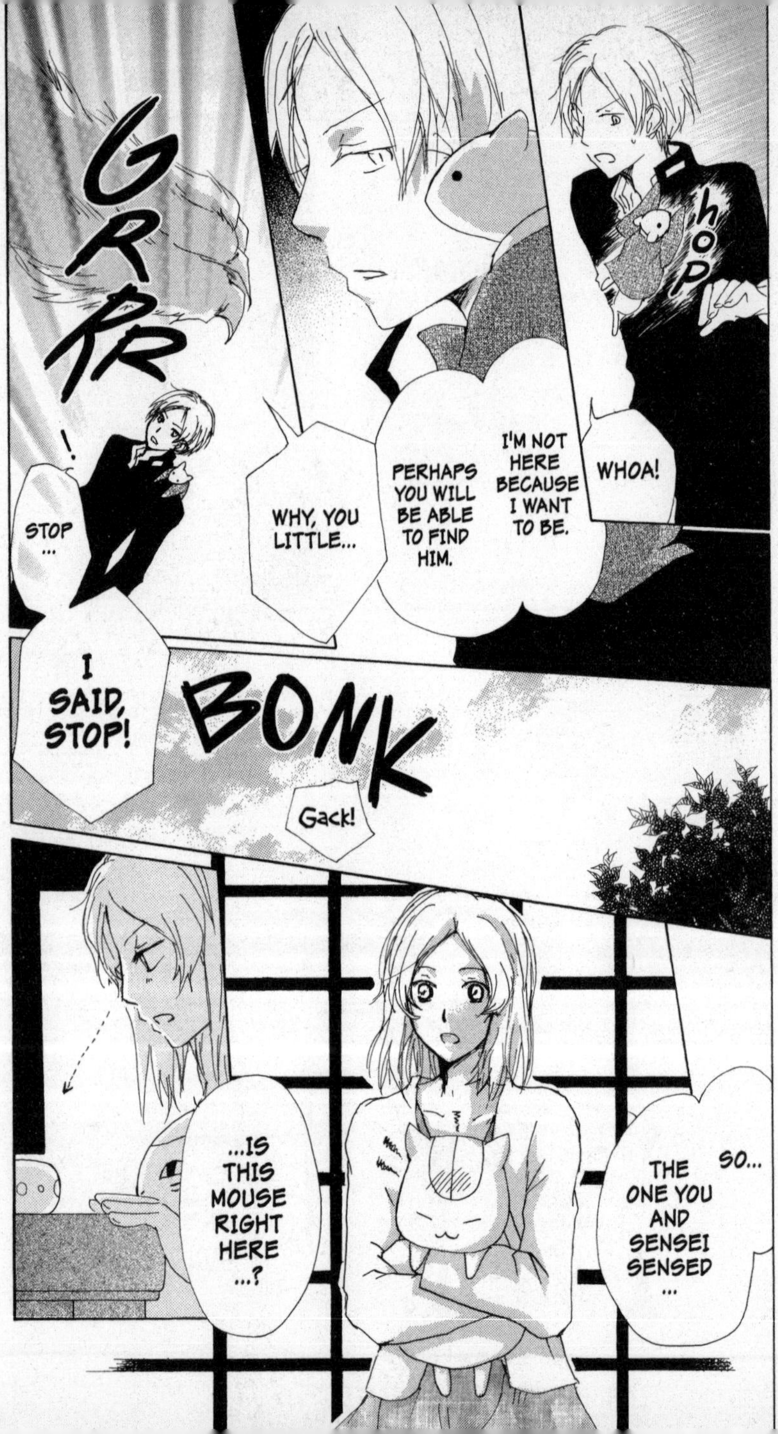

hop
WHOA!
I'M NOT HERE BECAUSE I WANT TO BE.
PERHAPS YOU WILL BE ABLE TO FIND HIM.
WHY, YOU LITTLE...
GRRR
!
STOP ...
I SAID, STOP!
BONK
Gack!
SO...
THE ONE YOU AND SENSEI SENSED ...
...IS THIS MOUSE RIGHT HERE ...?

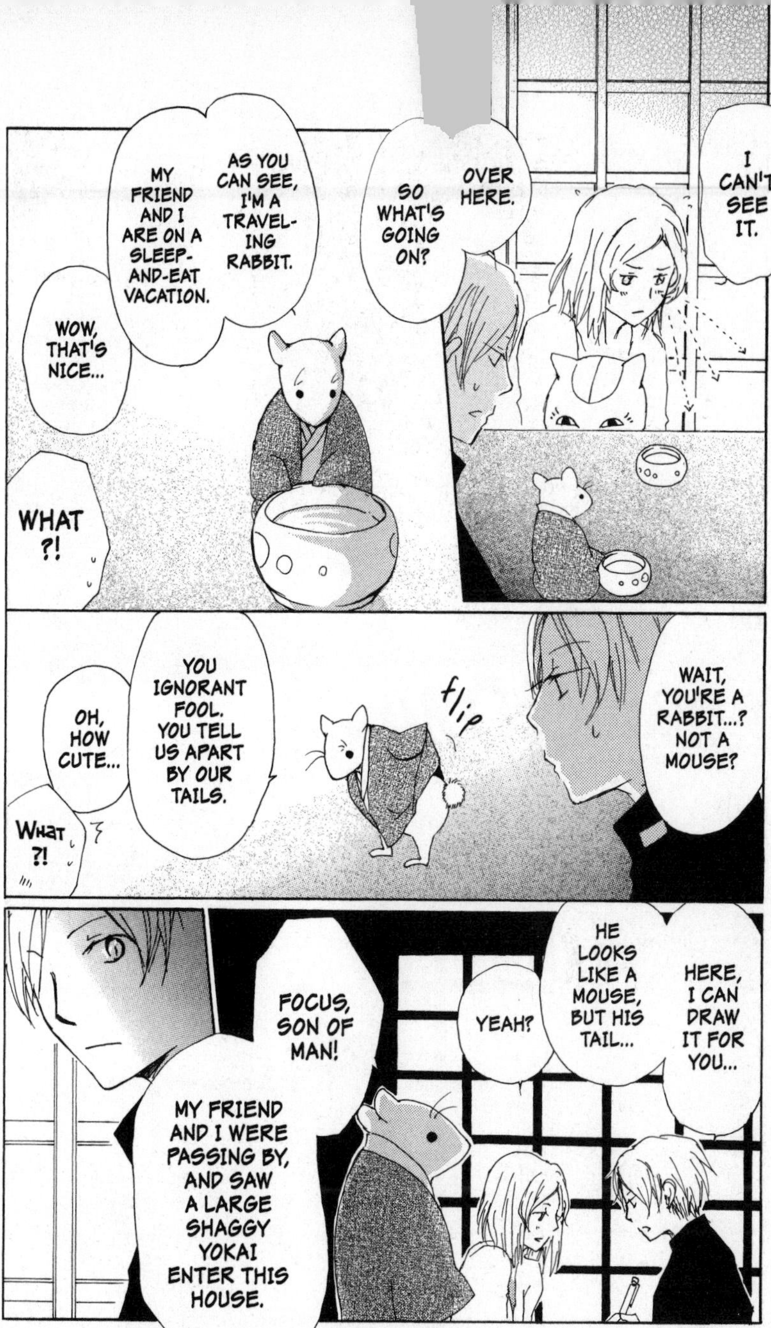
I CAN'T SEE IT.
OVER HERE.
SO WHAT'S GOING ON?
AS YOU CAN SEE, I'M A TRAVEL-ING RABBIT.
MY FRIEND AND I ARE ON A SLEEP-AND-EAT VACATION.
WOW, THAT'S NICE...
WHAT?!
WAIT, YOU'RE A RABBIT...? NOT A MOUSE?
flip
YOU IGNORANT FOOL. YOU TELL US APART BY OUR TAILS.
OH, HOW CUTE...
WHAT?!
HERE, I CAN DRAW IT FOR YOU...
HE LOOKS LIKE A MOUSE, BUT HIS TAIL...
YEAH?
FOCUS, SON OF MAN!
MY FRIEND AND I WERE PASSING BY, AND SAW A LARGE SHAGGY YOKAI ENTER THIS HOUSE.

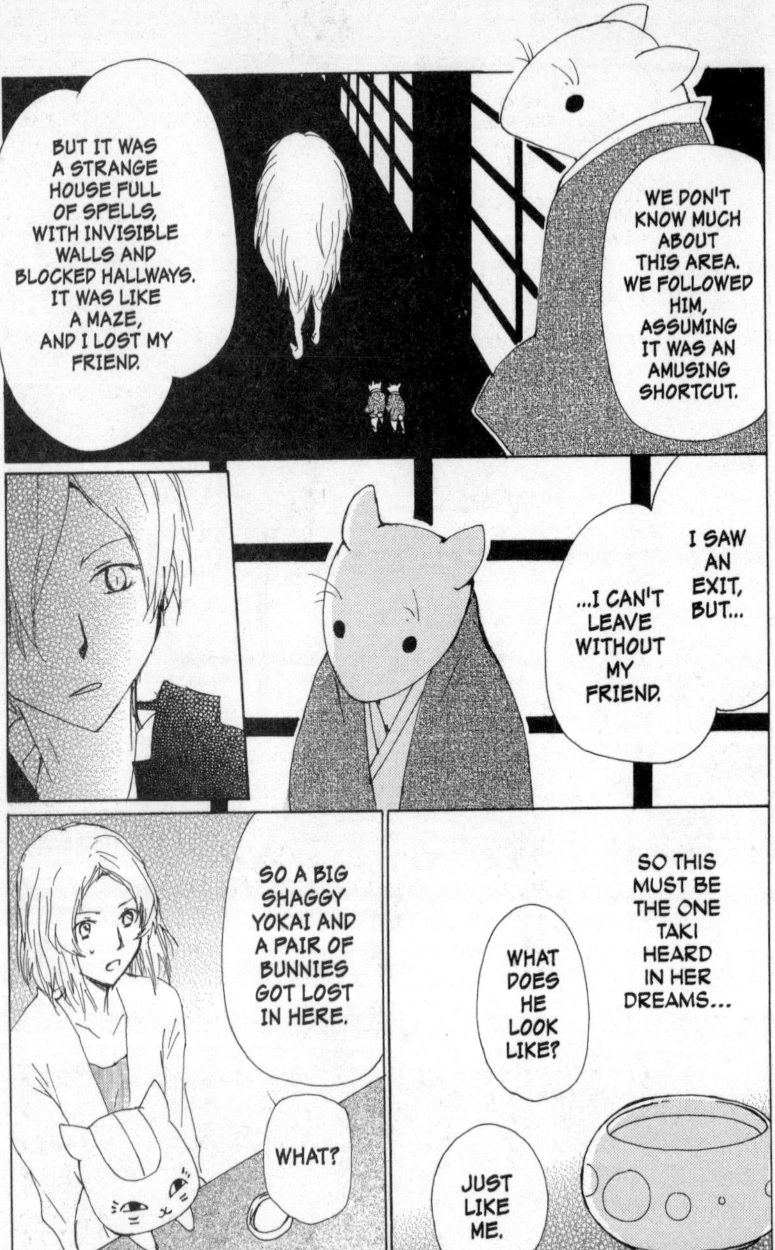

WE DON'T KNOW MUCH ABOUT THIS AREA. WE FOLLOWED HIM, ASSUMING IT WAS AN AMUSING SHORTCUT.
BUT IT WAS A STRANGE HOUSE FULL OF SPELLS, WITH INVISIBLE WALLS AND BLOCKED HALLWAYS. IT WAS LIKE A MAZE, AND I LOST MY FRIEND.
I SAW AN EXIT, BUT...
...I CAN'T LEAVE WITHOUT MY FRIEND.
SO THIS MUST BE THE ONE TAKI HEARD IN HER DREAMS...
WHAT DOES HE LOOK LIKE?
JUST LIKE ME.
SO A BIG SHAGGY YOKAI AND A PAIR OF BUNNIES GOT LOST IN HERE.
WHAT?

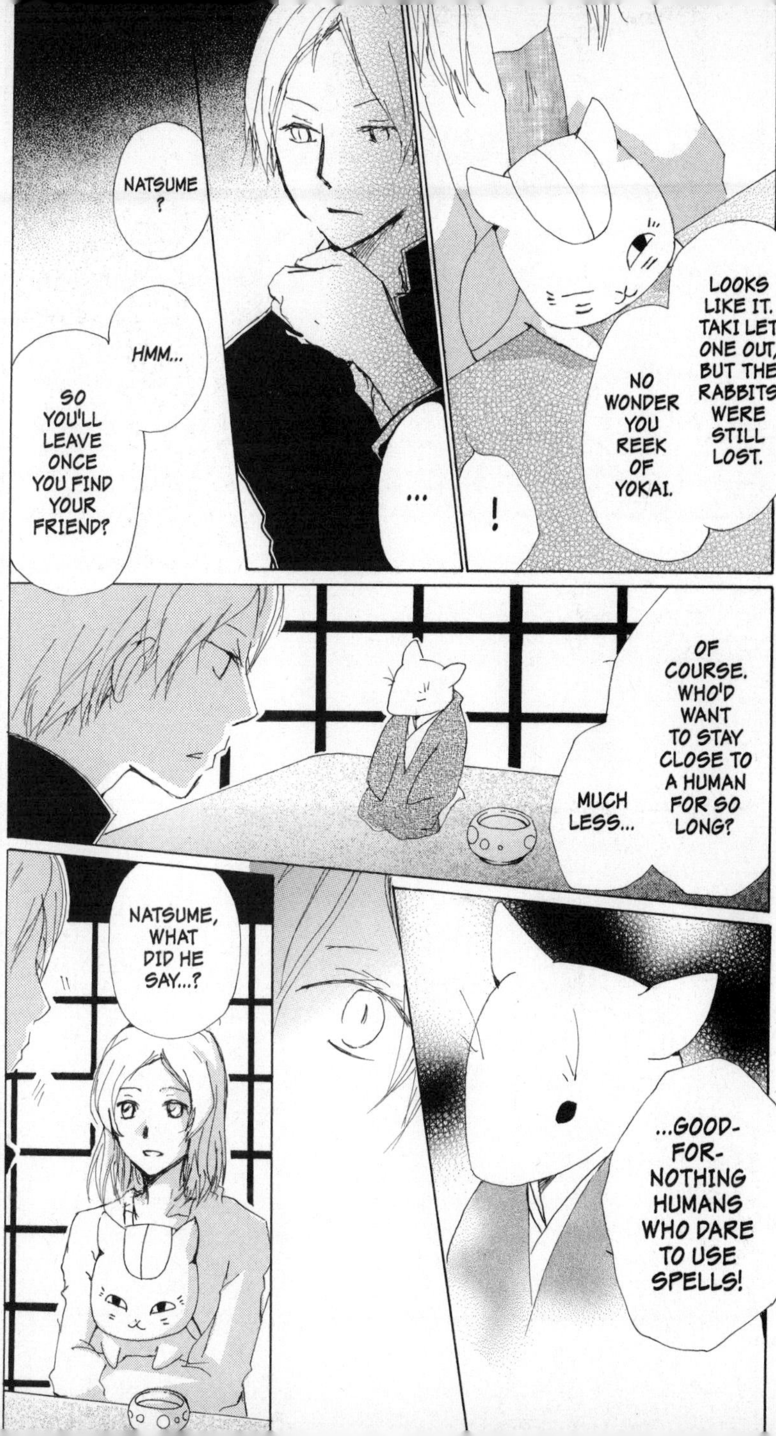
LOOKS LIKE IT. TAKI LET ONE OUT, BUT THE RABBITS WERE STILL LOST.
NO WONDER YOU REEK OF YOKAI.
!
...
NATSUME?
HMM...
SO YOU'LL LEAVE ONCE YOU FIND YOUR FRIEND?
OF COURSE. WHO'D WANT TO STAY CLOSE TO A HUMAN FOR SO LONG?
MUCH LESS...
...GOOD-FOR-NOTHING HUMANS WHO DARE TO USE SPELLS!
NATSUME, WHAT DID HE SAY...?

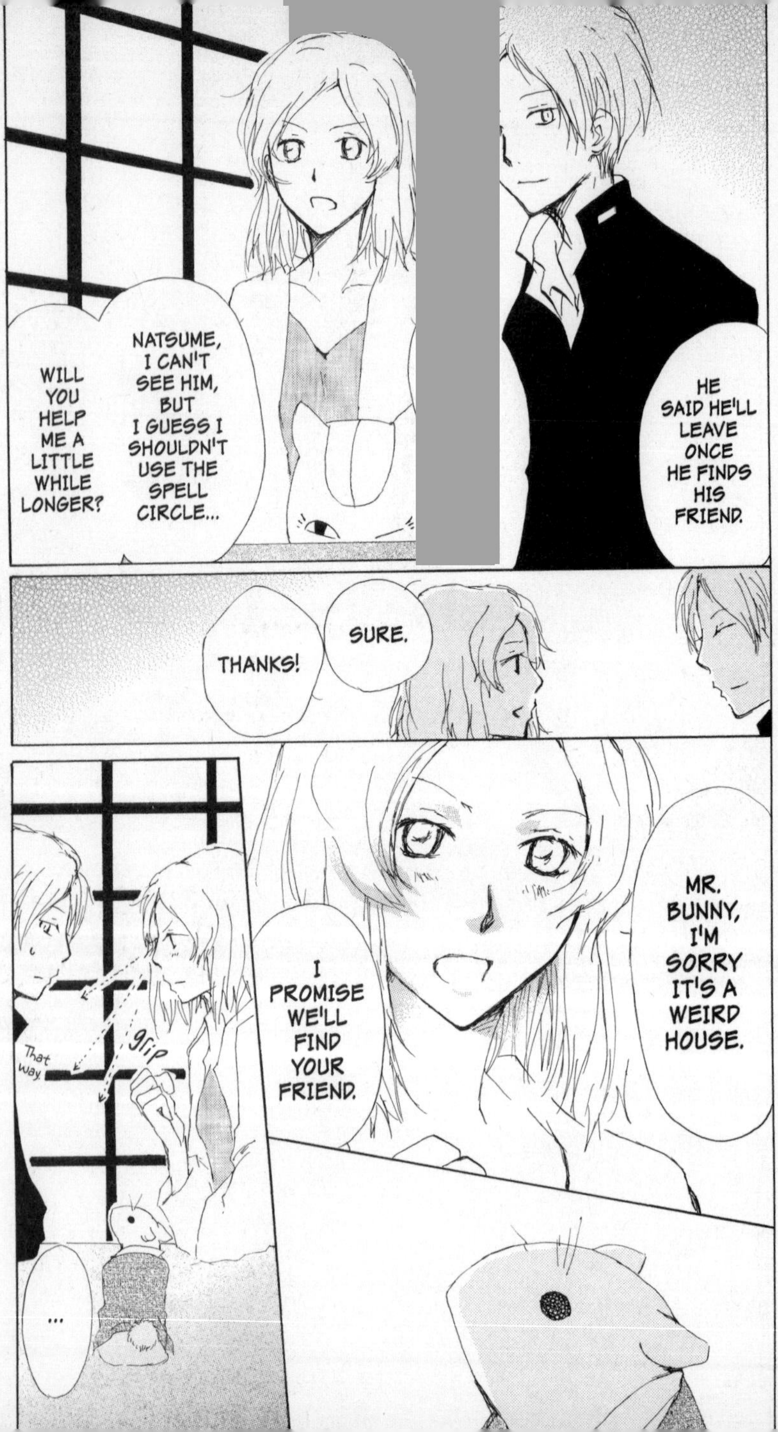
HE SAID HE'LL LEAVE ONCE HE FINDS HIS FRIEND.
NATSUME, I CAN'T SEE HIM, BUT I GUESS I SHOULDN'T USE THE SPELL CIRCLE...
WILL YOU HELP ME A LITTLE WHILE LONGER?
SURE.
THANKS!
MR. BUNNY, I'M SORRY IT'S A WEIRD HOUSE.
I PROMISE WE'LL FIND YOUR FRIEND.
grip
That way.
...

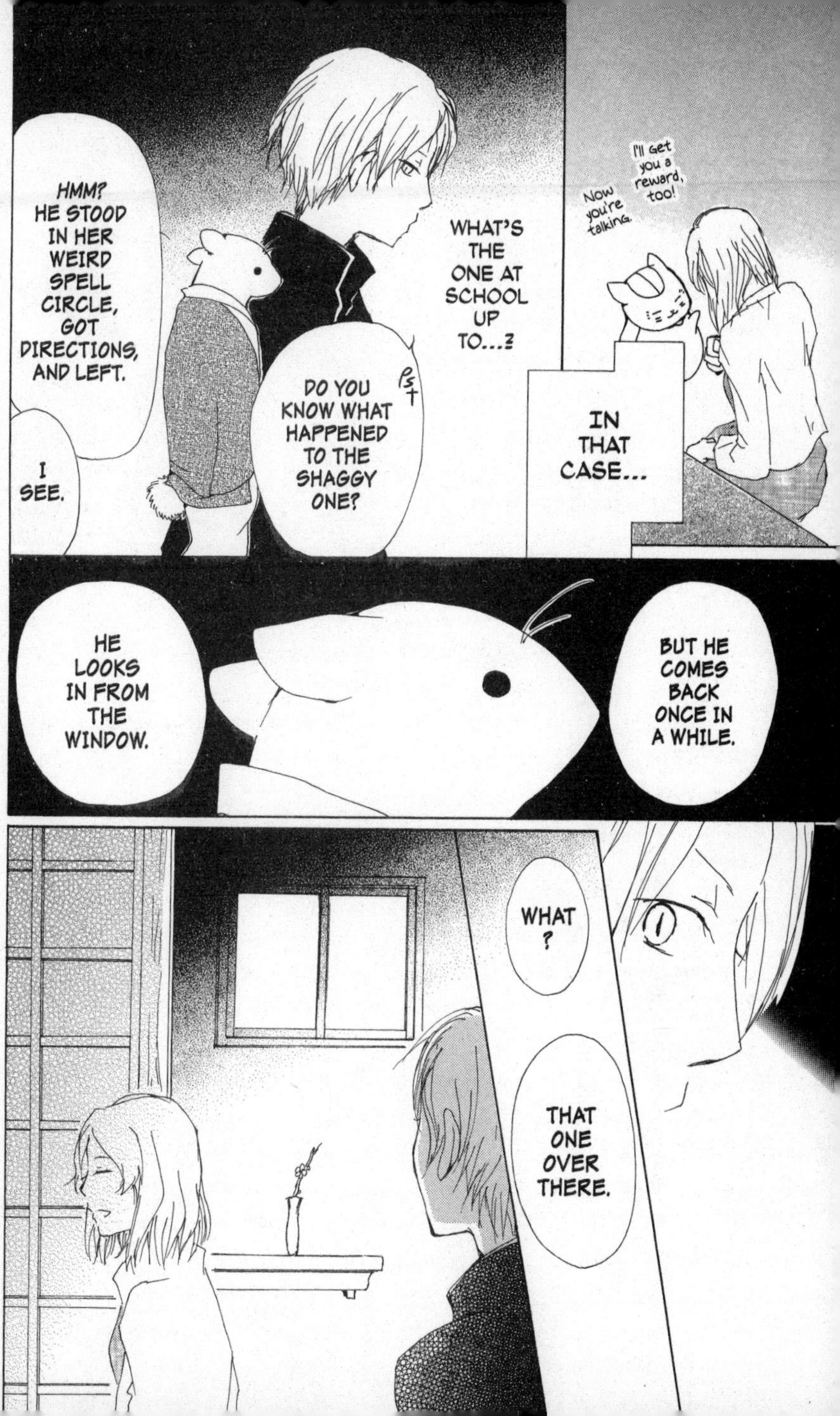
I'll Get you a reward, too!
Now you're talking.
IN THAT CASE...
WHAT'S THE ONE AT SCHOOL UP TO...?
Pst
DO YOU KNOW WHAT HAPPENED TO THE SHAGGY ONE?
HMM? HE STOOD IN HER WEIRD SPELL CIRCLE, GOT DIRECTIONS, AND LEFT.
I SEE.
BUT HE COMES BACK ONCE IN A WHILE.
HE LOOKS IN FROM THE WINDOW.
WHAT?
THAT ONE OVER THERE.

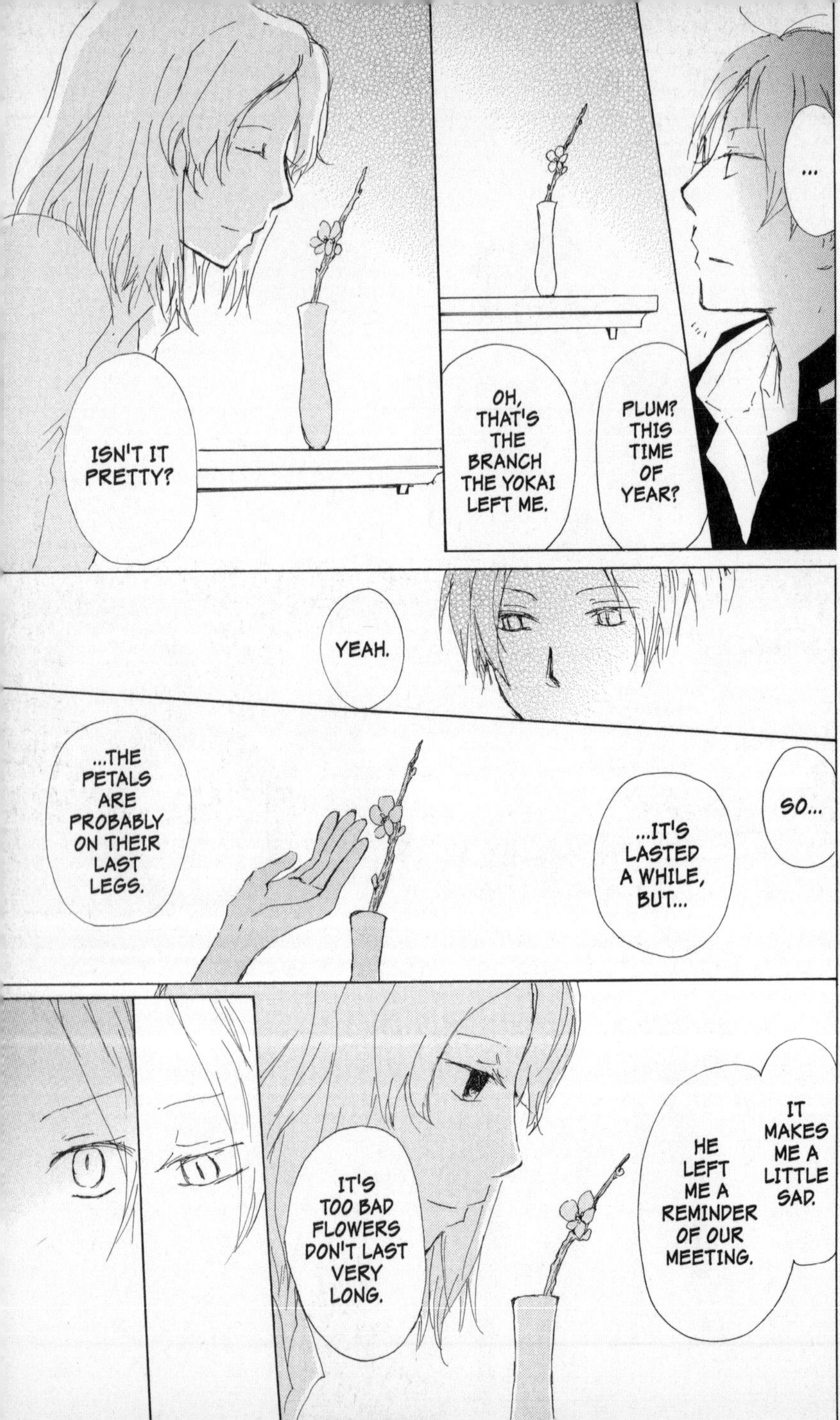
...
PLUM? THIS TIME OF YEAR?
OH, THAT'S THE BRANCH THE YOKAI LEFT ME.
ISN'T IT PRETTY?
YEAH.
SO...
...IT'S LASTED A WHILE, BUT...
...THE PETALS ARE PROBABLY ON THEIR LAST LEGS.
IT MAKES ME A LITTLE SAD.
HE LEFT ME A REMINDER OF OUR MEETING.
IT'S TOO BAD FLOWERS DON'T LAST VERY LONG.

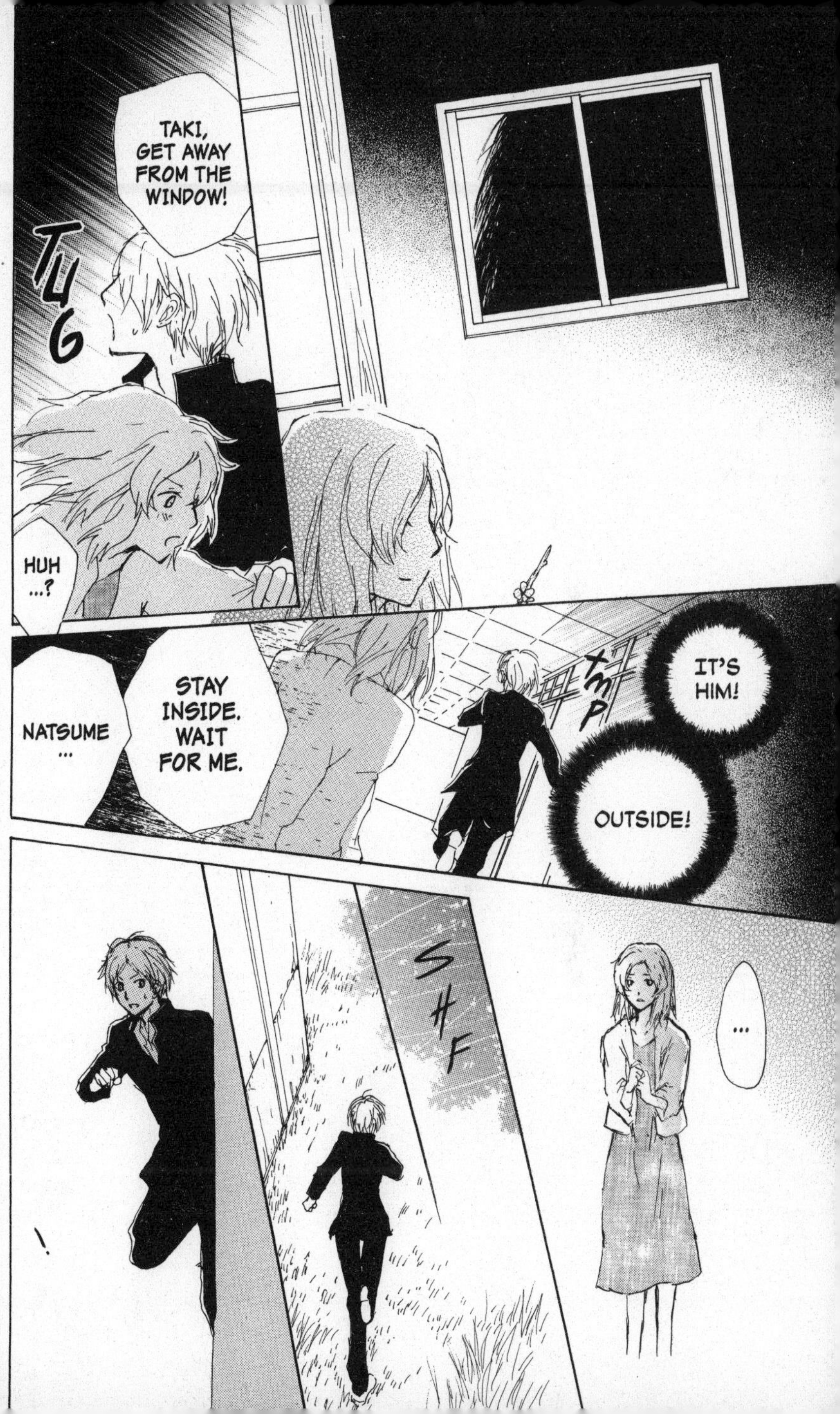
TAKI, GET AWAY FROM THE WINDOW!
TUG
HUH ...?
IT'S HIM!
OUTSIDE!
TMP
STAY INSIDE. WAIT FOR ME.
NATSUME ...
...
SHF
!

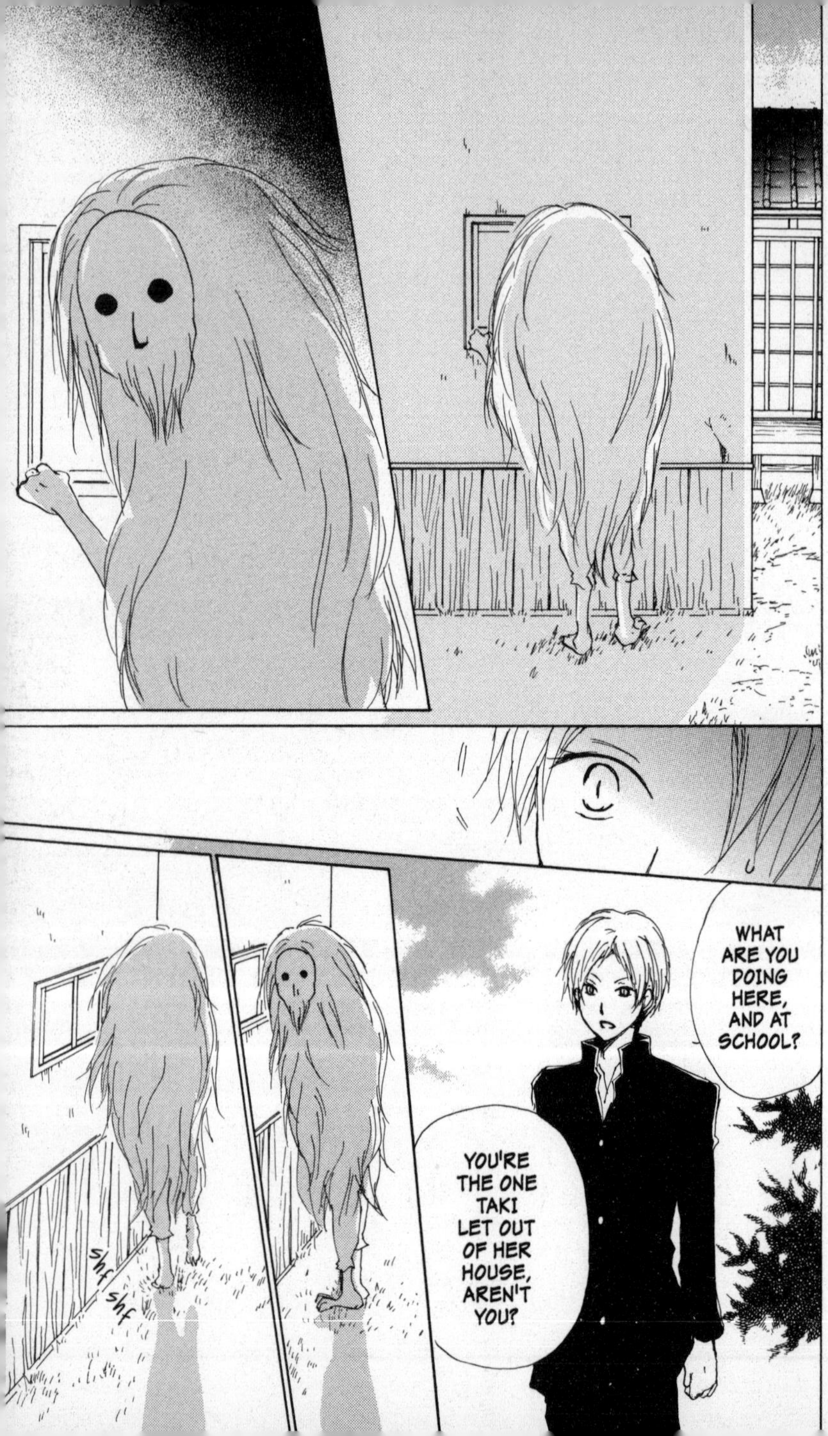
WHAT ARE YOU DOING HERE, AND AT SCHOOL?
YOU'RE THE ONE TAKI LET OUT OF HER HOUSE, AREN'T YOU?
shf shf

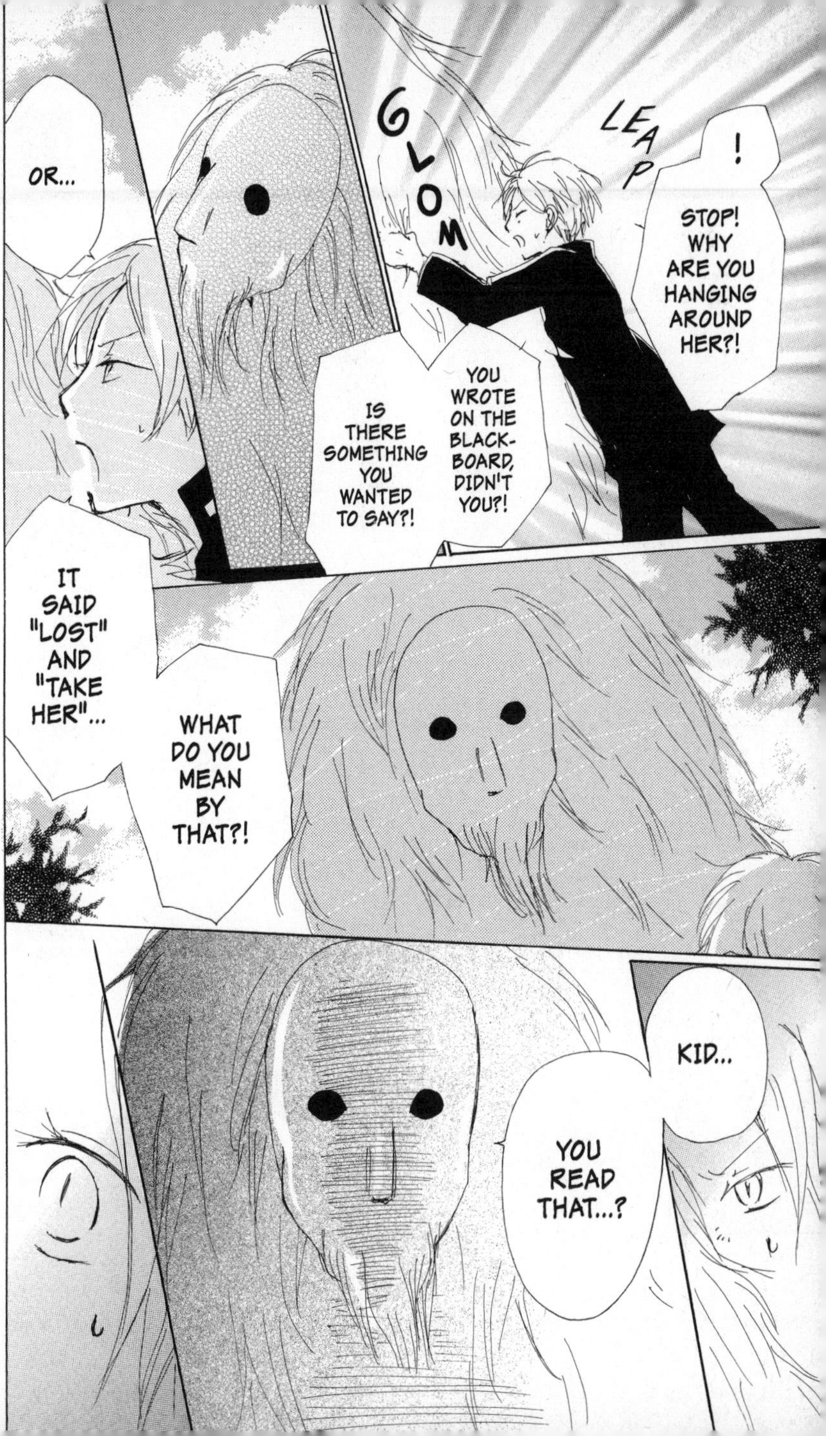
LEAP
!
STOP! WHY ARE YOU HANGING AROUND HER?!
GLOM
YOU WROTE ON THE BLACK-BOARD, DIDN'T YOU?!
IS THERE SOMETHING YOU WANTED TO SAY?!
OR...
IT SAID "LOST" AND "TAKE HER"...
WHAT DO YOU MEAN BY THAT?!
KID...
YOU READ THAT...?

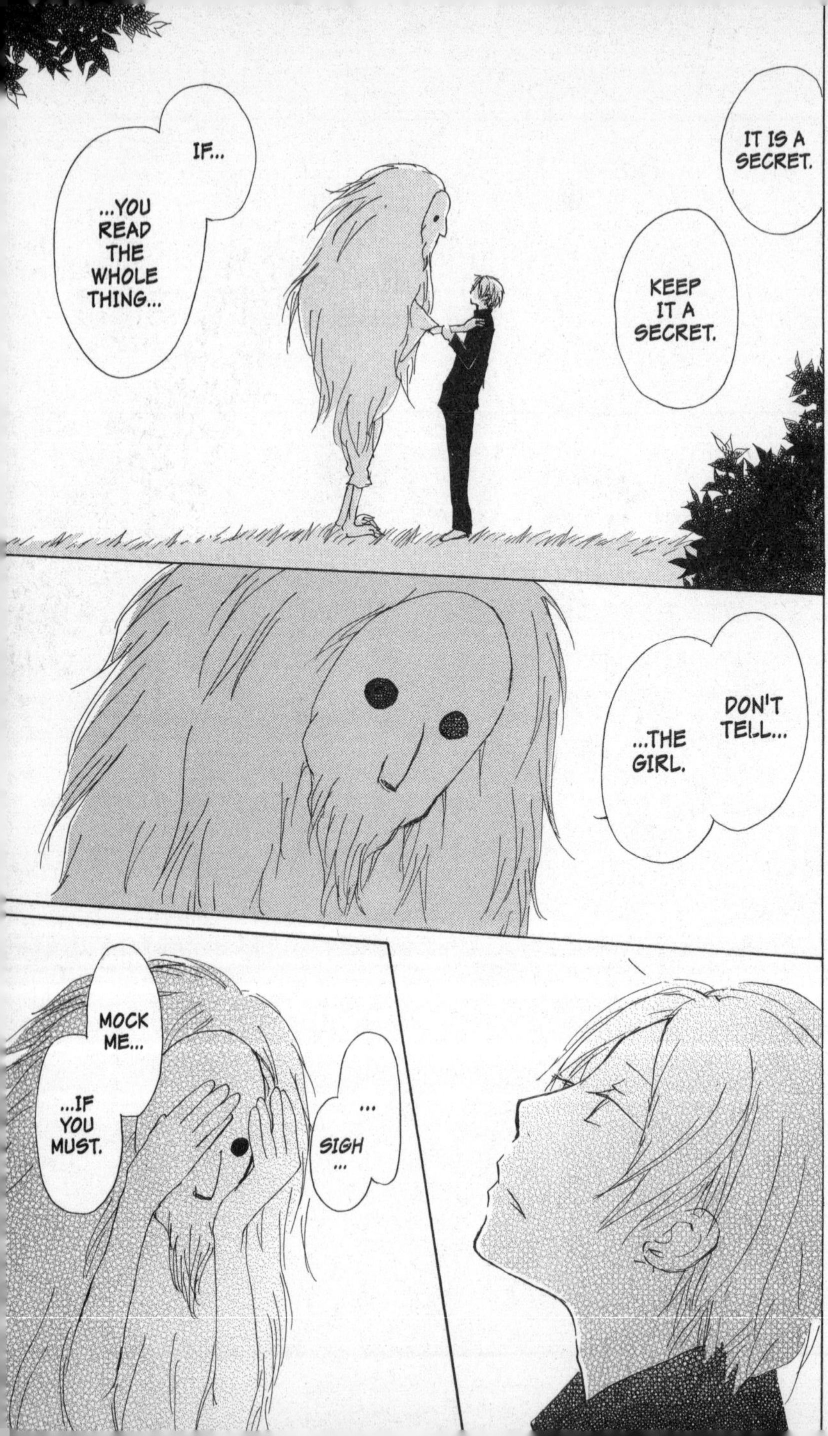
IT IS A SECRET.
KEEP IT A SECRET.
IF...
...YOU READ THE WHOLE THING...
DON'T TELL...
...THE GIRL.
... SIGH ...
MOCK ME...
...IF YOU MUST.

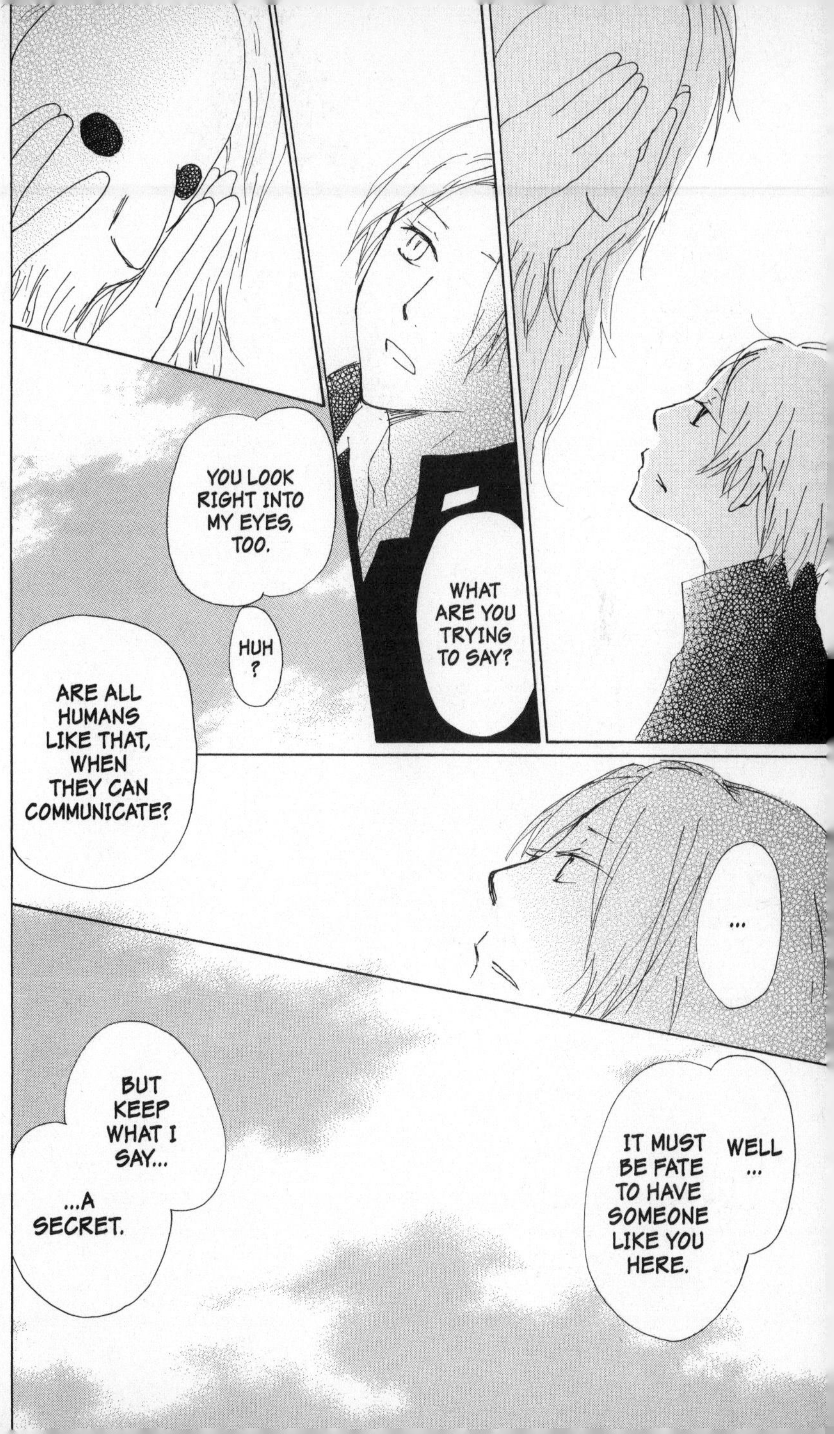
YOU LOOK RIGHT INTO MY EYES, TOO.
HUH?
ARE ALL HUMANS LIKE THAT, WHEN THEY CAN COMMUNICATE?
WHAT ARE YOU TRYING TO SAY?
...
WELL...
IT MUST BE FATE TO HAVE SOMEONE LIKE YOU HERE.
BUT KEEP WHAT I SAY...
...A SECRET.

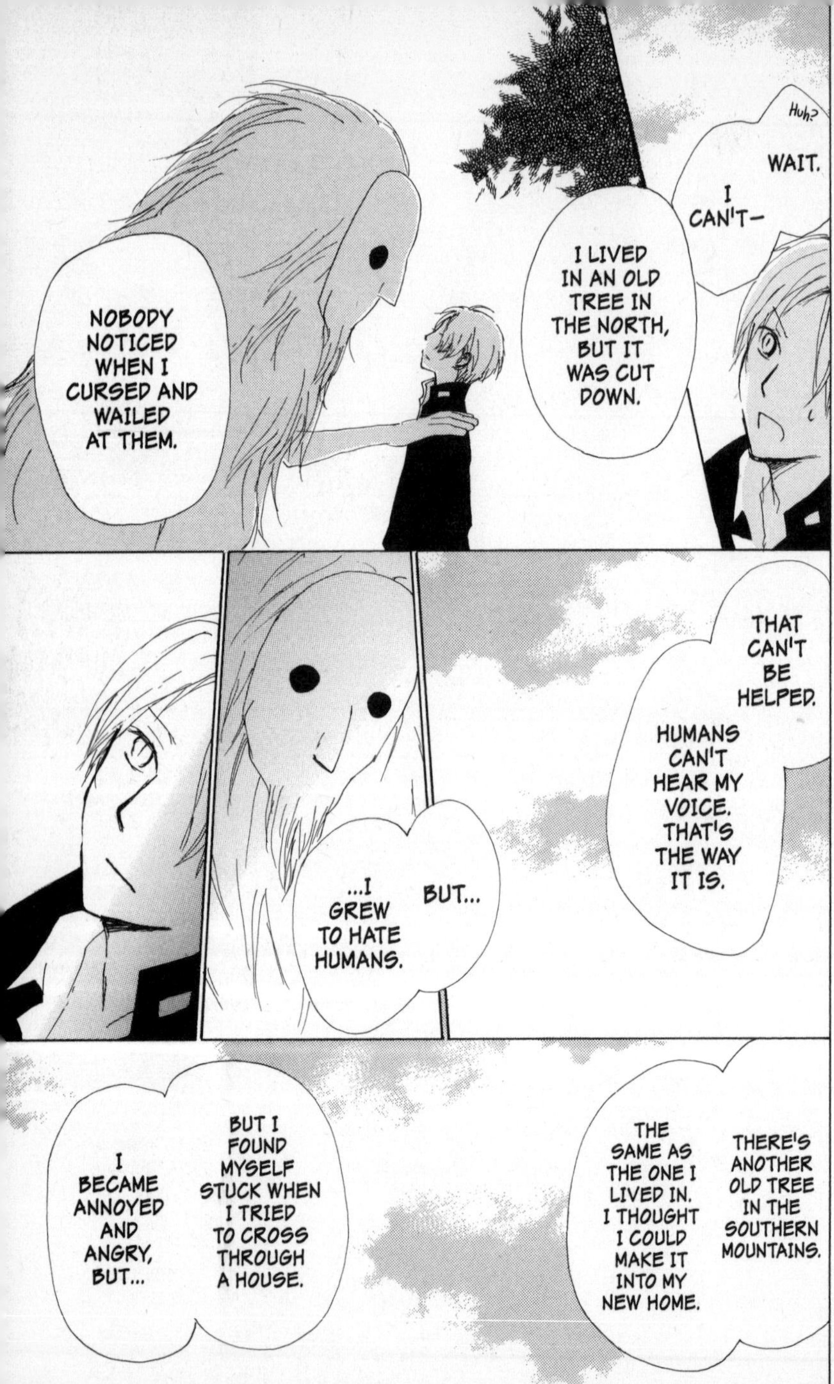
Huh?
WAIT.
I CAN'T—
I LIVED IN AN OLD TREE IN THE NORTH, BUT IT WAS CUT DOWN.
NOBODY NOTICED WHEN I CURSED AND WAILED AT THEM.
THAT CAN'T BE HELPED.
HUMANS CAN'T HEAR MY VOICE. THAT'S THE WAY IT IS.
BUT...
...I GREW TO HATE HUMANS.
THERE'S ANOTHER OLD TREE IN THE SOUTHERN MOUNTAINS.
THE SAME AS THE ONE I LIVED IN. I THOUGHT I COULD MAKE IT INTO MY NEW HOME.
BUT I FOUND MYSELF STUCK WHEN I TRIED TO CROSS THROUGH A HOUSE.
I BECAME ANNOYED AND ANGRY, BUT...

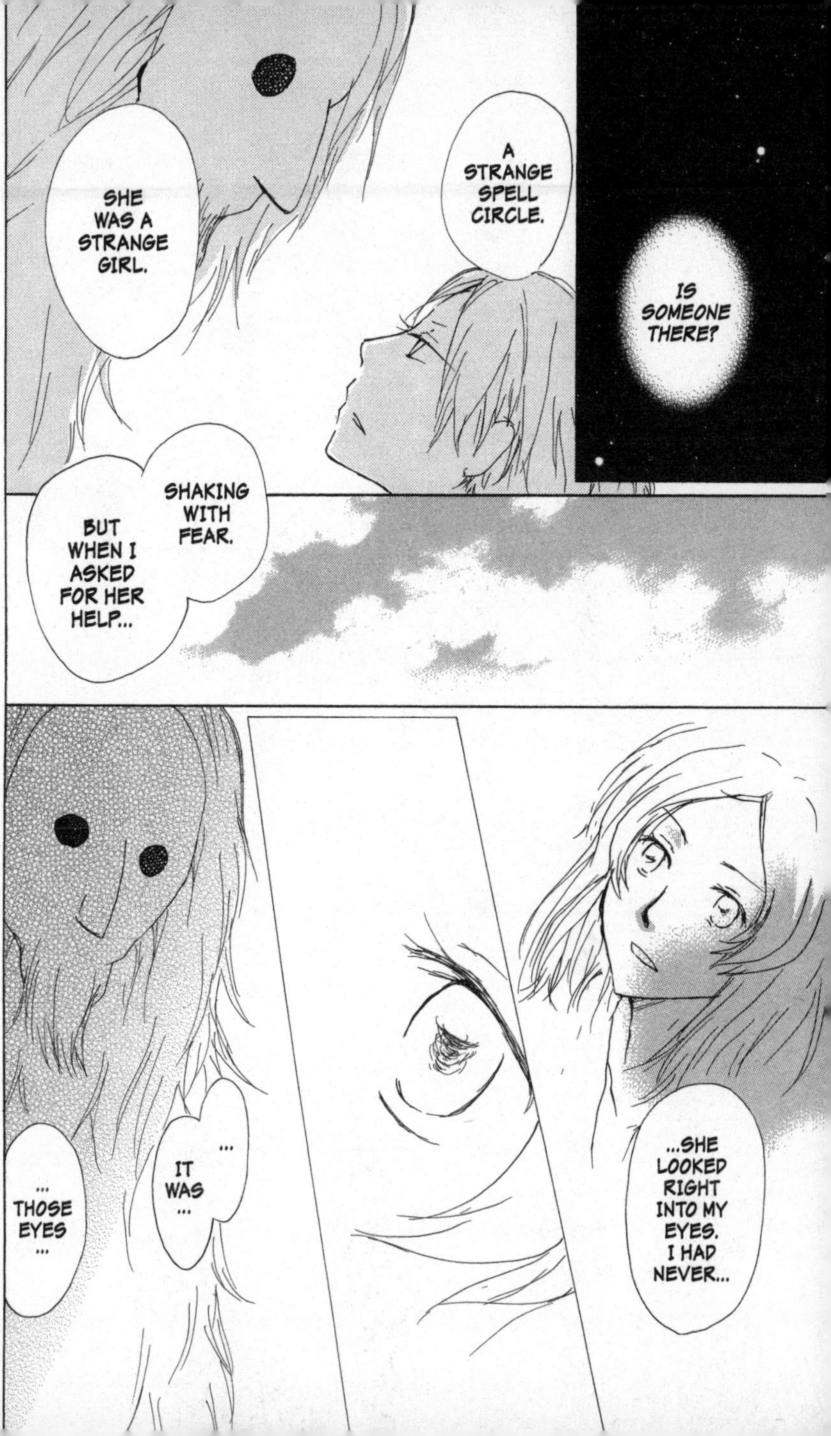
IS SOMEONE THERE?
A STRANGE SPELL CIRCLE.
SHE WAS A STRANGE GIRL.
SHAKING WITH FEAR.
BUT WHEN I ASKED FOR HER HELP...
...SHE LOOKED RIGHT INTO MY EYES. I HAD NEVER...
... IT WAS ...
... THOSE EYES ...

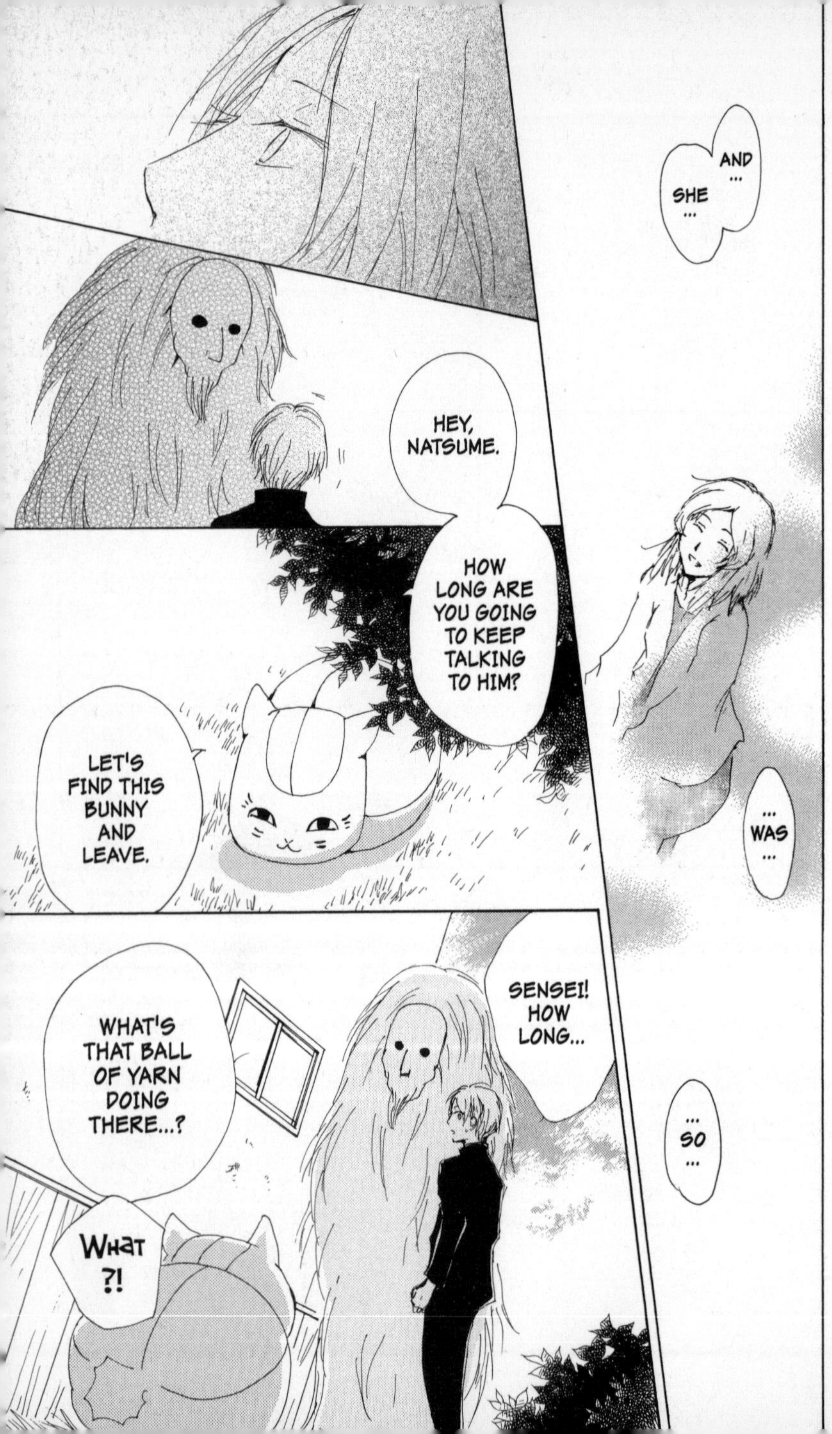
AND ... SHE ...
... WAS ...
... SO ...
HEY, NATSUME.
HOW LONG ARE YOU GOING TO KEEP TALKING TO HIM?
LET'S FIND THIS BUNNY AND LEAVE.
SENSEI! HOW LONG...
WHAT'S THAT BALL OF YARN DOING THERE...?
WHAT ?!

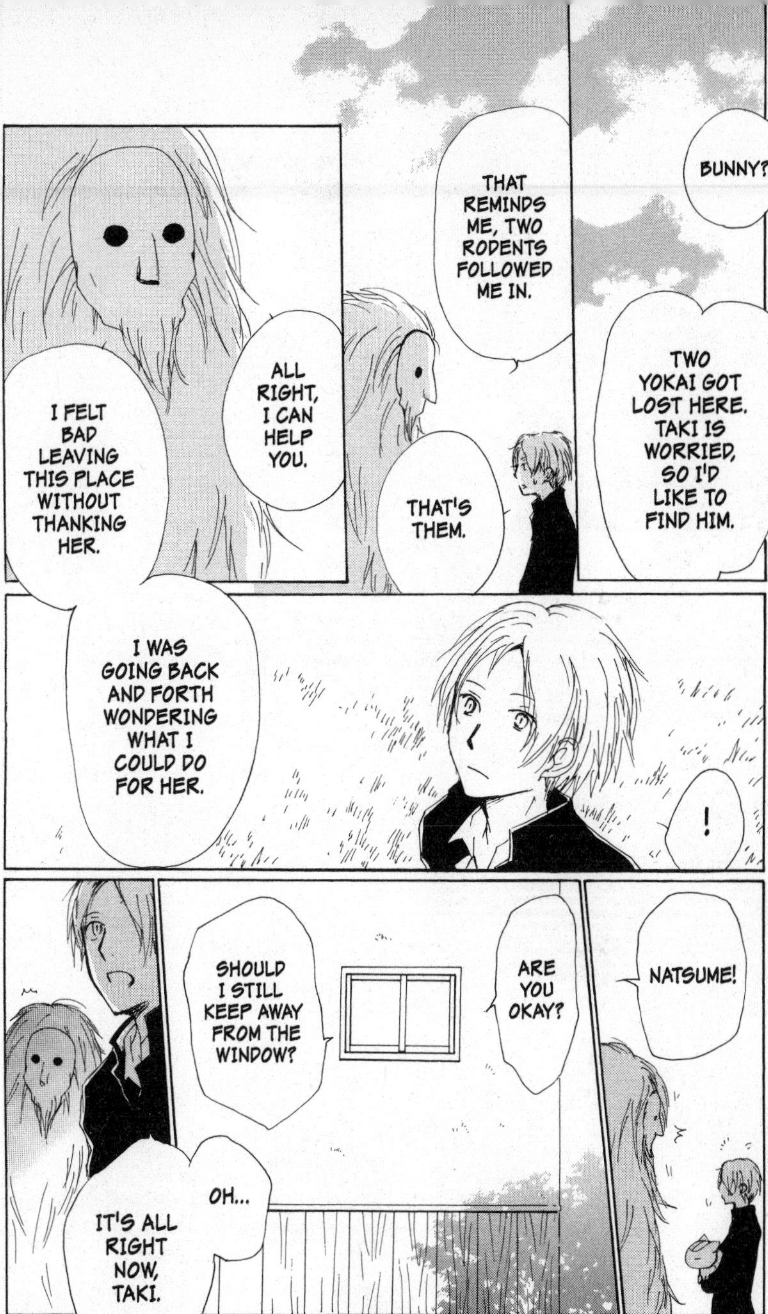
BUNNY?
TWO YOKAI GOT LOST HERE. TAKI IS WORRIED, SO I'D LIKE TO FIND HIM.
THAT REMINDS ME, TWO RODENTS FOLLOWED ME IN.
THAT'S THEM.
ALL RIGHT, I CAN HELP YOU.
I FELT BAD LEAVING THIS PLACE WITHOUT THANKING HER.
!
I WAS GOING BACK AND FORTH WONDERING WHAT I COULD DO FOR HER.
NATSUME!
ARE YOU OKAY?
SHOULD I STILL KEEP AWAY FROM THE WINDOW?
OH...
IT'S ALL RIGHT NOW, TAKI.

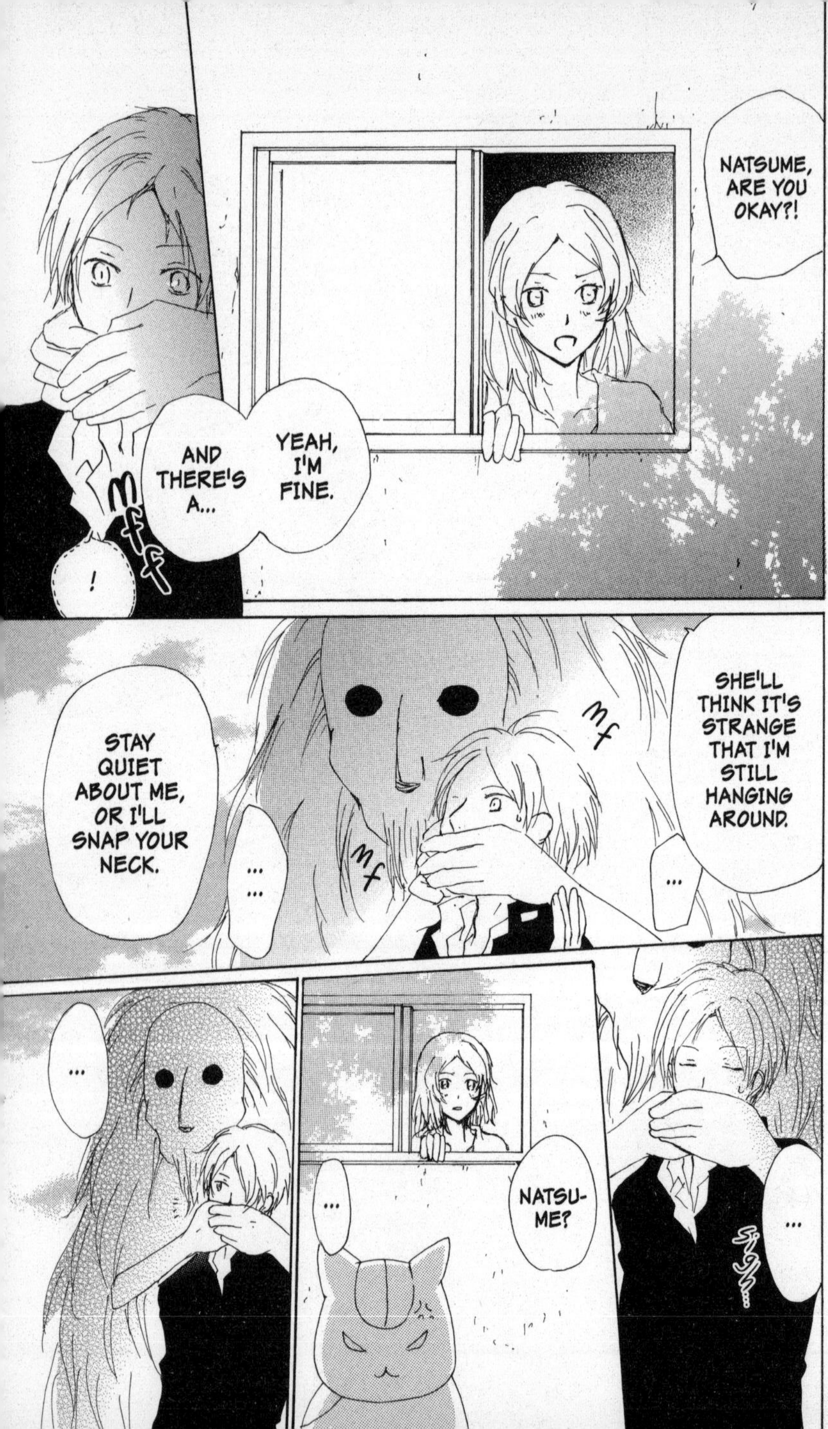
NATSUME, ARE YOU OKAY?!
YEAH, I'M FINE.
AND THERE'S A...
mff
!
SHE'LL THINK IT'S STRANGE THAT I'M STILL HANGING AROUND.
...
mf
mf
STAY QUIET ABOUT ME, OR I'LL SNAP YOUR NECK.
... ...
...
Sigh...
NATSU-ME?
...
...

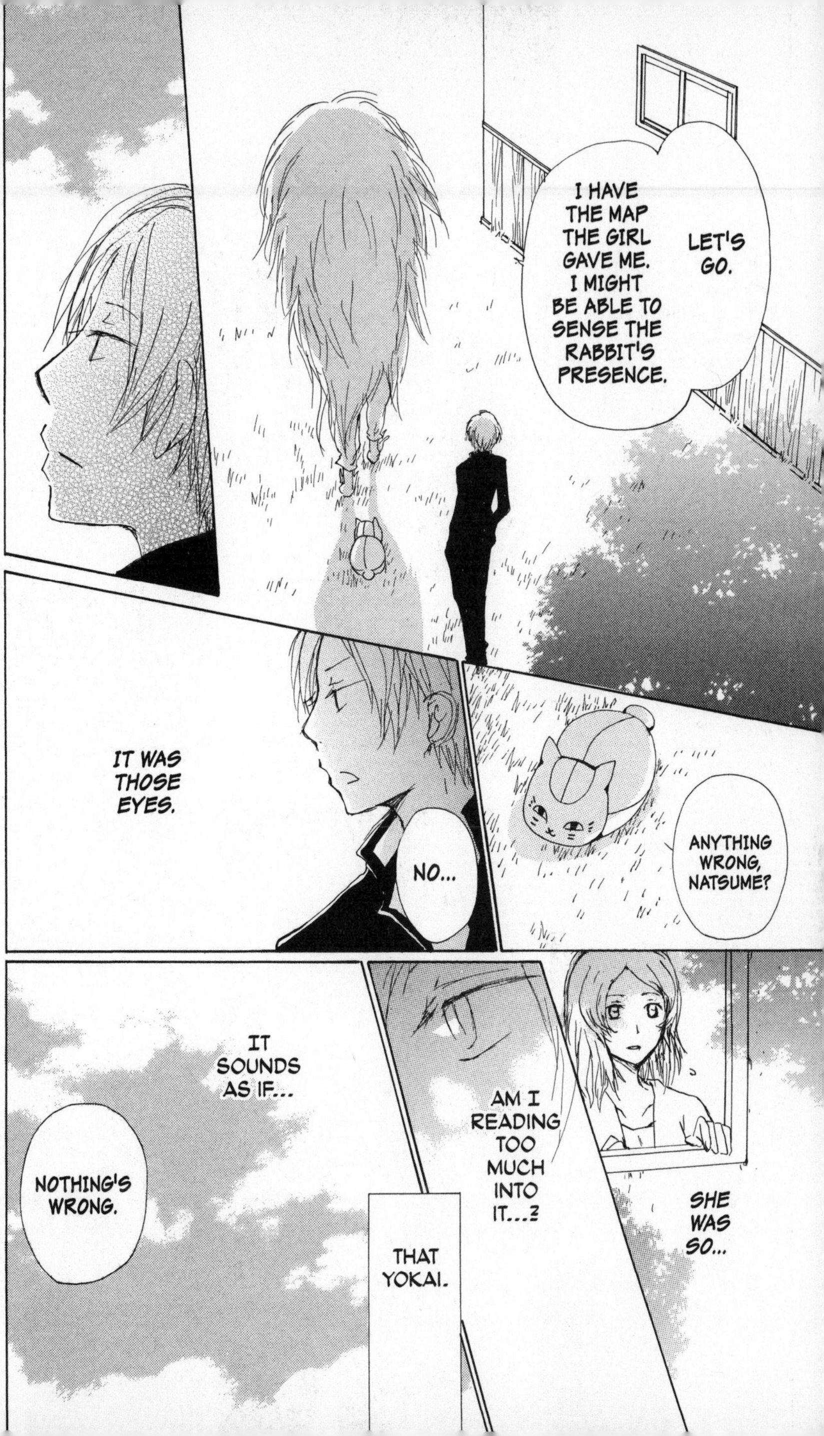
LET'S GO.
I HAVE THE MAP THE GIRL GAVE ME. I MIGHT BE ABLE TO SENSE THE RABBIT'S PRESENCE.
ANYTHING WRONG, NATSUME?
NO...
IT WAS THOSE EYES.
SHE WAS SO...
AM I READING TOO MUCH INTO IT...?
THAT YOKAI.
IT SOUNDS AS IF...
NOTHING'S WRONG.

02

Since it's our tenth anniversary, the magazine LaLa offered mail-in gifts like adorable figurines and a new DVD from the anime Natsume's Book of Friends, and they planned events like a stage reading by the voice actors and a gallery of my art. If you only read the graphic novels, please check out the LaLa and Hakusensha web-sites for details.

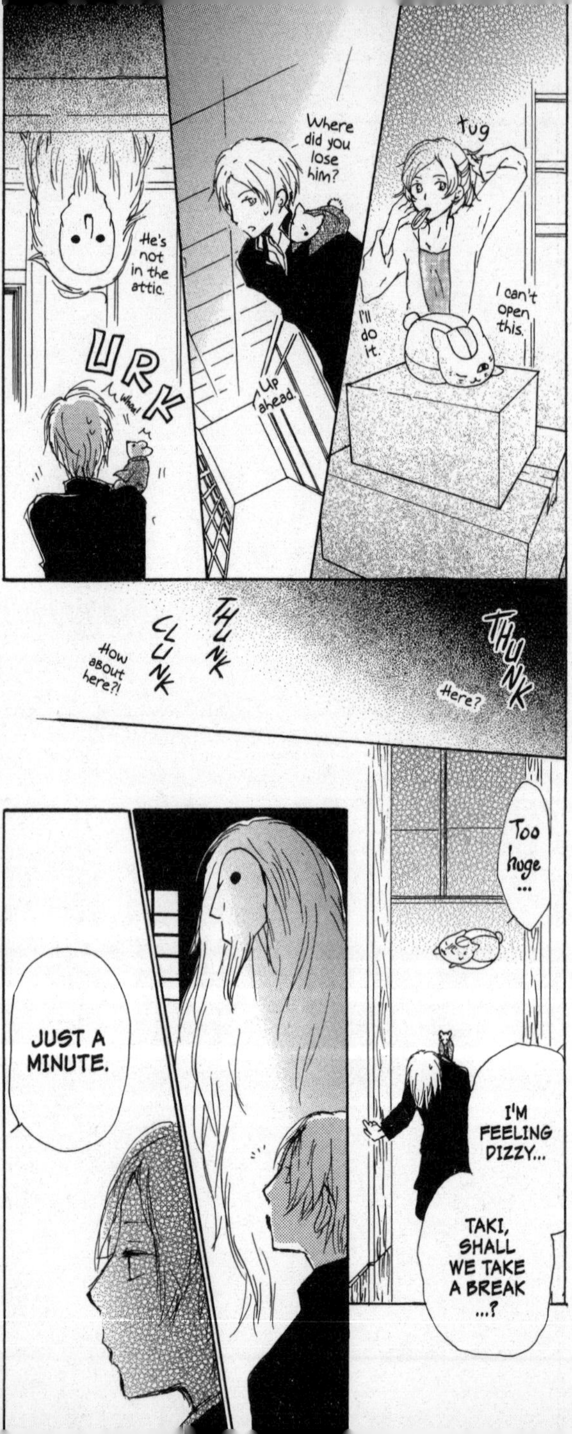
tug
I can't open this.
I'll do it.
Where did you lose him?
Up ahead.
He's not in the attic.
URK
Whoa!
THUNK
Here?
THUNK
CLUNK
How about here?!
Too huge...
I'M FEELING DIZZY...
TAKI, SHALL WE TAKE A BREAK ...?
JUST A MINUTE.

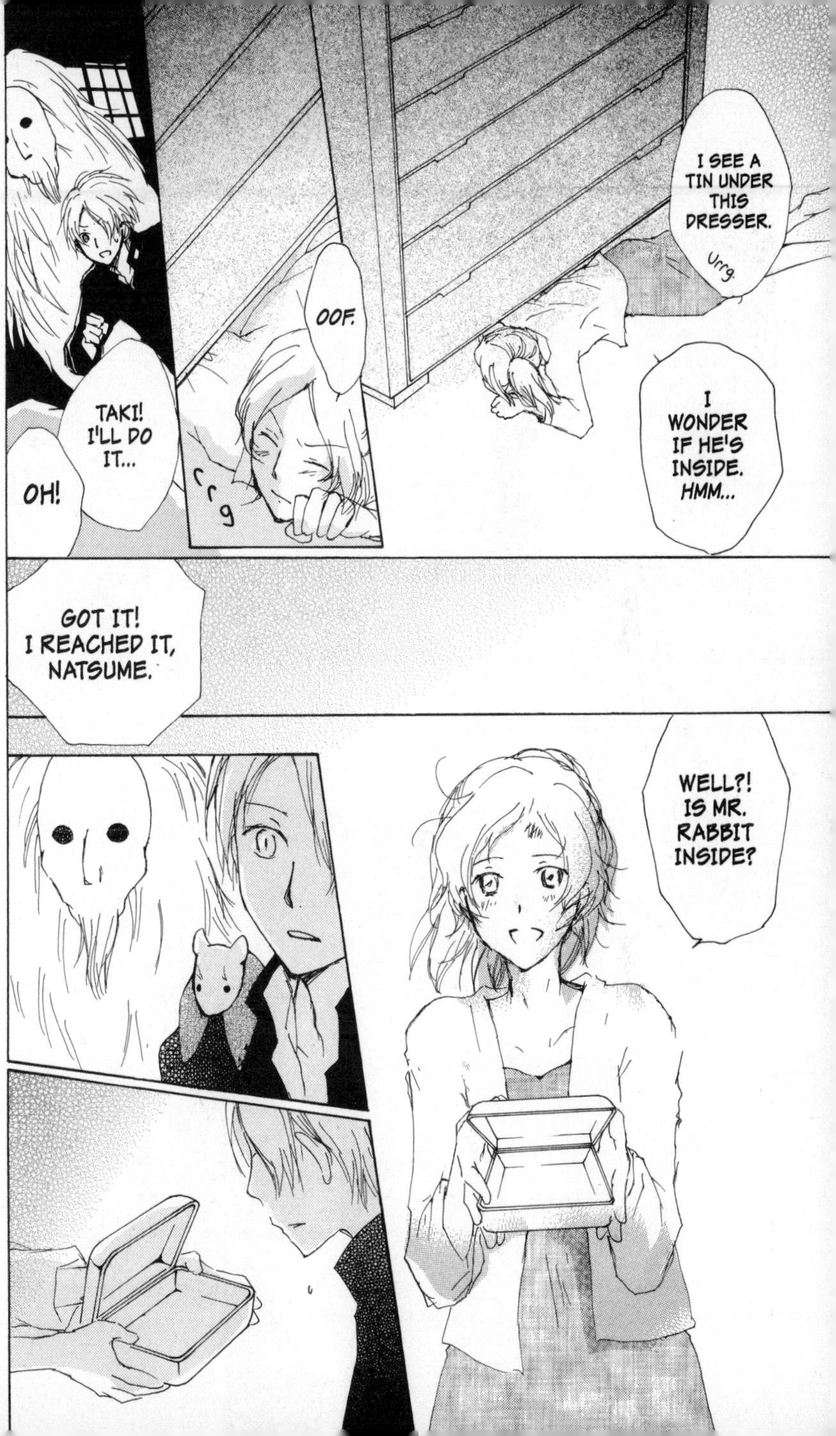
I SEE A TIN UNDER THIS DRESSER.
Urrg.
I WONDER IF HE'S INSIDE. HMM...
OOF.
TAKI! I'LL DO IT...
OH!
GOT IT! I REACHED IT, NATSUME.
WELL?! IS MR. RABBIT INSIDE?

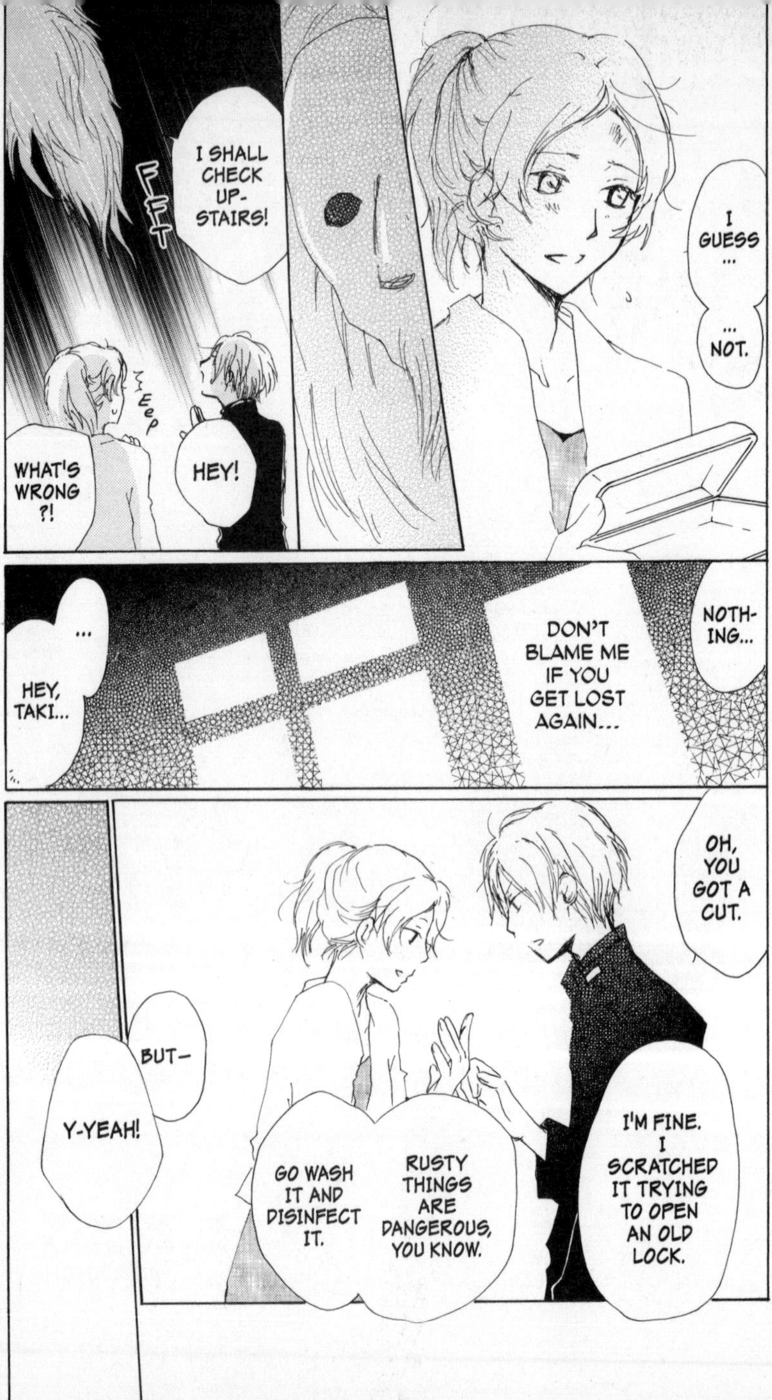
I GUESS... ...NOT.
I SHALL CHECK UP-STAIRS!
FFT
HEY!
Eep
WHAT'S WRONG?!
NOTH-ING...
DON'T BLAME ME IF YOU GET LOST AGAIN...
... HEY, TAKI...
OH, YOU GOT A CUT.
I'M FINE. I SCRATCHED IT TRYING TO OPEN AN OLD LOCK.
RUSTY THINGS ARE DANGEROUS, YOU KNOW.
GO WASH IT AND DISINFECT IT.
BUT—
Y-YEAH!

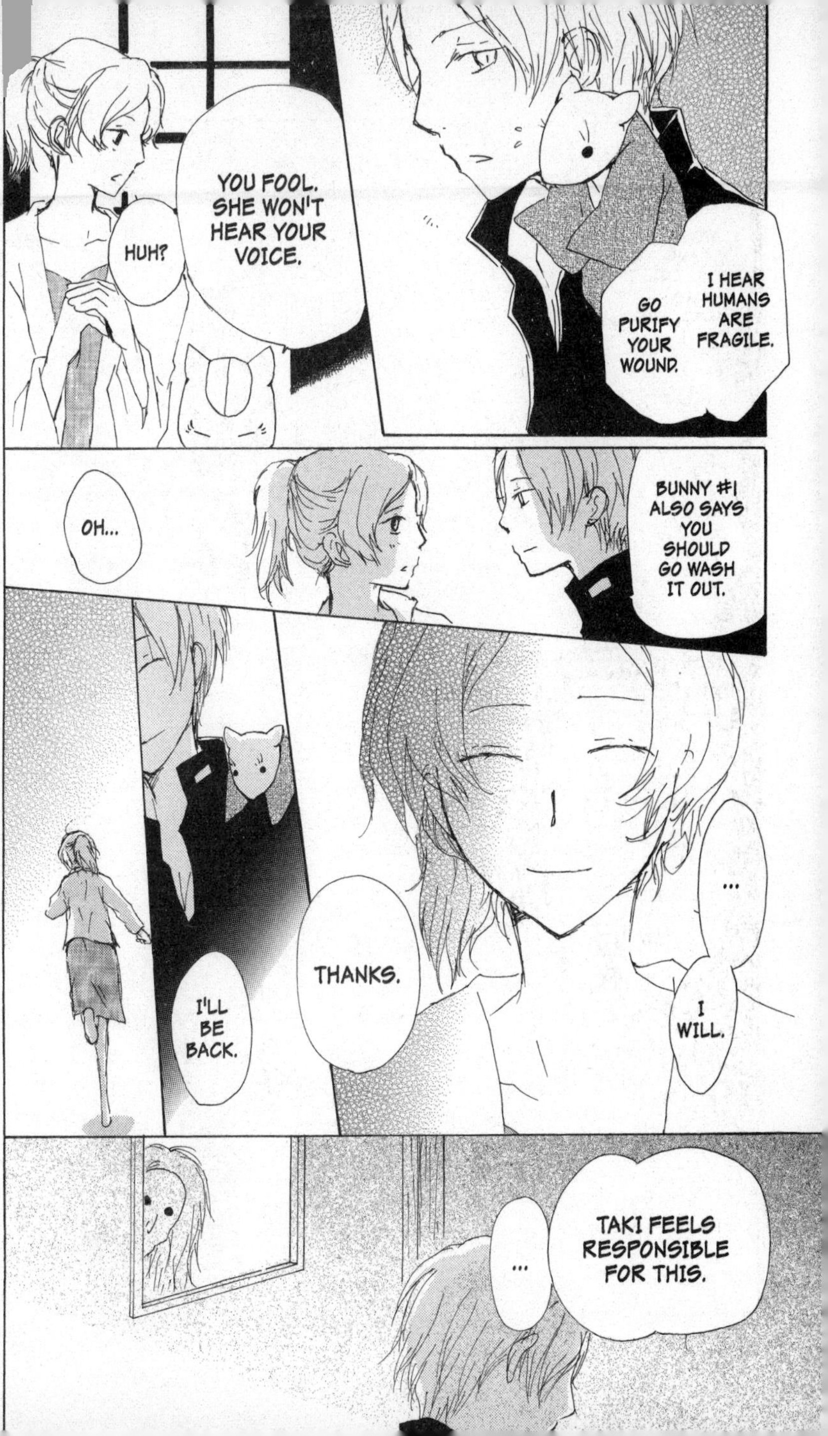
I HEAR HUMANS ARE FRAGILE.
GO PURIFY YOUR WOUND.
YOU FOOL. SHE WON'T HEAR YOUR VOICE.
HUH?
BUNNY #1 ALSO SAYS YOU SHOULD GO WASH IT OUT.
OH...
...
I WILL.
THANKS.
I'LL BE BACK.
TAKI FEELS RESPONSIBLE FOR THIS.
...

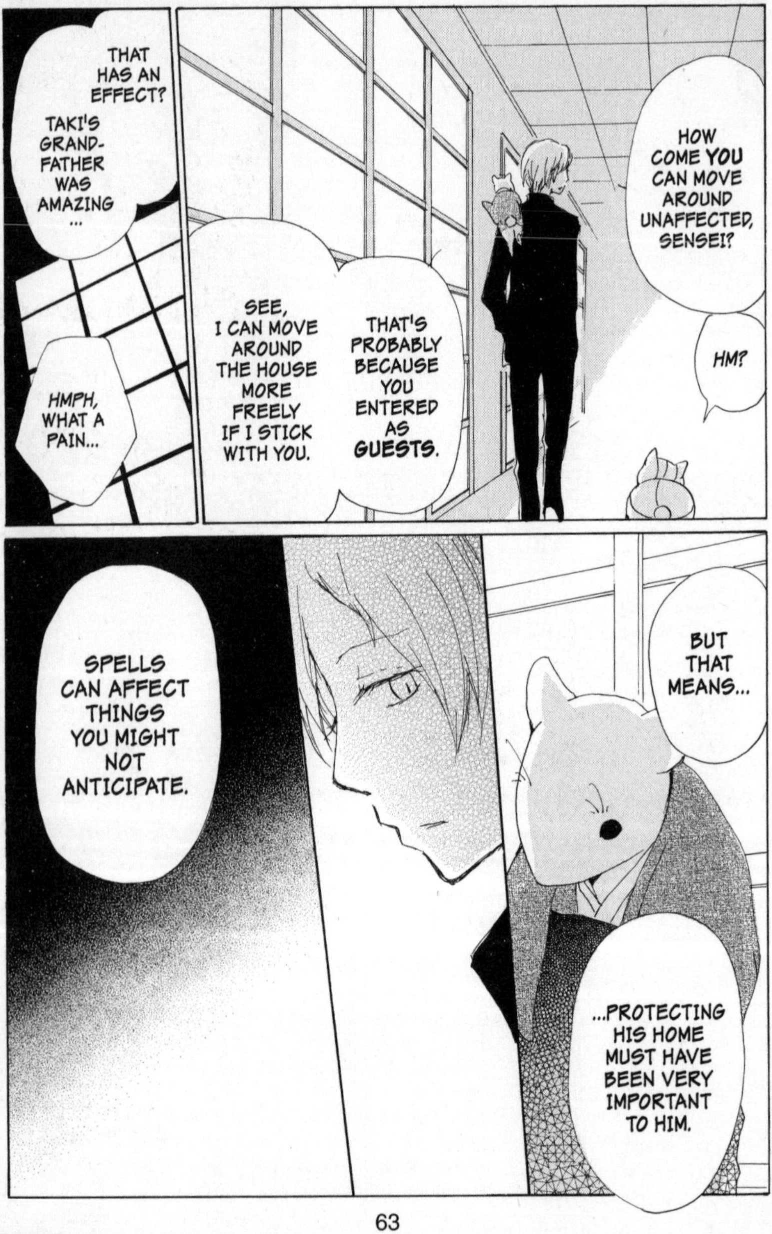
HOW COME YOU CAN MOVE AROUND UNAFFECTED, SENSEI?
HM?
THAT'S PROBABLY BECAUSE YOU ENTERED AS GUESTS.
SEE, I CAN MOVE AROUND THE HOUSE MORE FREELY IF I STICK WITH YOU.
THAT HAS AN EFFECT?
TAKI'S GRAND-FATHER WAS AMAZING ...
HMPH, WHAT A PAIN...
BUT THAT MEANS...
...PROTECTING HIS HOME MUST HAVE BEEN VERY IMPORTANT TO HIM.
SPELLS CAN AFFECT THINGS YOU MIGHT NOT ANTICIPATE.

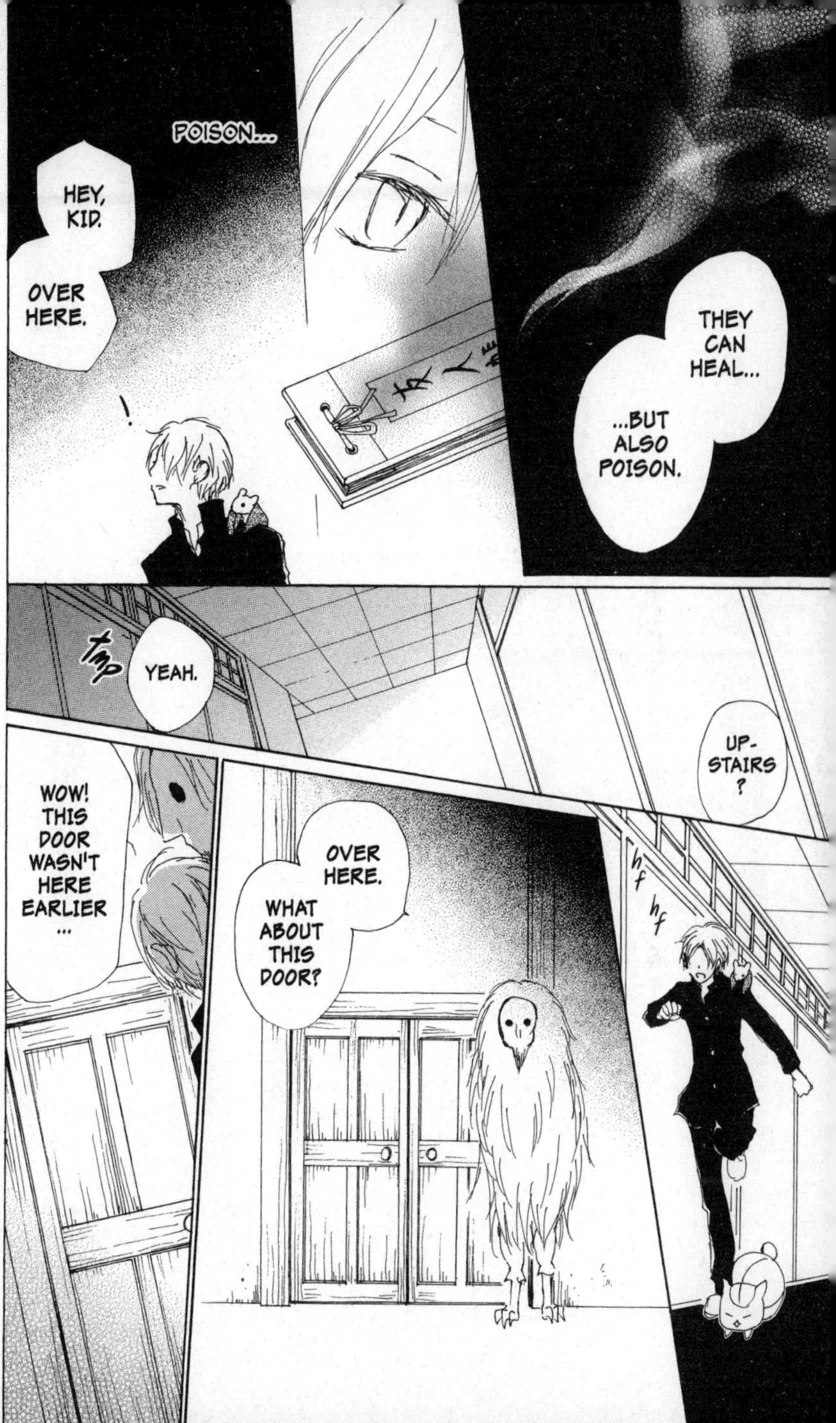
THEY CAN HEAL...
...BUT ALSO POISON.
POISON...
HEY, KID.
OVER HERE.
!
UP-STAIRS?
tmp
YEAH.
hf hf
OVER HERE.
WHAT ABOUT THIS DOOR?
WOW! THIS DOOR WASN'T HERE EARLIER...

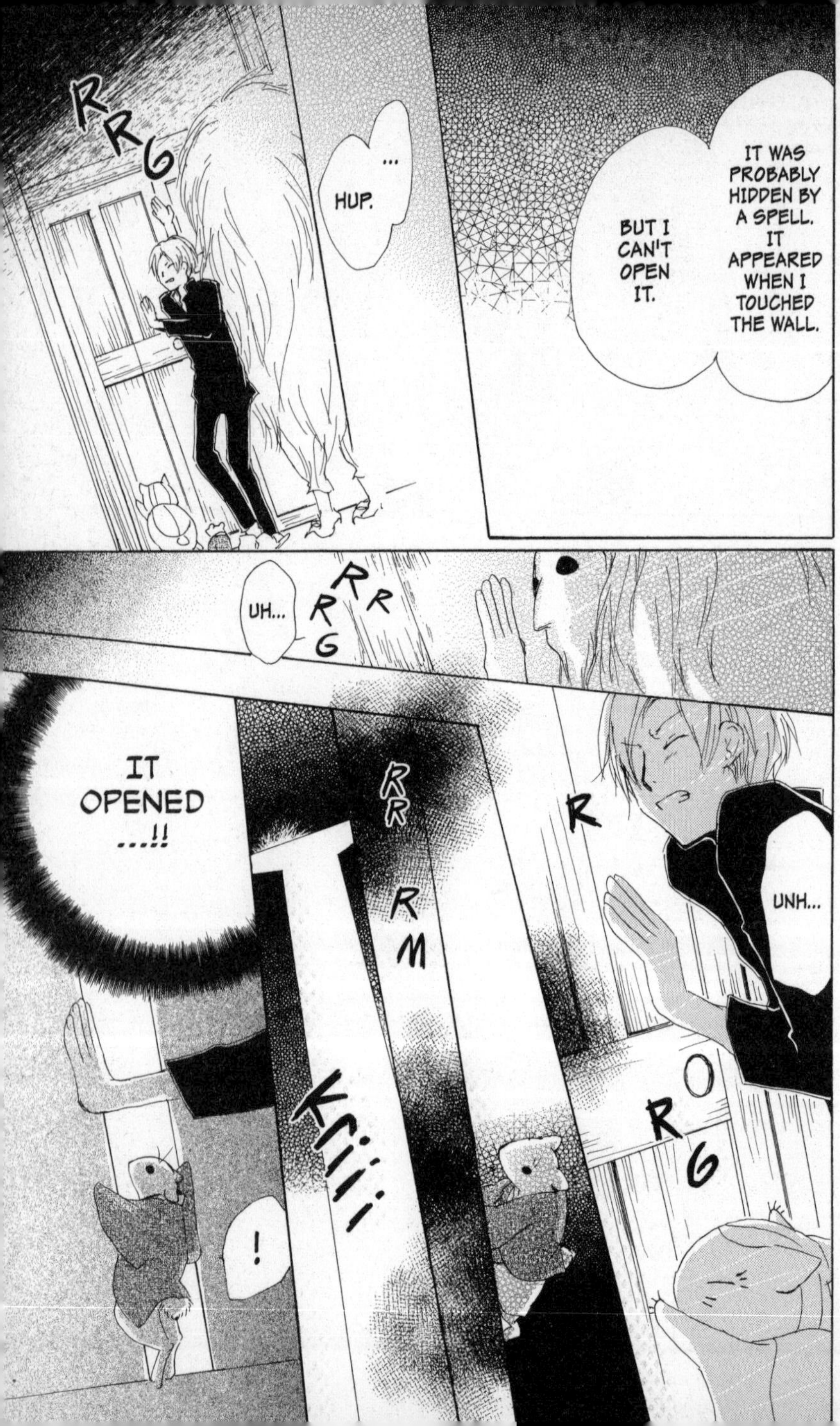
IT WAS PROBABLY HIDDEN BY A SPELL. IT APPEARED WHEN I TOUCHED THE WALL.
BUT I CAN'T OPEN IT.
... HUP.
RRG
RRRG
UH...
R
UNH...
ROG
RRRM
Kriiii
IT OPENED ...!!
!

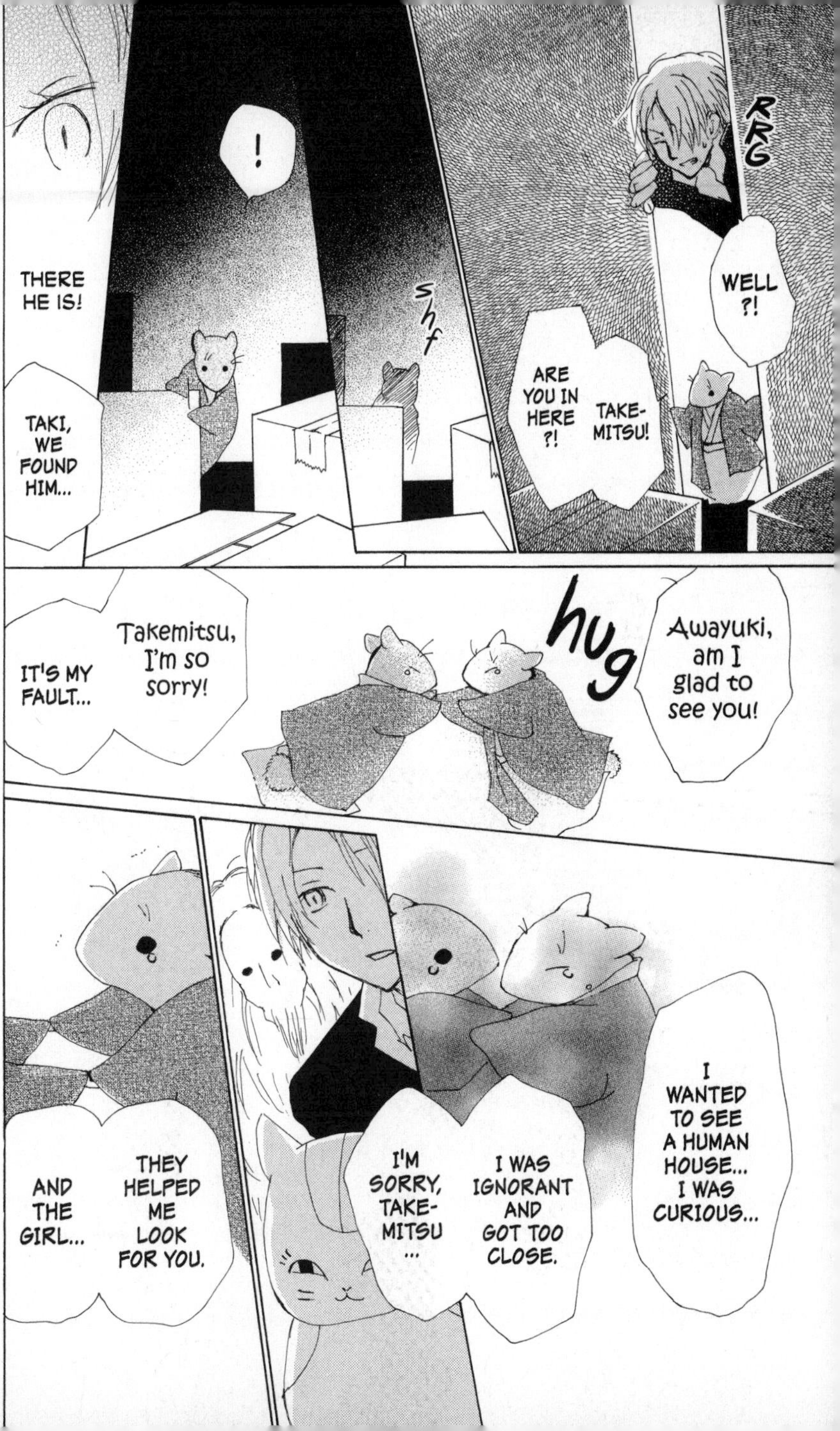
RRG
WELL?!
TAKEMITSU! ARE YOU IN HERE?!
!
shf
THERE HE IS!
TAKI, WE FOUND HIM...
Awayuki, am I glad to see you!
hug
Takemitsu, I'm so sorry!
IT'S MY FAULT...
I WANTED TO SEE A HUMAN HOUSE... I WAS CURIOUS...
I WAS IGNORANT AND GOT TOO CLOSE.
I'M SORRY, TAKEMITSU...
THEY HELPED ME LOOK FOR YOU.
AND THE GIRL...

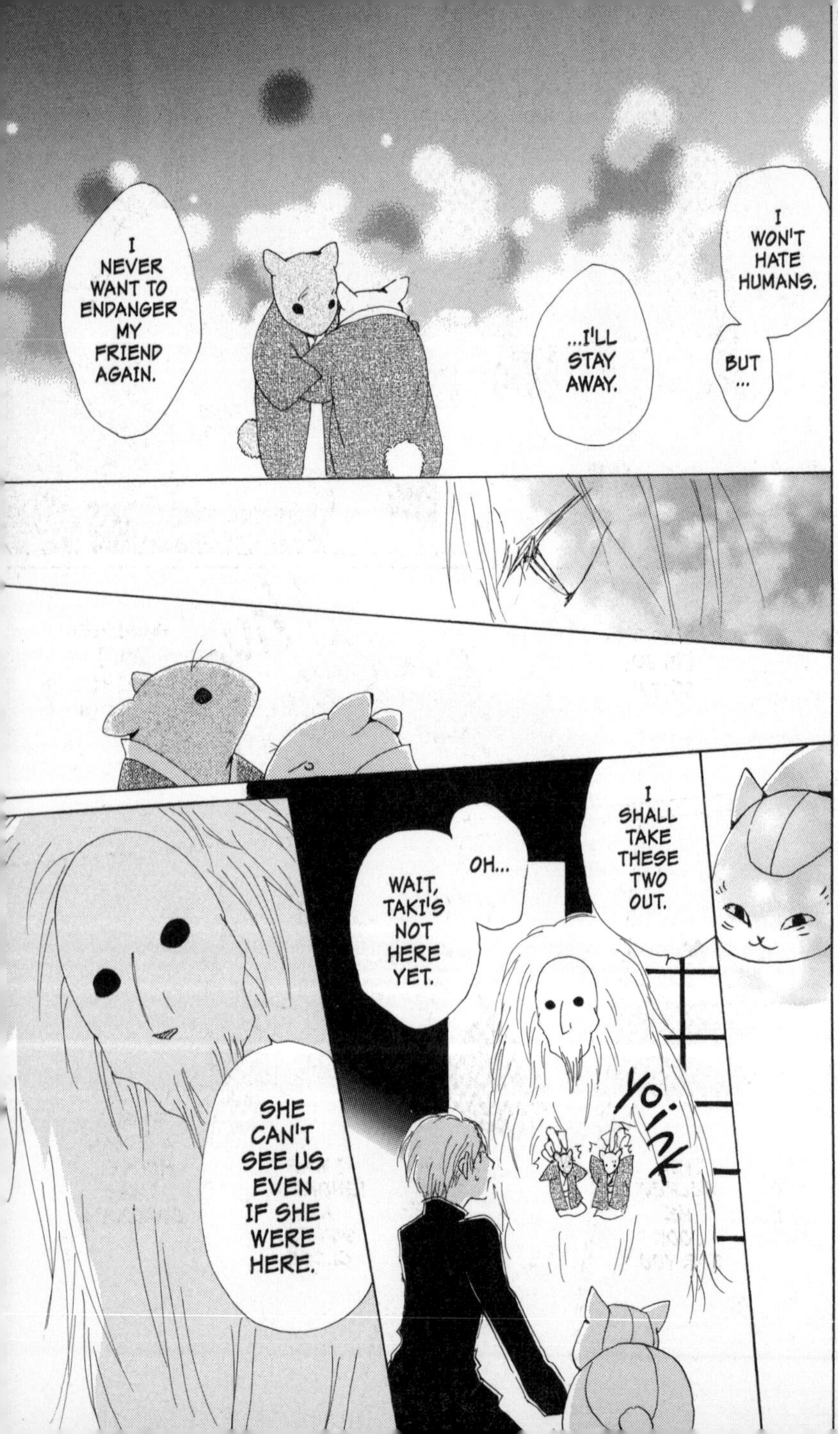
I WON'T HATE HUMANS.
BUT ...
...I'LL STAY AWAY.
I NEVER WANT TO ENDANGER MY FRIEND AGAIN.
I SHALL TAKE THESE TWO OUT.
OH...
WAIT, TAKI'S NOT HERE YET.
YOINK
SHE CAN'T SEE US EVEN IF SHE WERE HERE.

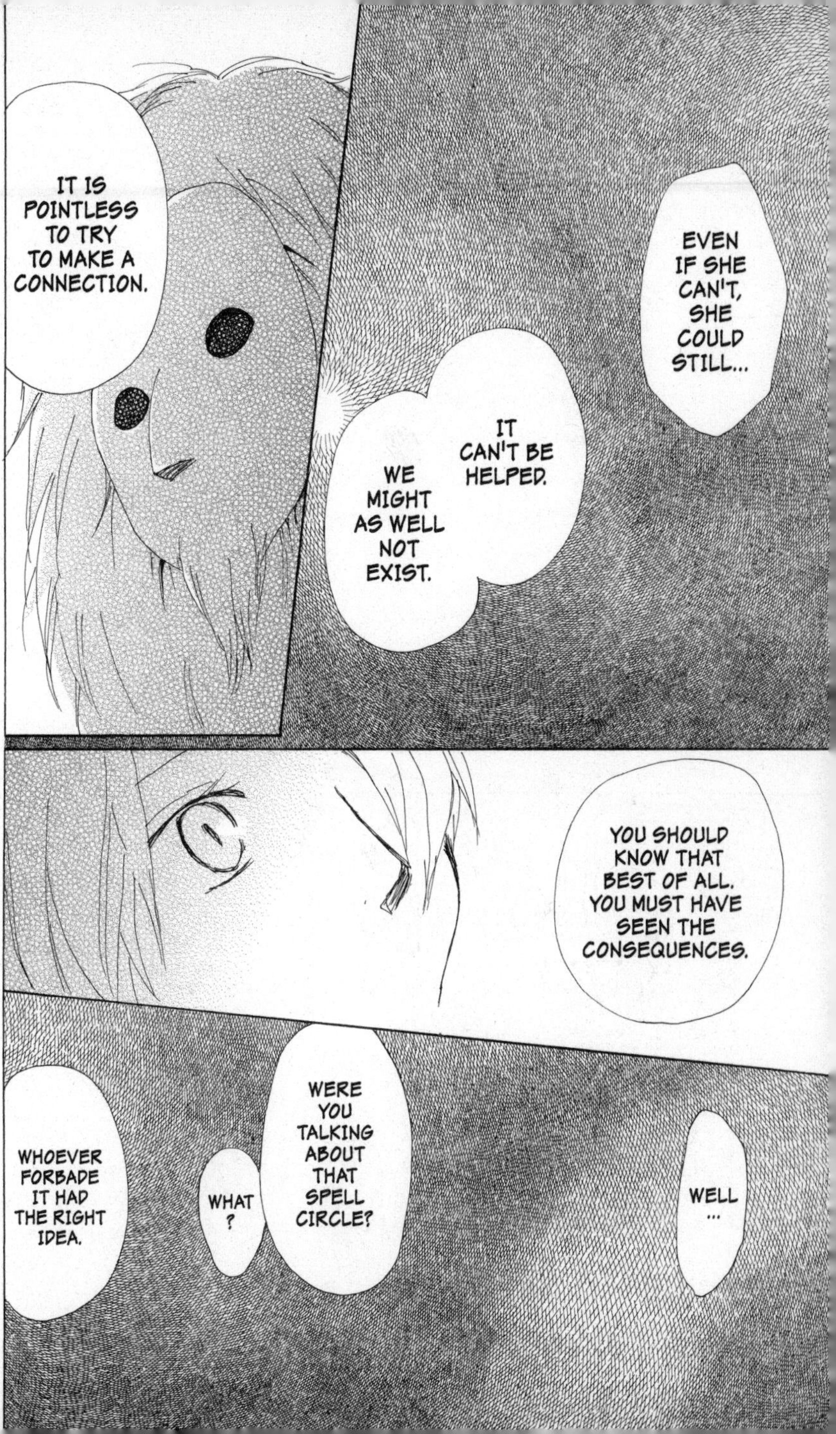
EVEN IF SHE CAN'T, SHE COULD STILL...
IT CAN'T BE HELPED.
WE MIGHT AS WELL NOT EXIST.
IT IS POINTLESS TO TRY TO MAKE A CONNECTION.
YOU SHOULD KNOW THAT BEST OF ALL. YOU MUST HAVE SEEN THE CONSEQUENCES.
WELL ...
WERE YOU TALKING ABOUT THAT SPELL CIRCLE?
WHAT ?
WHOEVER FORBADE IT HAD THE RIGHT IDEA.

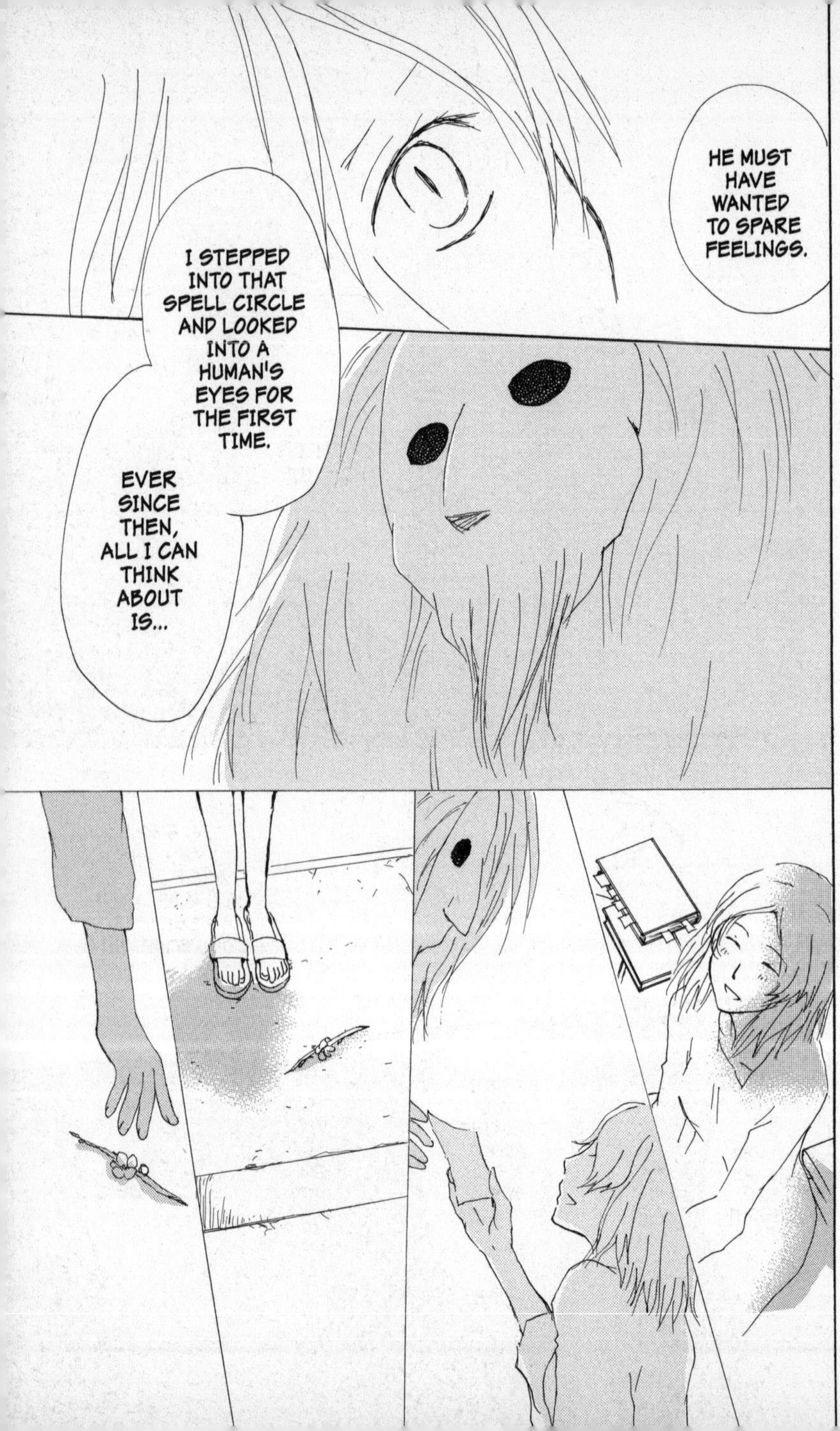
HE MUST HAVE WANTED TO SPARE FEELINGS.
I STEPPED INTO THAT SPELL CIRCLE AND LOOKED INTO A HUMAN'S EYES FOR THE FIRST TIME.
EVER SINCE THEN, ALL I CAN THINK ABOUT IS...

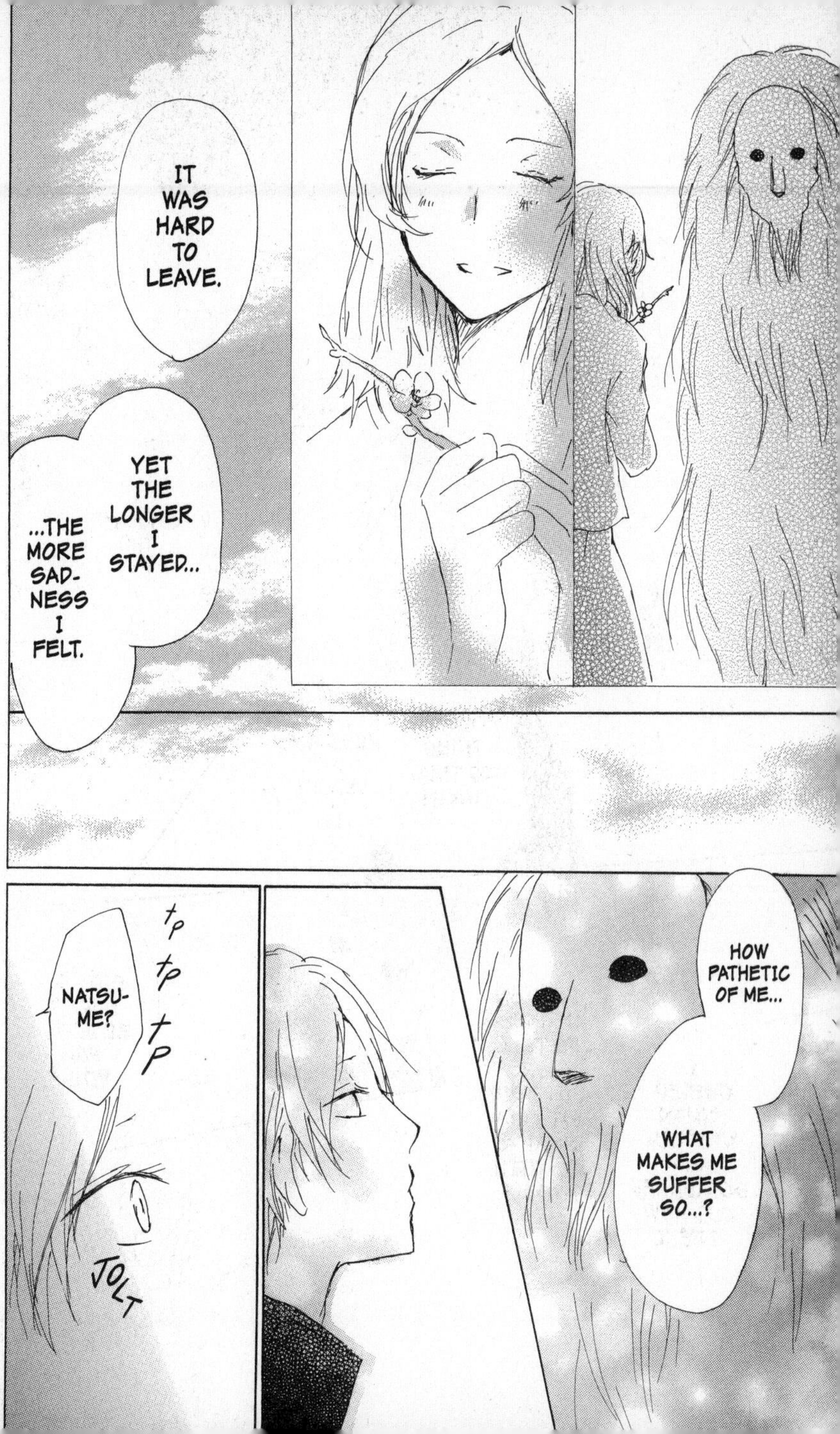
IT WAS HARD TO LEAVE.
YET THE LONGER I STAYED...
...THE MORE SAD-NESS I FELT.
HOW PATHETIC OF ME...
WHAT MAKES ME SUFFER SO...?
tp tp tp
NATSU-ME?
JOLT

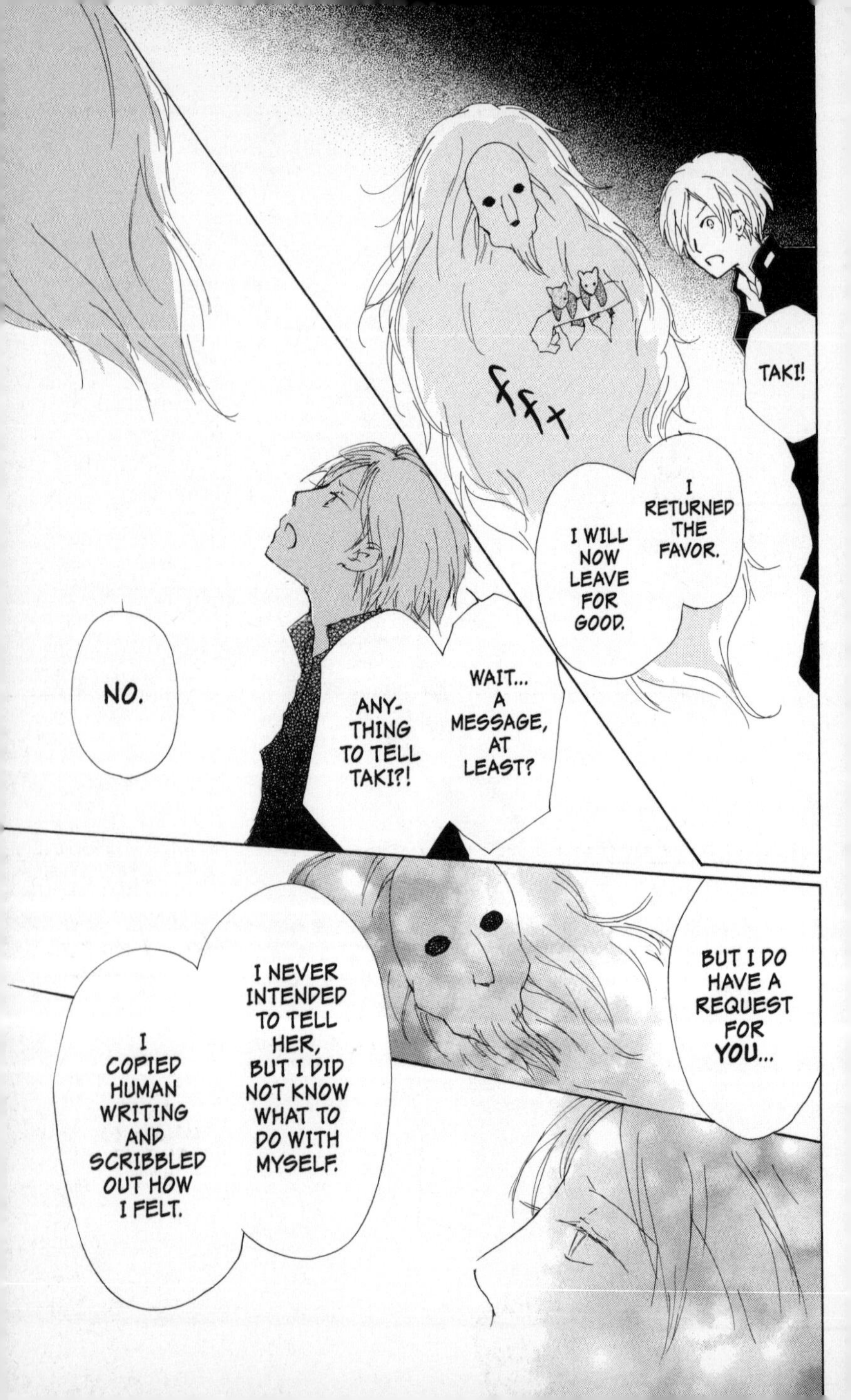
TAKI!
I RETURNED THE FAVOR.
I WILL NOW LEAVE FOR GOOD.
WAIT... A MESSAGE, AT LEAST?
ANYTHING TO TELL TAKI?!
NO.
BUT I DO HAVE A REQUEST FOR YOU...
I NEVER INTENDED TO TELL HER, BUT I DID NOT KNOW WHAT TO DO WITH MYSELF.
I COPIED HUMAN WRITING AND SCRIBBLED OUT HOW I FELT.

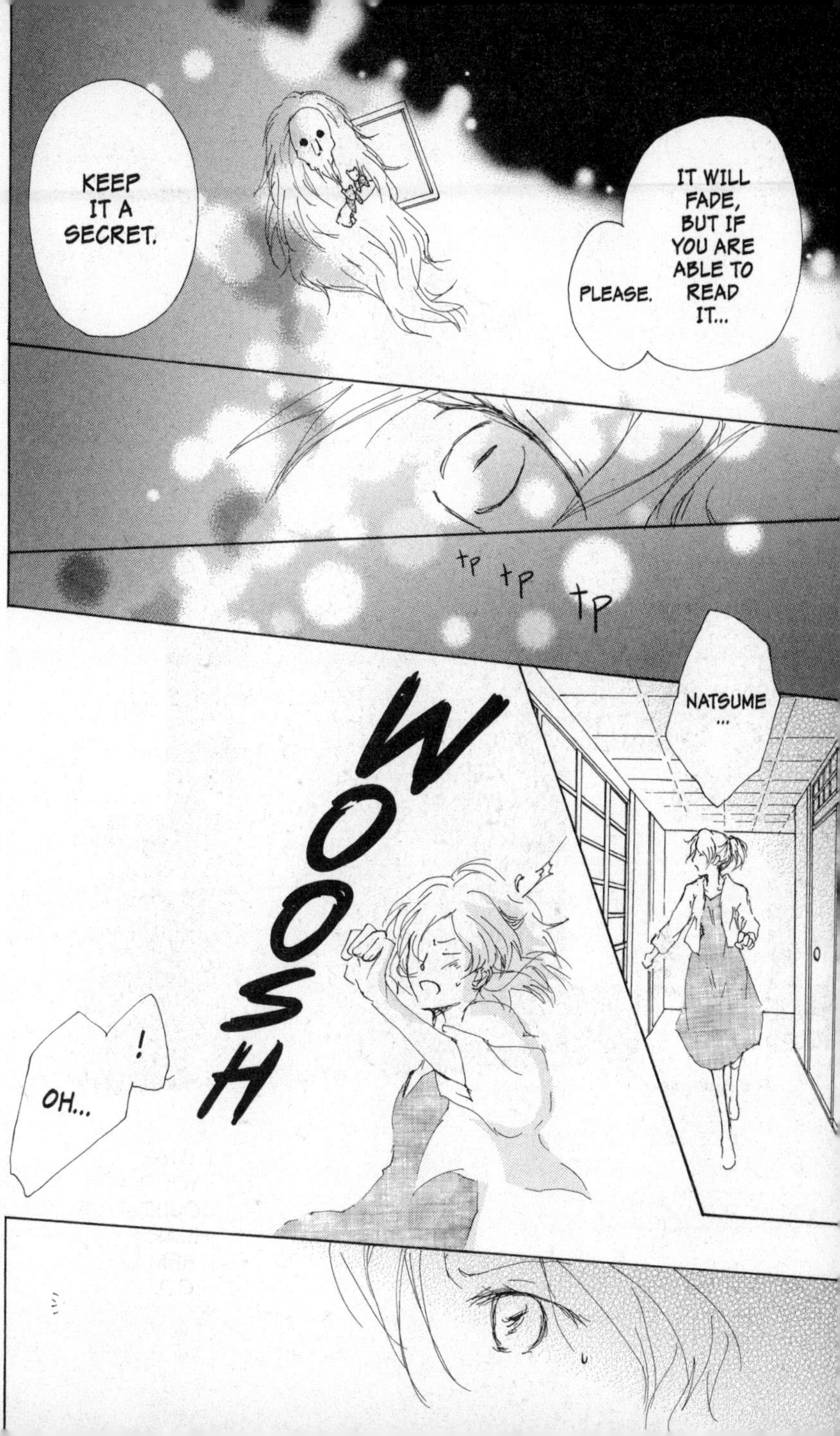
IT WILL FADE, BUT IF YOU ARE ABLE TO READ IT...
PLEASE.
KEEP IT A SECRET.
tp tp tp
NATSUME...
WOOSH
!
OH...

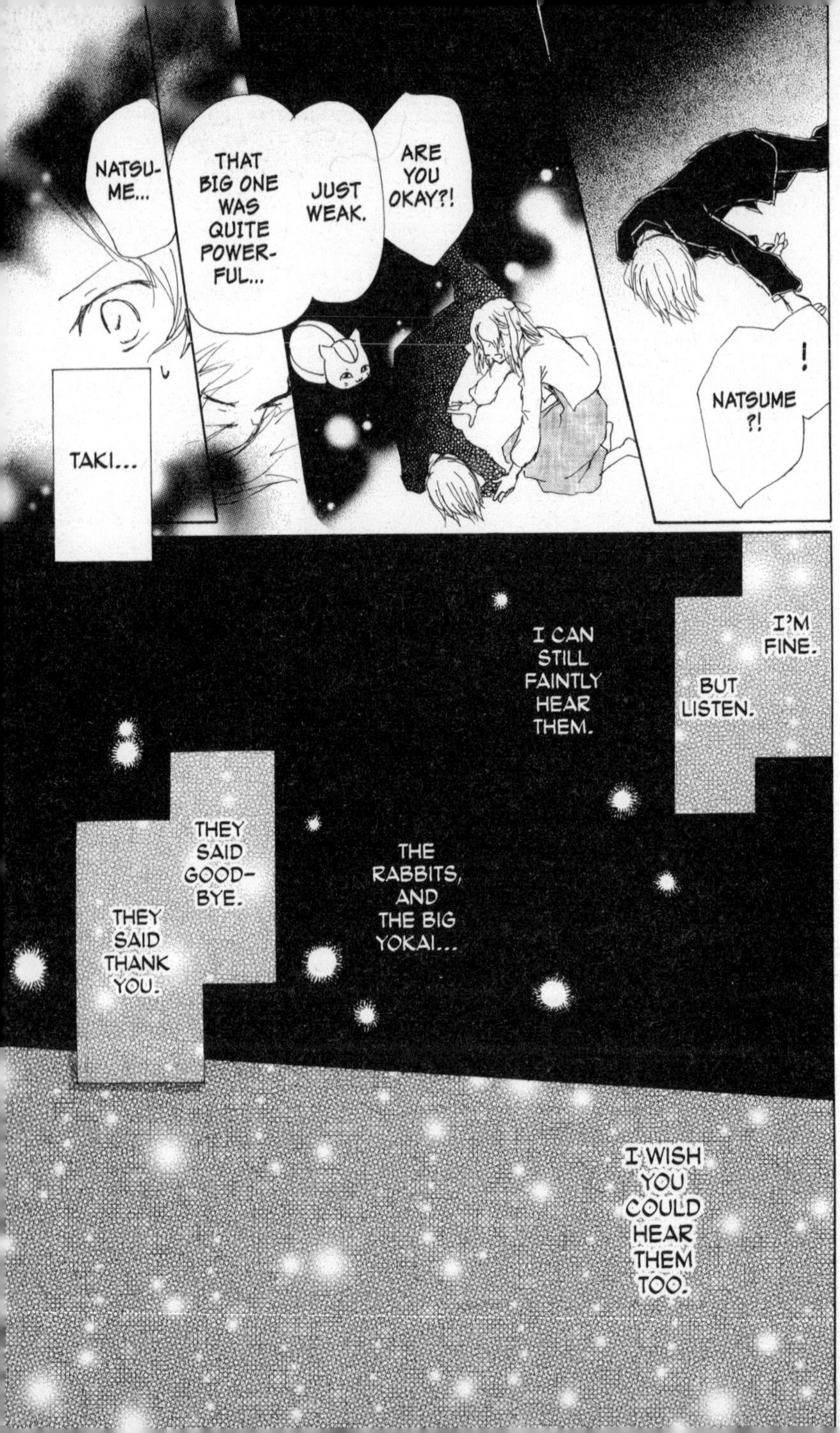
!
NATSUME ?!
ARE YOU OKAY?!
JUST WEAK.
THAT BIG ONE WAS QUITE POWERFUL...
NATSU-ME...
TAKI...
I'M FINE.
BUT LISTEN.
I CAN STILL FAINTLY HEAR THEM.
THE RABBITS, AND THE BIG YOKAI...
THEY SAID GOOD-BYE.
THEY SAID THANK YOU.
I WISH YOU COULD HEAR THEM TOO.

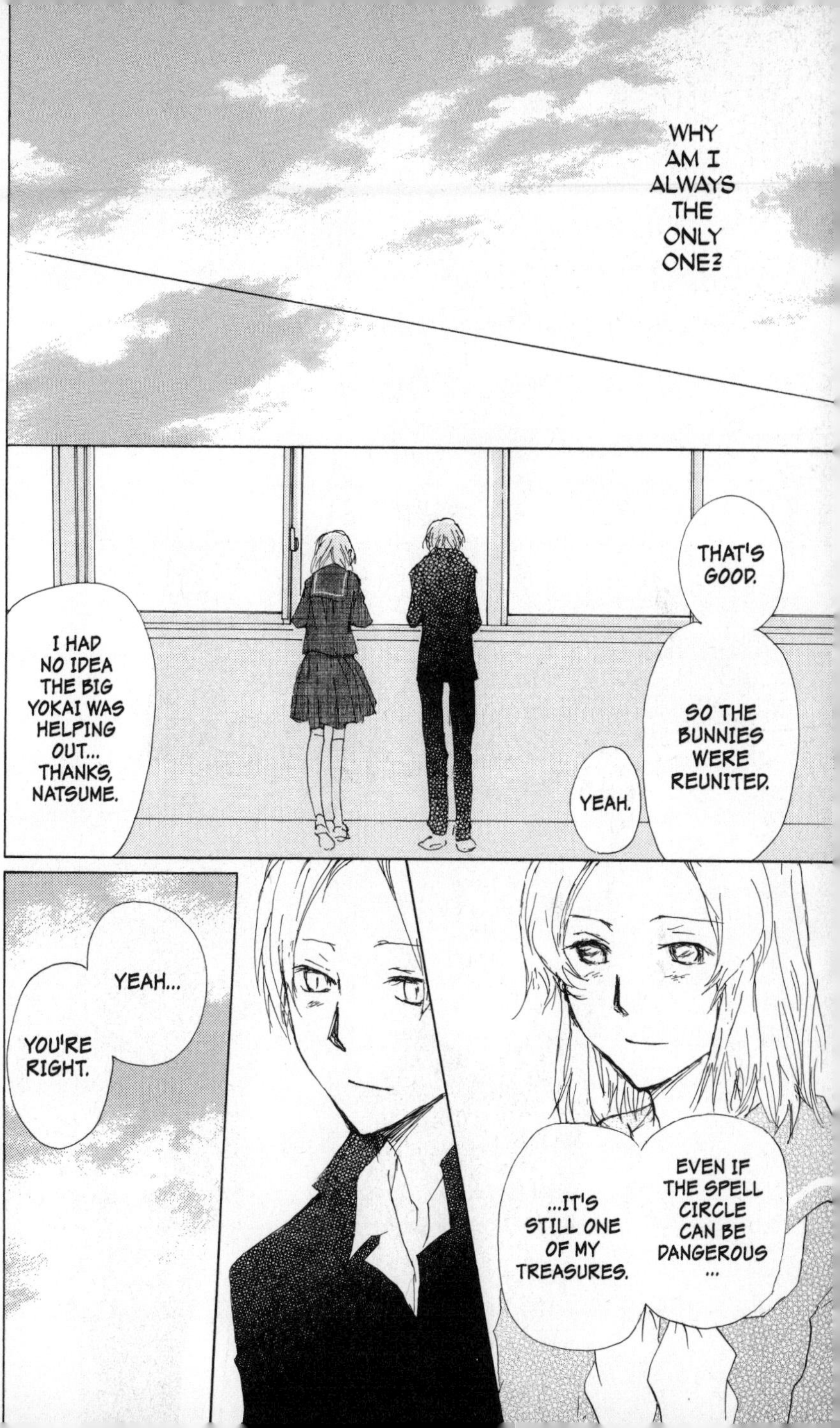
WHY AM I ALWAYS THE ONLY ONE?
THAT'S GOOD.
SO THE BUNNIES WERE REUNITED.
YEAH.
I HAD NO IDEA THE BIG YOKAI WAS HELPING OUT... THANKS, NATSUME.
EVEN IF THE SPELL CIRCLE CAN BE DANGEROUS...
...IT'S STILL ONE OF MY TREASURES.
YEAH...
YOU'RE RIGHT.

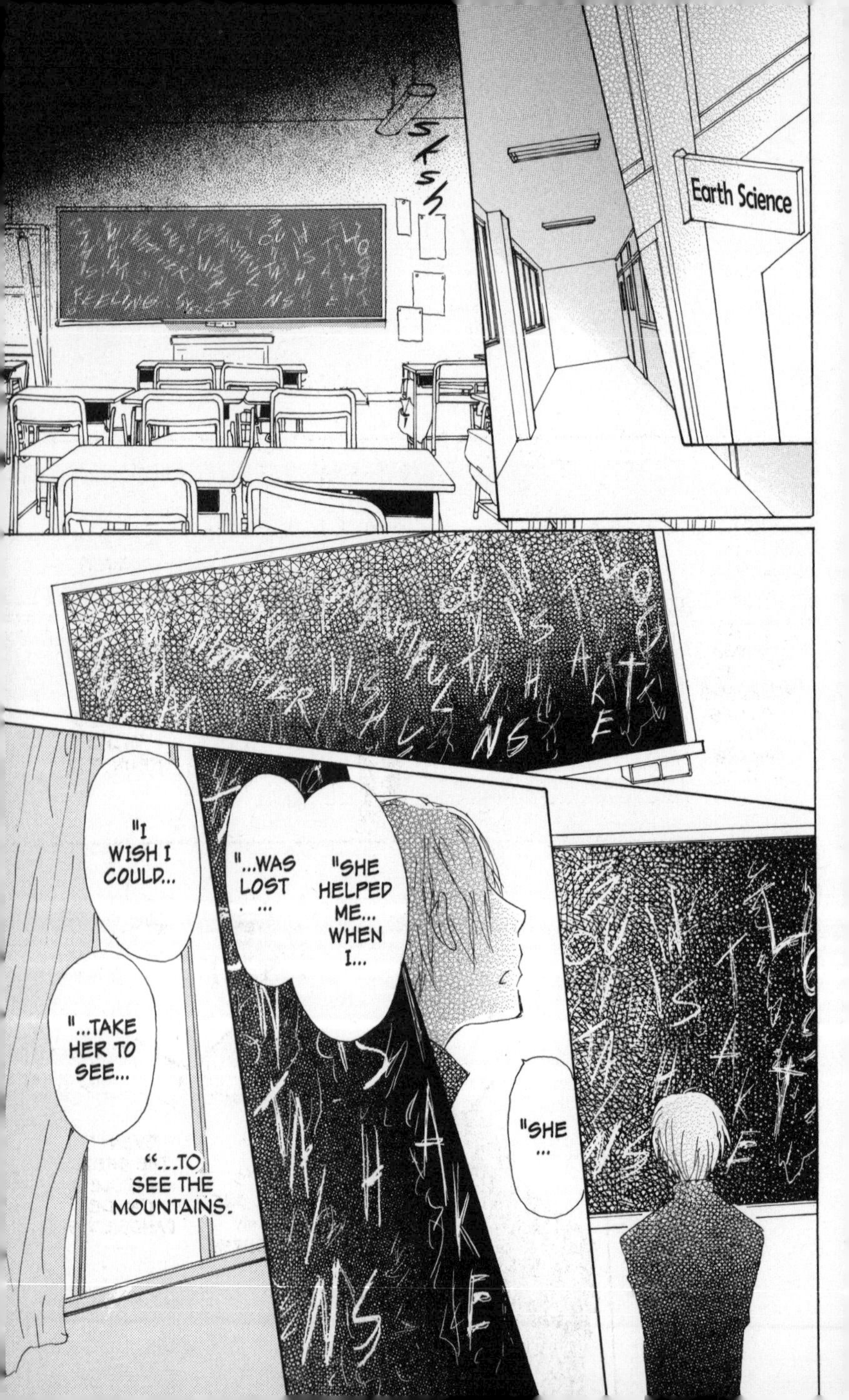
Earth Science
SKSH
"SHE ...
"SHE HELPED ME... WHEN I...
"...WAS LOST . ...
"I WISH I COULD...
"...TAKE HER TO SEE...
"...TO SEE THE MOUNTAINS.

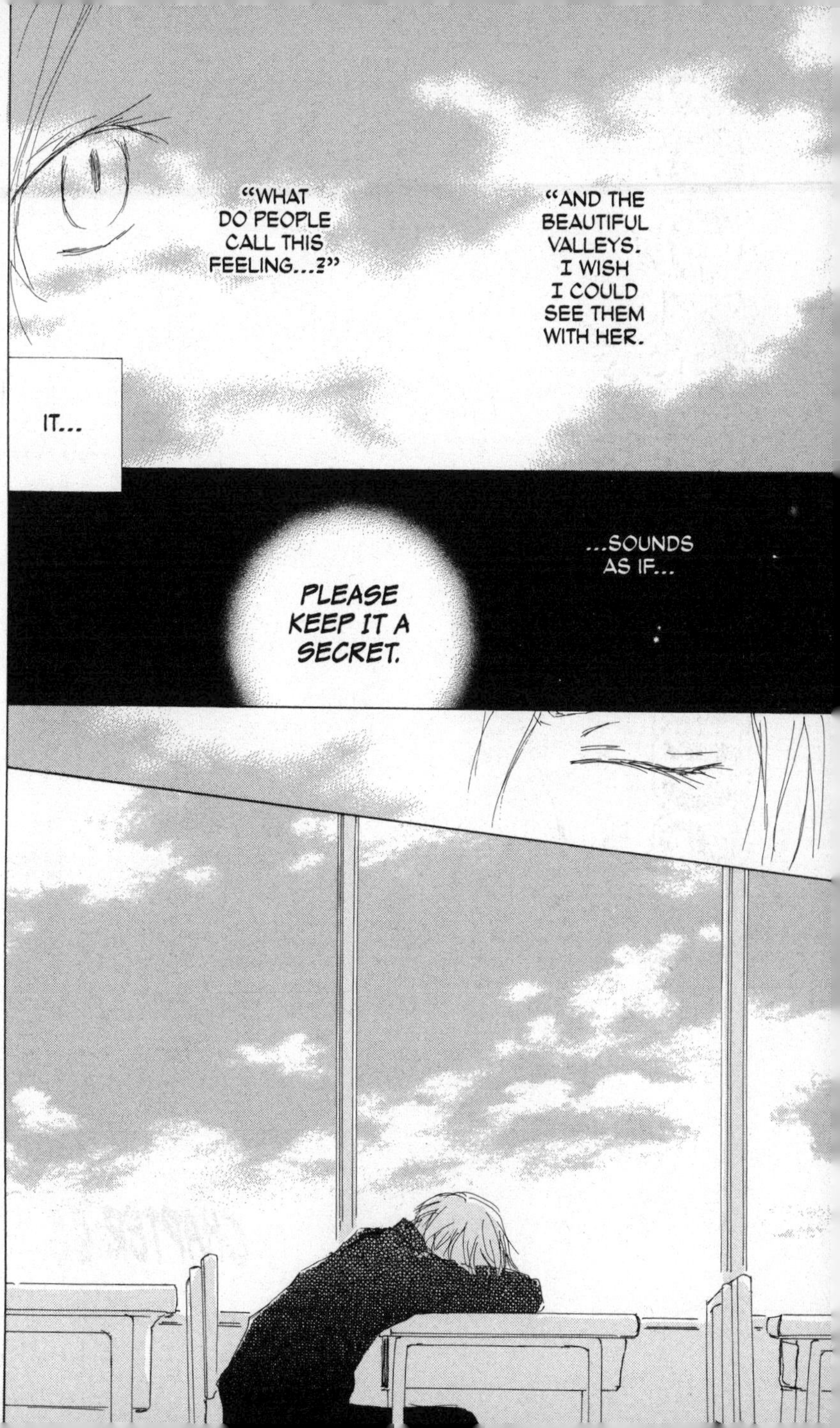
"AND THE BEAUTIFUL VALLEYS. I WISH I COULD SEE THEM WITH HER.
"WHAT DO PEOPLE CALL THIS FEELING...?"
IT...
...SOUNDS AS IF...
PLEASE KEEP IT A SECRET.

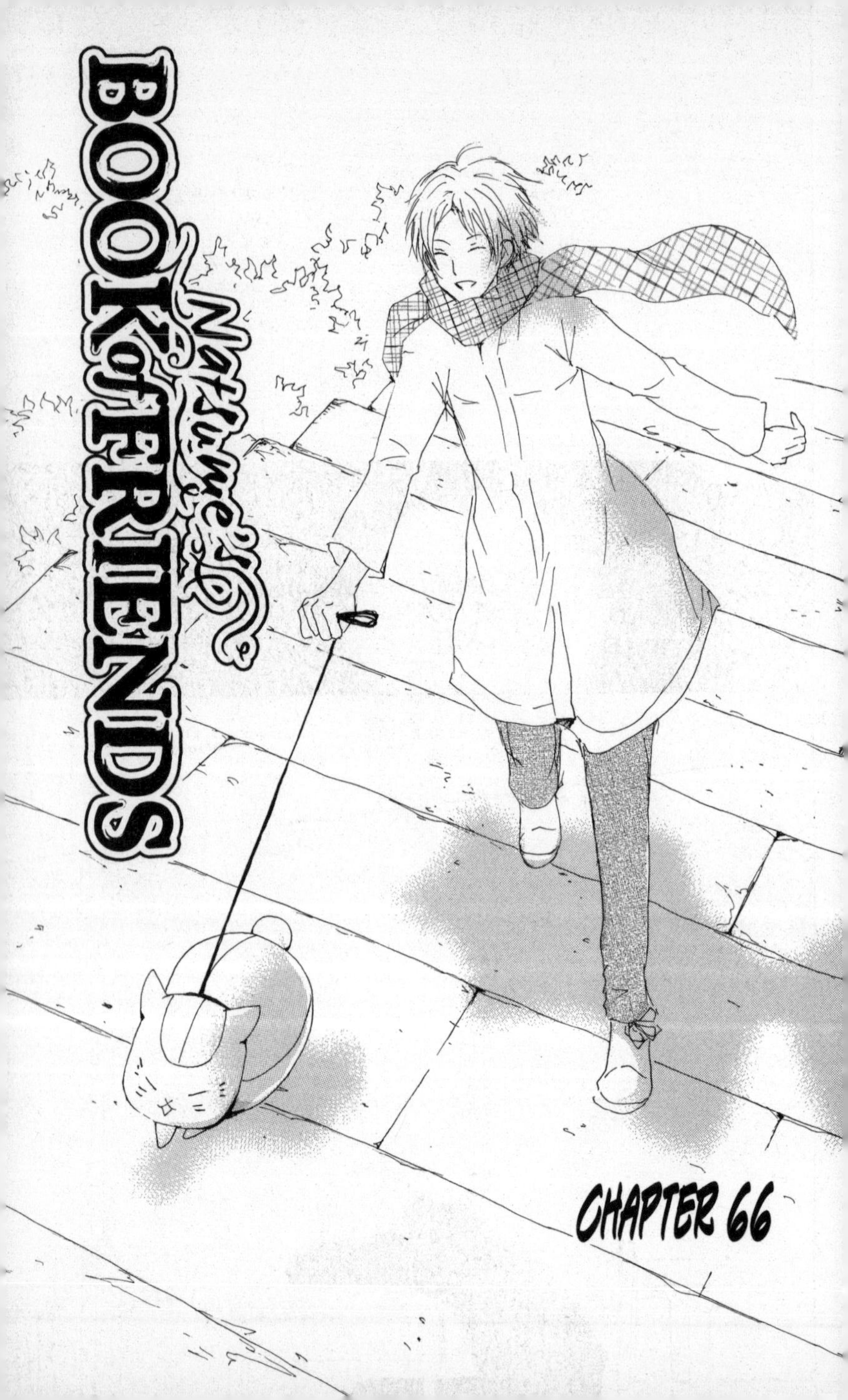
Natsume's
BOOK of FRIENDS
CHAPTER 66

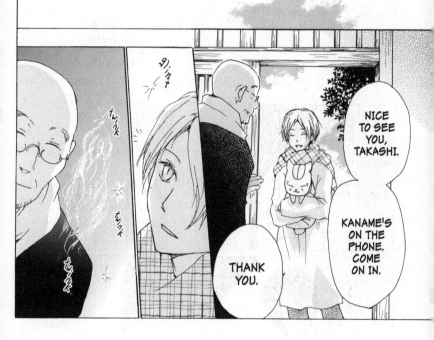

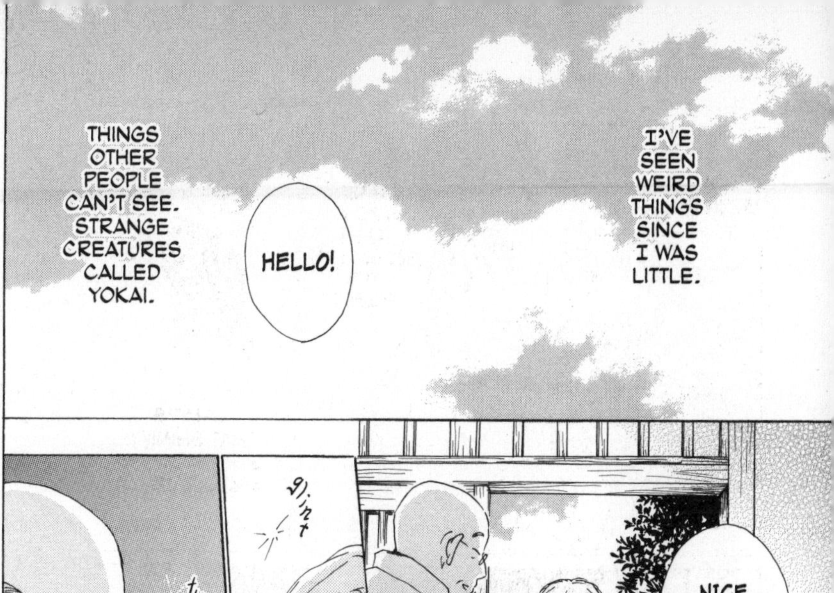
I'VE SEEN WEIRD THINGS SINCE I WAS LITTLE.
HELLO!
THINGS OTHER PEOPLE CAN'T SEE. STRANGE CREATURES CALLED YOKAI.
NICE TO SEE YOU, TAKASHI.
KANAME'S ON THE PHONE. COME ON IN.
THANK YOU.
glint
twink
twink
twink

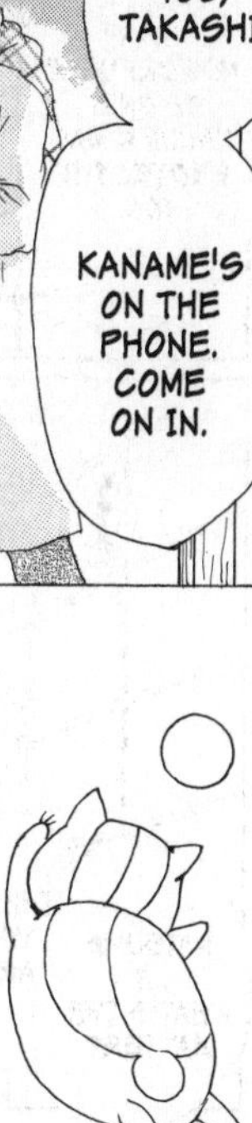

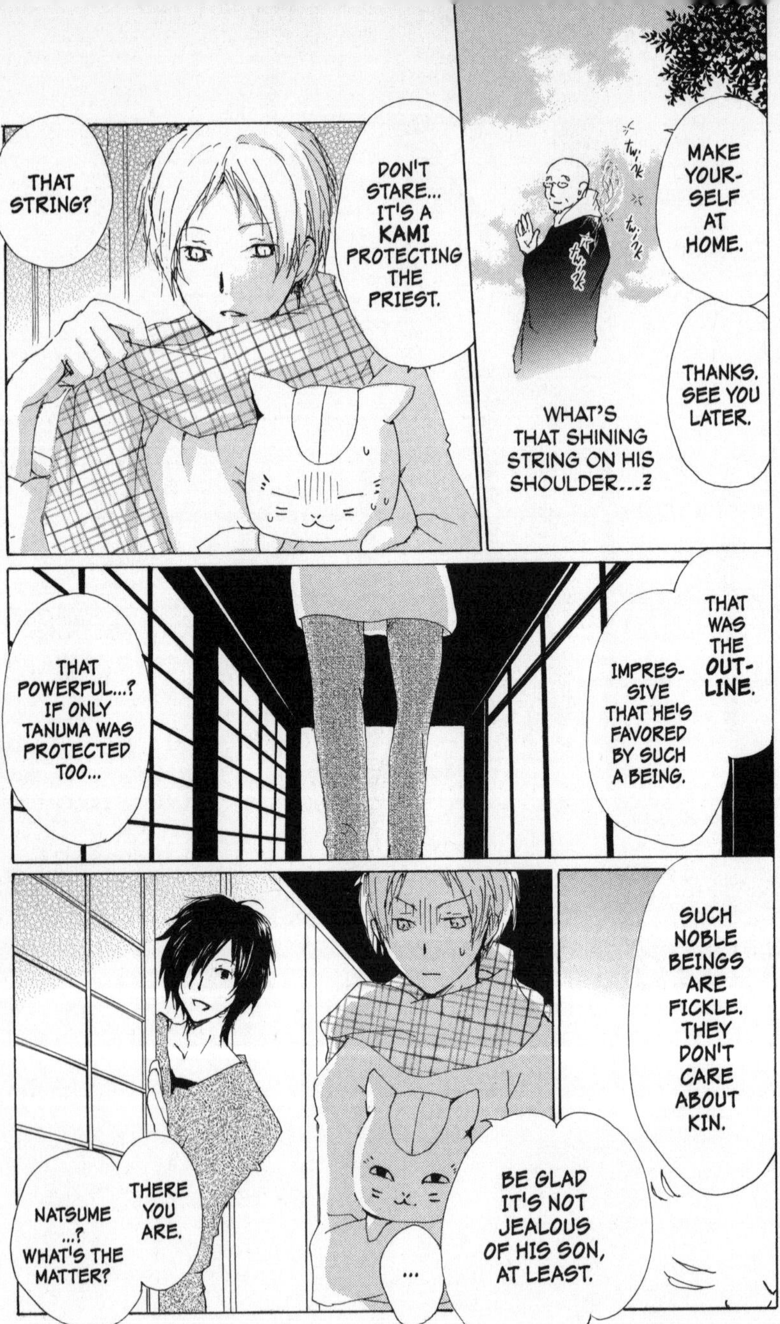
MAKE YOURSELF AT HOME.
twink twink
THANKS. SEE YOU LATER.
WHAT'S THAT SHINING STRING ON HIS SHOULDER...?
DON'T STARE... IT'S A KAMI PROTECTING THE PRIEST.
THAT STRING?
THAT WAS THE OUTLINE.
IMPRESSIVE THAT HE'S FAVORED BY SUCH A BEING.
THAT POWERFUL...? IF ONLY TANUMA WAS PROTECTED TOO...
SUCH NOBLE BEINGS ARE FICKLE. THEY DON'T CARE ABOUT KIN.
BE GLAD IT'S NOT JEALOUS OF HIS SON, AT LEAST.
...
THERE YOU ARE.
NATSUME ...? WHAT'S THE MATTER?

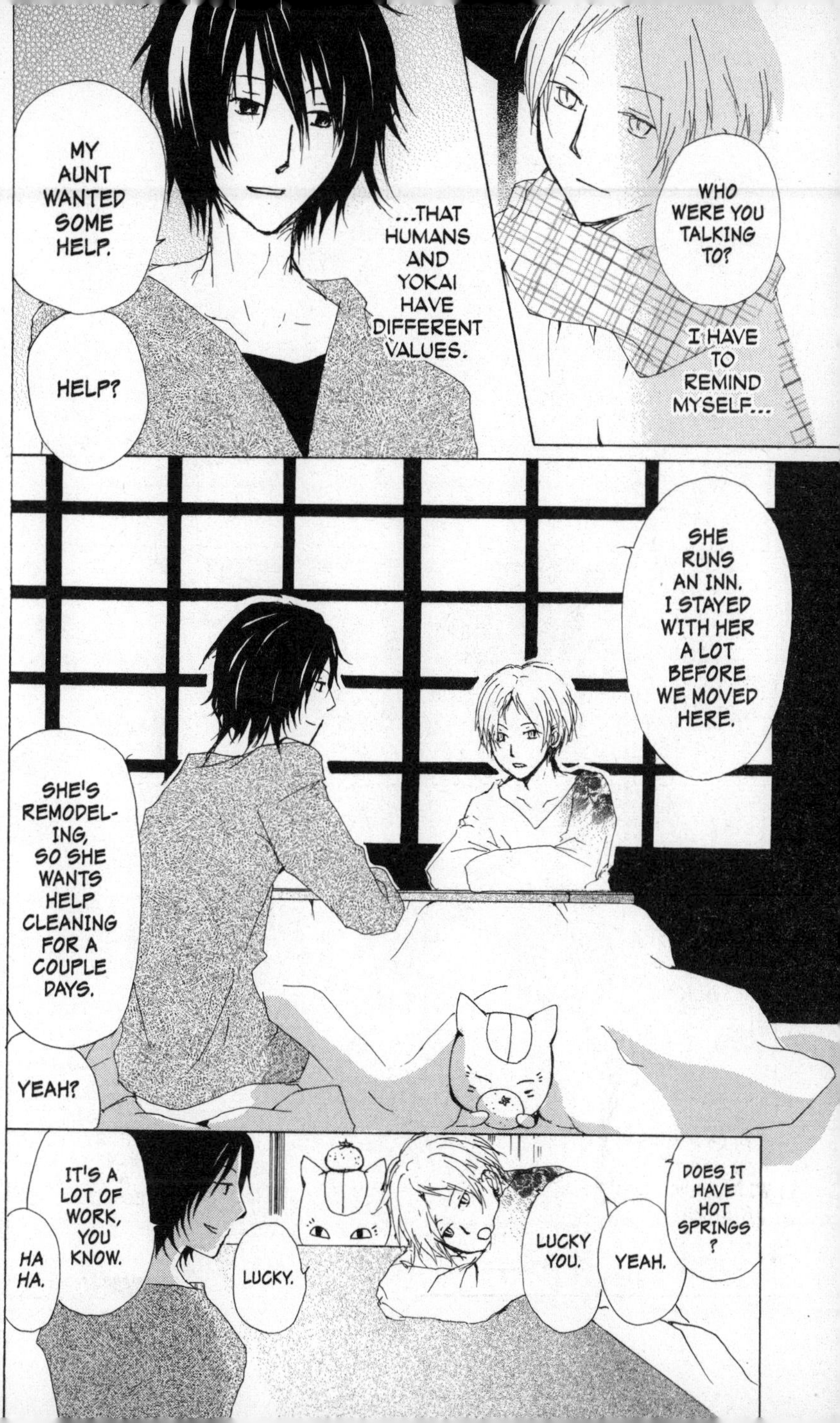
WHO WERE YOU TALKING TO?
I HAVE TO REMIND MYSELF...
...THAT HUMANS AND YOKAI HAVE DIFFERENT VALUES.
MY AUNT WANTED SOME HELP.
HELP?
SHE RUNS AN INN. I STAYED WITH HER A LOT BEFORE WE MOVED HERE.
SHE'S REMODEL-ING, SO SHE WANTS HELP CLEANING FOR A COUPLE DAYS.
YEAH?
DOES IT HAVE HOT SPRINGS?
YEAH.
LUCKY YOU.
LUCKY.
IT'S A LOT OF WORK, YOU KNOW.
HA HA.

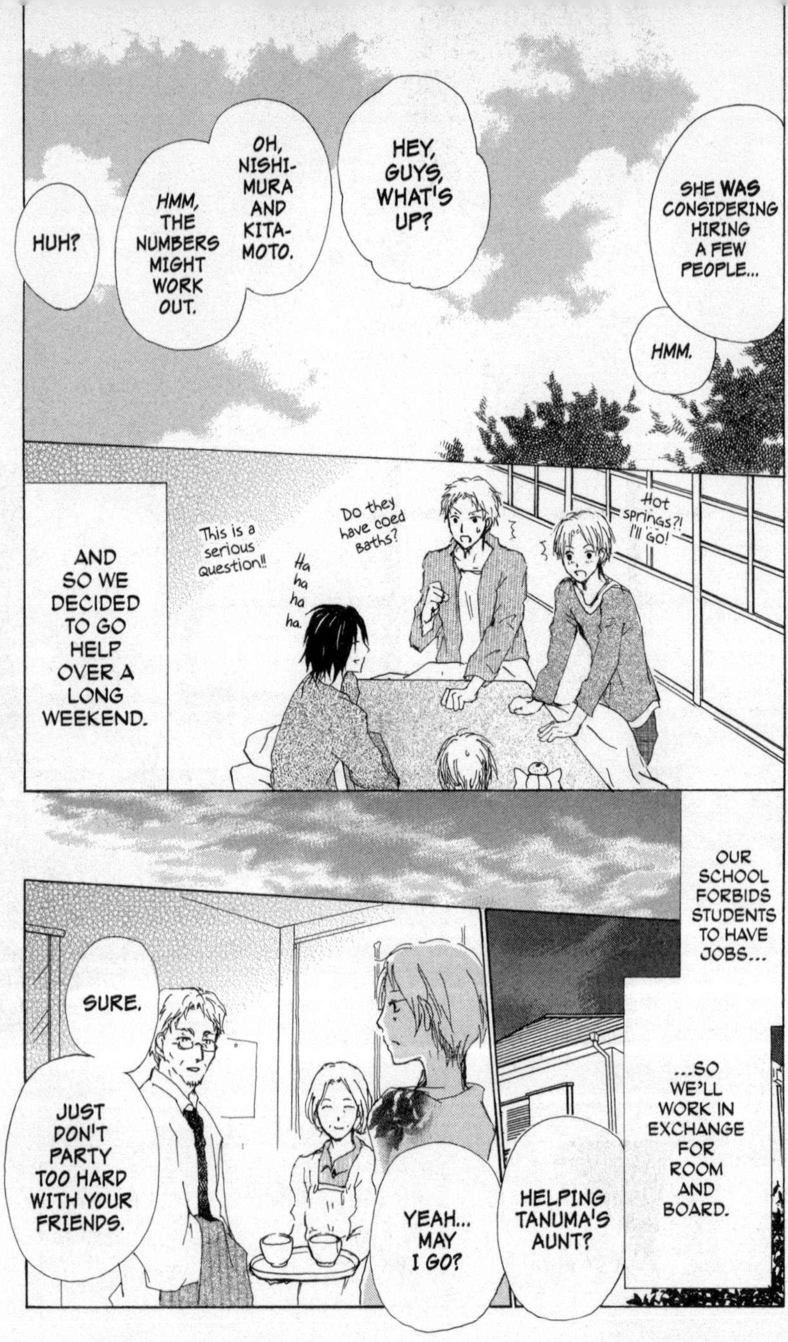
SHE WAS CONSIDERING HIRING A FEW PEOPLE...
HMM.
HEY, GUYS, WHAT'S UP?
OH, NISHIMURA AND KITAMOTO.
HMM, THE NUMBERS MIGHT WORK OUT.
HUH?
Hot springs?! I'll go!
Do they have coed baths?
Ha ha ha ha.
This is a serious question!!
AND SO WE DECIDED TO GO HELP OVER A LONG WEEKEND.
OUR SCHOOL FORBIDS STUDENTS TO HAVE JOBS...
...SO WE'LL WORK IN EXCHANGE FOR ROOM AND BOARD.
HELPING TANUMA'S AUNT?
YEAH... MAY I GO?
SURE.
JUST DON'T PARTY TOO HARD WITH YOUR FRIENDS.

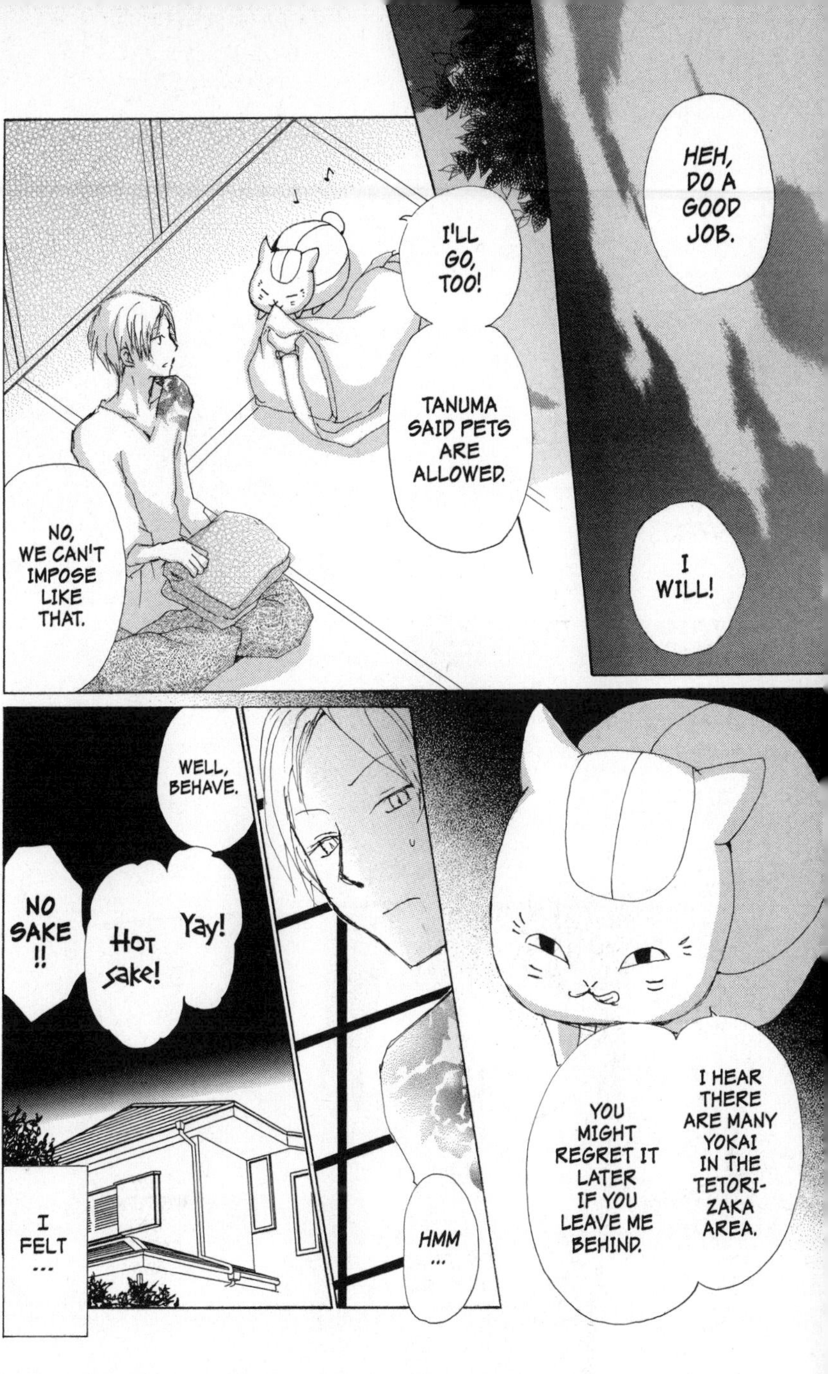
HEH, DO A GOOD JOB.
I WILL!
I'LL GO, TOO!
TANUMA SAID PETS ARE ALLOWED.
NO, WE CAN'T IMPOSE LIKE THAT.
I HEAR THERE ARE MANY YOKAI IN THE TETORI-ZAKA AREA.
YOU MIGHT REGRET IT LATER IF YOU LEAVE ME BEHIND.
HMM...
WELL, BEHAVE.
Yay!
Hot sake!
NO SAKE!!
I FELT...

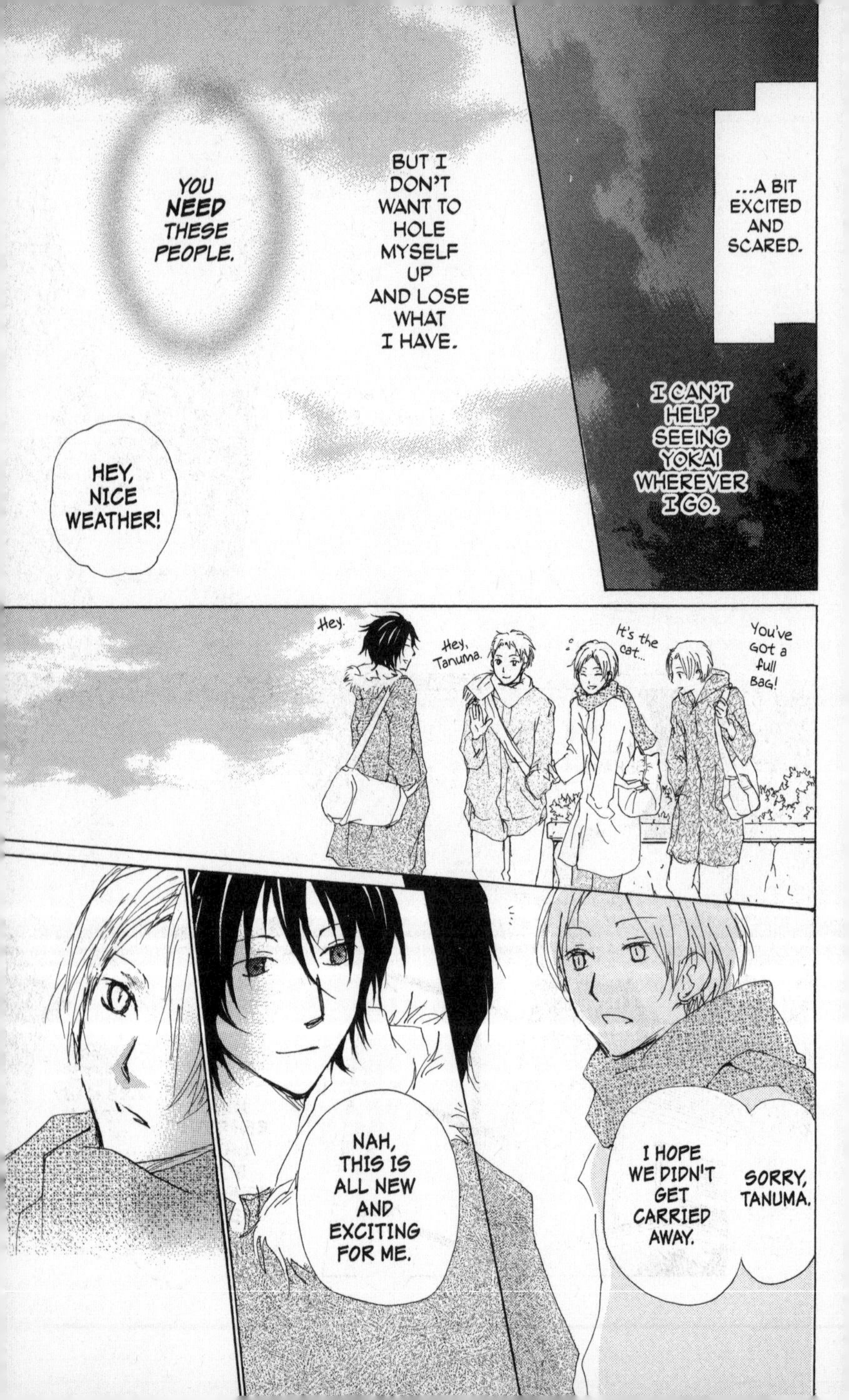
...A BIT EXCITED AND SCARED.
I CAN'T HELP SEEING YOKAI WHEREVER I GO.
BUT I DON'T WANT TO HOLE MYSELF UP AND LOSE WHAT I HAVE.
YOU NEED THESE PEOPLE.
HEY, NICE WEATHER!
You've got a full bag!
It's the cat...
Hey, Tanuma.
Hey.
SORRY, TANUMA.
I HOPE WE DIDN'T GET CARRIED AWAY.
NAH, THIS IS ALL NEW AND EXCITING FOR ME.

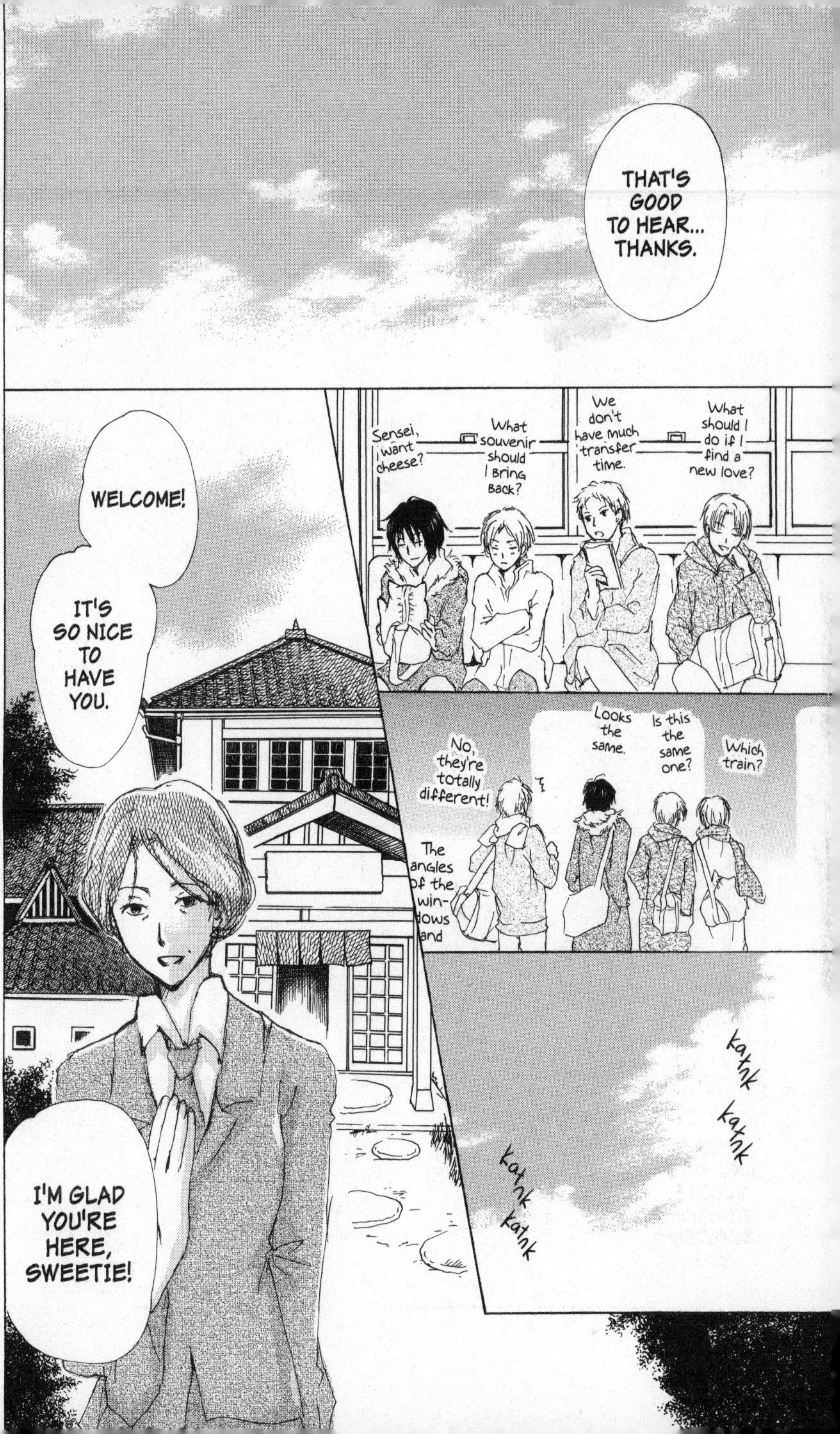
THAT'S GOOD TO HEAR... THANKS.
What should I do if I find a new love?
We don't have much transfer time.
What souvenir should I bring back?
Sensei, I want cheese?
Which train?
Is this the same one?
Looks the same.
No, they're totally different!
The angles of the win-dows and
katnk
katnk
katnk
katnk
WELCOME!
IT'S SO NICE TO HAVE YOU.
I'M GLAD YOU'RE HERE, SWEETIE!

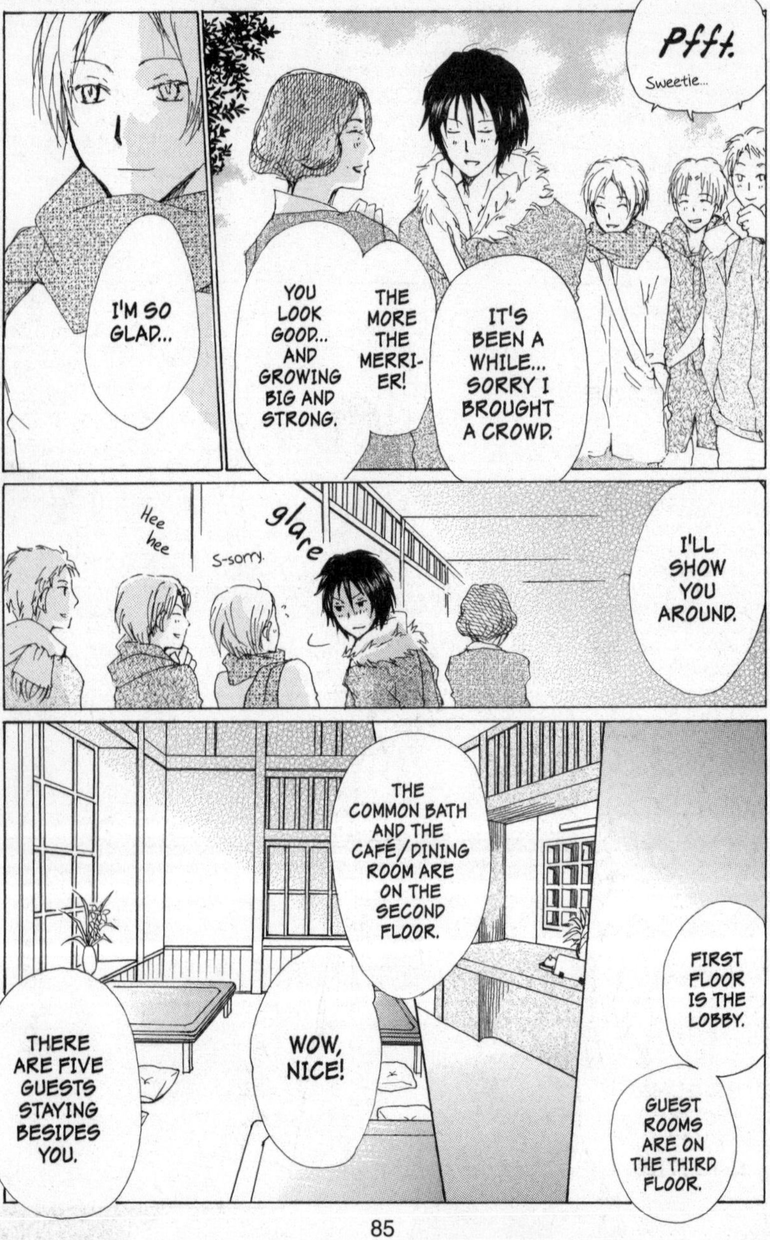
Pfft.
Sweetie...
IT'S BEEN A WHILE... SORRY I BROUGHT A CROWD.
THE MORE THE MERRIER!
YOU LOOK GOOD... AND GROWING BIG AND STRONG.
I'M SO GLAD...
I'LL SHOW YOU AROUND.
glare
S-sorry.
Hee hee
FIRST FLOOR IS THE LOBBY.
GUEST ROOMS ARE ON THE THIRD FLOOR.
THE COMMON BATH AND THE CAFÉ/DINING ROOM ARE ON THE SECOND FLOOR.
WOW, NICE!
THERE ARE FIVE GUESTS STAYING BESIDES YOU.

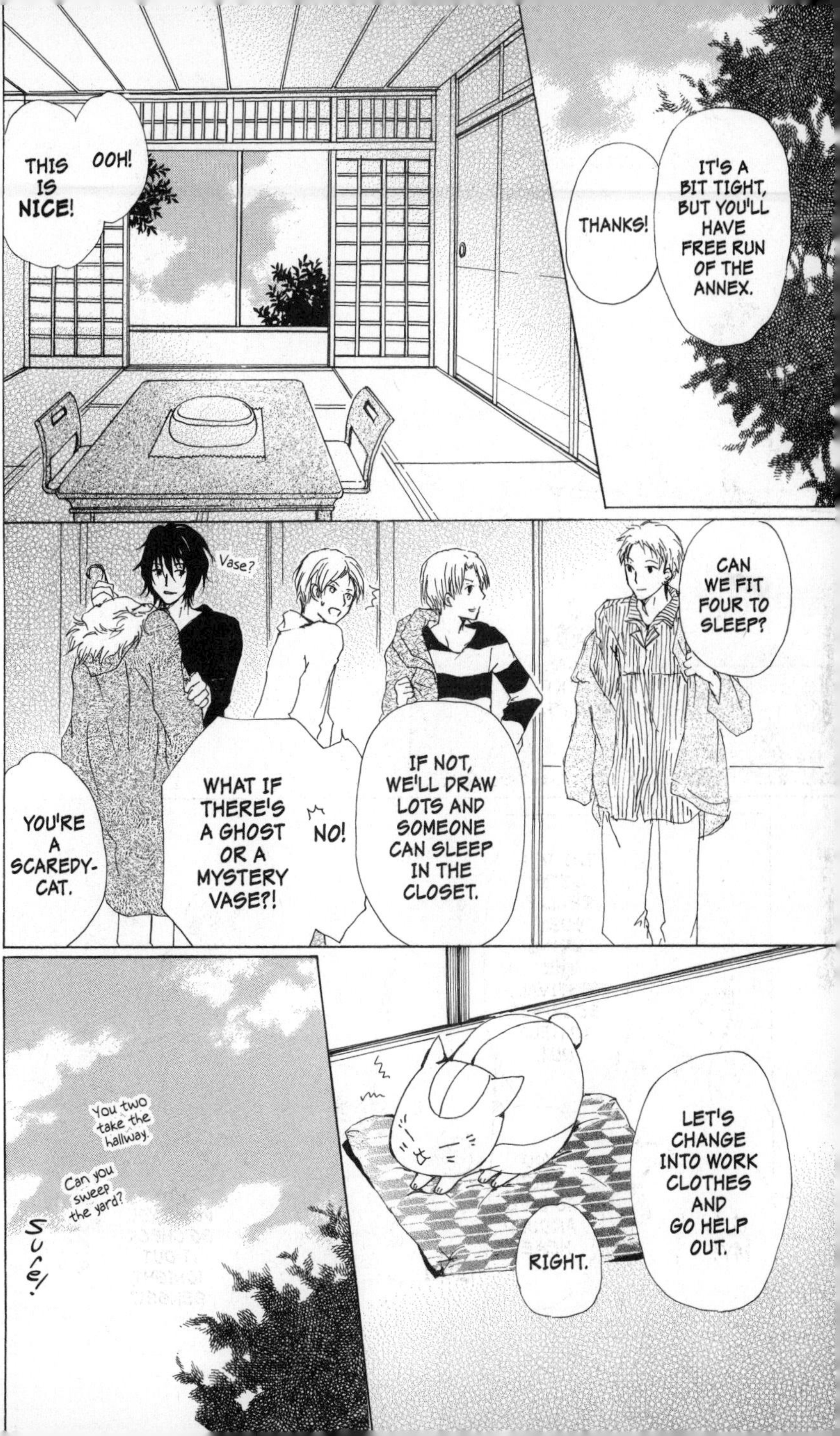
IT'S A BIT TIGHT, BUT YOU'LL HAVE FREE RUN OF THE ANNEX.
THANKS!
OOH!
THIS IS NICE!
CAN WE FIT FOUR TO SLEEP?
IF NOT, WE'LL DRAW LOTS AND SOMEONE CAN SLEEP IN THE CLOSET.
NO!
WHAT IF THERE'S A GHOST OR A MYSTERY VASE?!
Vase?
YOU'RE A SCAREDY-CAT.
LET'S CHANGE INTO WORK CLOTHES AND GO HELP OUT.
RIGHT.
You two take the hallway.
Can you sweep the yard?
Sure!

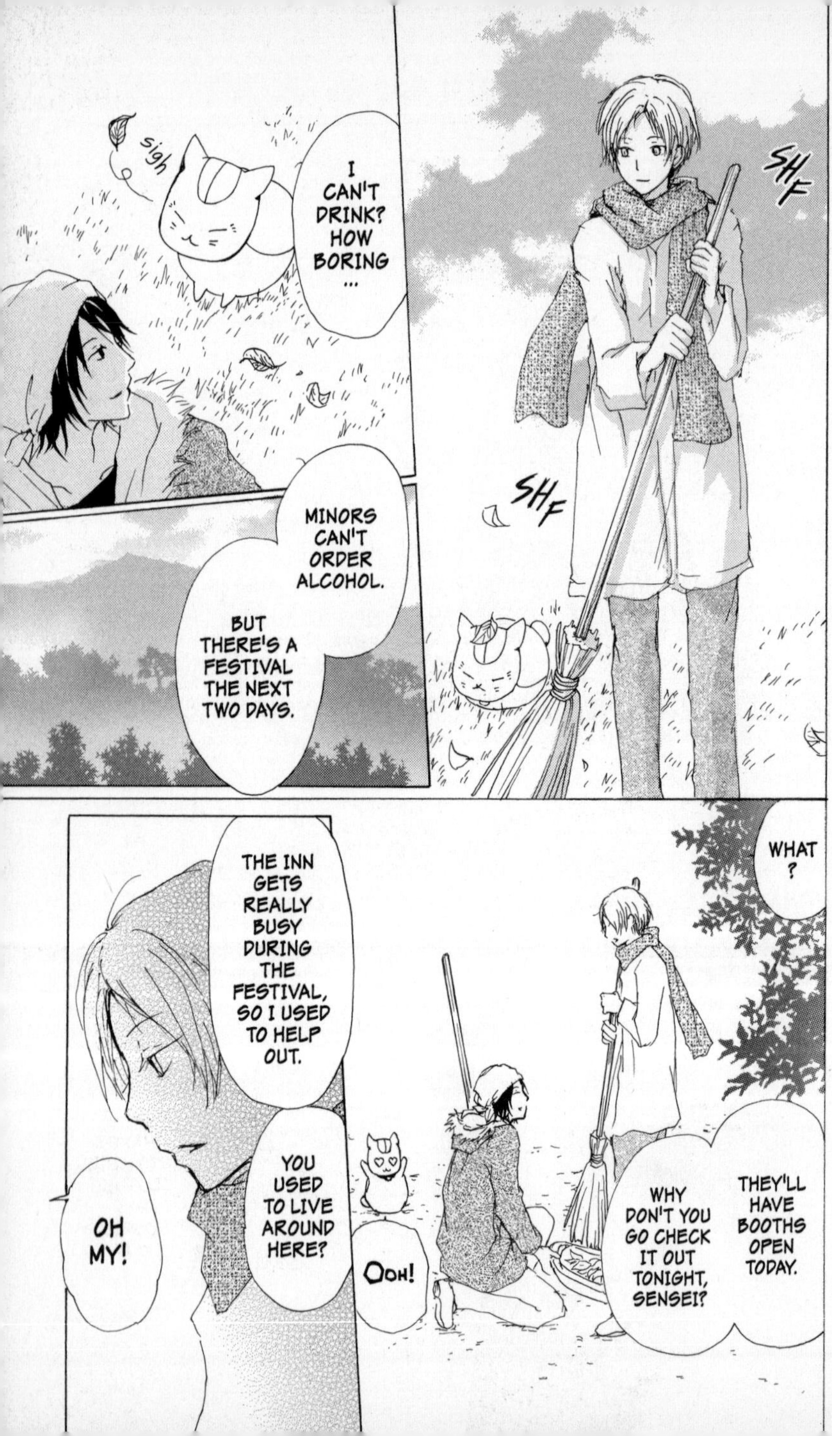
SHF
SHF
sigh
I CAN'T DRINK? HOW BORING ...
MINORS CAN'T ORDER ALCOHOL.
BUT THERE'S A FESTIVAL THE NEXT TWO DAYS.
WHAT?
THEY'LL HAVE BOOTHS OPEN TODAY.
WHY DON'T YOU GO CHECK IT OUT TONIGHT, SENSEI?
OOH!
THE INN GETS REALLY BUSY DURING THE FESTIVAL, SO I USED TO HELP OUT.
YOU USED TO LIVE AROUND HERE?
OH MY!

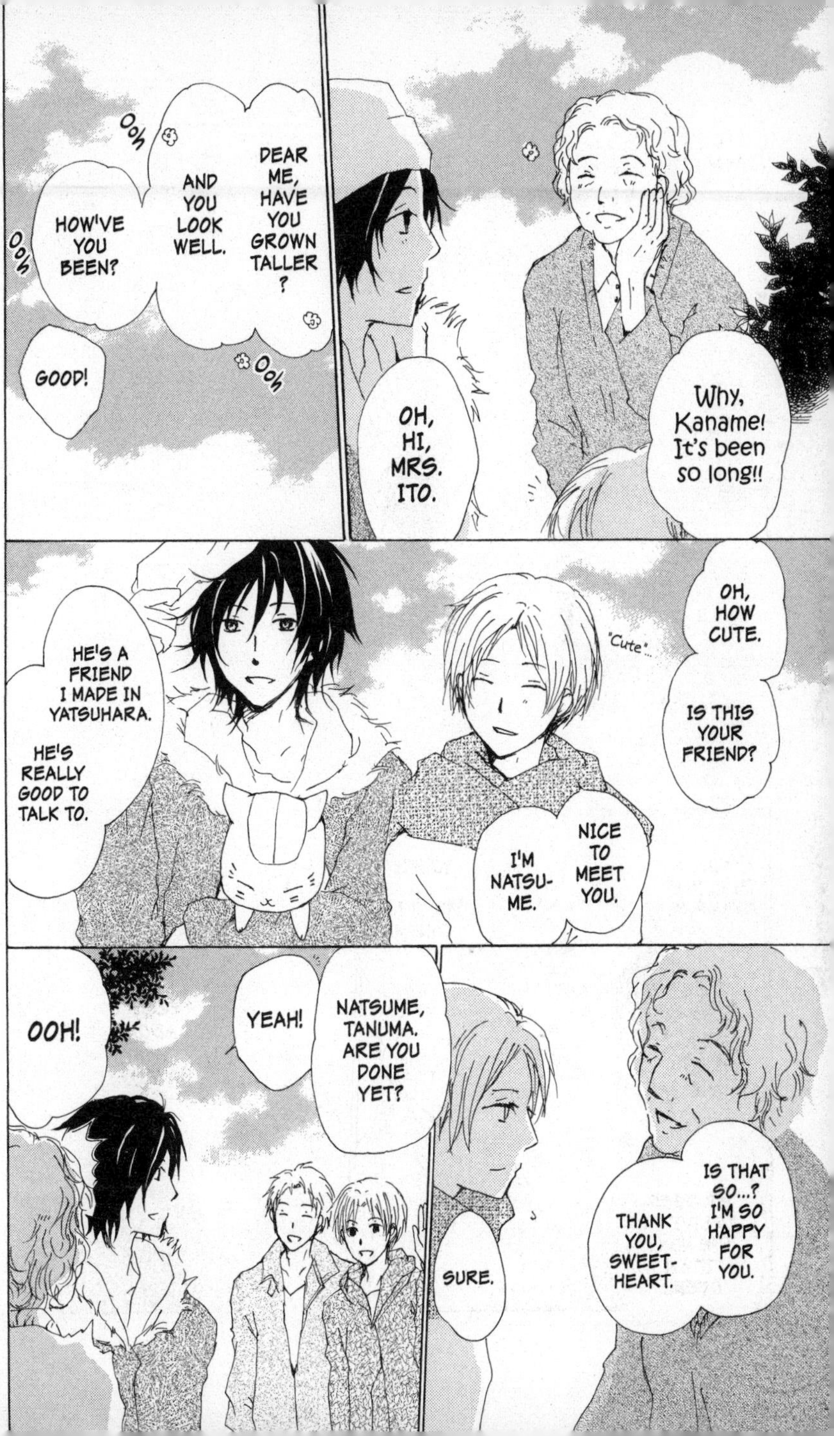
Why, Kaname! It's been so long!!
OH, HI, MRS. ITO.
DEAR ME, HAVE YOU GROWN TALLER?
Ooh
AND YOU LOOK WELL.
Ooh
HOW'VE YOU BEEN?
Ooh
GOOD!
OH, HOW CUTE.
"Cute"...
IS THIS YOUR FRIEND?
HE'S A FRIEND I MADE IN YATSUHARA.
HE'S REALLY GOOD TO TALK TO.
NICE TO MEET YOU.
I'M NATSUME.
IS THAT SO...? I'M SO HAPPY FOR YOU.
THANK YOU, SWEETHEART.
SURE.
NATSUME, TANUMA. ARE YOU DONE YET?
YEAH!
OOH!

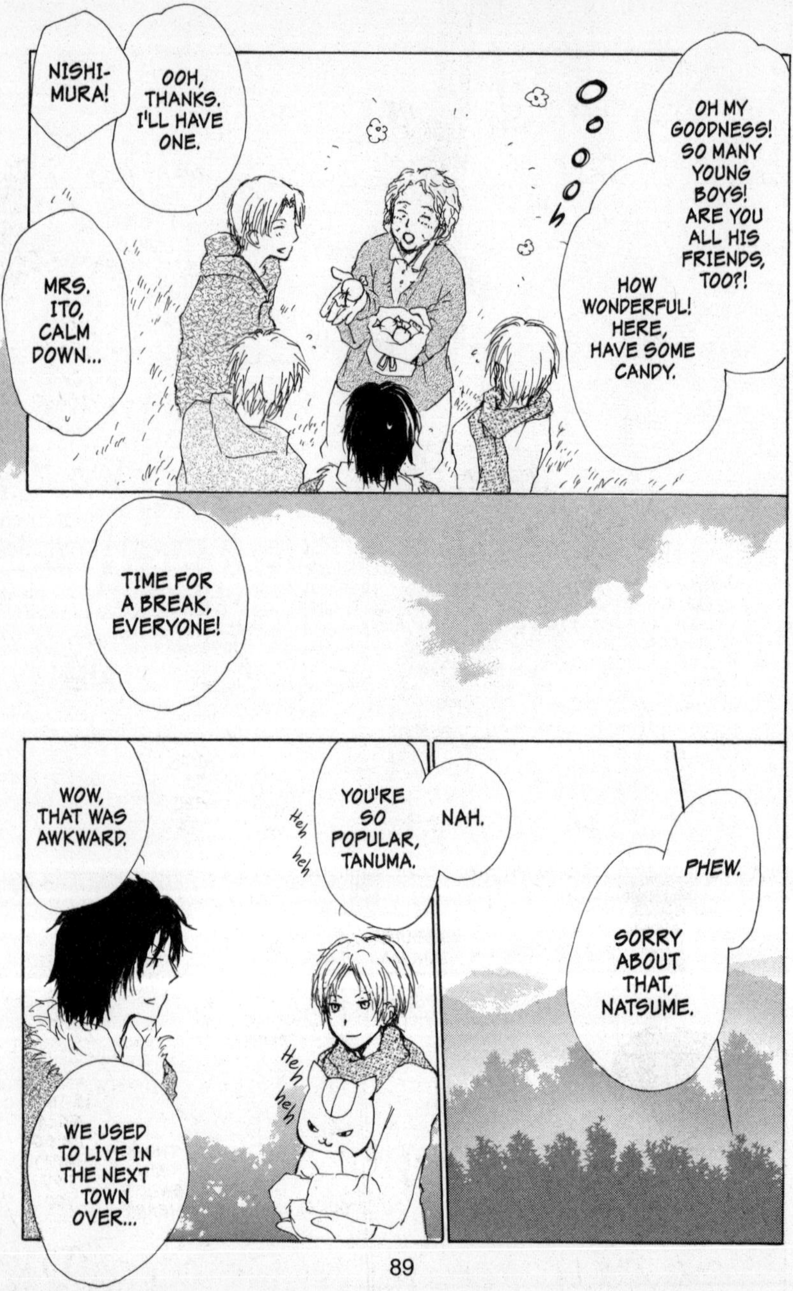
OH MY GOODNESS! SO MANY YOUNG BOYS! ARE YOU ALL HIS FRIENDS, TOO?!
Ooooh
HOW WONDERFUL! HERE, HAVE SOME CANDY.
OOH, THANKS. I'LL HAVE ONE.
NISHI-MURA!
MRS. ITO, CALM DOWN...
TIME FOR A BREAK, EVERYONE!
PHEW.
SORRY ABOUT THAT, NATSUME.
NAH.
YOU'RE SO POPULAR, TANUMA.
Heh heh
WOW, THAT WAS AWKWARD.
Heh heh
WE USED TO LIVE IN THE NEXT TOWN OVER...

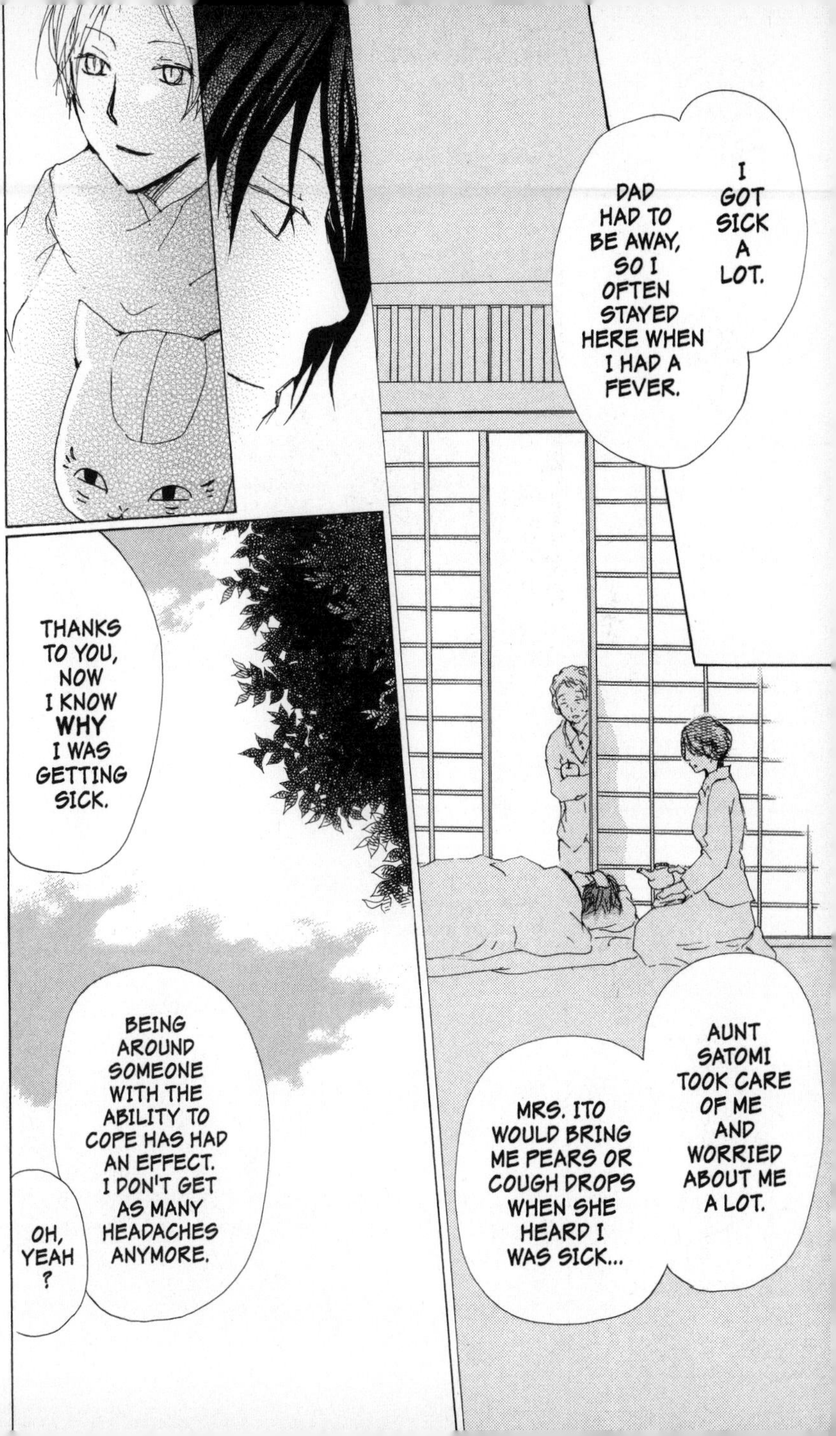
I GOT SICK A LOT.
DAD HAD TO BE AWAY, SO I OFTEN STAYED HERE WHEN I HAD A FEVER.
AUNT SATOMI TOOK CARE OF ME AND WORRIED ABOUT ME A LOT.
MRS. ITO WOULD BRING ME PEARS OR COUGH DROPS WHEN SHE HEARD I WAS SICK...
THANKS TO YOU, NOW I KNOW **WHY** I WAS GETTING SICK.
BEING AROUND SOMEONE WITH THE ABILITY TO COPE HAS HAD AN EFFECT. I DON'T GET AS MANY HEADACHES ANYMORE.
OH, YEAH ?

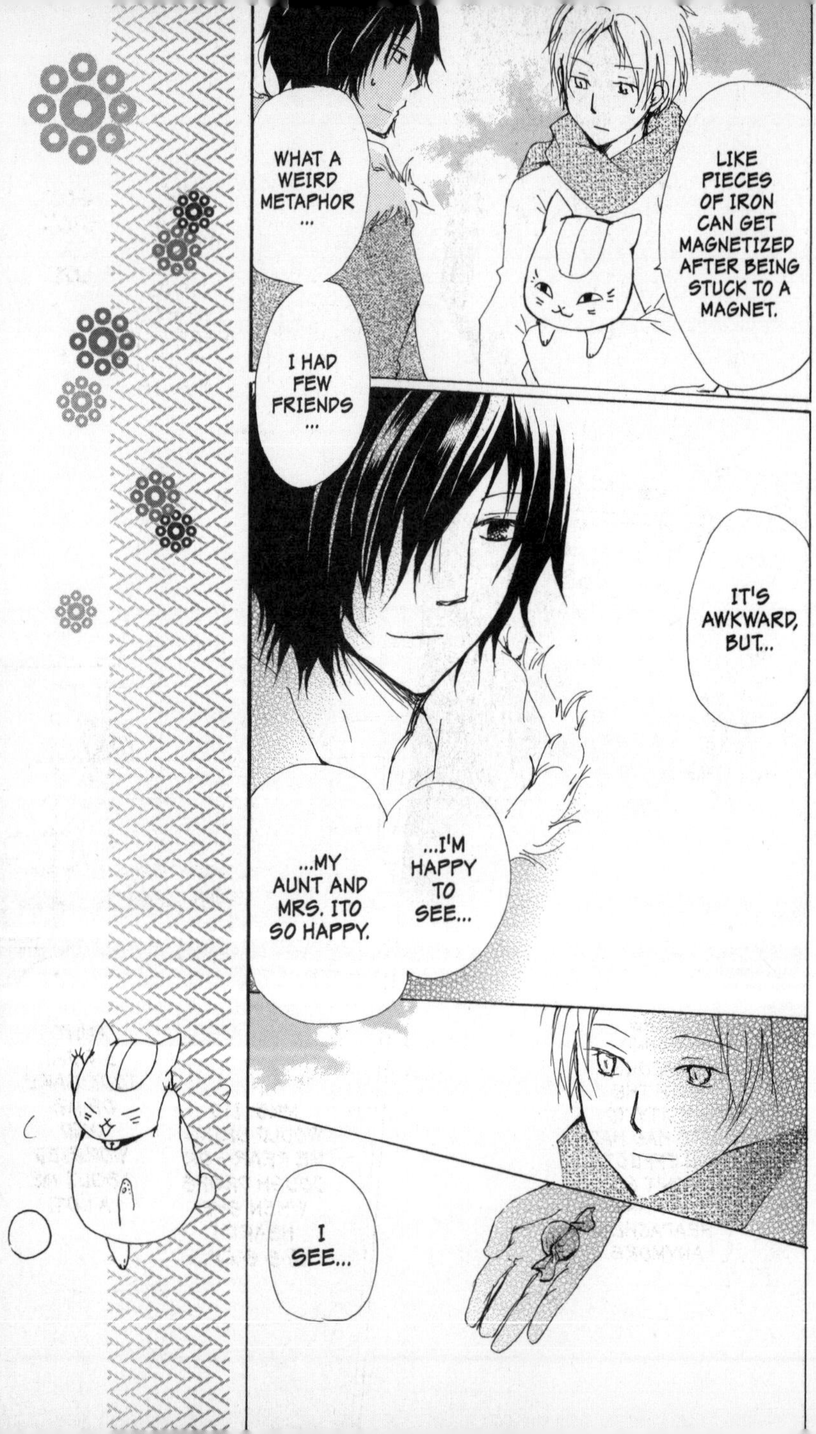
LIKE PIECES OF IRON CAN GET MAGNETIZED AFTER BEING STUCK TO A MAGNET.
WHAT A WEIRD METAPHOR ...
I HAD FEW FRIENDS ...
IT'S AWKWARD, BUT...
...I'M HAPPY TO SEE...
...MY AUNT AND MRS. ITO SO HAPPY.
I SEE...

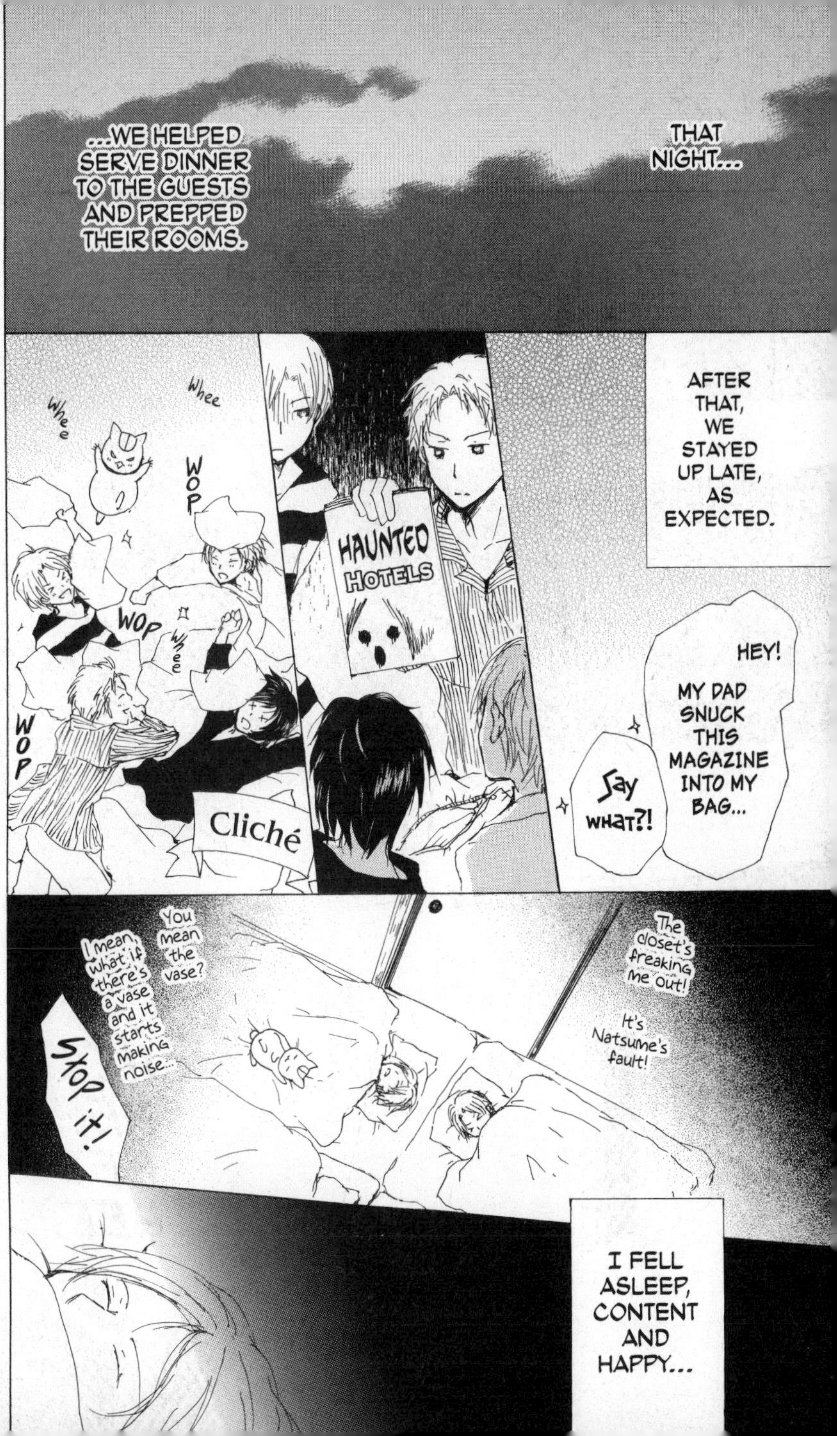
THAT NIGHT...
...WE HELPED SERVE DINNER TO THE GUESTS AND PREPPED THEIR ROOMS.
AFTER THAT, WE STAYED UP LATE, AS EXPECTED.
HEY! MY DAD SNUCK THIS MAGAZINE INTO MY BAG...
Say WHAT?!
HAUNTED HOTELS
Whee
Whee
WOP
WOP
Whee
WOP
Cliché
The closet's freaking me out!
It's Natsume's fault!
You mean the vase?
I mean, what if there's a vase and it starts making noise...
Stop it!
I FELL ASLEEP, CONTENT AND HAPPY...

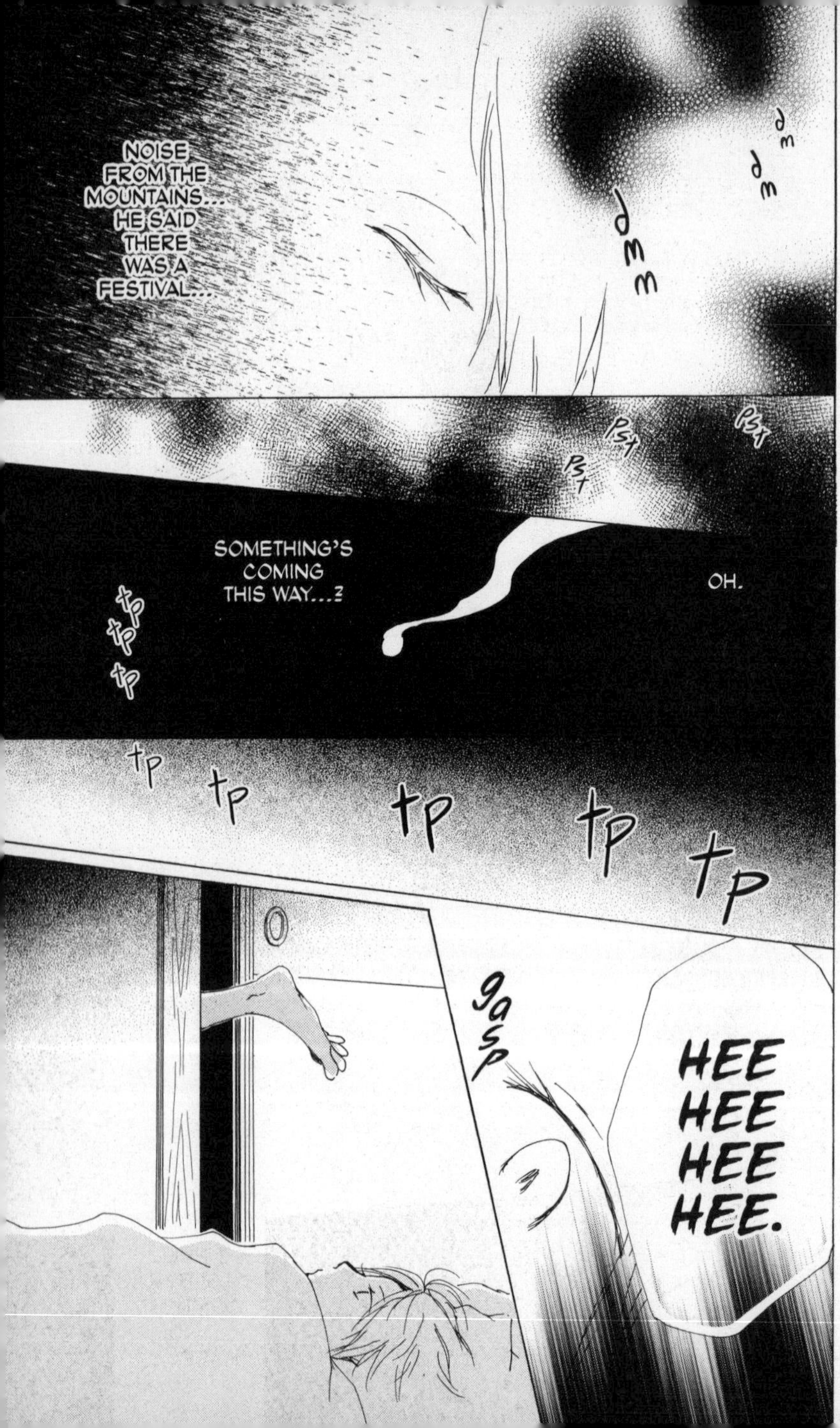
dmm
dmm
dmm
NOISE FROM THE MOUNTAINS... HE SAID THERE WAS A FESTIVAL...
pst
pst
pst
OH.
SOMETHING'S COMING THIS WAY...?
tp
tp
tp
tp
tp
tp
tp
tp
HEE HEE HEE HEE.
gasp

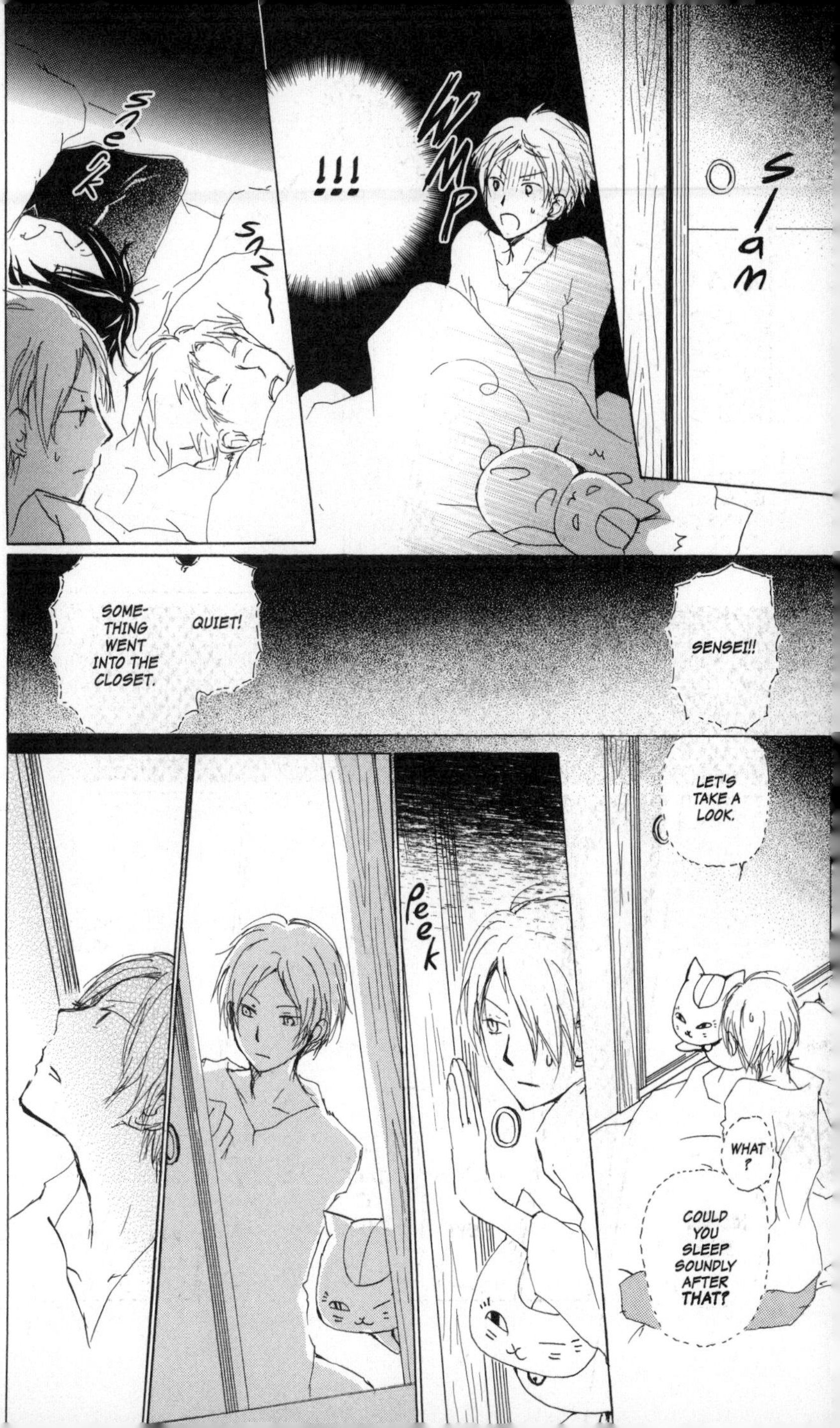
slam
WUMP
!!!
sneak
snz~
SENSEI!!
QUIET!
SOME-THING WENT INTO THE CLOSET.
LET'S TAKE A LOOK.
WHAT?
COULD YOU SLEEP SOUNDLY AFTER THAT?
Peek

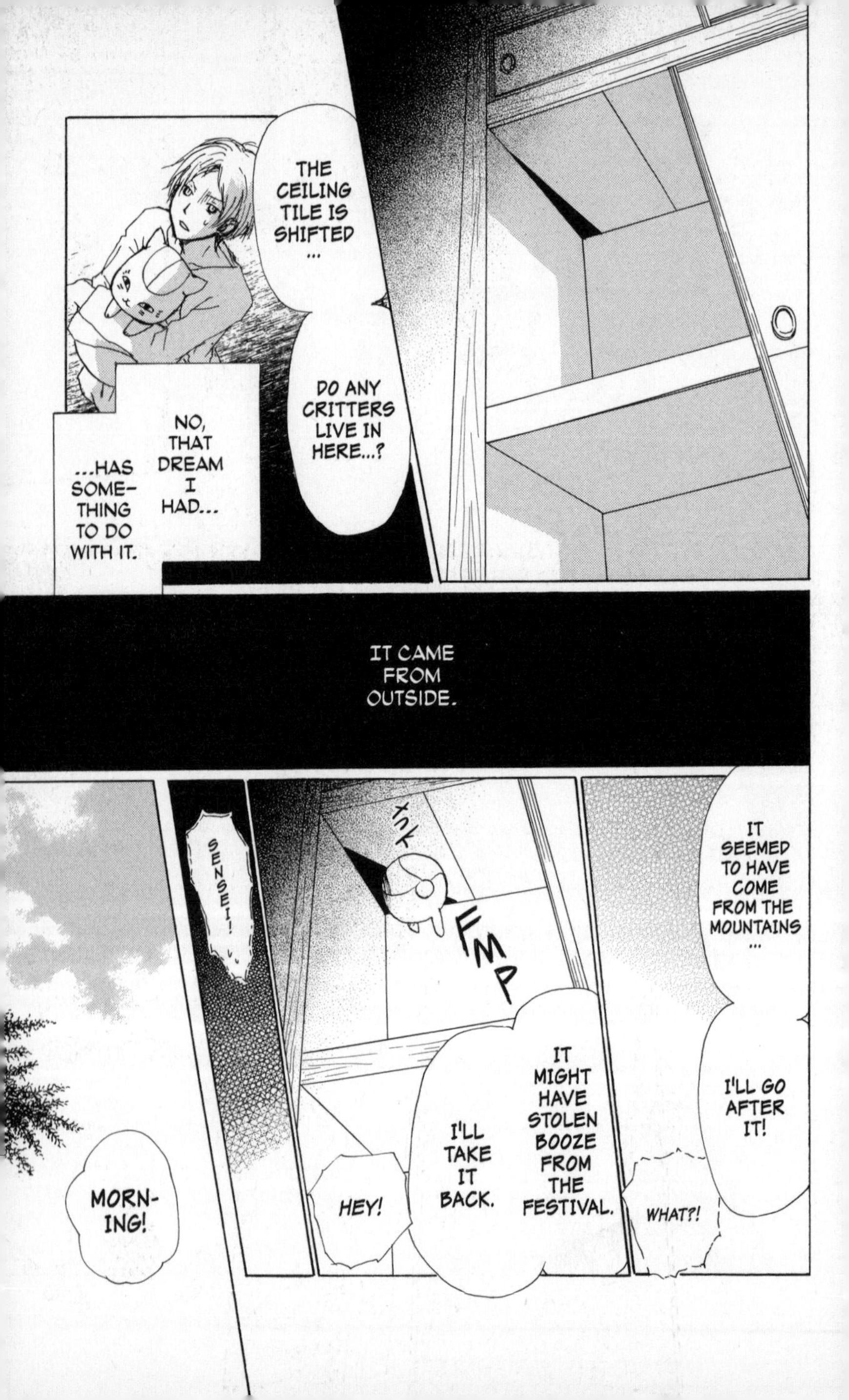
THE CEILING TILE IS SHIFTED...
DO ANY CRITTERS LIVE IN HERE...?
NO, THAT DREAM I HAD...
...HAS SOMETHING TO DO WITH IT.
IT CAME FROM OUTSIDE.
IT SEEMED TO HAVE COME FROM THE MOUNTAINS...
I'LL GO AFTER IT!
WHAT?!
FMP
IT MIGHT HAVE STOLEN BOOZE FROM THE FESTIVAL.
I'LL TAKE IT BACK.
HEY!
SENSEI!
MORNING!

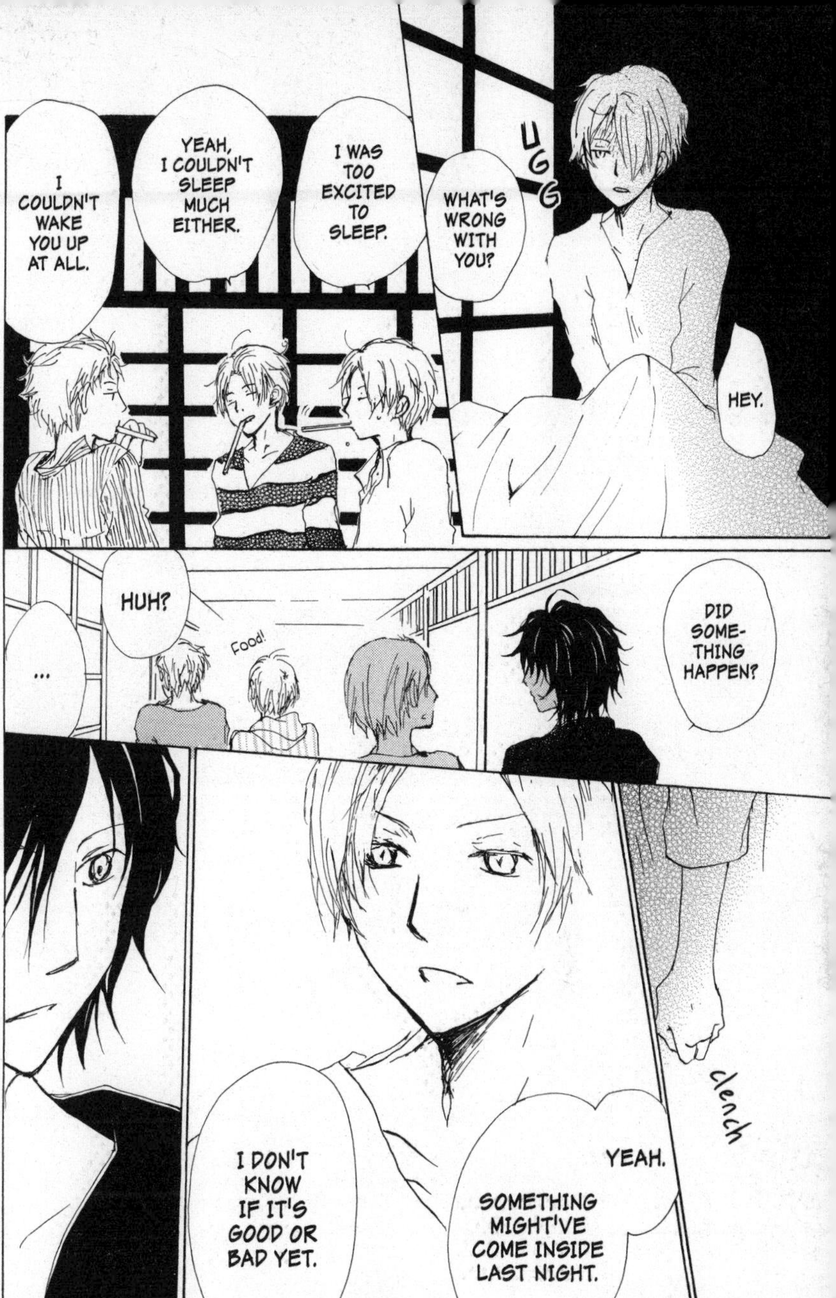

HEY.
UGG
WHAT'S WRONG WITH YOU?
I WAS TOO EXCITED TO SLEEP.
YEAH, I COULDN'T SLEEP MUCH EITHER.
I COULDN'T WAKE YOU UP AT ALL.
DID SOME-THING HAPPEN?
HUH?
Food!
...
clench
YEAH.
SOMETHING MIGHT'VE COME INSIDE LAST NIGHT.
I DON'T KNOW IF IT'S GOOD OR BAD YET.

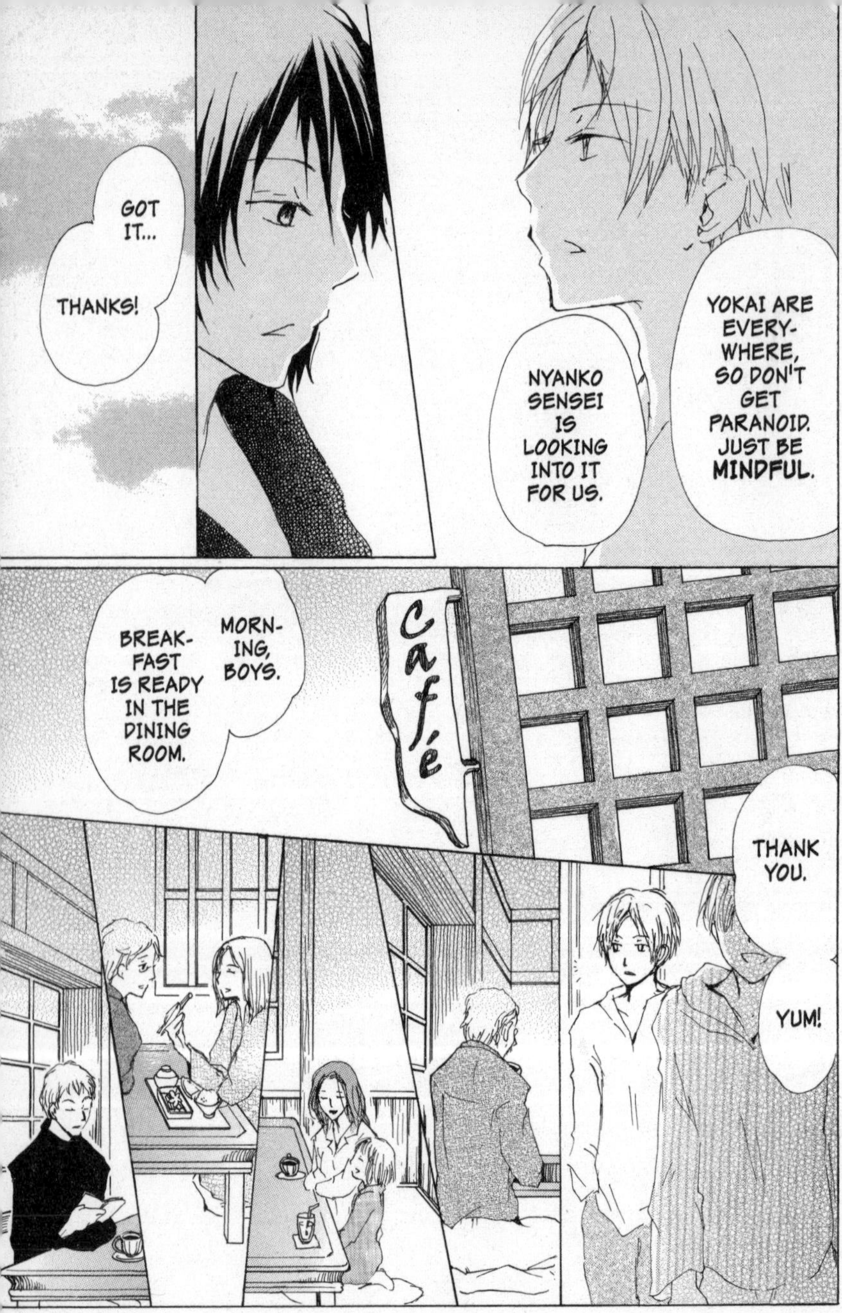
YOKAI ARE EVERY-WHERE, SO DON'T GET PARANOID. JUST BE **MINDFUL.**
NYANKO SENSEI IS LOOKING INTO IT FOR US.
GOT IT...
THANKS!
Café
MORN-ING, BOYS.
BREAK-FAST IS READY IN THE DINING ROOM.
THANK YOU.
YUM!

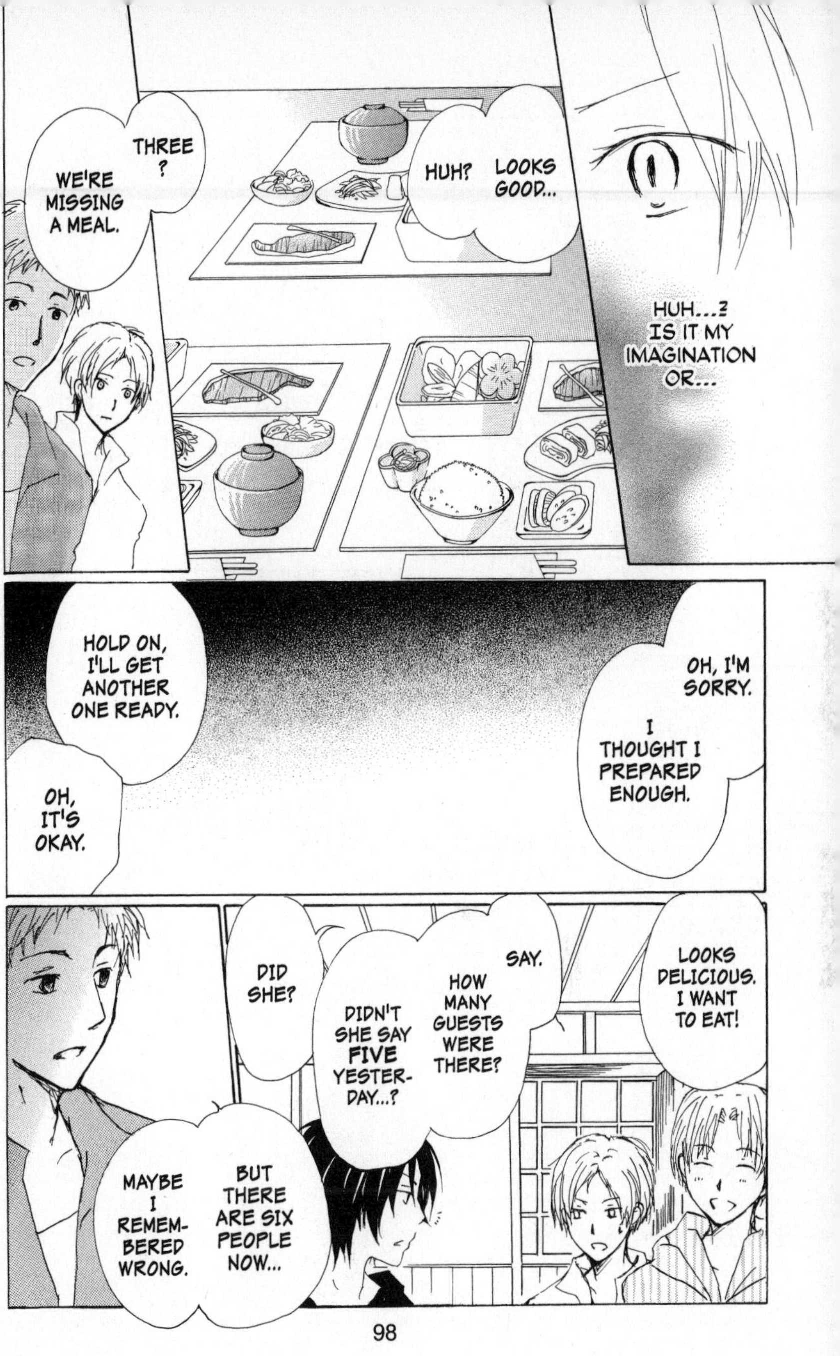

HUH...? IS IT MY IMAGINATION OR...
HUH? LOOKS GOOD...
THREE?
WE'RE MISSING A MEAL.
OH, I'M SORRY.
I THOUGHT I PREPARED ENOUGH.
HOLD ON, I'LL GET ANOTHER ONE READY.
OH, IT'S OKAY.
LOOKS DELICIOUS. I WANT TO EAT!
SAY.
HOW MANY GUESTS WERE THERE?
DIDN'T SHE SAY FIVE YESTER-DAY...?
DID SHE?
BUT THERE ARE SIX PEOPLE NOW...
MAYBE I REMEM-BERED WRONG.

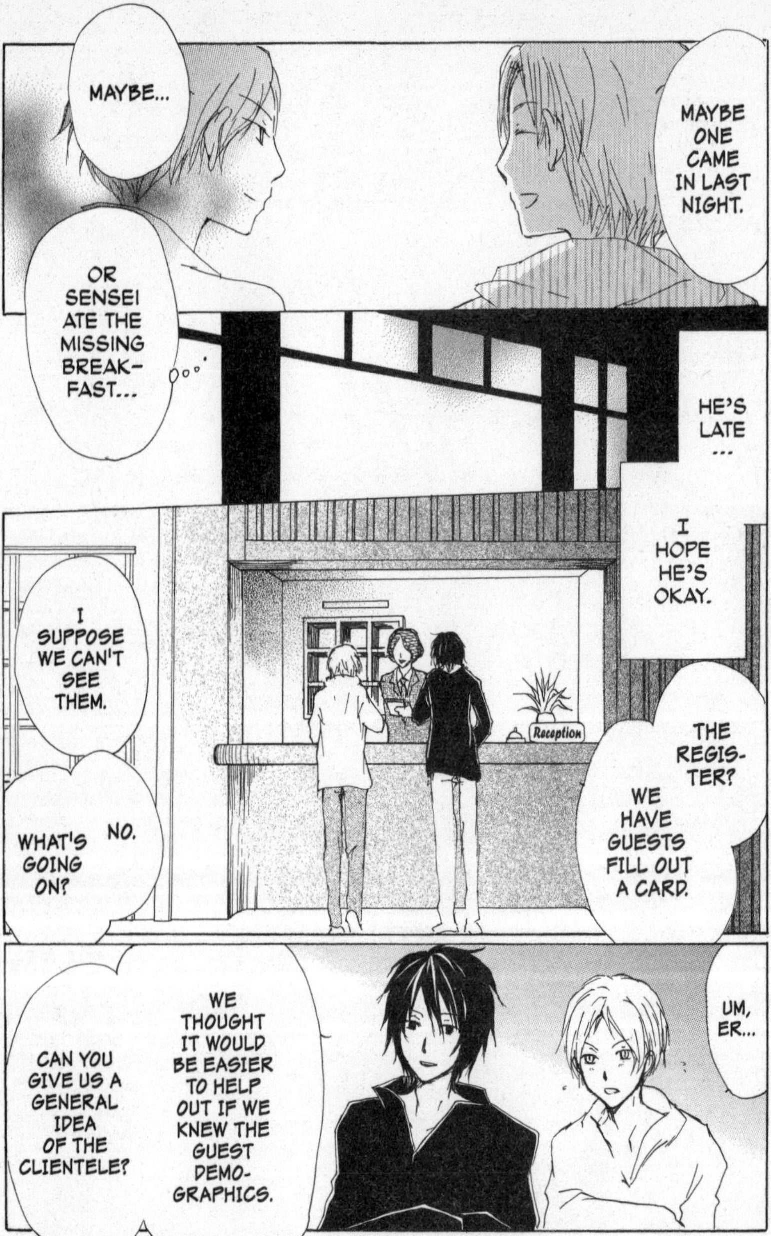
MAYBE ONE CAME IN LAST NIGHT.
MAYBE...
OR SENSEI ATE THE MISSING BREAKFAST...
HE'S LATE...
I HOPE HE'S OKAY.
THE REGISTER?
WE HAVE GUESTS FILL OUT A CARD.
Reception
I SUPPOSE WE CAN'T SEE THEM.
NO.
WHAT'S GOING ON?
UM, ER...
WE THOUGHT IT WOULD BE EASIER TO HELP OUT IF WE KNEW THE GUEST DEMOGRAPHICS.
CAN YOU GIVE US A GENERAL IDEA OF THE CLIENTELE?

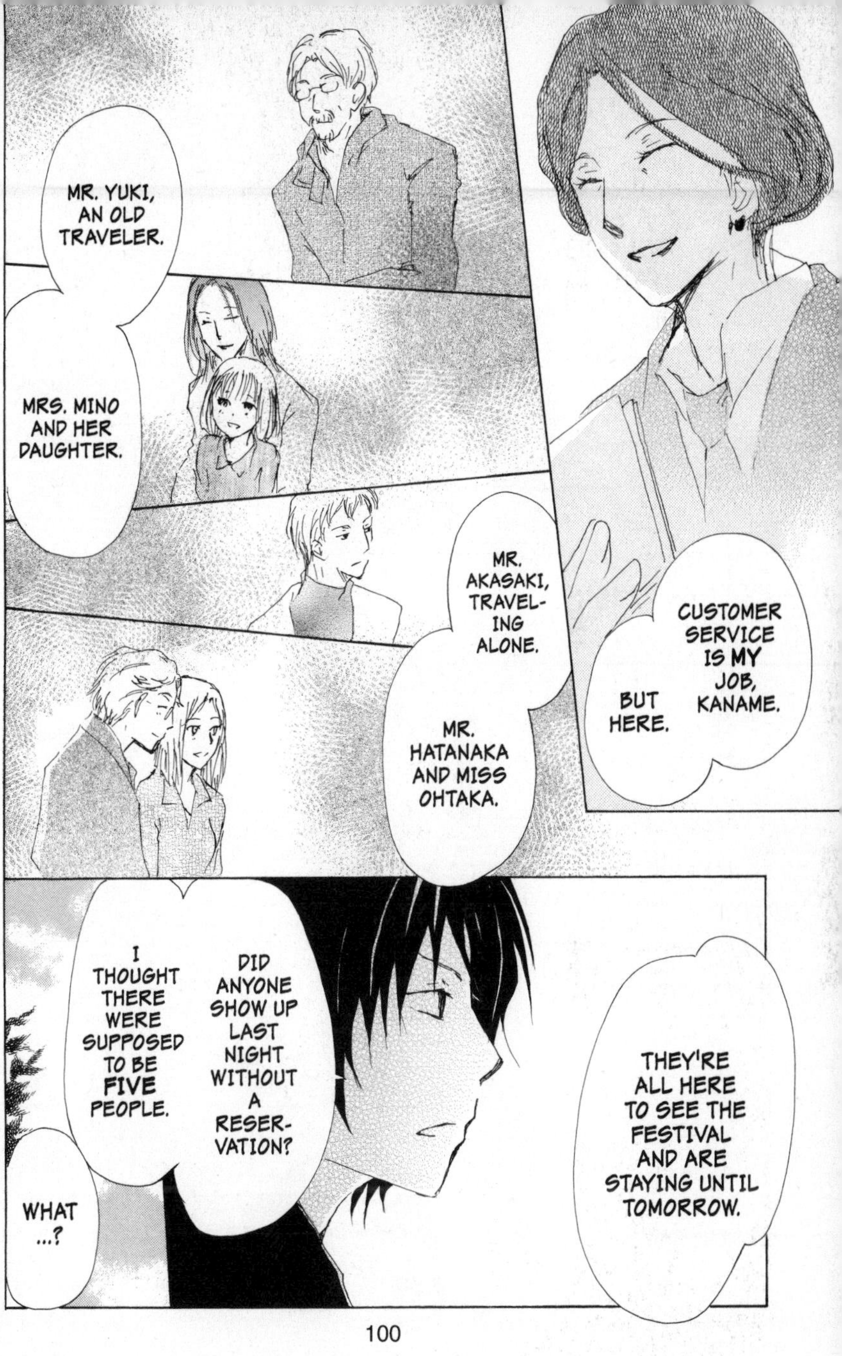

CUSTOMER SERVICE IS MY JOB, KANAME.
BUT HERE.
MR. YUKI, AN OLD TRAVELER.
MRS. MINO AND HER DAUGHTER.
MR. AKASAKI, TRAVEL-ING ALONE.
MR. HATANAKA AND MISS OHTAKA.
THEY'RE ALL HERE TO SEE THE FESTIVAL AND ARE STAYING UNTIL TOMORROW.
DID ANYONE SHOW UP LAST NIGHT WITHOUT A RESER-VATION?
I THOUGHT THERE WERE SUPPOSED TO BE FIVE PEOPLE.
WHAT ...?

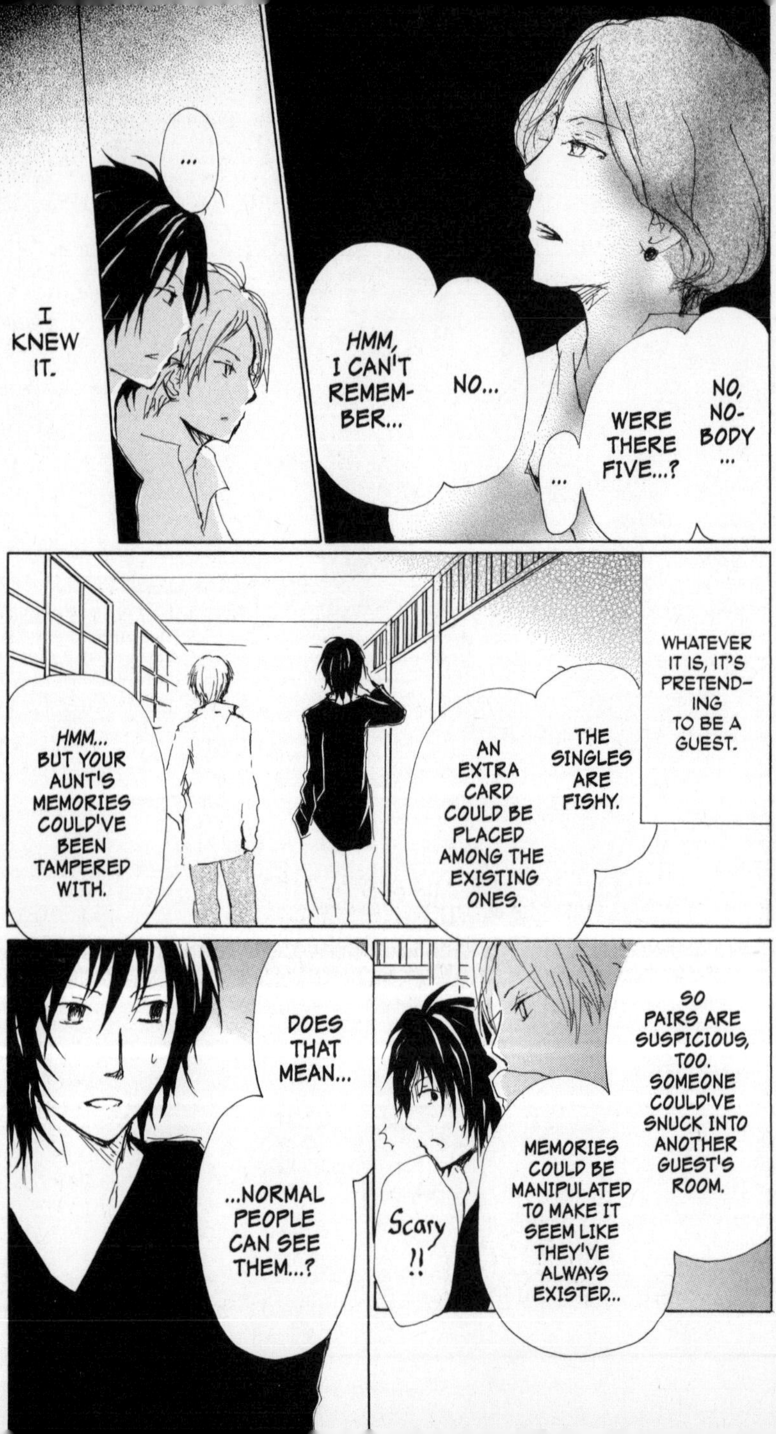
NO, NOBODY ...
WERE THERE FIVE...?
...
NO...
HMM, I CAN'T REMEMBER...
...
I KNEW IT.
WHATEVER IT IS, IT'S PRETENDING TO BE A GUEST.
THE SINGLES ARE FISHY.
AN EXTRA CARD COULD BE PLACED AMONG THE EXISTING ONES.
HMM... BUT YOUR AUNT'S MEMORIES COULD'VE BEEN TAMPERED WITH.
SO PAIRS ARE SUSPICIOUS, TOO. SOMEONE COULD'VE SNUCK INTO ANOTHER GUEST'S ROOM.
MEMORIES COULD BE MANIPULATED TO MAKE IT SEEM LIKE THEY'VE ALWAYS EXISTED...
Scary !!
DOES THAT MEAN...
...NORMAL PEOPLE CAN SEE THEM...?

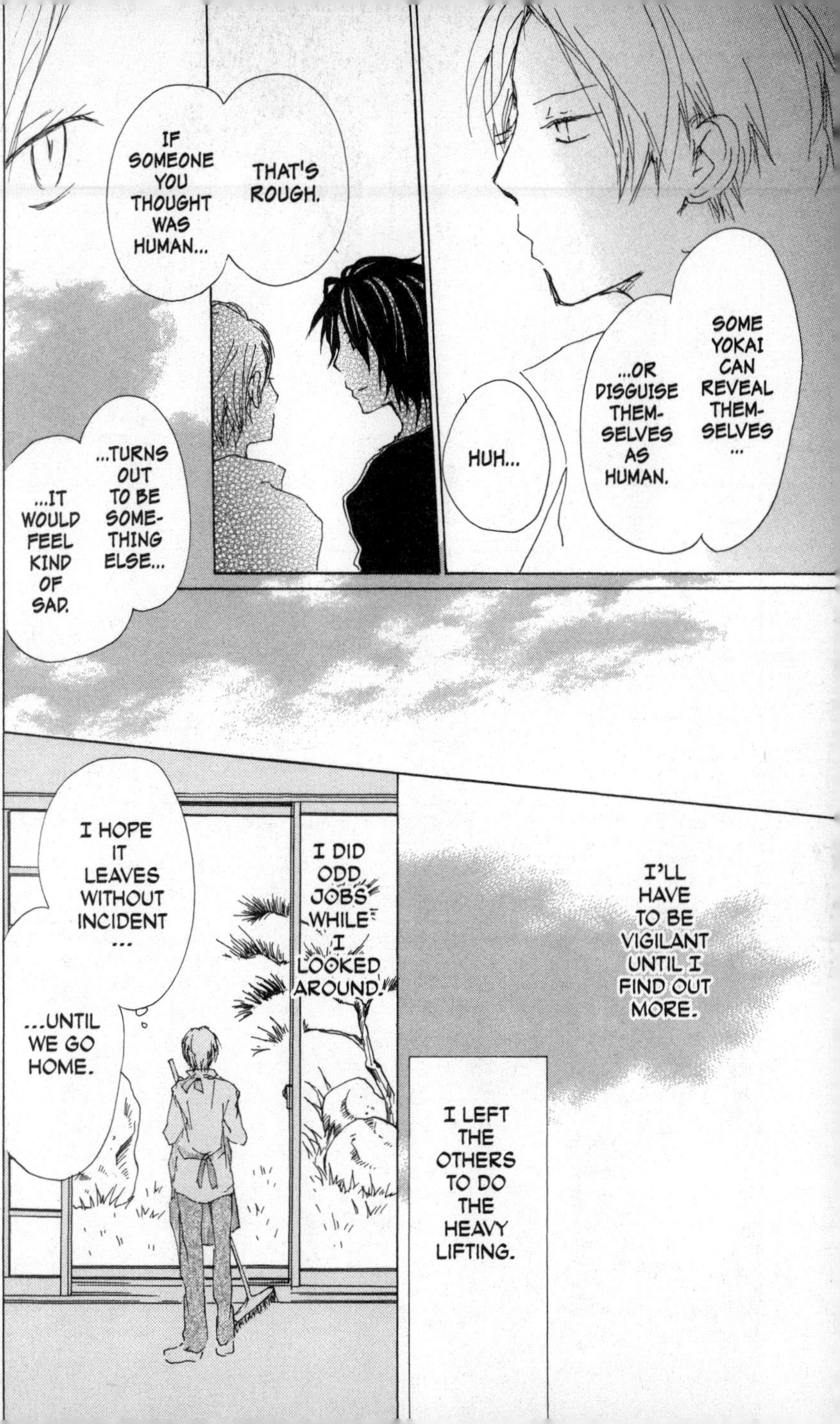
SOME YOKAI CAN REVEAL THEMSELVES...
...OR DISGUISE THEMSELVES AS HUMAN.
HUH...
THAT'S ROUGH.
IF SOMEONE YOU THOUGHT WAS HUMAN...
...TURNS OUT TO BE SOMETHING ELSE...
...IT WOULD FEEL KIND OF SAD.
I'LL HAVE TO BE VIGILANT UNTIL I FIND OUT MORE.
I LEFT THE OTHERS TO DO THE HEAVY LIFTING.
I DID ODD JOBS WHILE I LOOKED AROUND.
I HOPE IT LEAVES WITHOUT INCIDENT...
...UNTIL WE GO HOME.

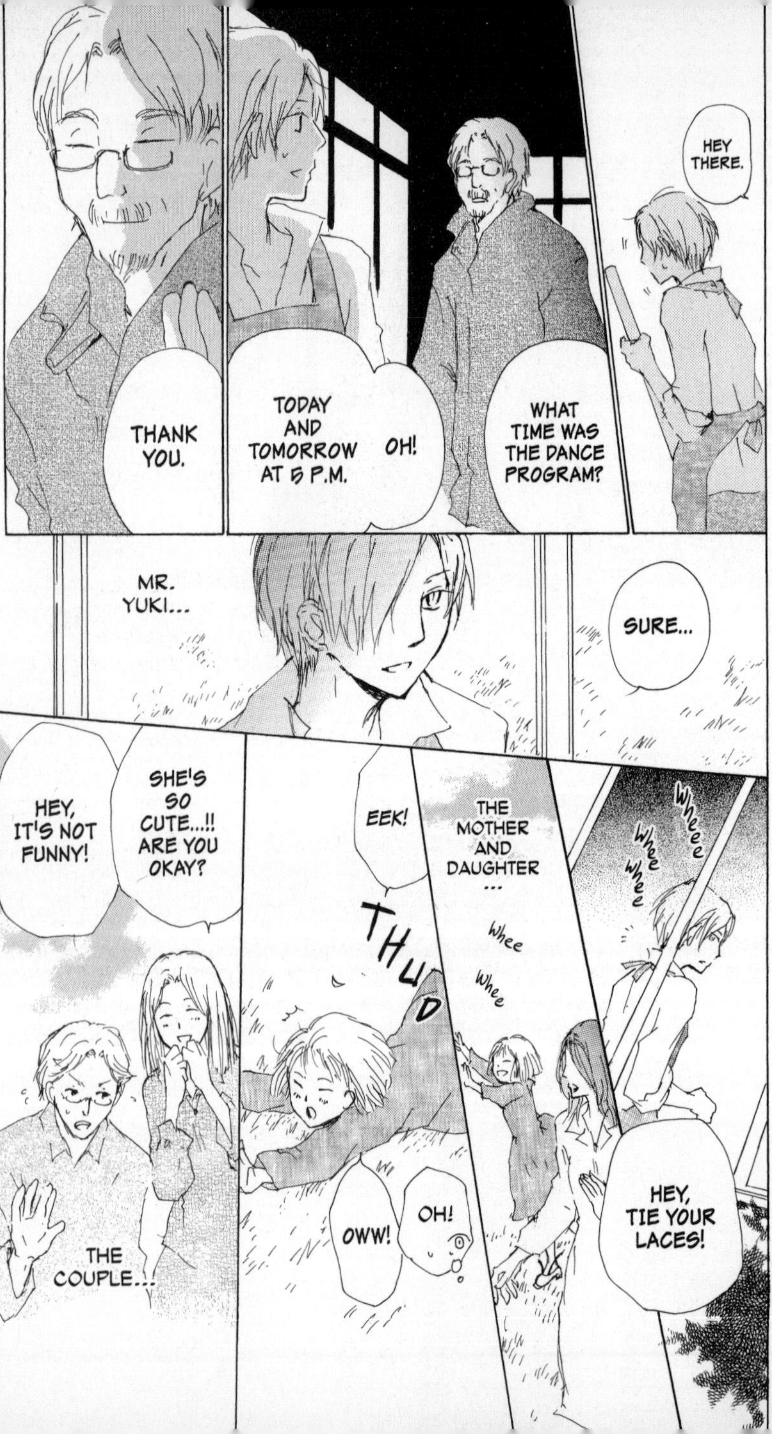
HEY THERE.
WHAT TIME WAS THE DANCE PROGRAM?
OH!
TODAY AND TOMORROW AT 5 P.M.
THANK YOU.
SURE...
MR. YUKI...
Wheee
whee
whee
HEY, TIE YOUR LACES!
THE MOTHER AND DAUGHTER...
Whee
Whee
EEK!
THUD
OH!
OWW!
SHE'S SO CUTE...!! ARE YOU OKAY?
HEY, IT'S NOT FUNNY!
THE COUPLE...

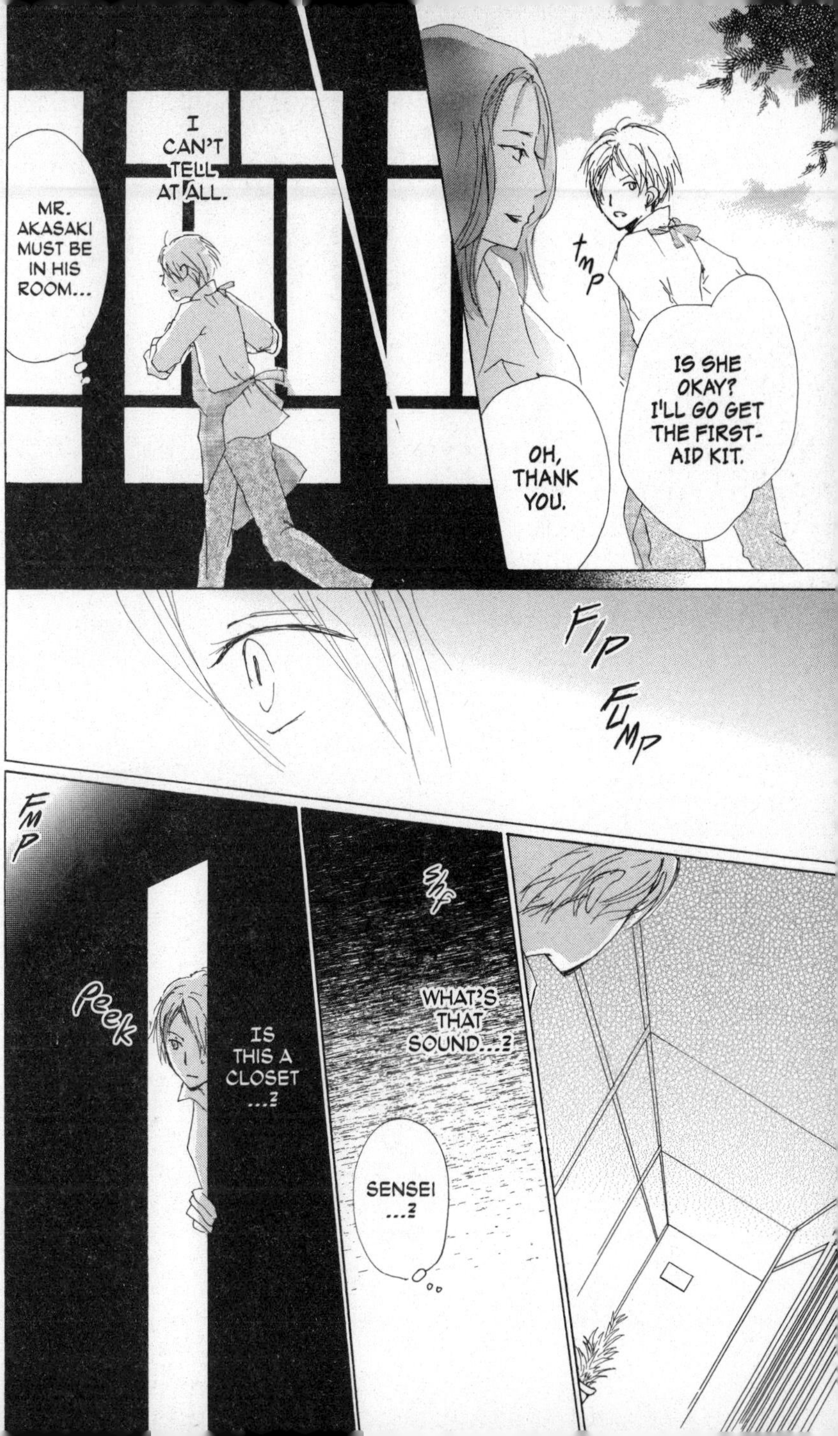
tmp
IS SHE OKAY? I'LL GO GET THE FIRST-AID KIT.
OH, THANK YOU.
I CAN'T TELL AT ALL.
MR. AKASAKI MUST BE IN HIS ROOM...
FLIP
FUMP
shf
WHAT'S THAT SOUND...?
SENSEI...?
FMP
Peek
IS THIS A CLOSET...?

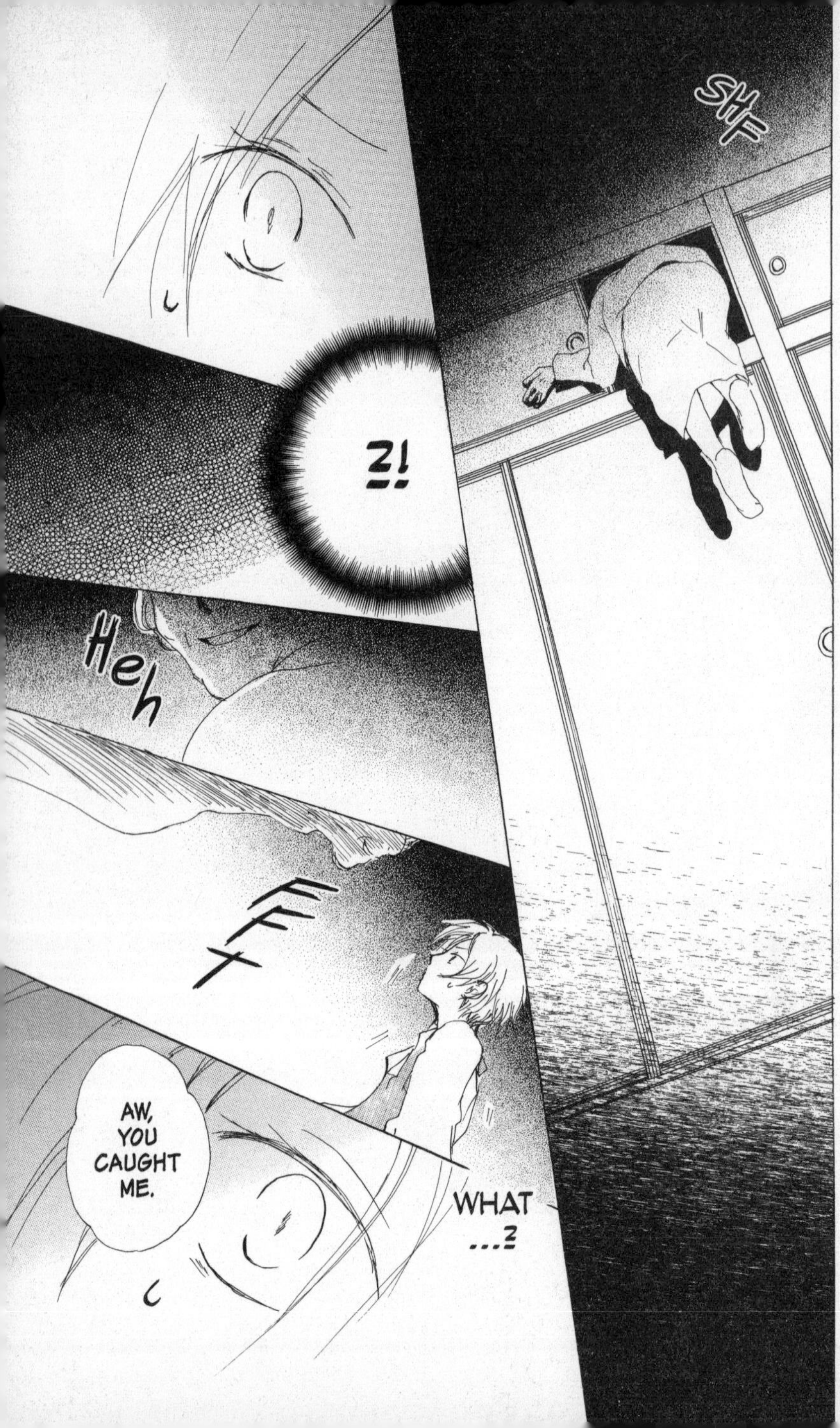
SHF
WHAT ...?
!?
Heh
FFT
AW, YOU CAUGHT ME.

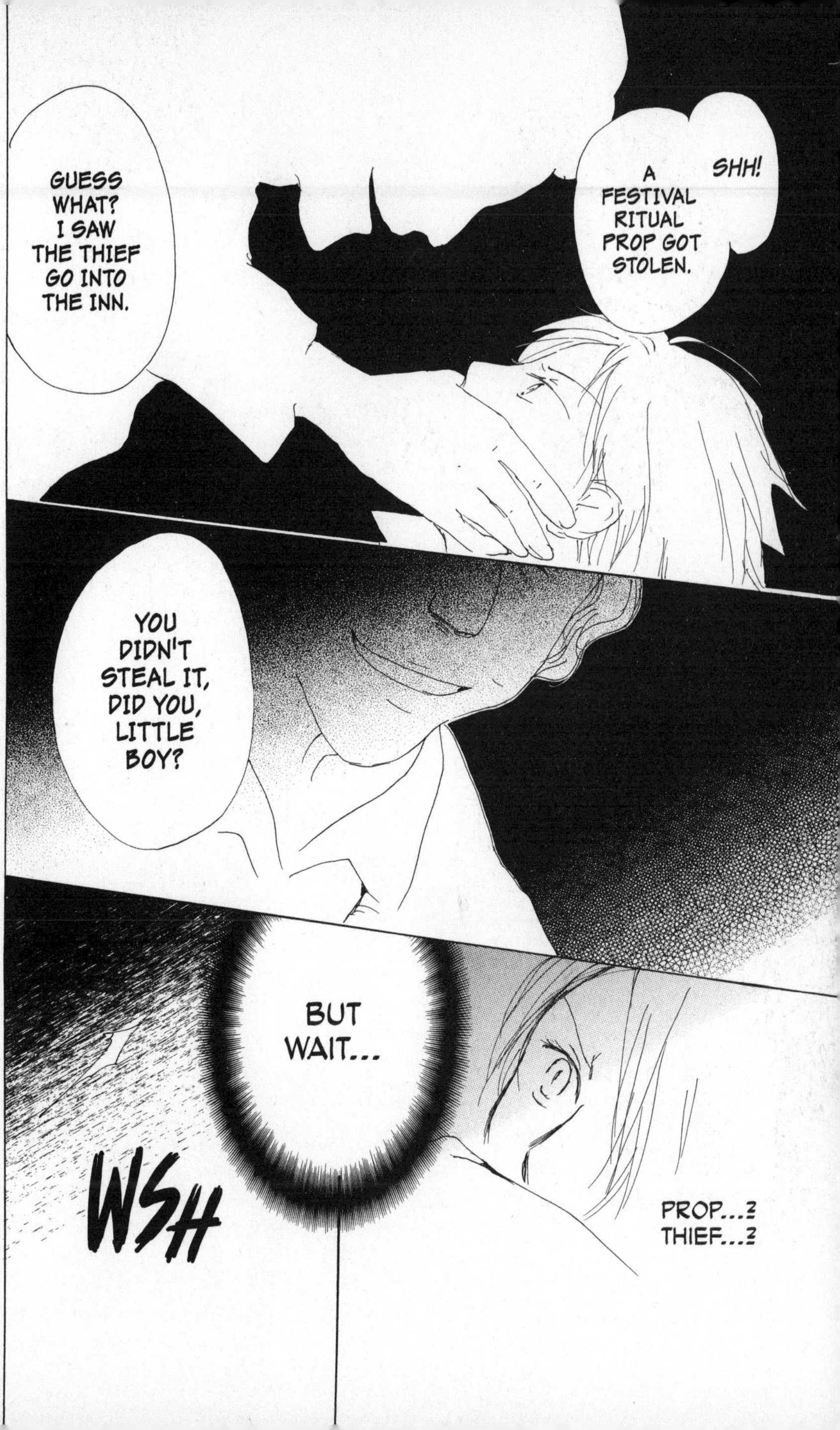
SHH!
A FESTIVAL RITUAL PROP GOT STOLEN.
GUESS WHAT? I SAW THE THIEF GO INTO THE INN.
YOU DIDN'T STEAL IT, DID YOU, LITTLE BOY?
BUT WAIT...
PROP...? THIEF...?
WSH

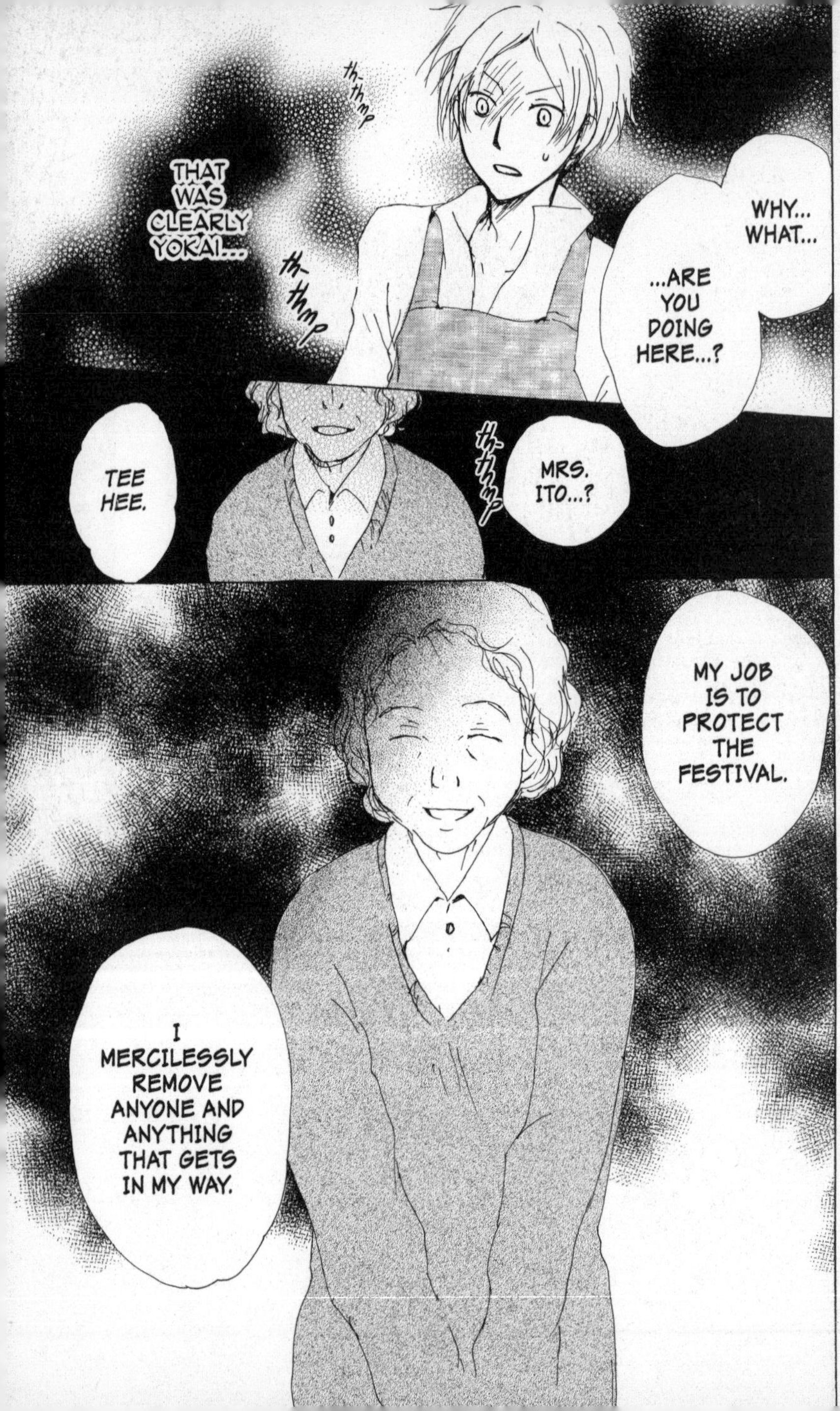
WHY... WHAT...
...ARE YOU DOING HERE...?
th-thmp
THAT WAS CLEARLY YOKAI...
th-thmp
MRS. ITO...?
th-thmp
TEE HEE.
MY JOB IS TO PROTECT THE FESTIVAL.
I MERCILESSLY REMOVE ANYONE AND ANYTHING THAT GETS IN MY WAY.

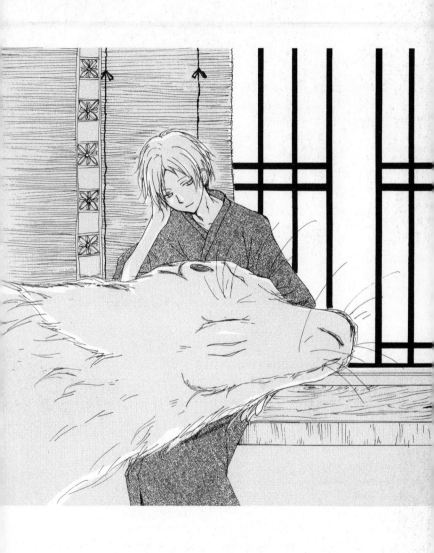

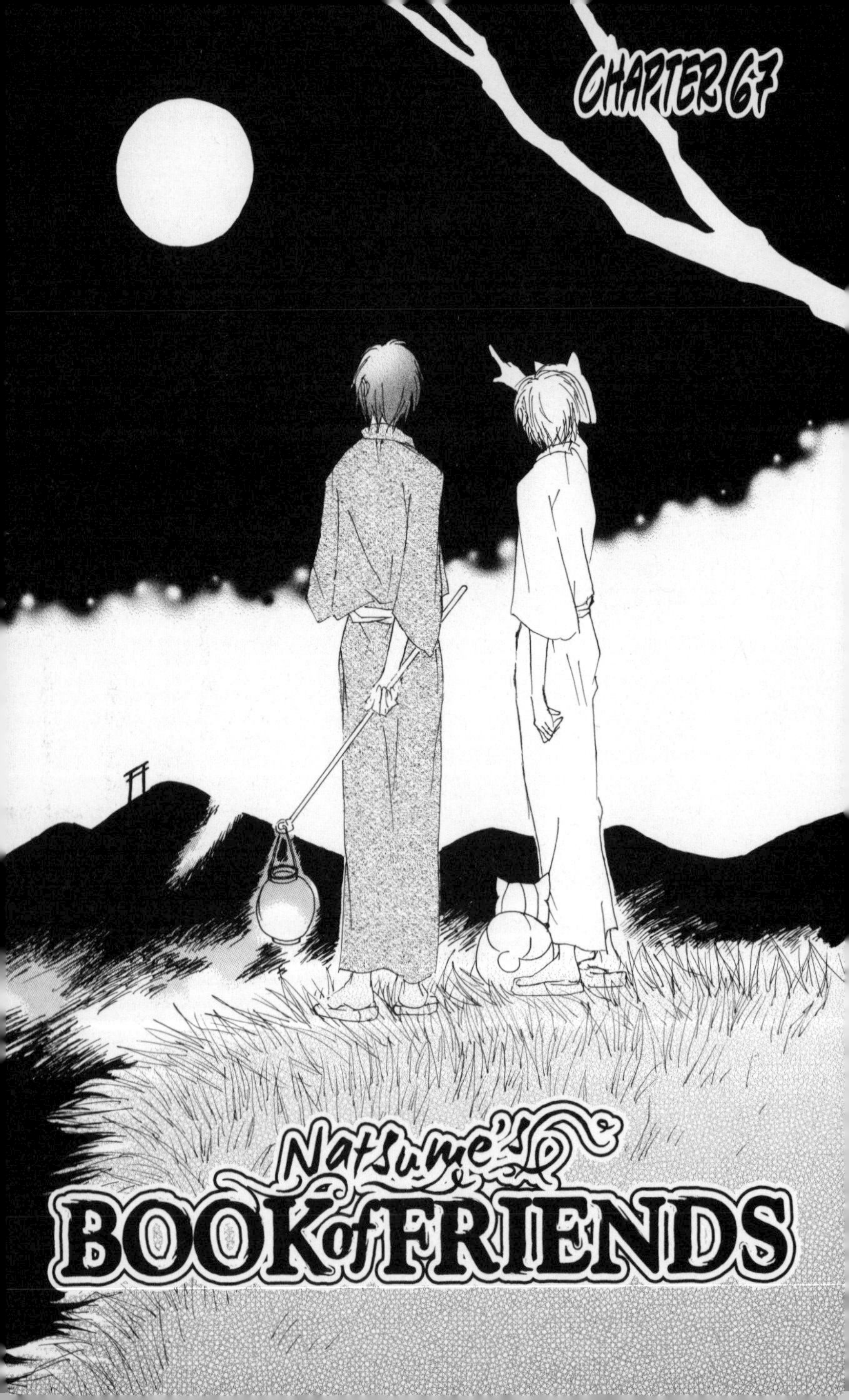
CHAPTER 67
Natsume's
BOOK of FRIENDS

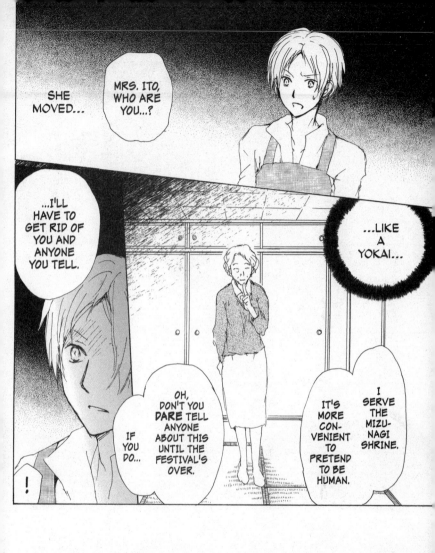

MRS. ITO, WHO ARE YOU...?
SHE MOVED...
...LIKE A YOKAI...
I SERVE THE MIZUNAGI SHRINE.
IT'S MORE CONVENIENT TO PRETEND TO BE HUMAN.
OH, DON'T YOU **DARE** TELL ANYONE ABOUT THIS UNTIL THE FESTIVAL'S OVER.
IF YOU DO...
...I'LL HAVE TO GET RID OF YOU AND ANYONE YOU TELL.
!

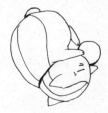

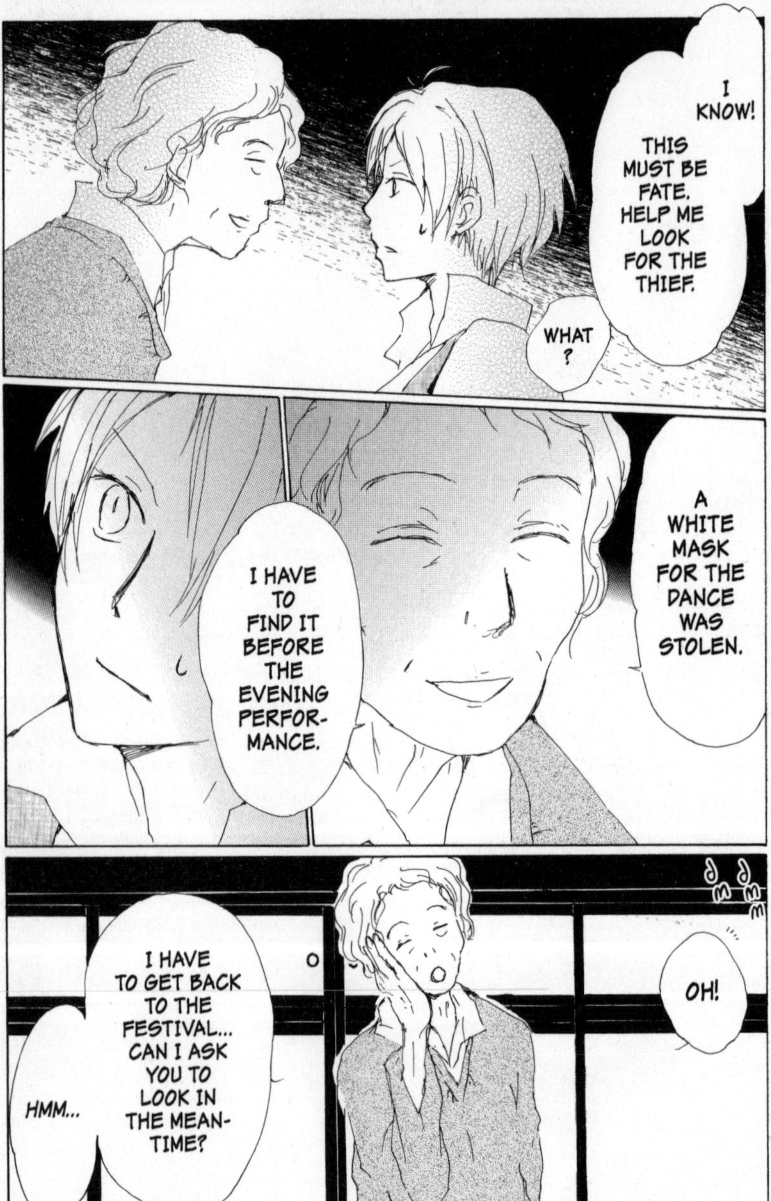
I KNOW!
THIS MUST BE FATE. HELP ME LOOK FOR THE THIEF.
WHAT?
A WHITE MASK FOR THE DANCE WAS STOLEN.
I HAVE TO FIND IT BEFORE THE EVENING PERFORMANCE.
OH!
I HAVE TO GET BACK TO THE FESTIVAL... CAN I ASK YOU TO LOOK IN THE MEAN-TIME?
HMM...

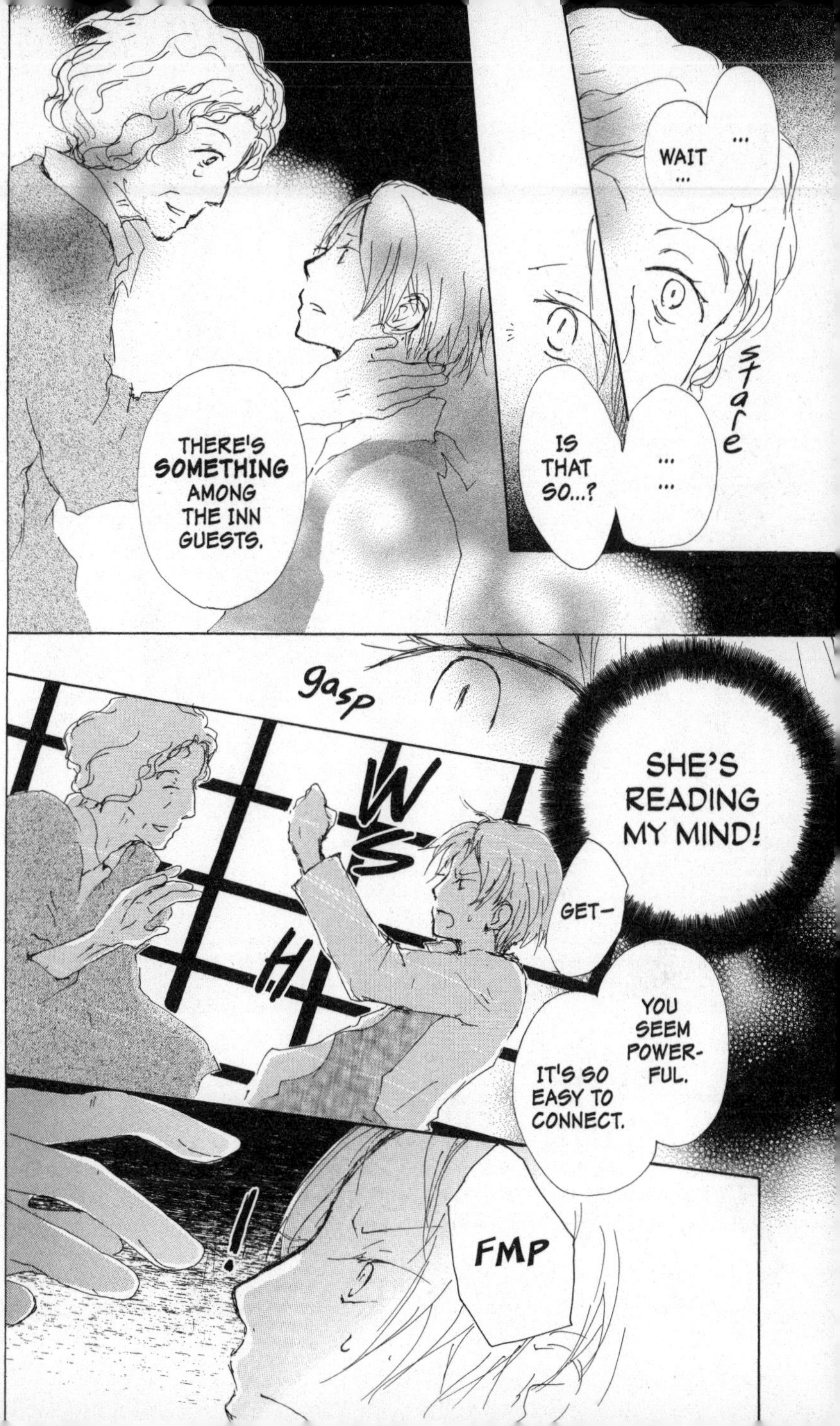

... WAIT ...
stare
... ...
IS THAT SO...?
THERE'S **SOMETHING** AMONG THE INN GUESTS.
gasp
SHE'S READING MY MIND!
WHS
GET—
YOU SEEM POWER-FUL.
IT'S SO EASY TO CONNECT.
FMP
!

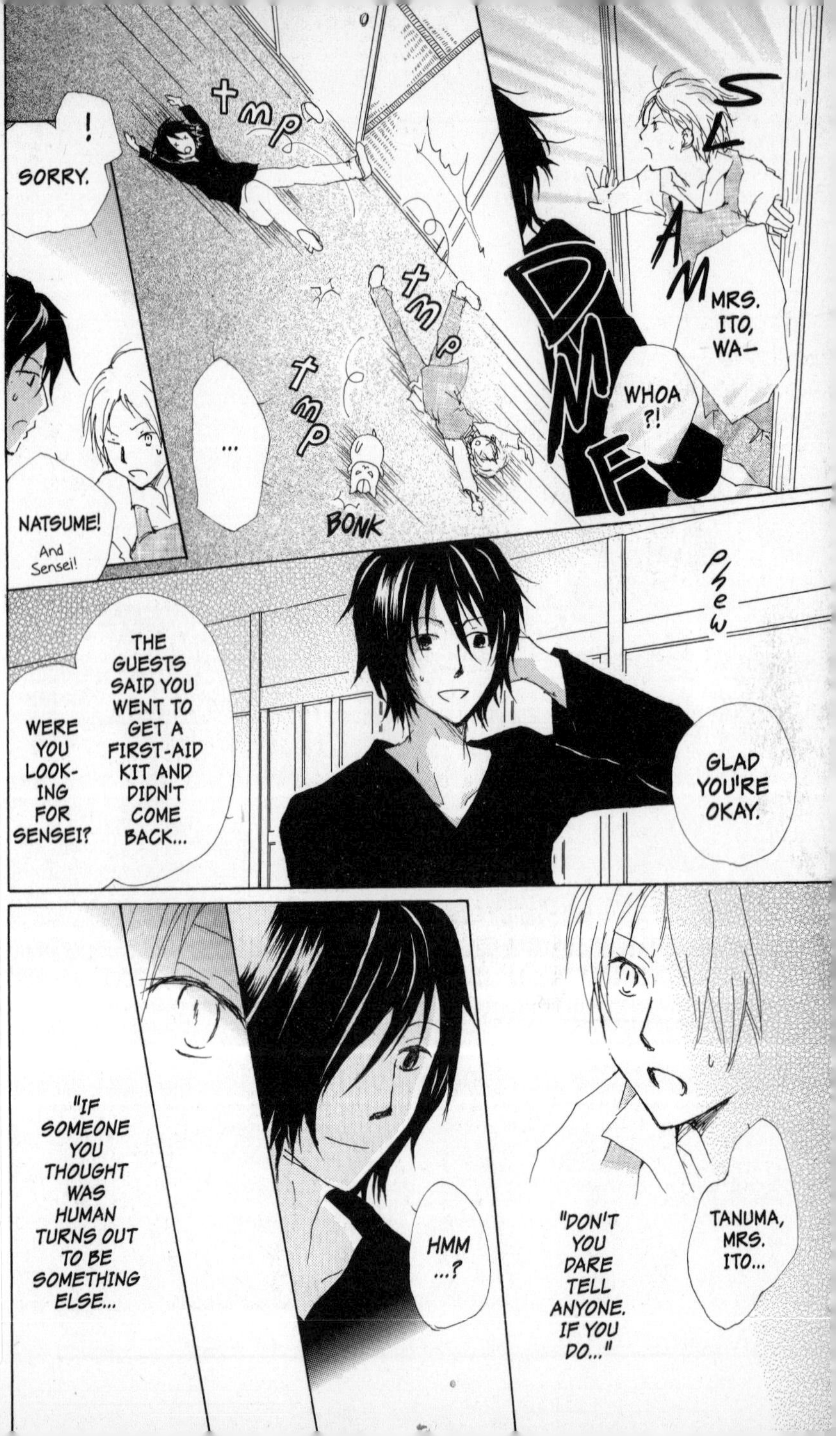
SLAM
MRS. ITO, WA—
WHOA?!
DMMF
tmp tmp tmp tmp
BONK
...
!
SORRY.
NATSUME!
And Sensei!
Phew
GLAD YOU'RE OKAY.
THE GUESTS SAID YOU WENT TO GET A FIRST-AID KIT AND DIDN'T COME BACK...
WERE YOU LOOKING FOR SENSEI?
TANUMA, MRS. ITO...
"DON'T YOU DARE TELL ANYONE. IF YOU DO..."
HMM ...?
"IF SOMEONE YOU THOUGHT WAS HUMAN TURNS OUT TO BE SOMETHING ELSE...

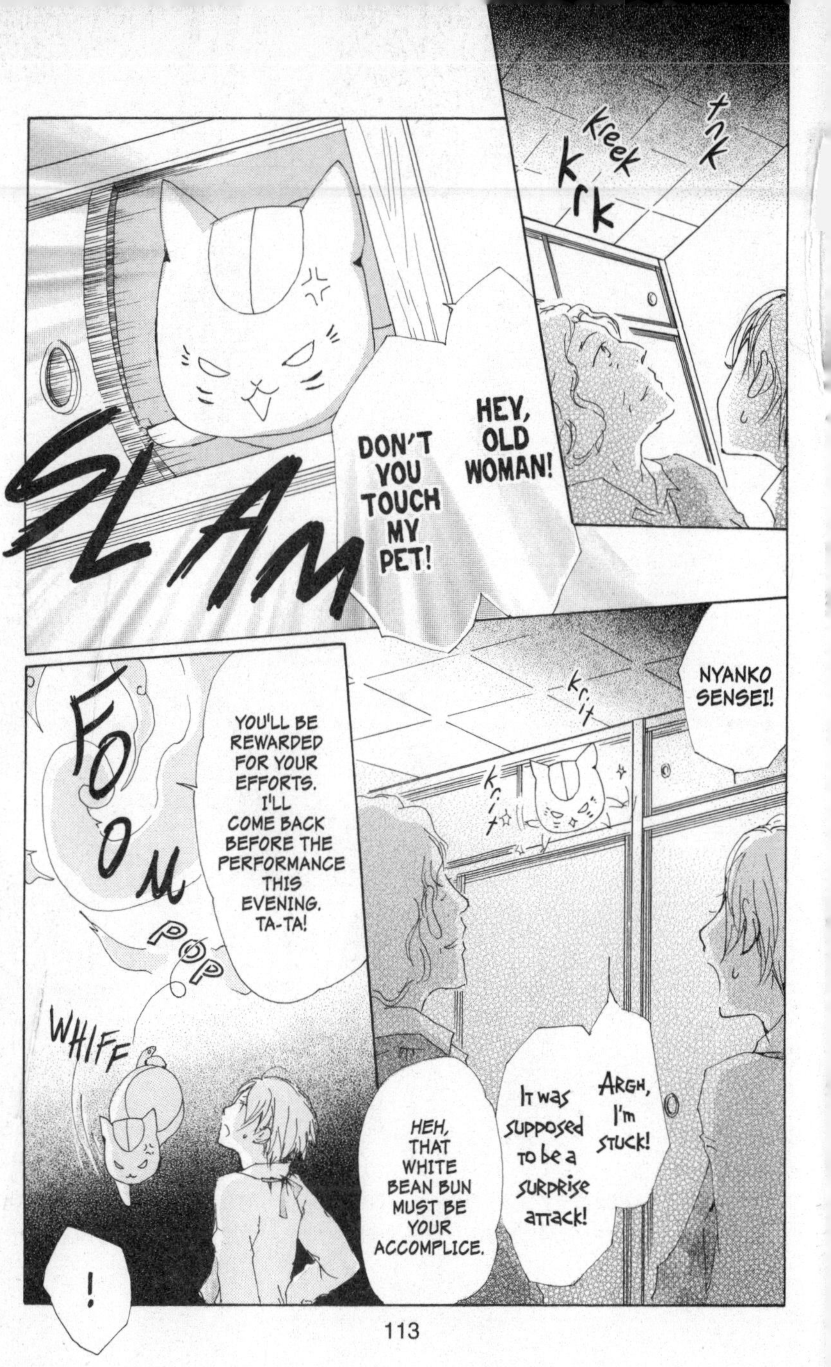
tnk
kreek
krk
SLAM
HEY, OLD WOMAN! DON'T YOU TOUCH MY PET!
NYANKO SENSEI!
krit
krit
ARGH, I'm STUCK!
It was supposed to be a surprise attack!
HEH, THAT WHITE BEAN BUN MUST BE YOUR ACCOMPLICE.
YOU'LL BE REWARDED FOR YOUR EFFORTS. I'LL COME BACK BEFORE THE PERFORMANCE THIS EVENING. TA-TA!
FOOOM
POP
WHIFF
!

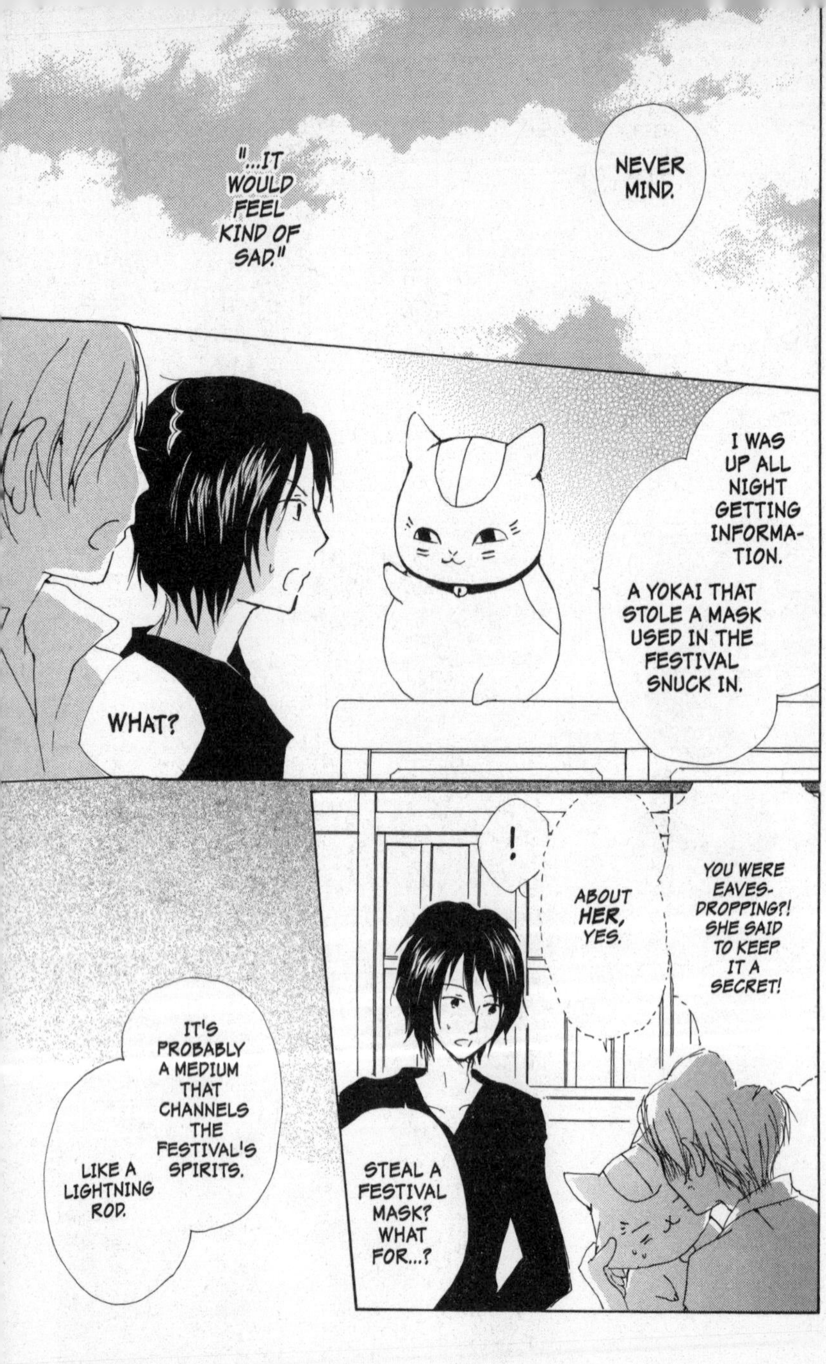
NEVER MIND.
"...IT WOULD FEEL KIND OF SAD."
I WAS UP ALL NIGHT GETTING INFORMA-TION.
A YOKAI THAT STOLE A MASK USED IN THE FESTIVAL SNUCK IN.
WHAT?
YOU WERE EAVES-DROPPING?! SHE SAID TO KEEP IT A SECRET!
ABOUT HER, YES.
!
STEAL A FESTIVAL MASK? WHAT FOR...?
IT'S PROBABLY A MEDIUM THAT CHANNELS THE FESTIVAL'S SPIRITS.
LIKE A LIGHTNING ROD.

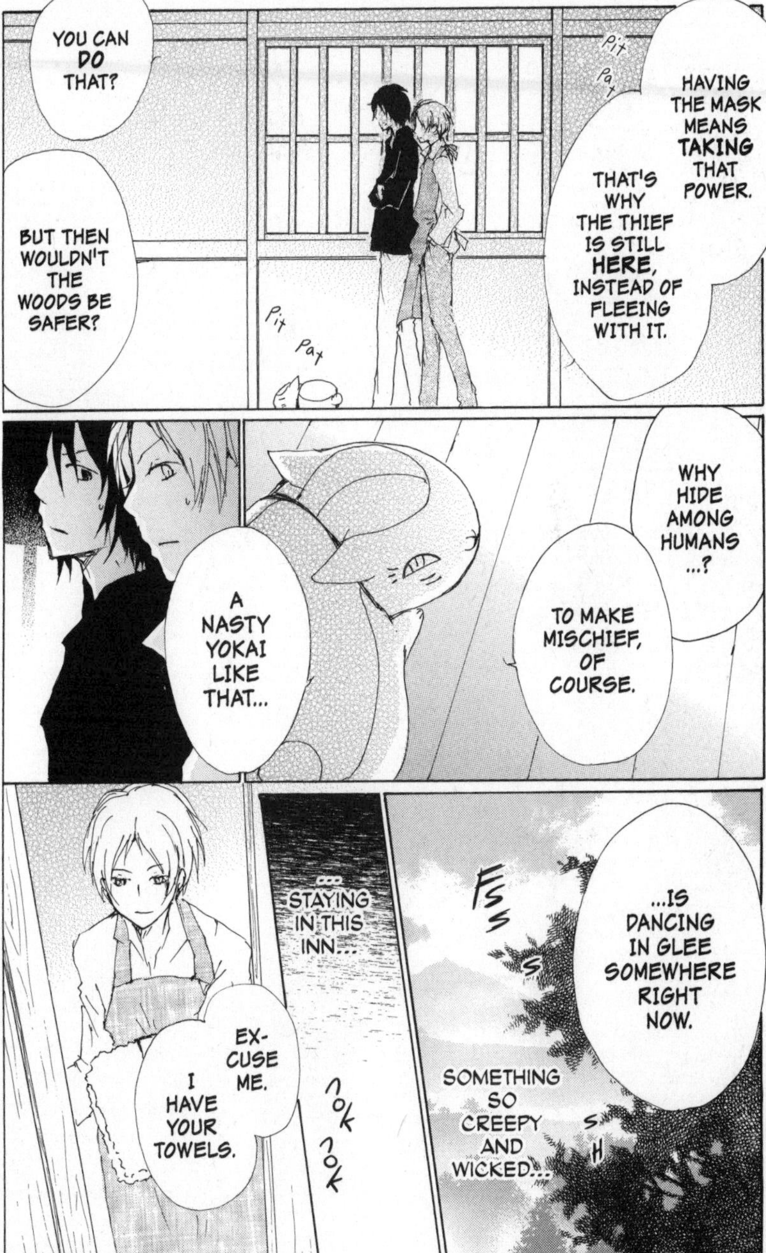
HAVING THE MASK MEANS TAKING THAT POWER.
THAT'S WHY THE THIEF IS STILL HERE, INSTEAD OF FLEEING WITH IT.
Pit Pat
YOU CAN DO THAT?
BUT THEN WOULDN'T THE WOODS BE SAFER?
Pit Pat
WHY HIDE AMONG HUMANS ...?
TO MAKE MISCHIEF, OF COURSE.
A NASTY YOKAI LIKE THAT...
...IS DANCING IN GLEE SOMEWHERE RIGHT NOW.
FSS
S
SOMETHING SO CREEPY AND WICKED...
SH
...STAYING IN THIS INN...
nok nok
EX-CUSE ME. I HAVE YOUR TOWELS.

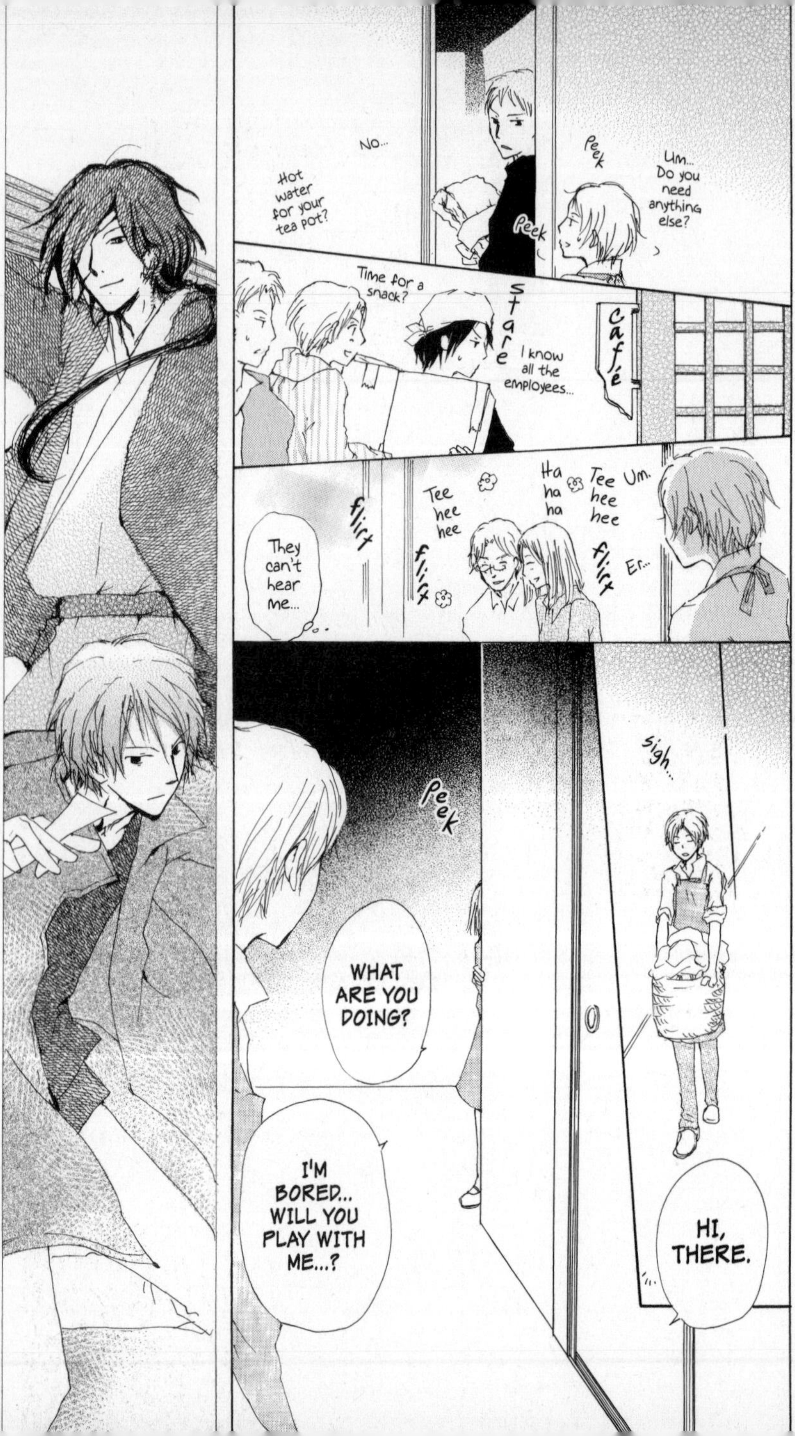

Um... Do you need anything else?
Peek
Peek
No...
Hot water for your tea pot?
Café
stare
I know all the employees...
Time for a snack?
Um.
Tee hee hee
Ha ha ha
Er...
flirt
Tee hee hee
flirt
flirt
They can't hear me...
sigh...
HI, THERE.
Peek
WHAT ARE YOU DOING?
I'M BORED... WILL YOU PLAY WITH ME...?

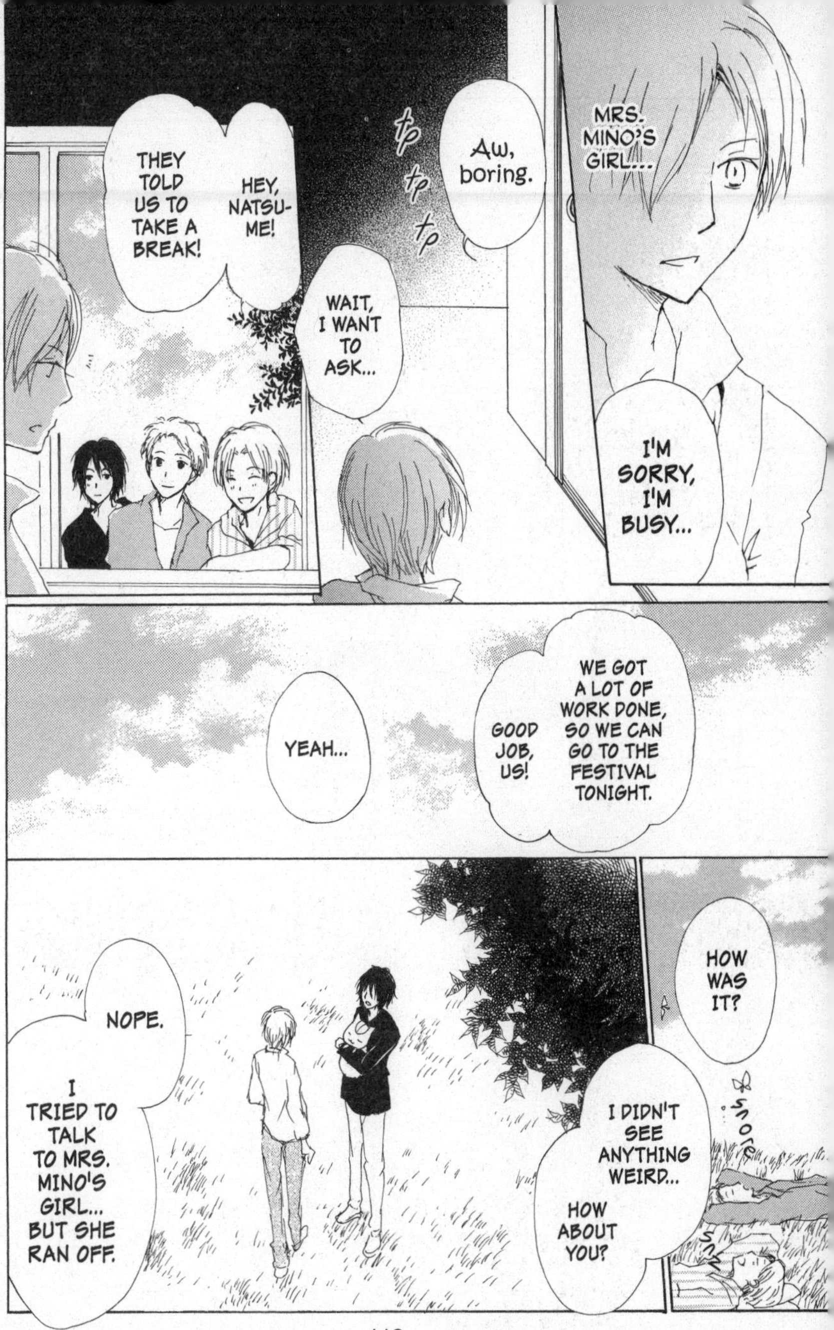
MRS. MINO'S GIRL...
I'M SORRY, I'M BUSY...
Aw, boring.
tp tp tp
HEY, NATSUME!
THEY TOLD US TO TAKE A BREAK!
WAIT, I WANT TO ASK...
WE GOT A LOT OF WORK DONE, SO WE CAN GO TO THE FESTIVAL TONIGHT.
GOOD JOB, US!
YEAH...
HOW WAS IT?
snore
I DIDN'T SEE ANYTHING WEIRD...
HOW ABOUT YOU?
snz
NOPE.
I TRIED TO TALK TO MRS. MINO'S GIRL... BUT SHE RAN OFF.

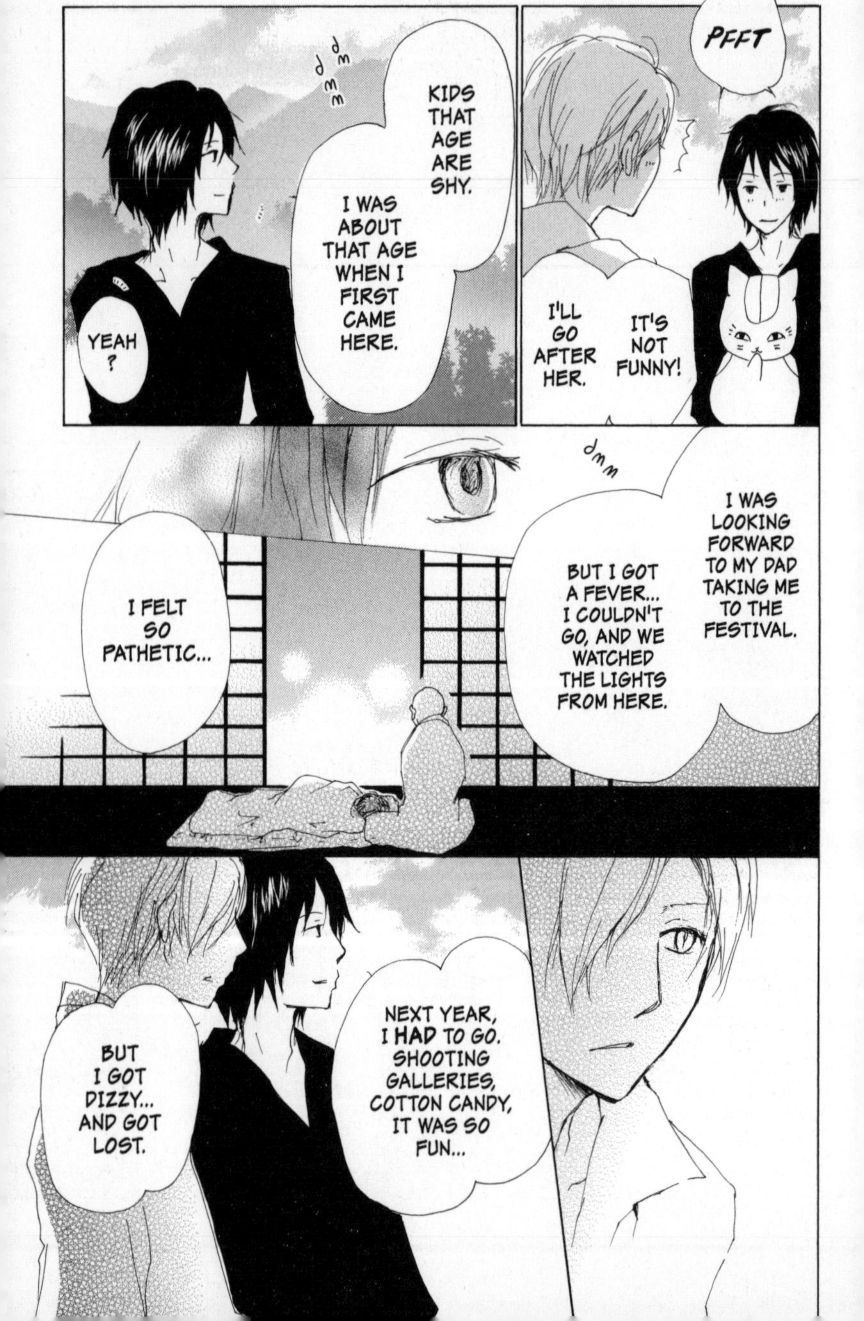
PFFT
IT'S NOT FUNNY!
I'LL GO AFTER HER.
KIDS THAT AGE ARE SHY.
I WAS ABOUT THAT AGE WHEN I FIRST CAME HERE.
YEAH?
I WAS LOOKING FORWARD TO MY DAD TAKING ME TO THE FESTIVAL.
BUT I GOT A FEVER... I COULDN'T GO, AND WE WATCHED THE LIGHTS FROM HERE.
I FELT SO PATHETIC...
NEXT YEAR, I HAD TO GO. SHOOTING GALLERIES, COTTON CANDY, IT WAS SO FUN...
BUT I GOT DIZZY... AND GOT LOST.

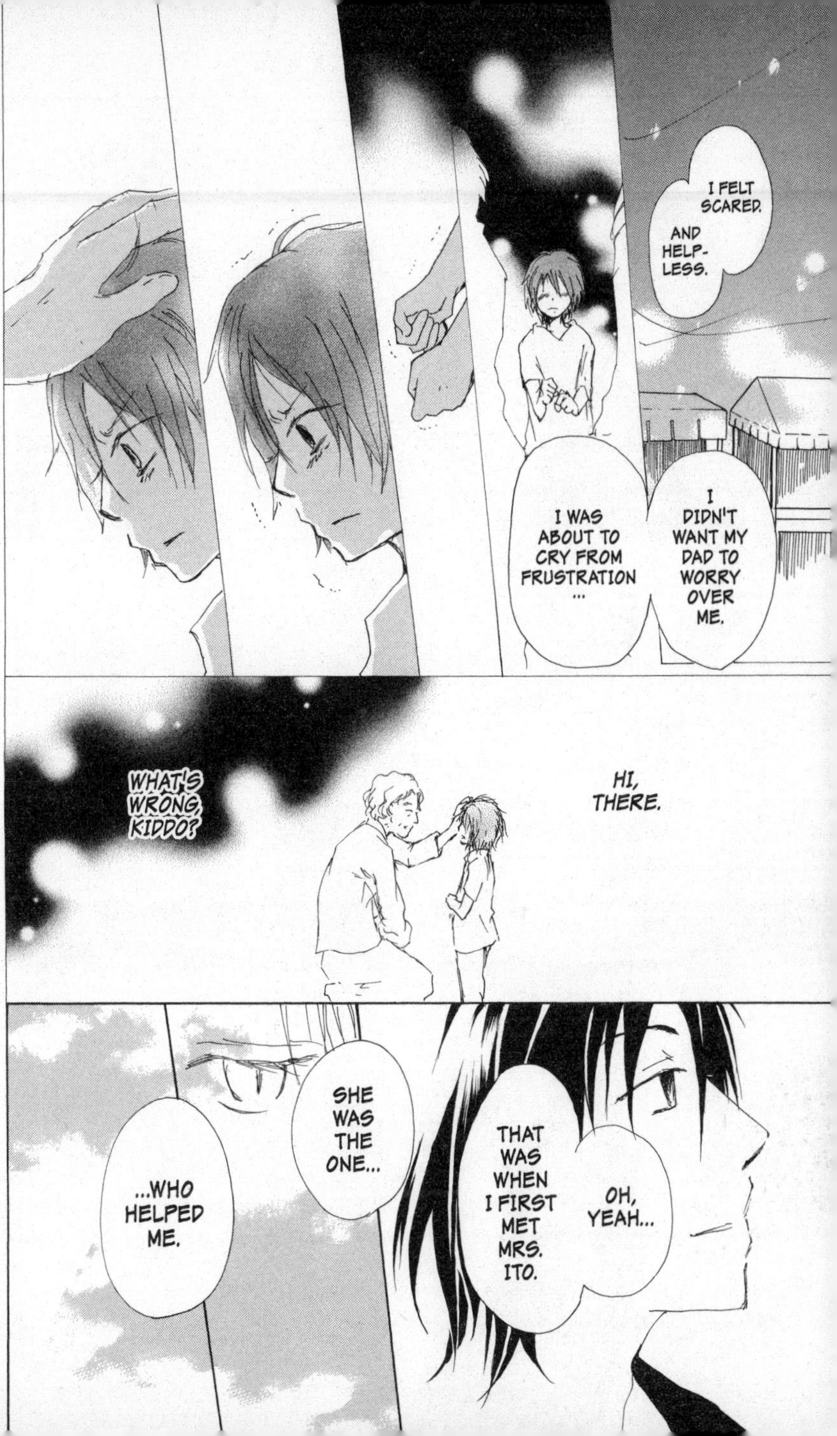
I FELT SCARED.
AND HELP-LESS.
I DIDN'T WANT MY DAD TO WORRY OVER ME.
I WAS ABOUT TO CRY FROM FRUSTRATION...
HI, THERE.
WHAT'S WRONG, KIDDO?
OH, YEAH...
THAT WAS WHEN I FIRST MET MRS. ITO.
SHE WAS THE ONE...
...WHO HELPED ME.

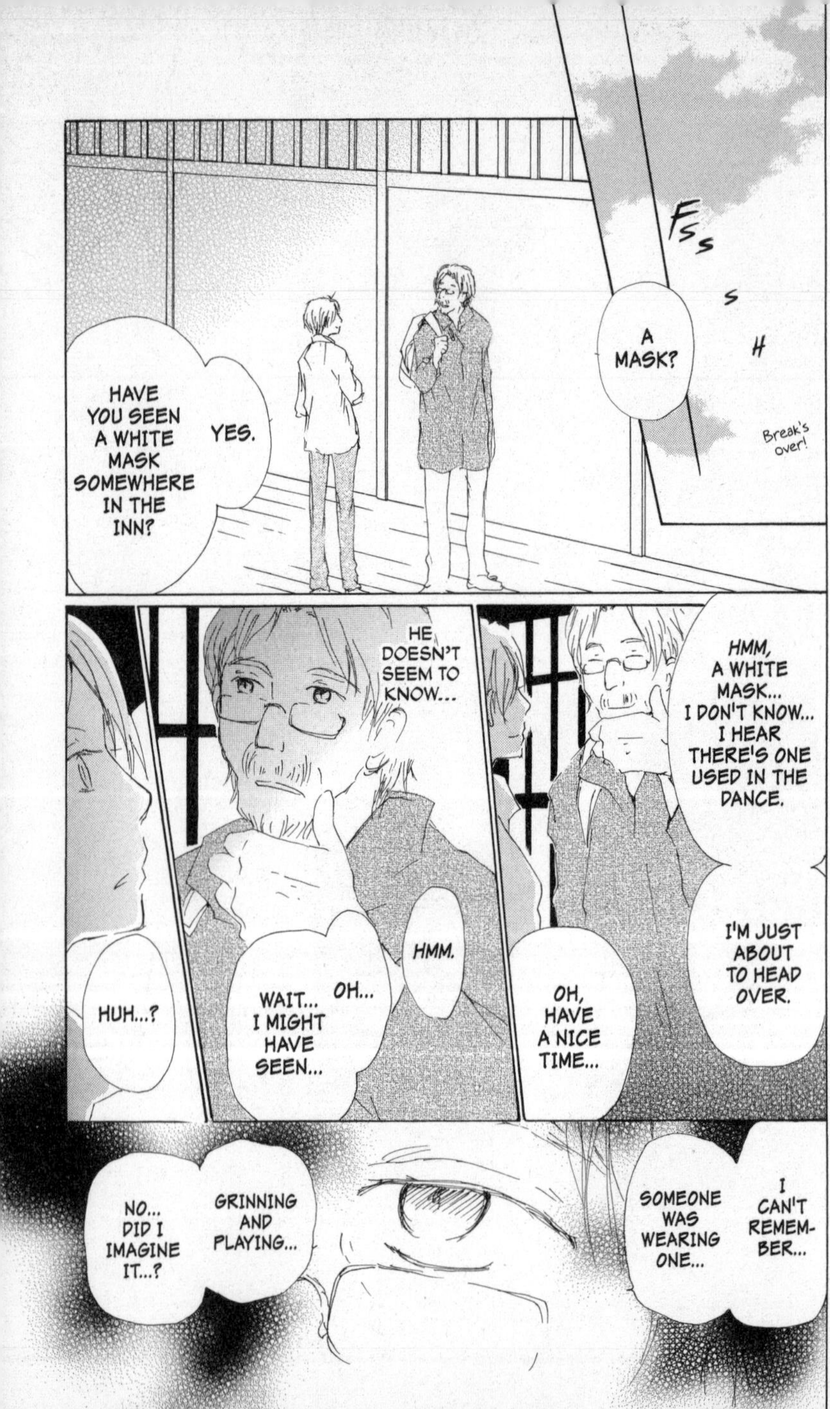
FSSS
SH
Break's over!
A MASK?
YES.
HAVE YOU SEEN A WHITE MASK SOMEWHERE IN THE INN?
HMM, A WHITE MASK... I DON'T KNOW... I HEAR THERE'S ONE USED IN THE DANCE.
I'M JUST ABOUT TO HEAD OVER.
OH, HAVE A NICE TIME...
HE DOESN'T SEEM TO KNOW...
HMM.
OH...
WAIT... I MIGHT HAVE SEEN...
HUH...?
I CAN'T REMEM-BER...
SOMEONE WAS WEARING ONE...
GRINNING AND PLAYING...
NO... DID I IMAGINE IT...?

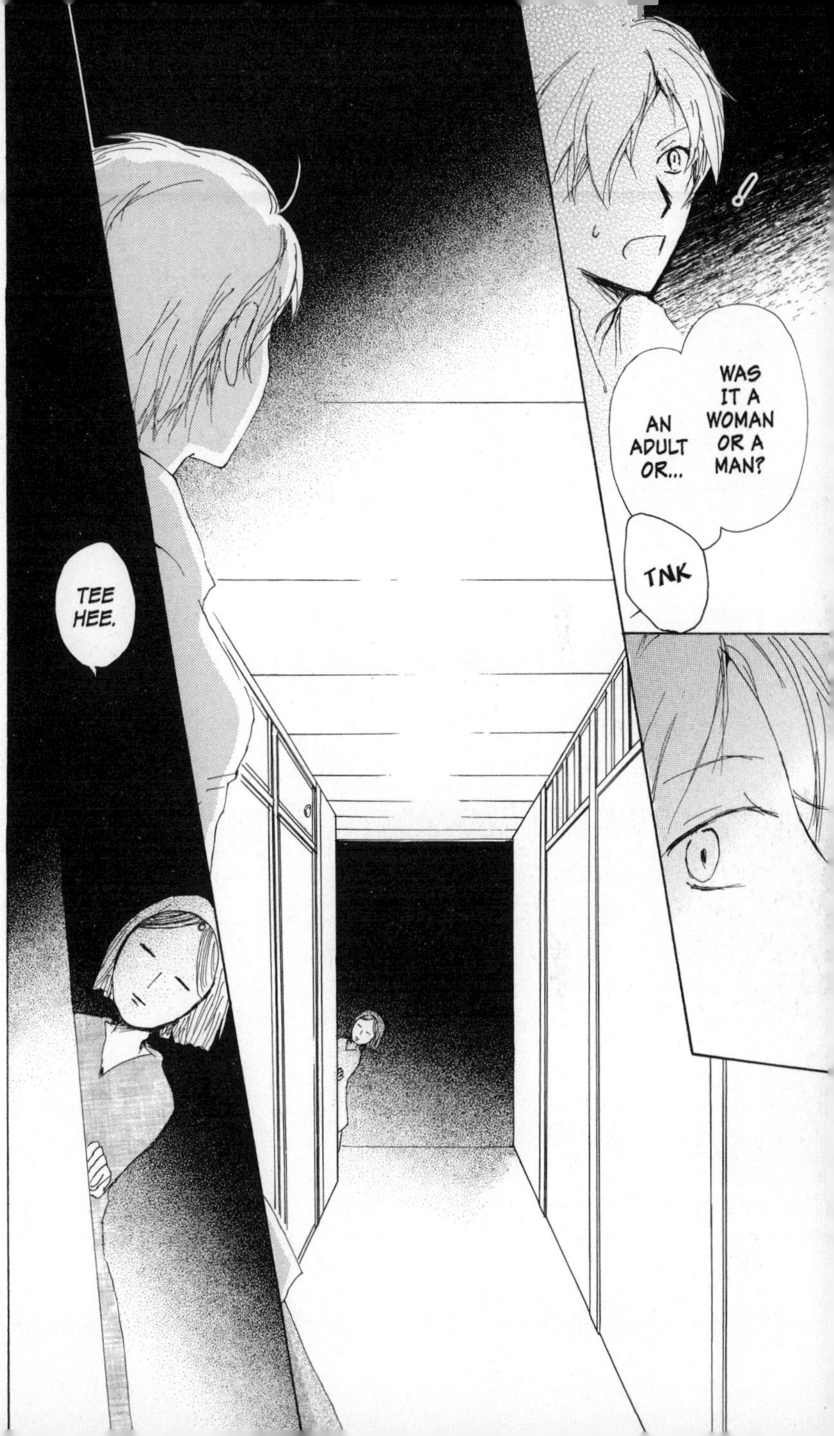
WAS IT A WOMAN OR A MAN?
AN ADULT OR...
TNK
TEE HEE.

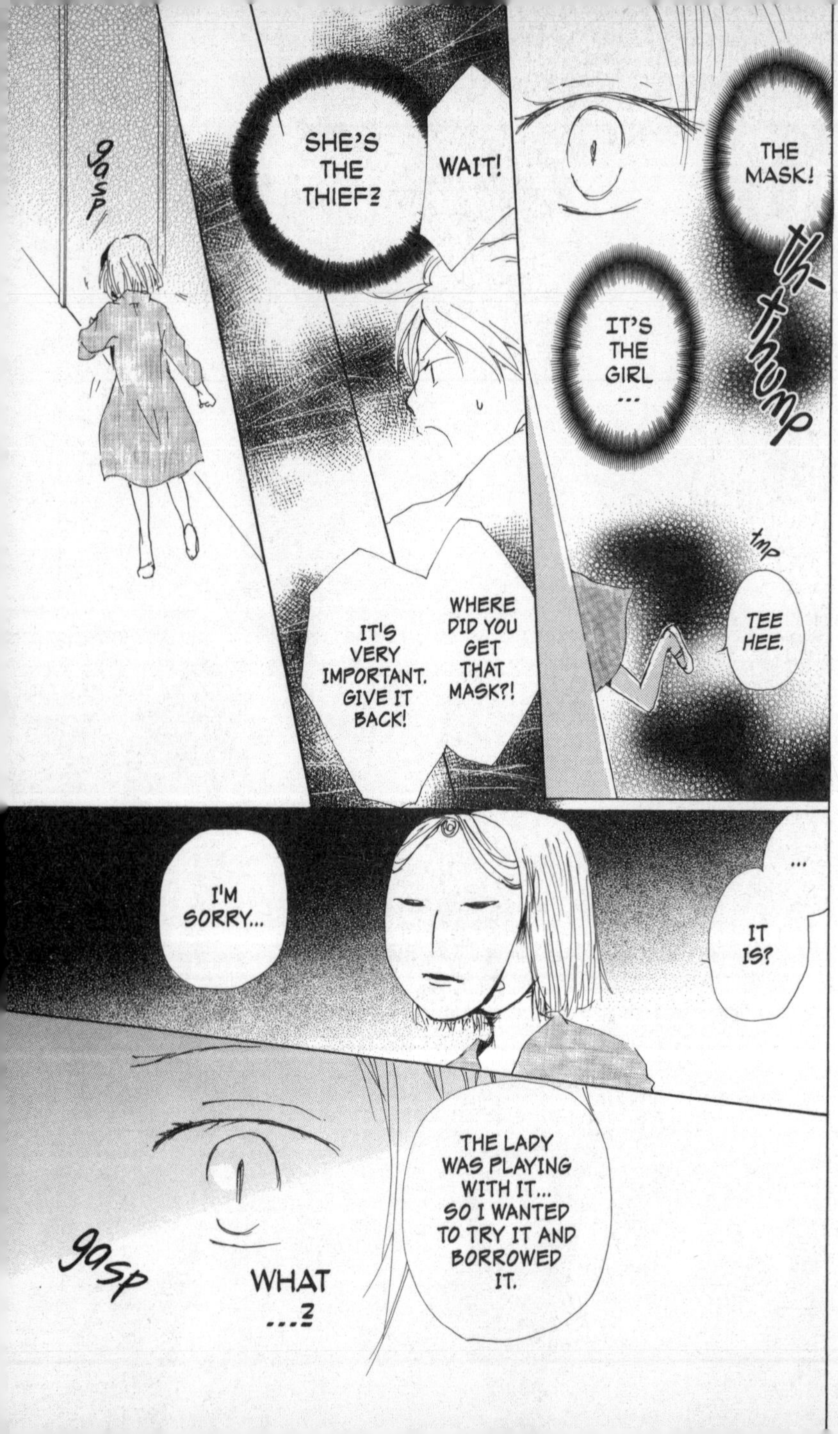
THE MASK!
th-thump
IT'S THE GIRL...
tmp
TEE HEE.
SHE'S THE THIEF?
WAIT!
WHERE DID YOU GET THAT MASK?!
IT'S VERY IMPORTANT. GIVE IT BACK!
gasp
...
IT IS?
I'M SORRY...
THE LADY WAS PLAYING WITH IT... SO I WANTED TO TRY IT AND BORROWED IT.
WHAT...?
gasp

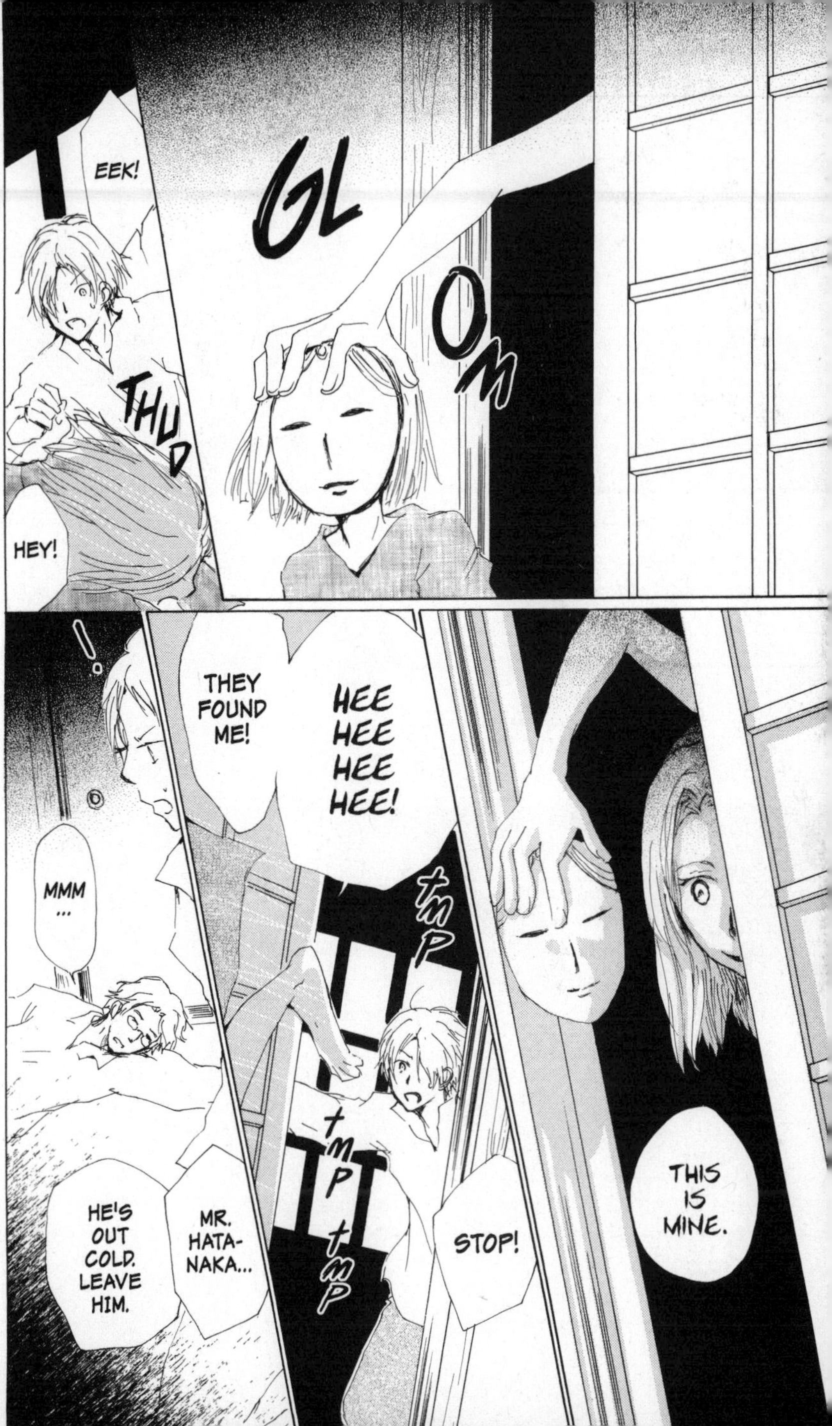
GLOM
EEK!
THUD
HEY!
THIS IS MINE.
HEE HEE HEE HEE!
THEY FOUND ME!
tmp
STOP!
tmp tmp
!
MMM...
MR. HATA-NAKA...
HE'S OUT COLD. LEAVE HIM.

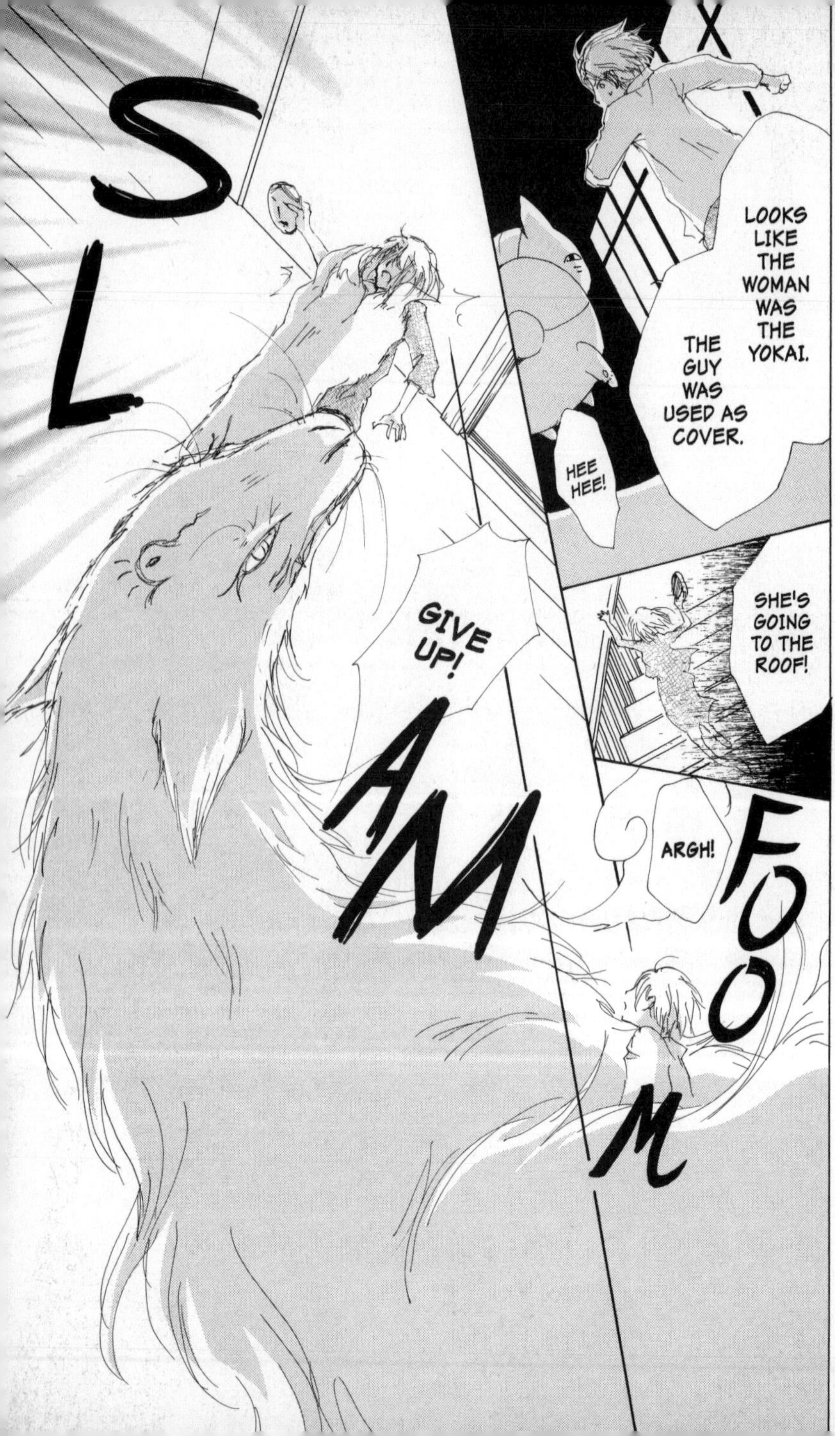
LOOKS LIKE THE WOMAN WAS THE YOKAI.
THE GUY WAS USED AS COVER.
HEE HEE!
SHE'S GOING TO THE ROOF!
ARGH!
FOOOM
SLAM
GIVE UP!

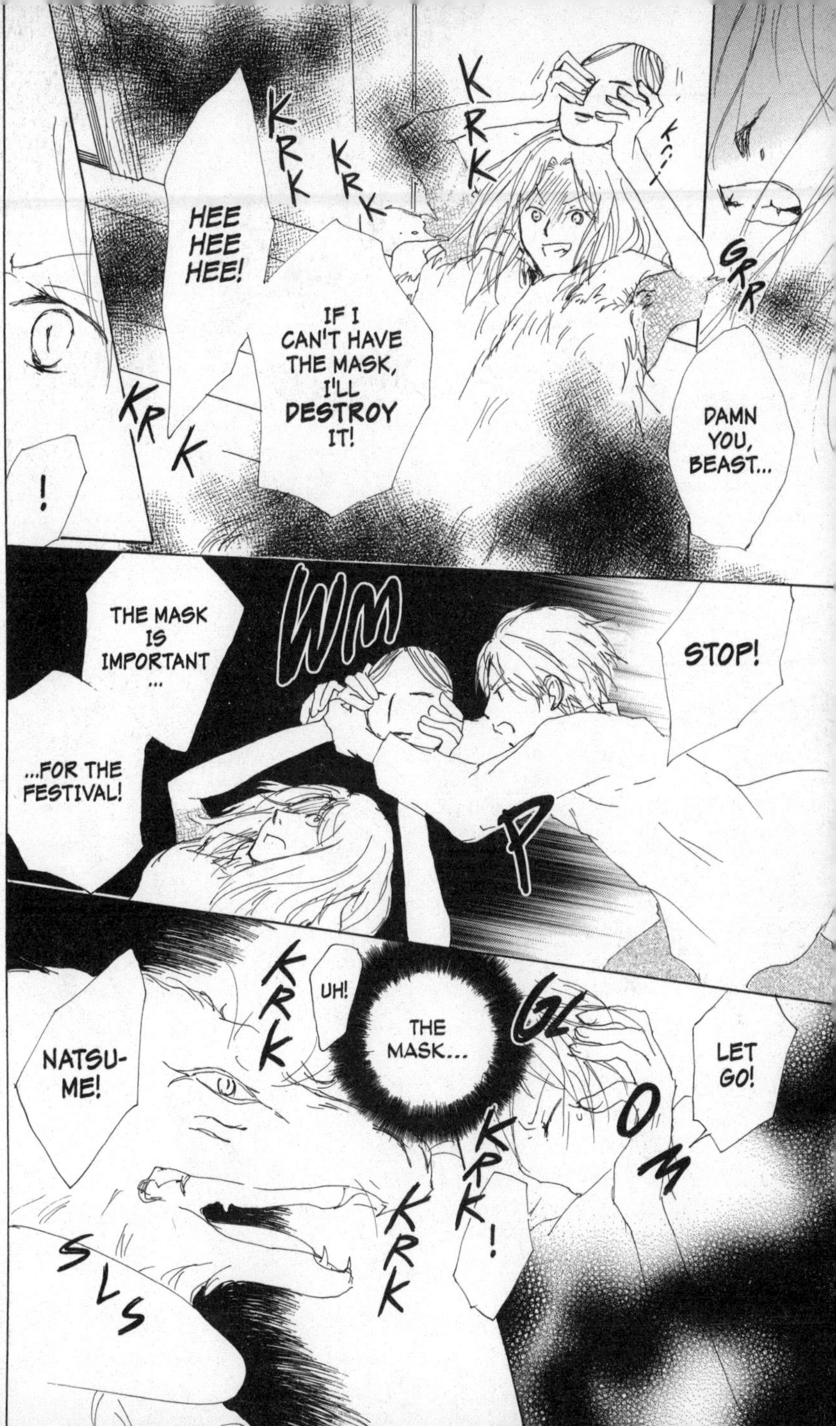
GRR
DAMN YOU, BEAST...
KRK
KRK
KRK
HEE HEE HEE!
IF I CAN'T HAVE THE MASK, I'LL DESTROY IT!
KRK
!
STOP!
WM
P
THE MASK IS IMPORTANT ...
...FOR THE FESTIVAL!
LET GO!
GLOOM
THE MASK...
UH!
KRK
KRK!
KRK
NATSU-ME!
SLS

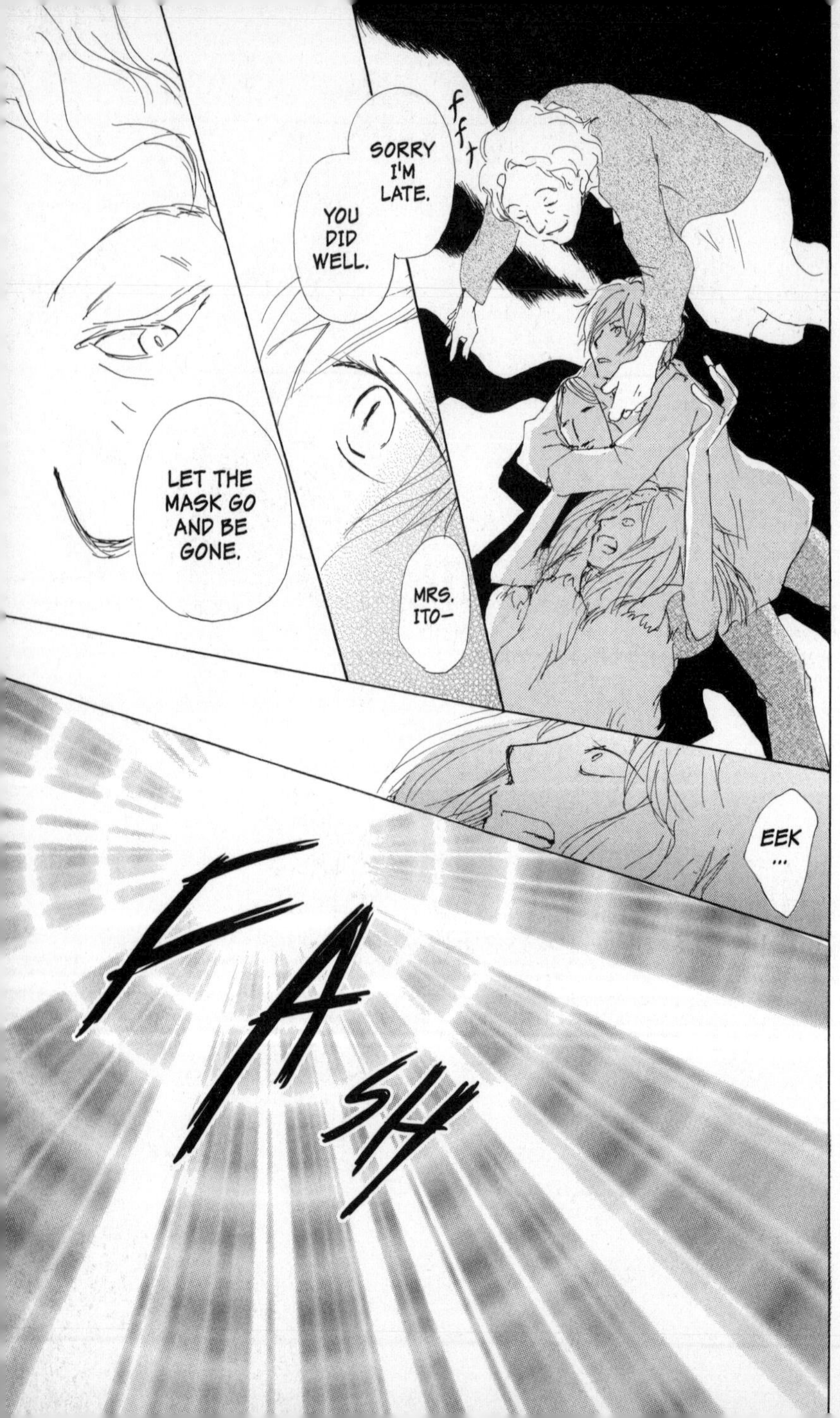
fff
SORRY I'M LATE.
YOU DID WELL.
MRS. ITO—
LET THE MASK GO AND BE GONE.
EEK ...
FASH

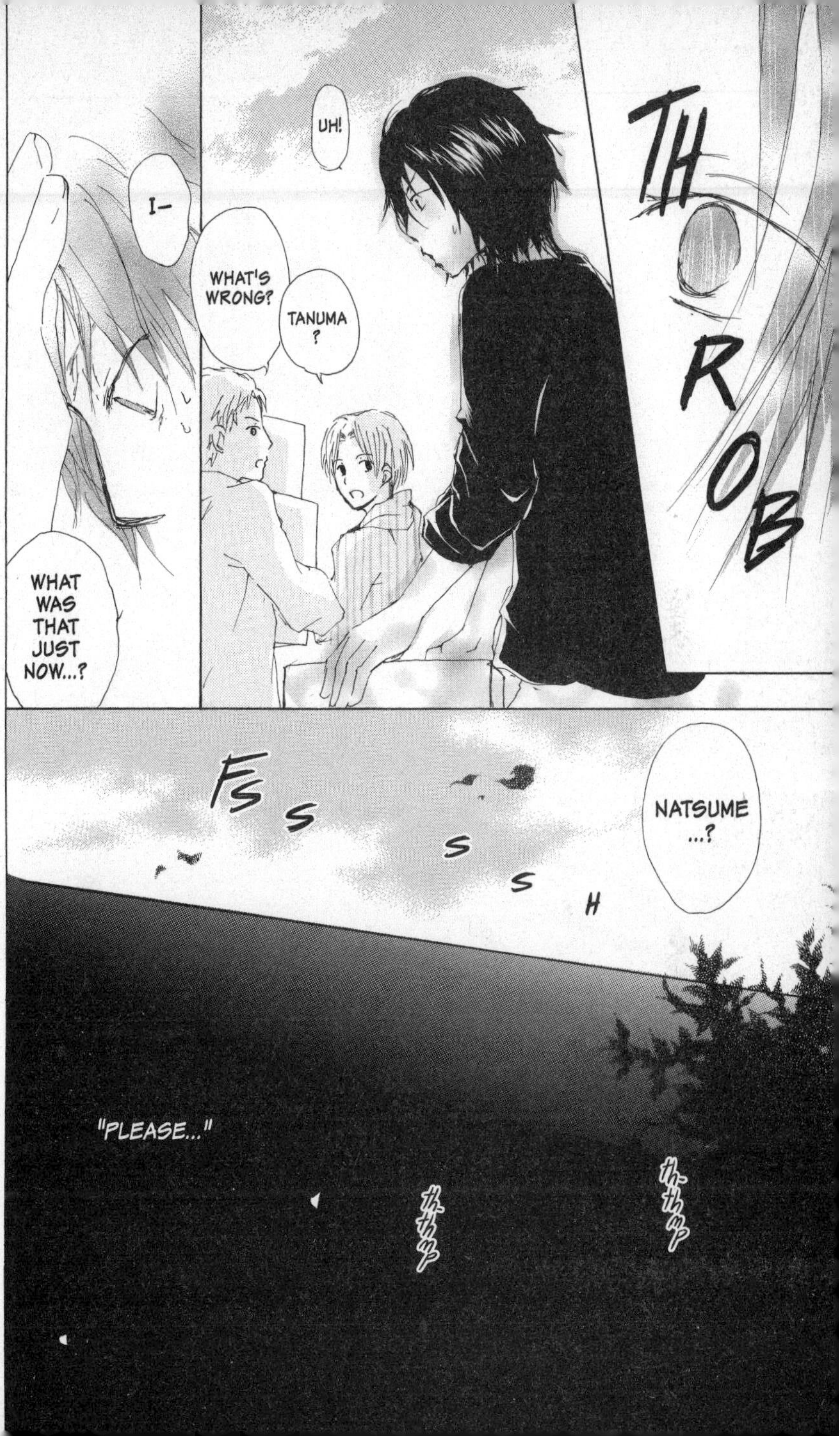
THROB
UH!
TANUMA?
WHAT'S WRONG?
I—
WHAT WAS THAT JUST NOW...?
NATSUME...?
FSSSSH
"PLEASE..."
th-thmp
th-thmp

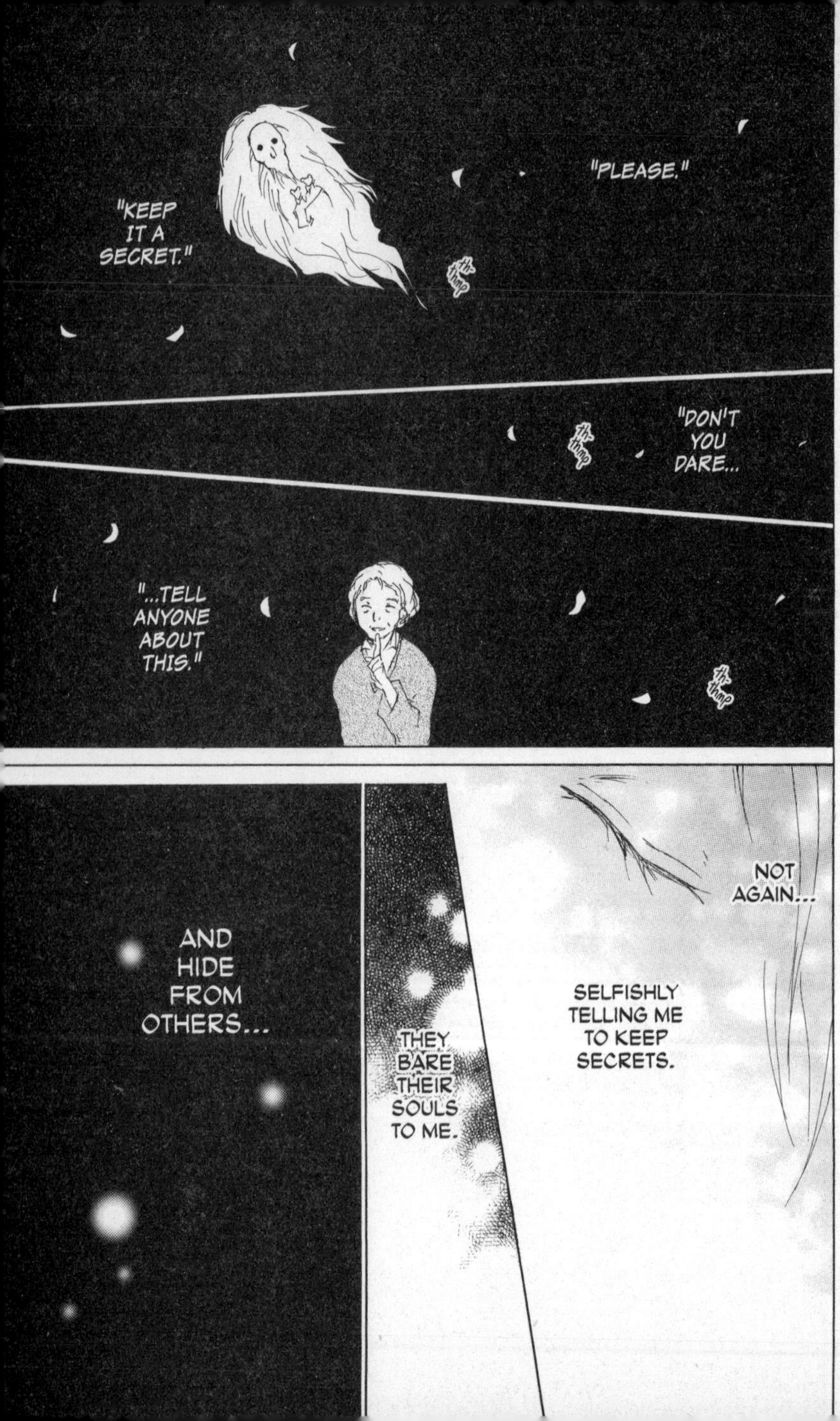
"PLEASE."
"KEEP IT A SECRET."
"DON'T YOU DARE...
"...TELL ANYONE ABOUT THIS."
NOT AGAIN...
SELFISHLY TELLING ME TO KEEP SECRETS.
THEY BARE THEIR SOULS TO ME.
AND HIDE FROM OTHERS...

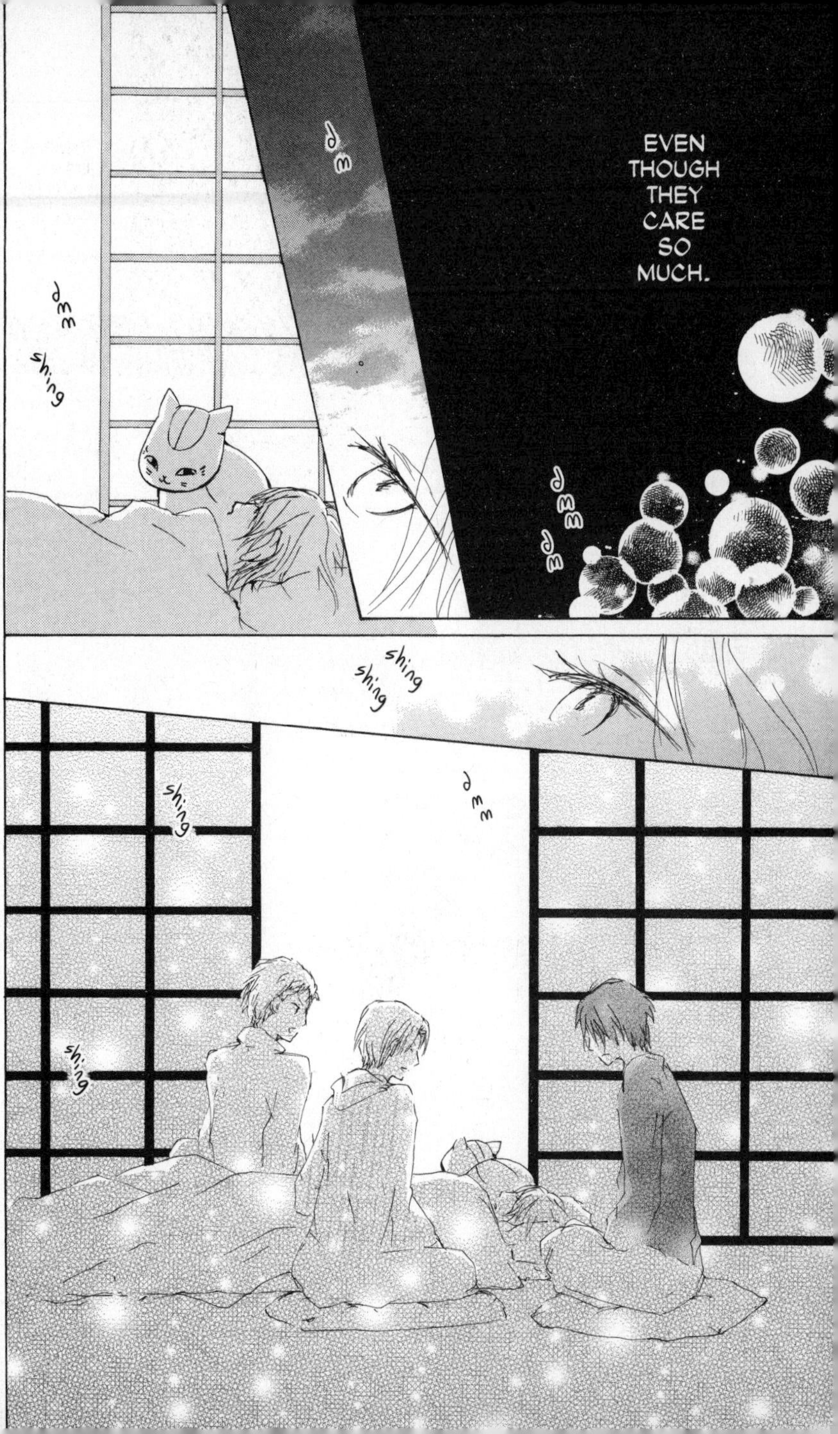
EVEN THOUGH THEY CARE SO MUCH.
shing
shing
shing
shing
shing

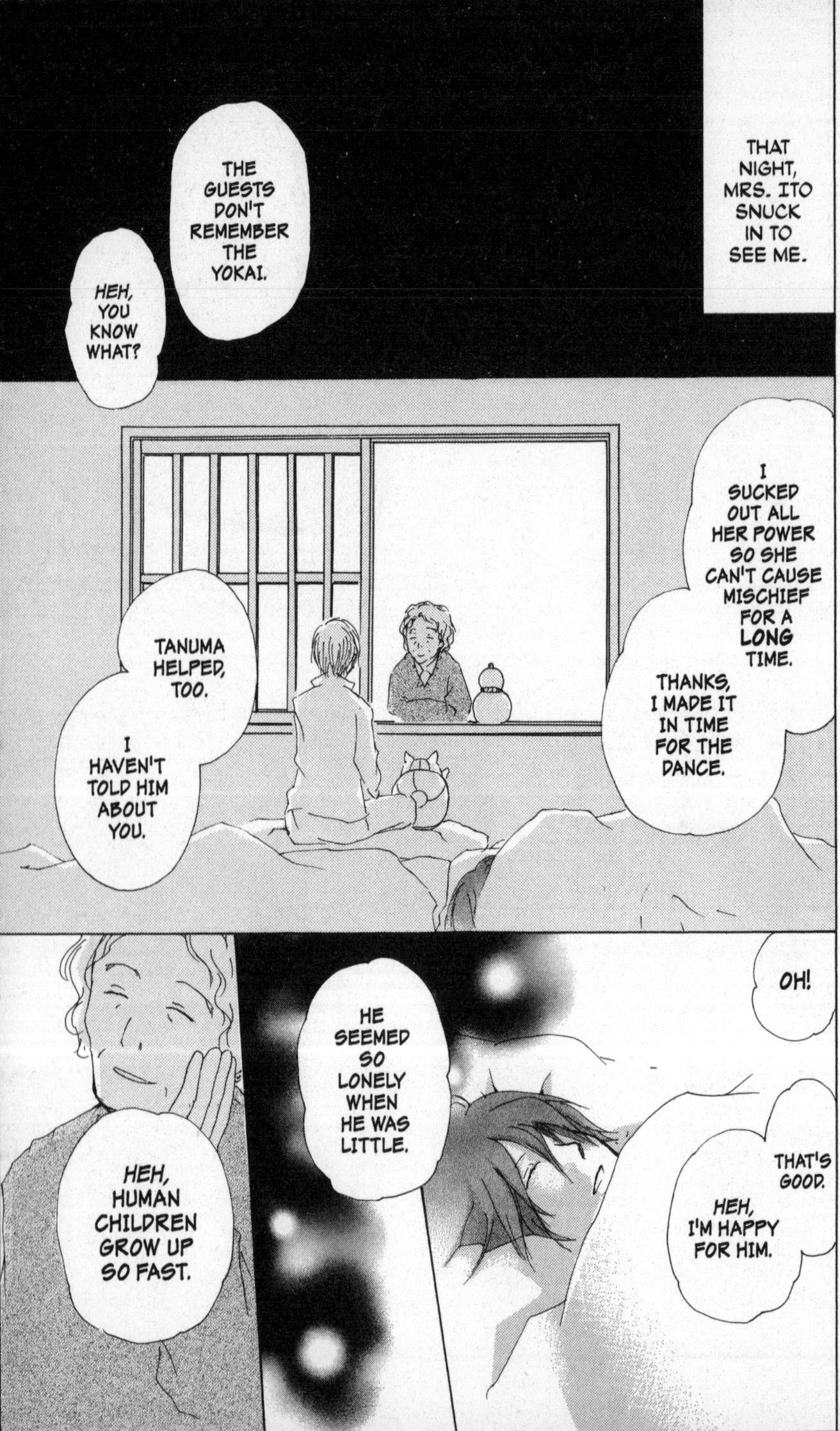
THAT NIGHT, MRS. ITO SNUCK IN TO SEE ME.
THE GUESTS DON'T REMEMBER THE YOKAI.
HEH, YOU KNOW WHAT?
I SUCKED OUT ALL HER POWER SO SHE CAN'T CAUSE MISCHIEF FOR A LONG TIME.
THANKS, I MADE IT IN TIME FOR THE DANCE.
TANUMA HELPED, TOO.
I HAVEN'T TOLD HIM ABOUT YOU.
OH!
THAT'S GOOD.
HEH, I'M HAPPY FOR HIM.
HE SEEMED SO LONELY WHEN HE WAS LITTLE.
HEH, HUMAN CHILDREN GROW UP SO FAST.

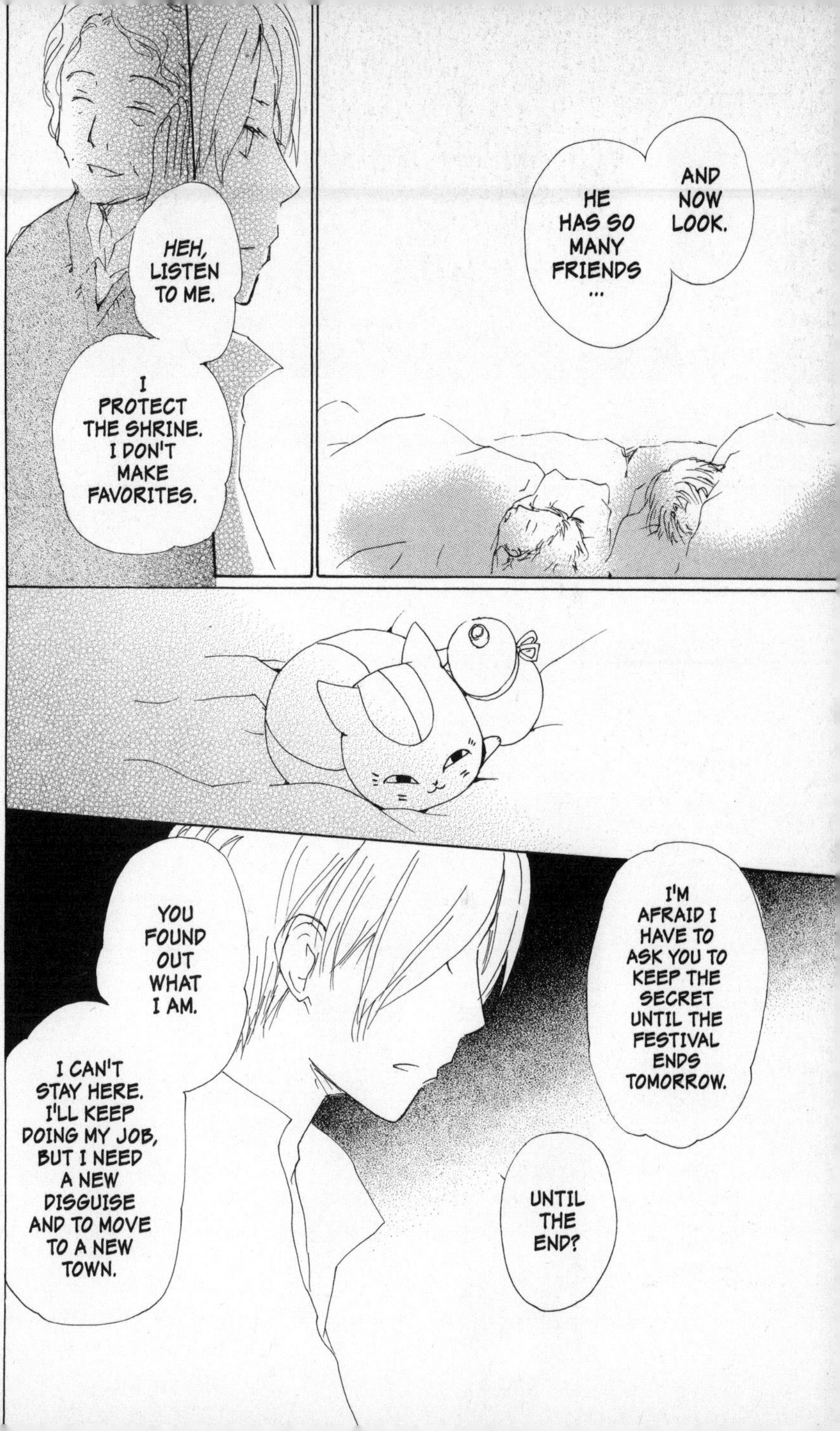
AND NOW LOOK. HE HAS SO MANY FRIENDS...
HEH, LISTEN TO ME.
I PROTECT THE SHRINE. I DON'T MAKE FAVORITES.
I'M AFRAID I HAVE TO ASK YOU TO KEEP THE SECRET UNTIL THE FESTIVAL ENDS TOMORROW.
UNTIL THE END?
YOU FOUND OUT WHAT I AM.
I CAN'T STAY HERE. I'LL KEEP DOING MY JOB, BUT I NEED A NEW DISGUISE AND TO MOVE TO A NEW TOWN.

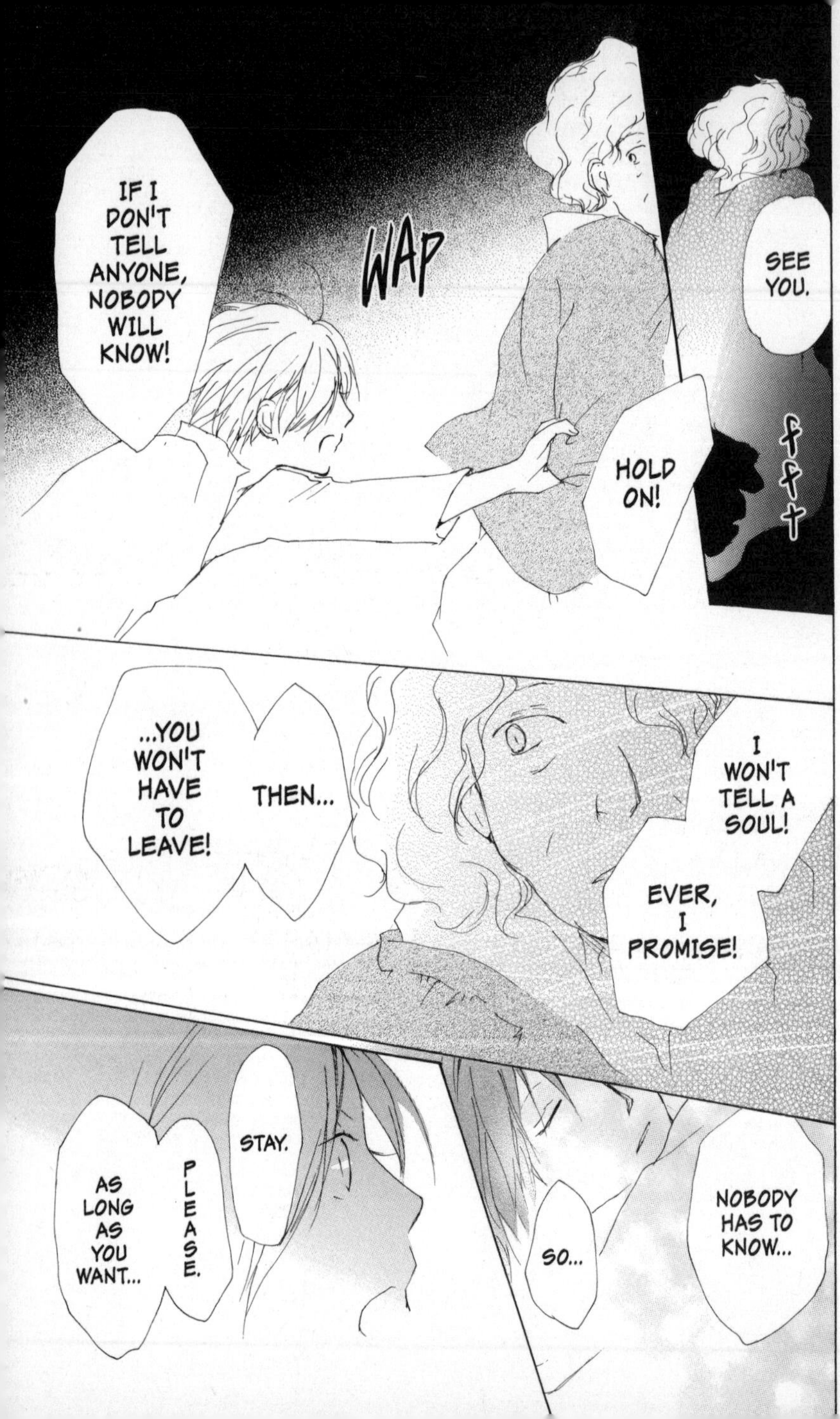
SEE YOU.
fft
WAP
HOLD ON!
IF I DON'T TELL ANYONE, NOBODY WILL KNOW!
I WON'T TELL A SOUL!
EVER, I PROMISE!
THEN...
...YOU WON'T HAVE TO LEAVE!
NOBODY HAS TO KNOW...
SO...
STAY.
PLEASE.
AS LONG AS YOU WANT...

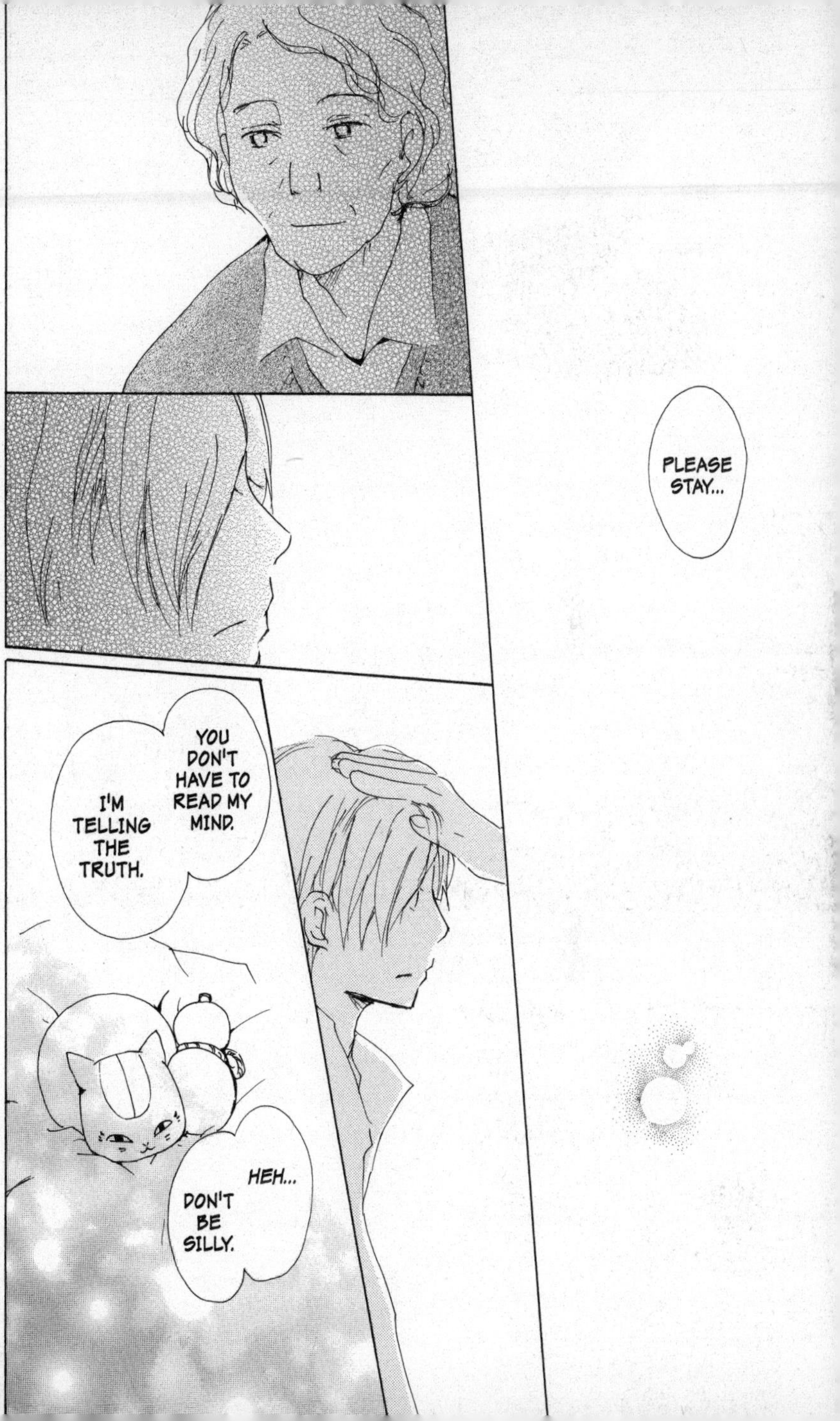
PLEASE STAY...
YOU DON'T HAVE TO READ MY MIND.
I'M TELLING THE TRUTH.
HEH... DON'T BE SILLY.

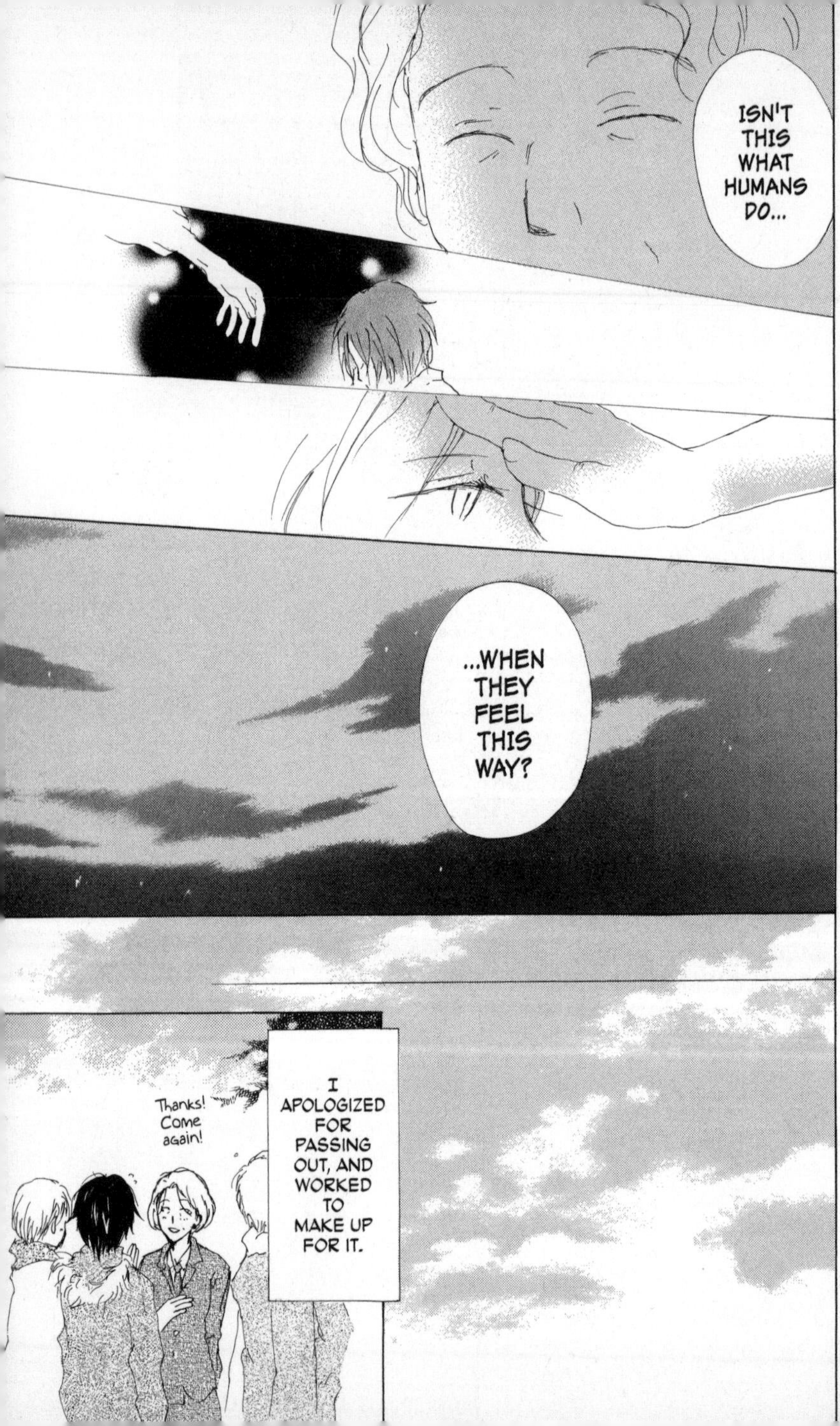
ISN'T THIS WHAT HUMANS DO...
...WHEN THEY FEEL THIS WAY?
I APOLOGIZED FOR PASSING OUT, AND WORKED TO MAKE UP FOR IT.
Thanks! Come again!

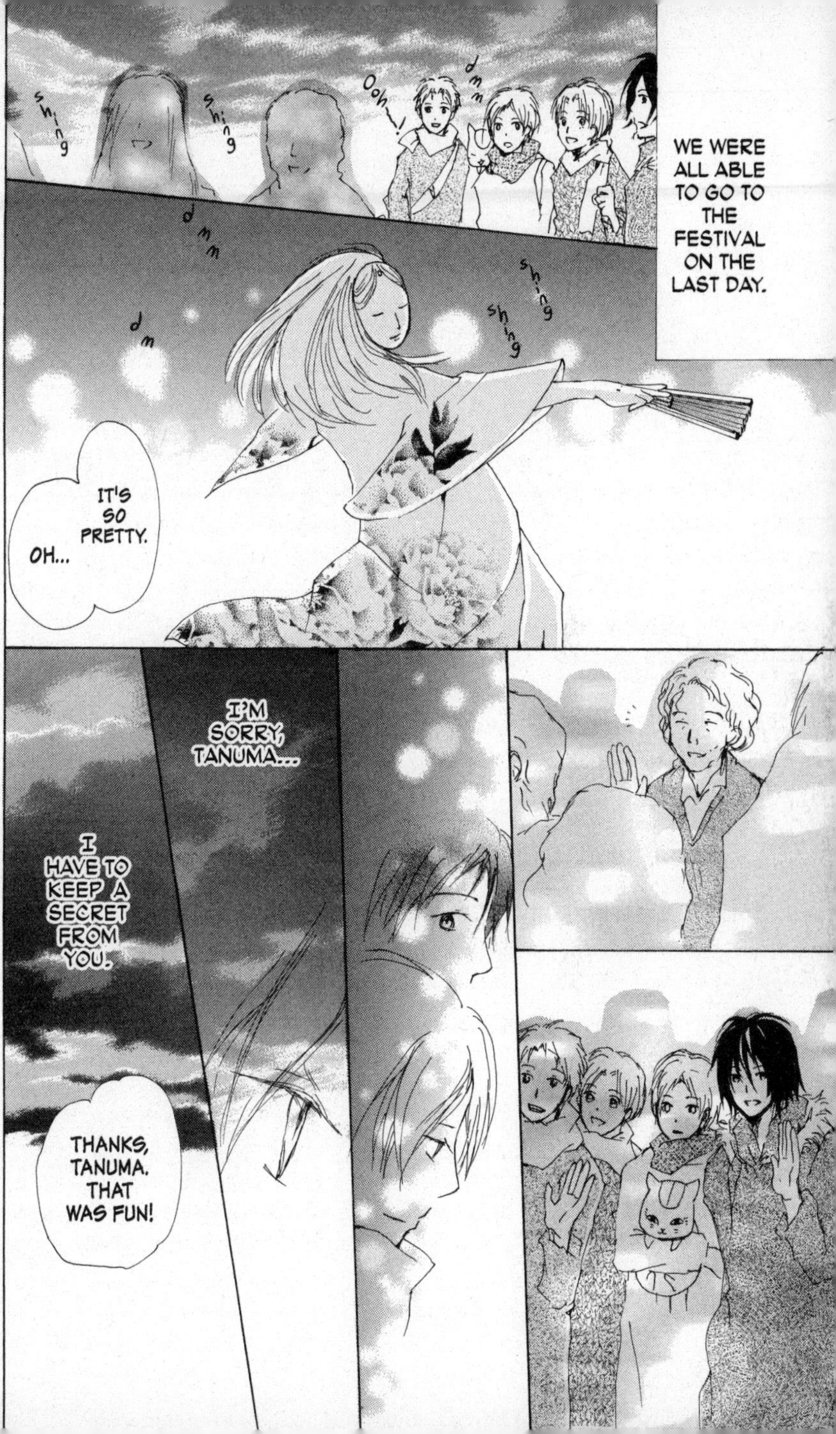
WE WERE ALL ABLE TO GO TO THE FESTIVAL ON THE LAST DAY.
Ooh...!
dmm
shing
shing
shing
dmm
shing
shing
dm
IT'S SO PRETTY.
OH...
I'M SORRY, TANUMA...
I HAVE TO KEEP A SECRET FROM YOU.
THANKS, TANUMA. THAT WAS FUN!

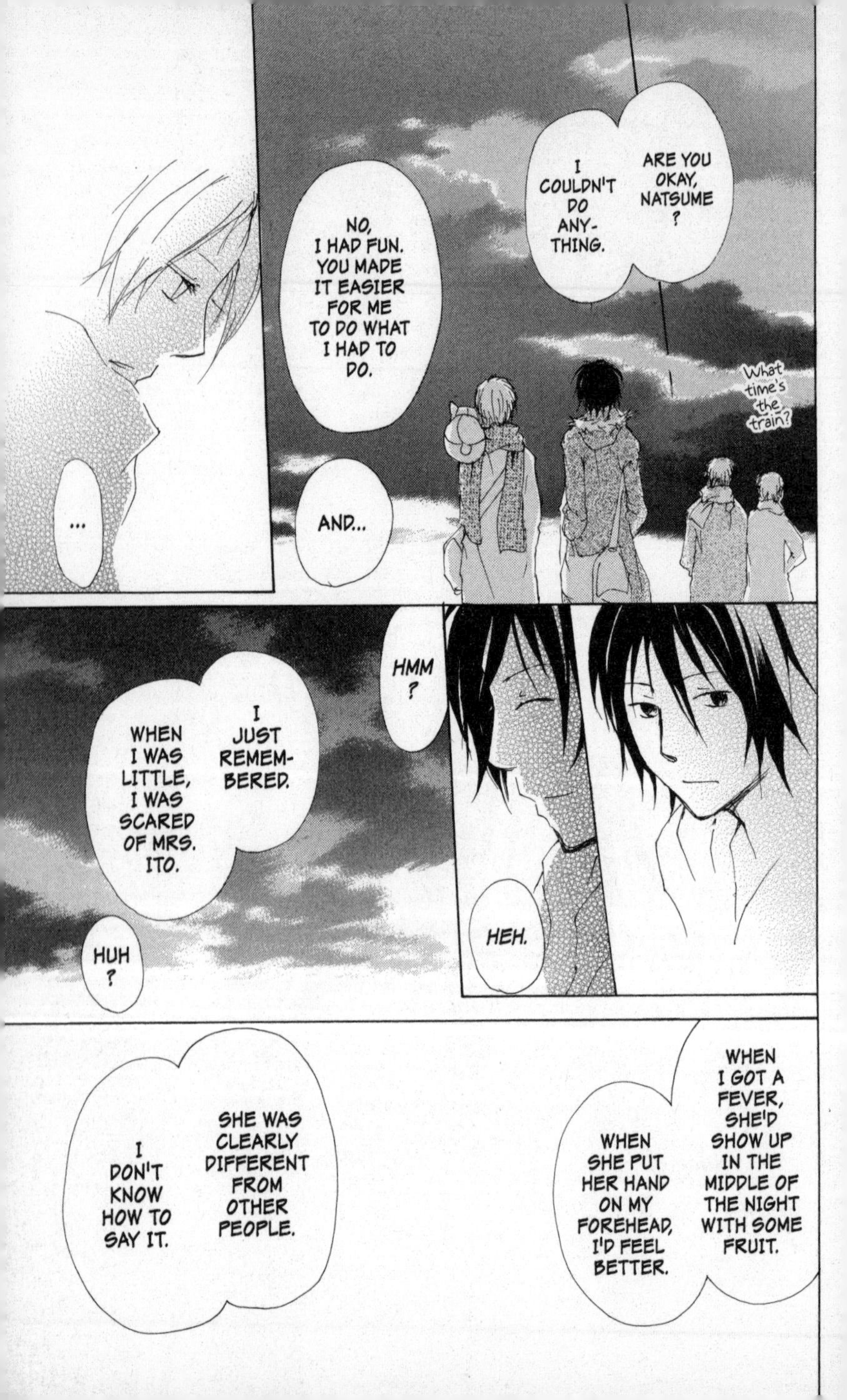
ARE YOU OKAY, NATSUME?
I COULDN'T DO ANYTHING.
What time's the train?
NO, I HAD FUN. YOU MADE IT EASIER FOR ME TO DO WHAT I HAD TO DO.
AND...
...
HMM?
HEH.
I JUST REMEMBERED.
WHEN I WAS LITTLE, I WAS SCARED OF MRS. ITO.
HUH?
WHEN I GOT A FEVER, SHE'D SHOW UP IN THE MIDDLE OF THE NIGHT WITH SOME FRUIT.
WHEN SHE PUT HER HAND ON MY FOREHEAD, I'D FEEL BETTER.
SHE WAS CLEARLY DIFFERENT FROM OTHER PEOPLE.
I DON'T KNOW HOW TO SAY IT.

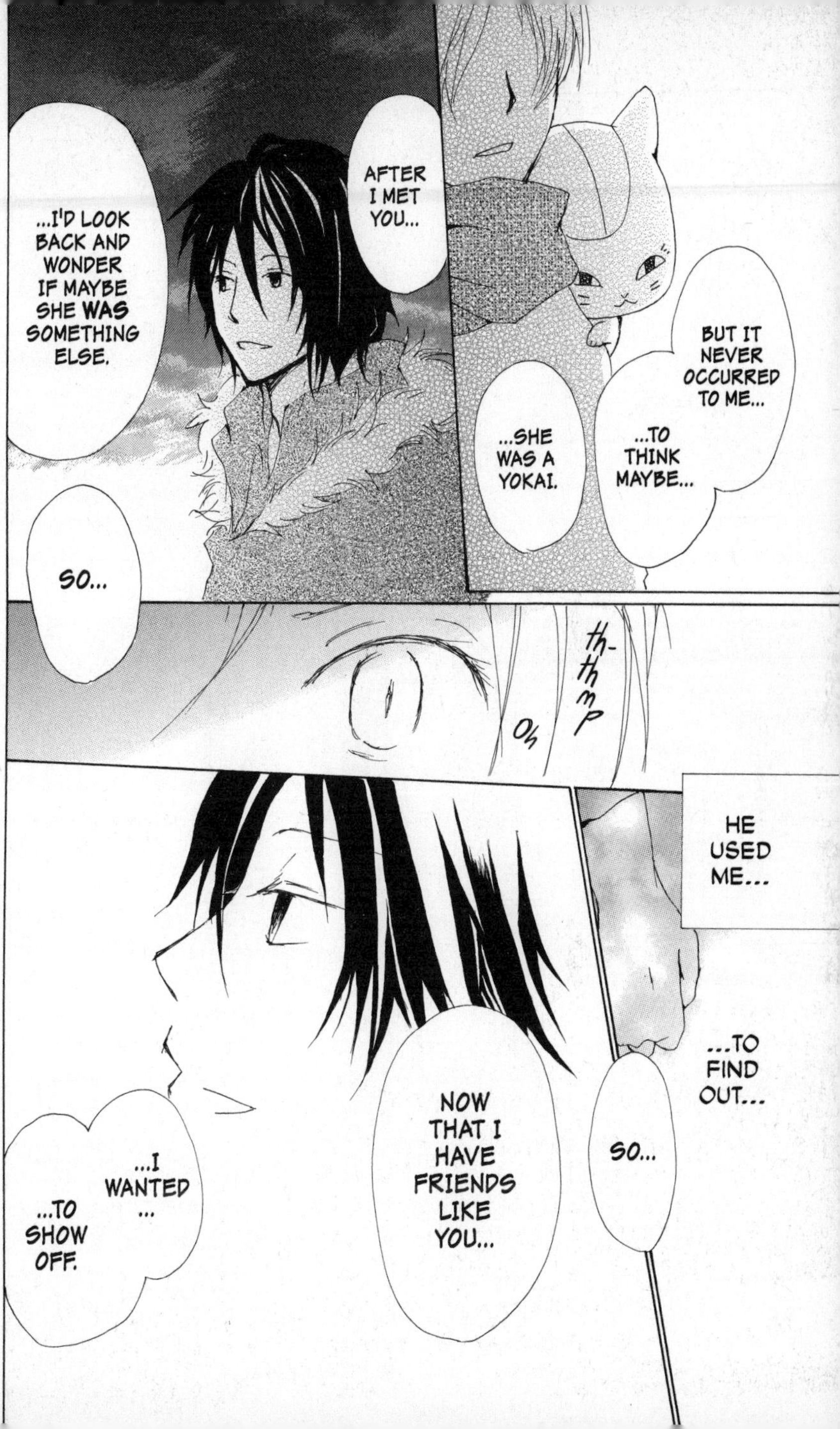
BUT IT NEVER OCCURRED TO ME...
...TO THINK MAYBE...
...SHE WAS A YOKAI.
AFTER I MET YOU...
...I'D LOOK BACK AND WONDER IF MAYBE SHE WAS SOMETHING ELSE.
SO...
th-thmp
Oh
HE USED ME...
...TO FIND OUT...
SO...
NOW THAT I HAVE FRIENDS LIKE YOU...
...I WANTED...
...TO SHOW OFF.

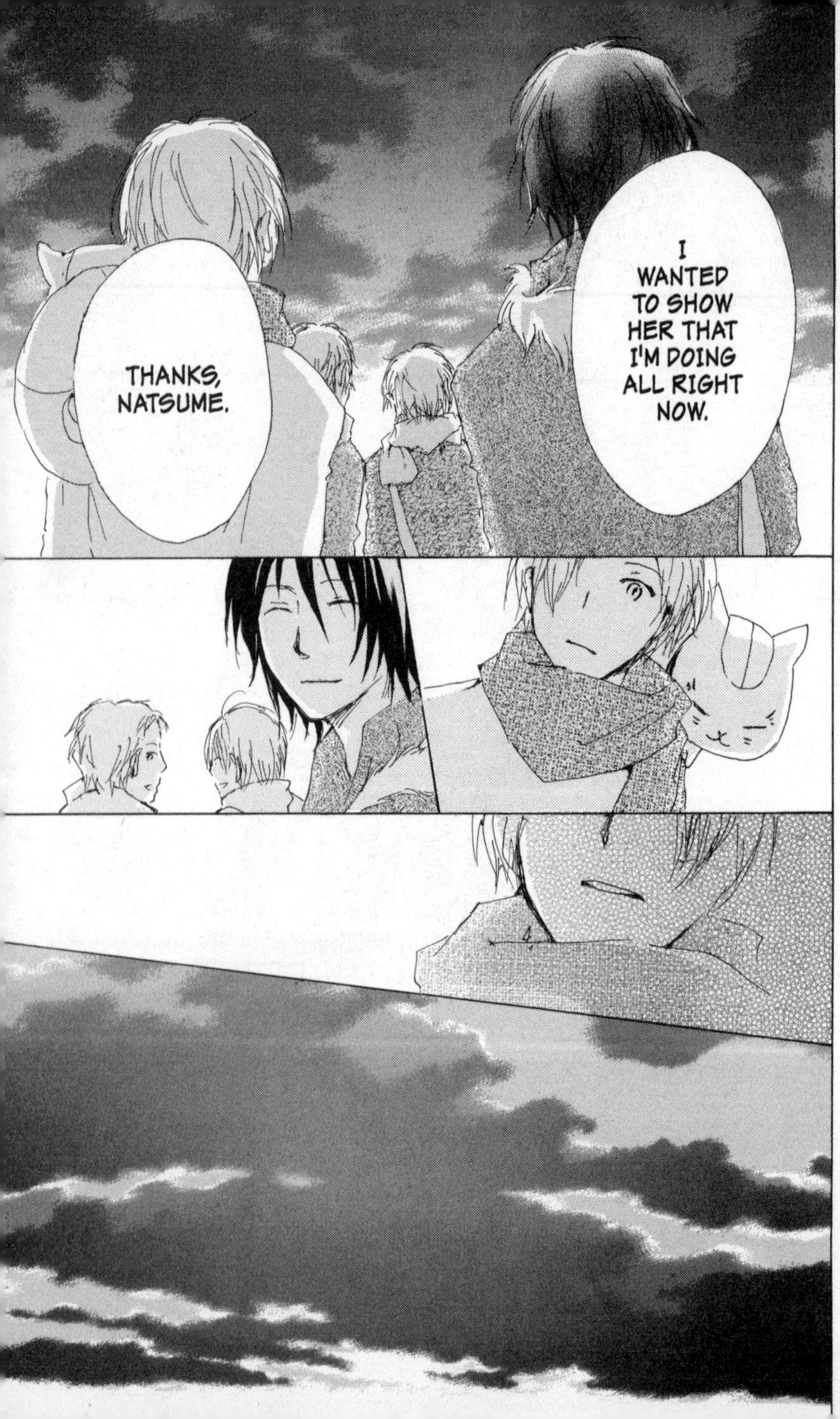
I WANTED TO SHOW HER THAT I'M DOING ALL RIGHT NOW.
THANKS, NATSUME.

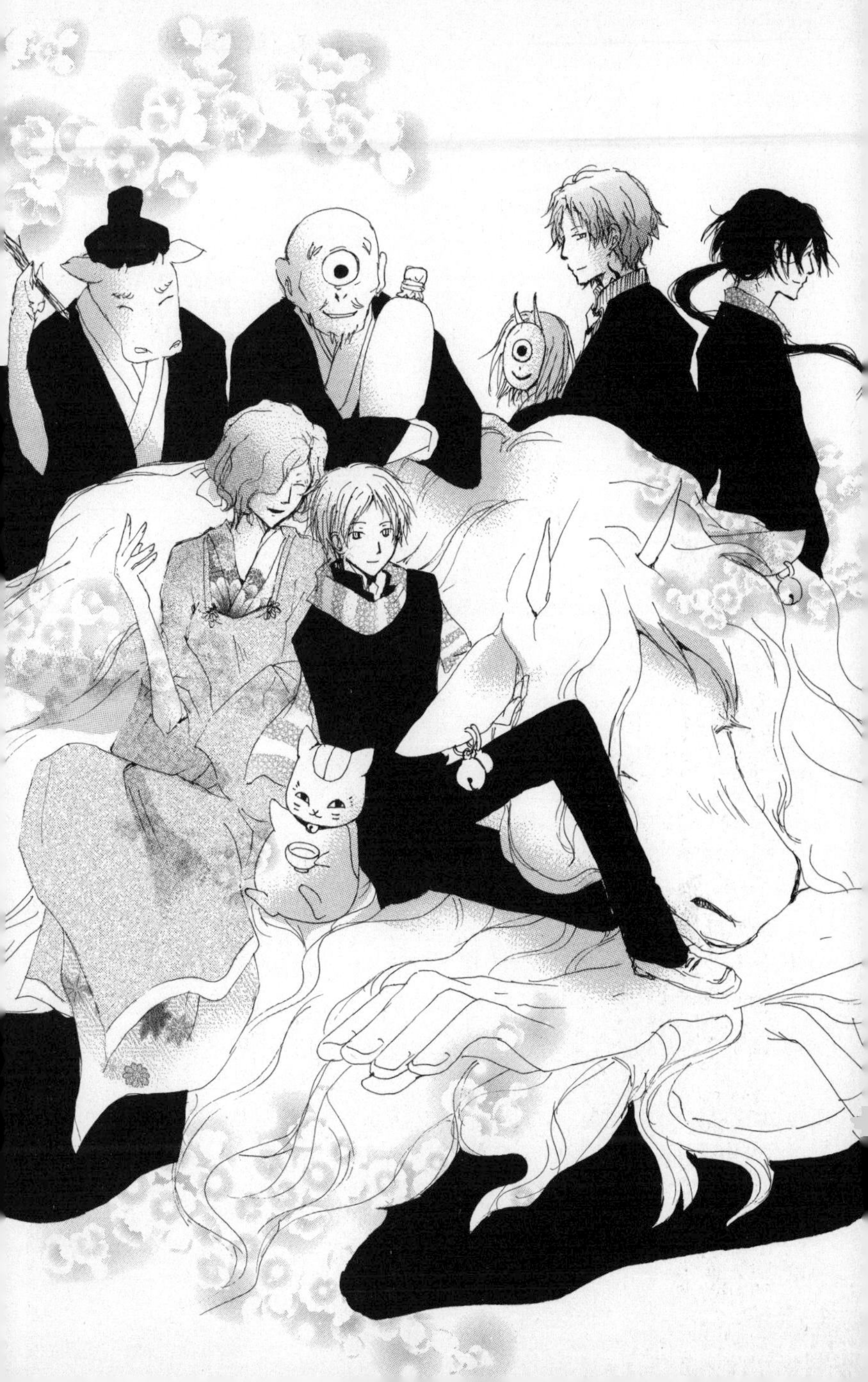

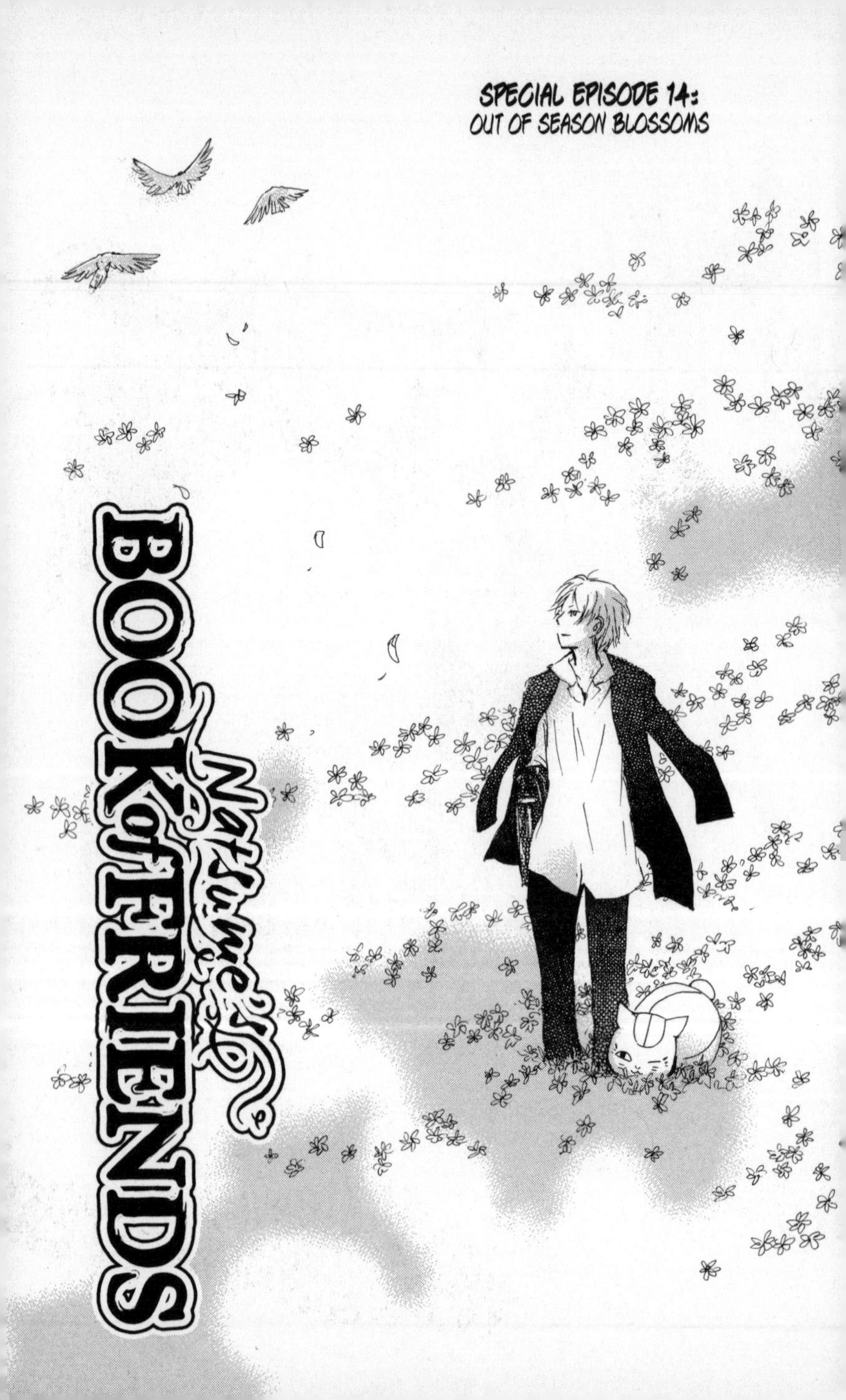
SPECIAL EPISODE 14:
OUT OF SEASON BLOSSOMS
Natsume's BOOK of FRIENDS

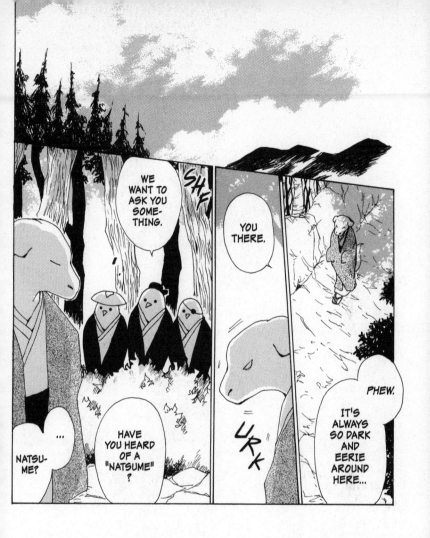

PHEW.
IT'S ALWAYS SO DARK AND EERIE AROUND HERE...
YOU THERE.
URK
SHF
WE WANT TO ASK YOU SOME-THING.
HAVE YOU HEARD OF A "NATSUME" ?
... NATSU-ME?

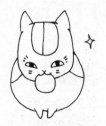

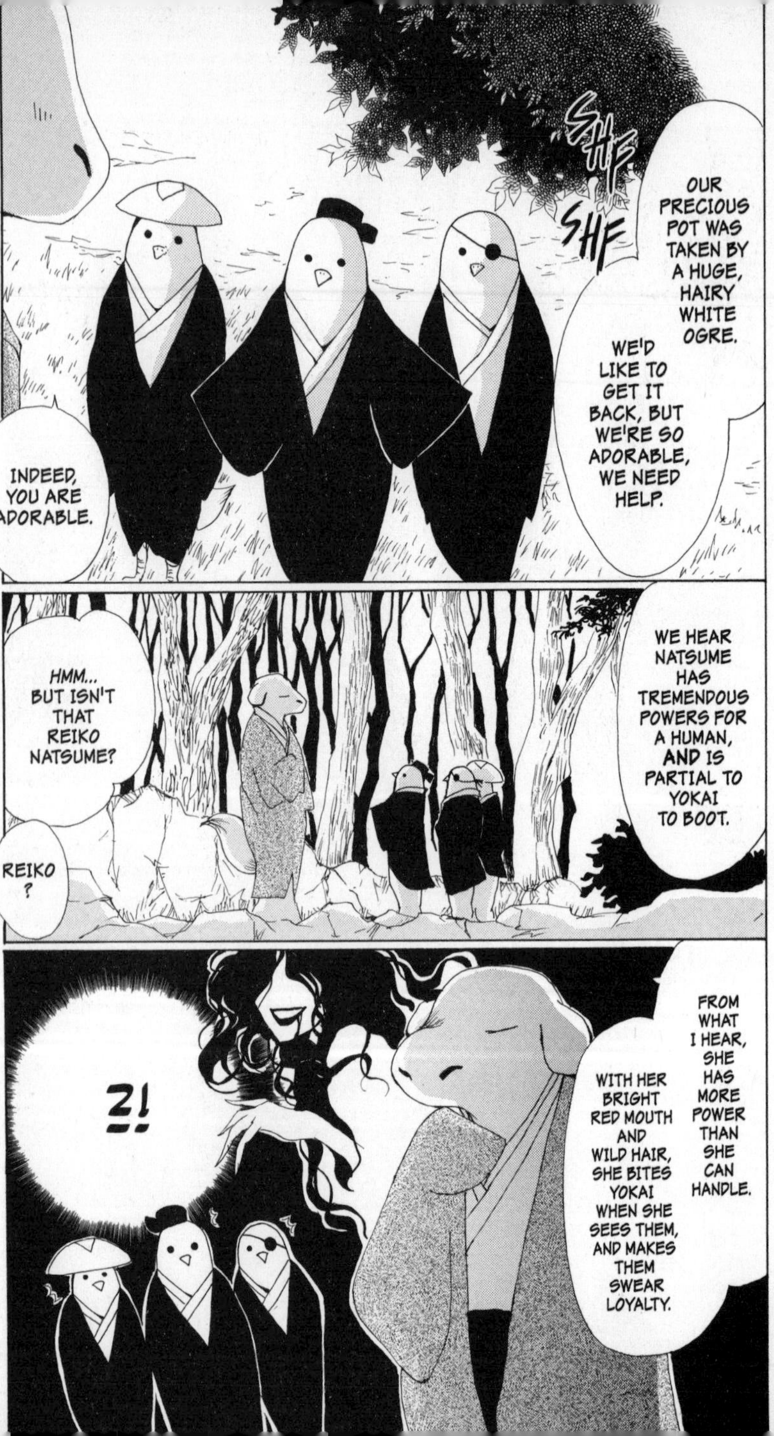
SHF SHF
OUR PRECIOUS POT WAS TAKEN BY A HUGE, HAIRY WHITE OGRE.
WE'D LIKE TO GET IT BACK, BUT WE'RE SO ADORABLE, WE NEED HELP.
INDEED, YOU ARE ADORABLE.
WE HEAR NATSUME HAS TREMENDOUS POWERS FOR A HUMAN, AND IS PARTIAL TO YOKAI TO BOOT.
HMM... BUT ISN'T THAT REIKO NATSUME?
REIKO ?
FROM WHAT I HEAR, SHE HAS MORE POWER THAN SHE CAN HANDLE.
WITH HER BRIGHT RED MOUTH AND WILD HAIR, SHE BITES YOKAI WHEN SHE SEES THEM, AND MAKES THEM SWEAR LOYALTY.
?!

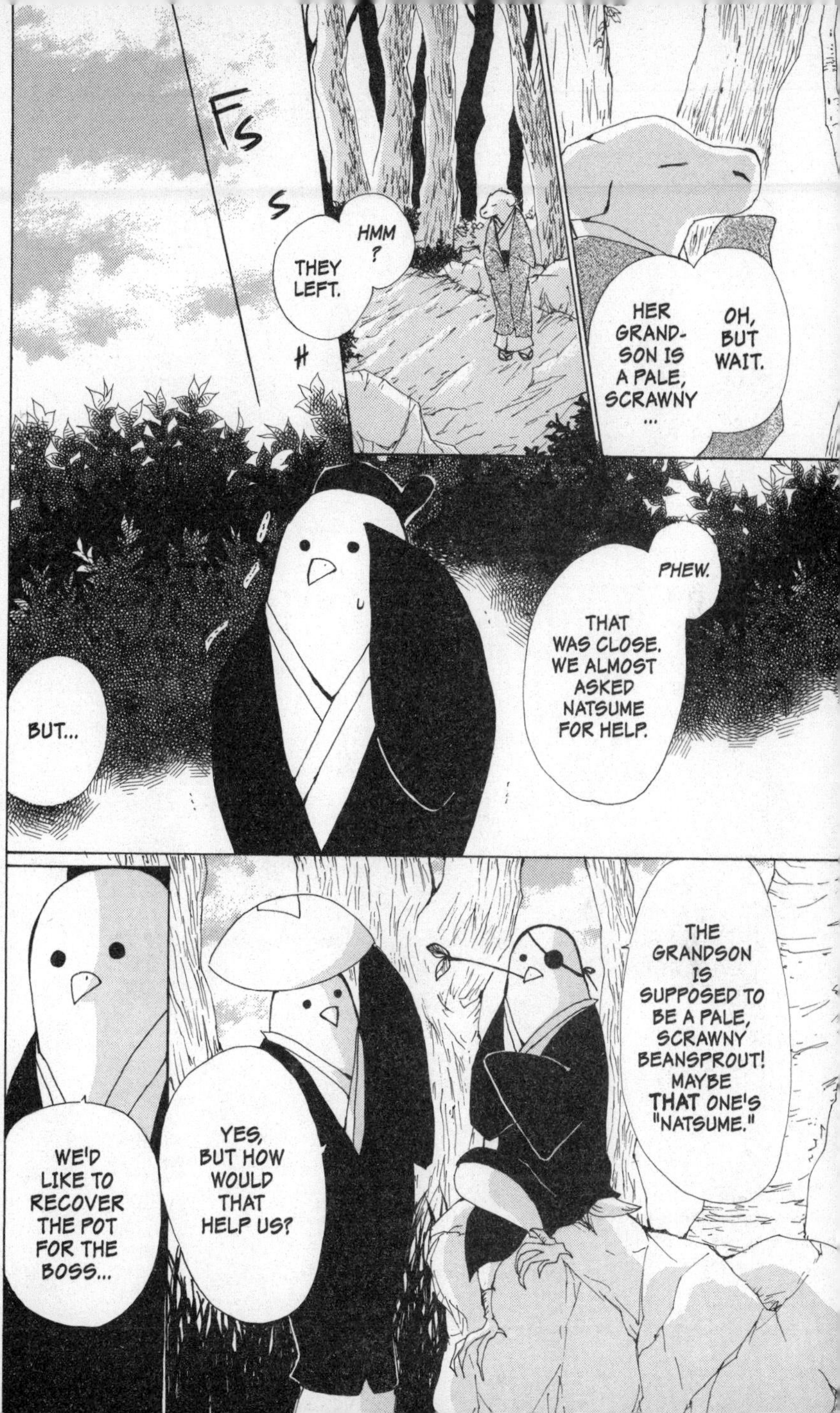
OH, BUT WAIT.
HER GRANDSON IS A PALE, SCRAWNY...
HMM?
THEY LEFT.
FSSH
PHEW.
THAT WAS CLOSE. WE ALMOST ASKED NATSUME FOR HELP.
BUT...
THE GRANDSON IS SUPPOSED TO BE A PALE, SCRAWNY BEANSPROUT! MAYBE THAT ONE'S "NATSUME."
YES, BUT HOW WOULD THAT HELP US?
WE'D LIKE TO RECOVER THE POT FOR THE BOSS...

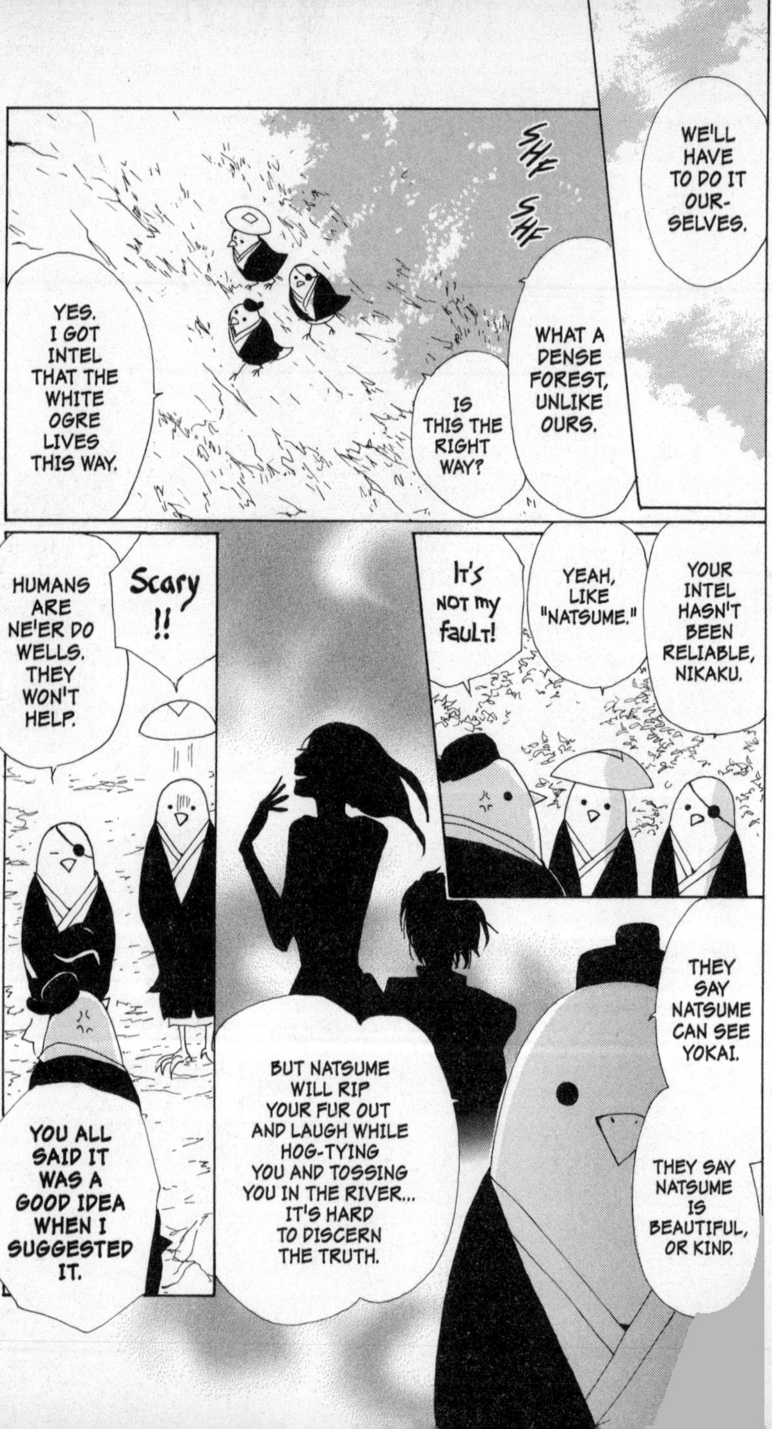
WE'LL HAVE TO DO IT OURSELVES.
SHF SHF
WHAT A DENSE FOREST, UNLIKE OURS.
IS THIS THE RIGHT WAY?
YES. I GOT INTEL THAT THE WHITE OGRE LIVES THIS WAY.
YOUR INTEL HASN'T BEEN RELIABLE, NIKAKU.
YEAH, LIKE "NATSUME."
It's not my fault!
Scary!!
HUMANS ARE NE'ER DO WELLS. THEY WON'T HELP.
THEY SAY NATSUME CAN SEE YOKAI.
THEY SAY NATSUME IS BEAUTIFUL, OR KIND.
BUT NATSUME WILL RIP YOUR FUR OUT AND LAUGH WHILE HOG-TYING YOU AND TOSSING YOU IN THE RIVER... IT'S HARD TO DISCERN THE TRUTH.
YOU ALL SAID IT WAS A GOOD IDEA WHEN I SUGGESTED IT.

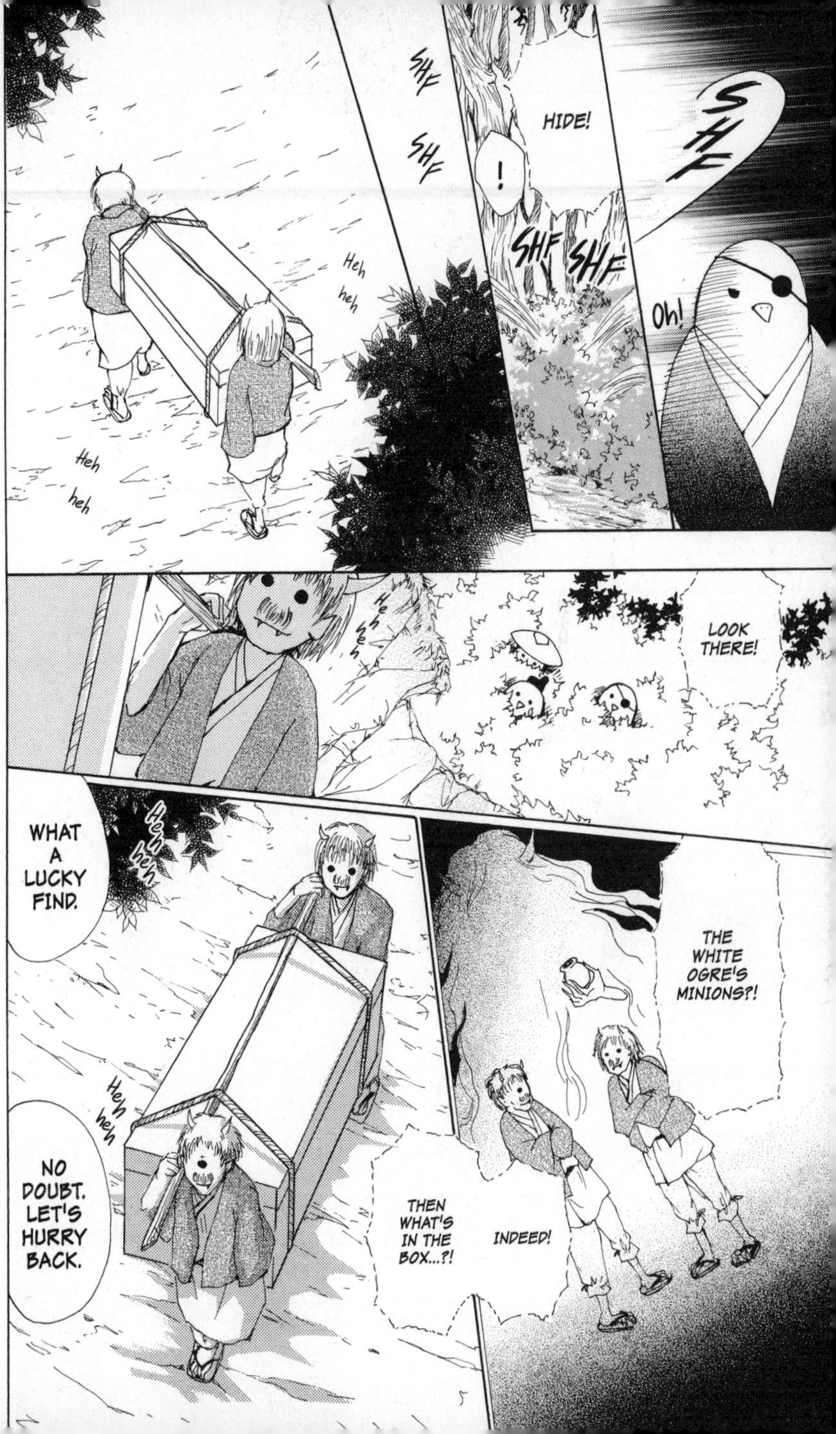
SHF
Oh!
HIDE!
!
SHF
SHF
SHF
SHF
Heh heh
Heh heh
LOOK THERE!
Heh heh
THE WHITE OGRE'S MINIONS?!
INDEED!
THEN WHAT'S IN THE BOX...?!
WHAT A LUCKY FIND.
Heh heh
Heh heh
NO DOUBT. LET'S HURRY BACK.

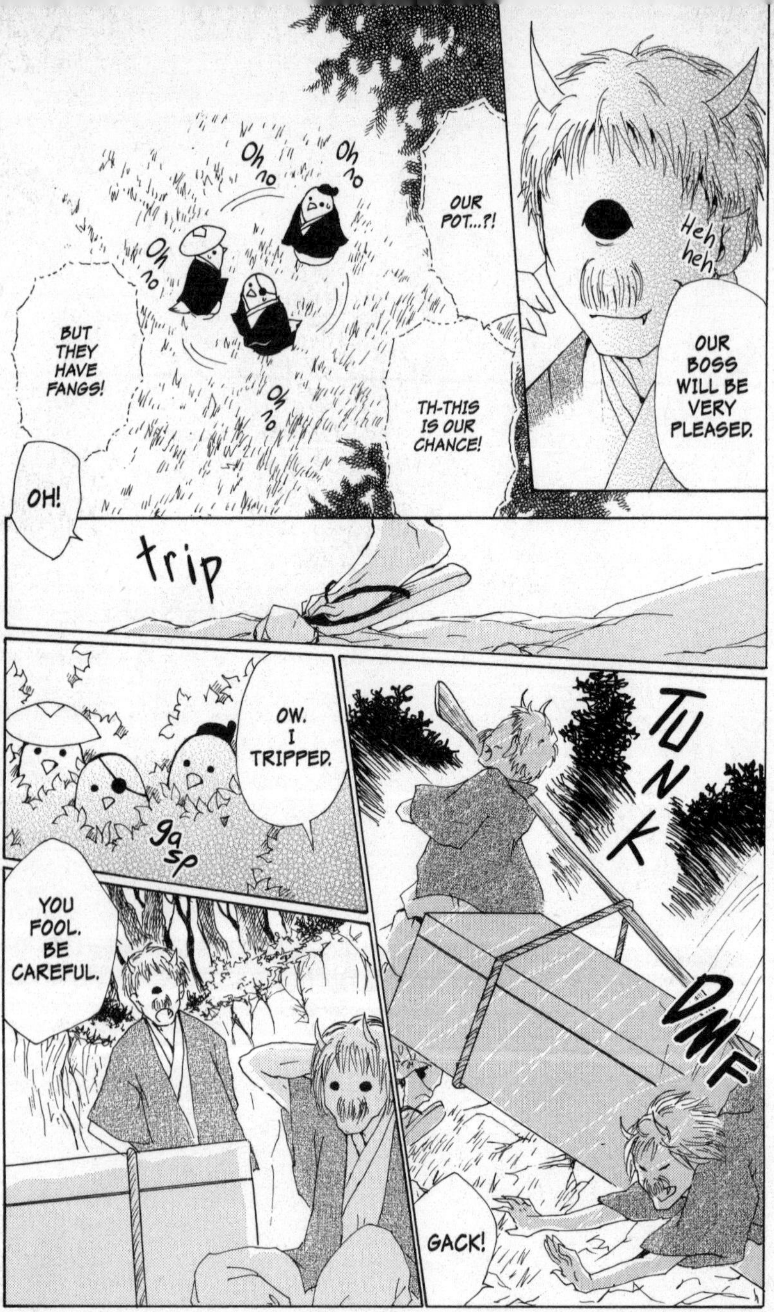
Heh heh
OUR BOSS WILL BE VERY PLEASED.
OUR POT...?!
Oh no
Oh no
Oh no
TH-THIS IS OUR CHANCE!
Oh no
BUT THEY HAVE FANGS!
OH!
trip
TUNK
DMF
GACK!
OW. I TRIPPED.
gasp
YOU FOOL. BE CAREFUL.

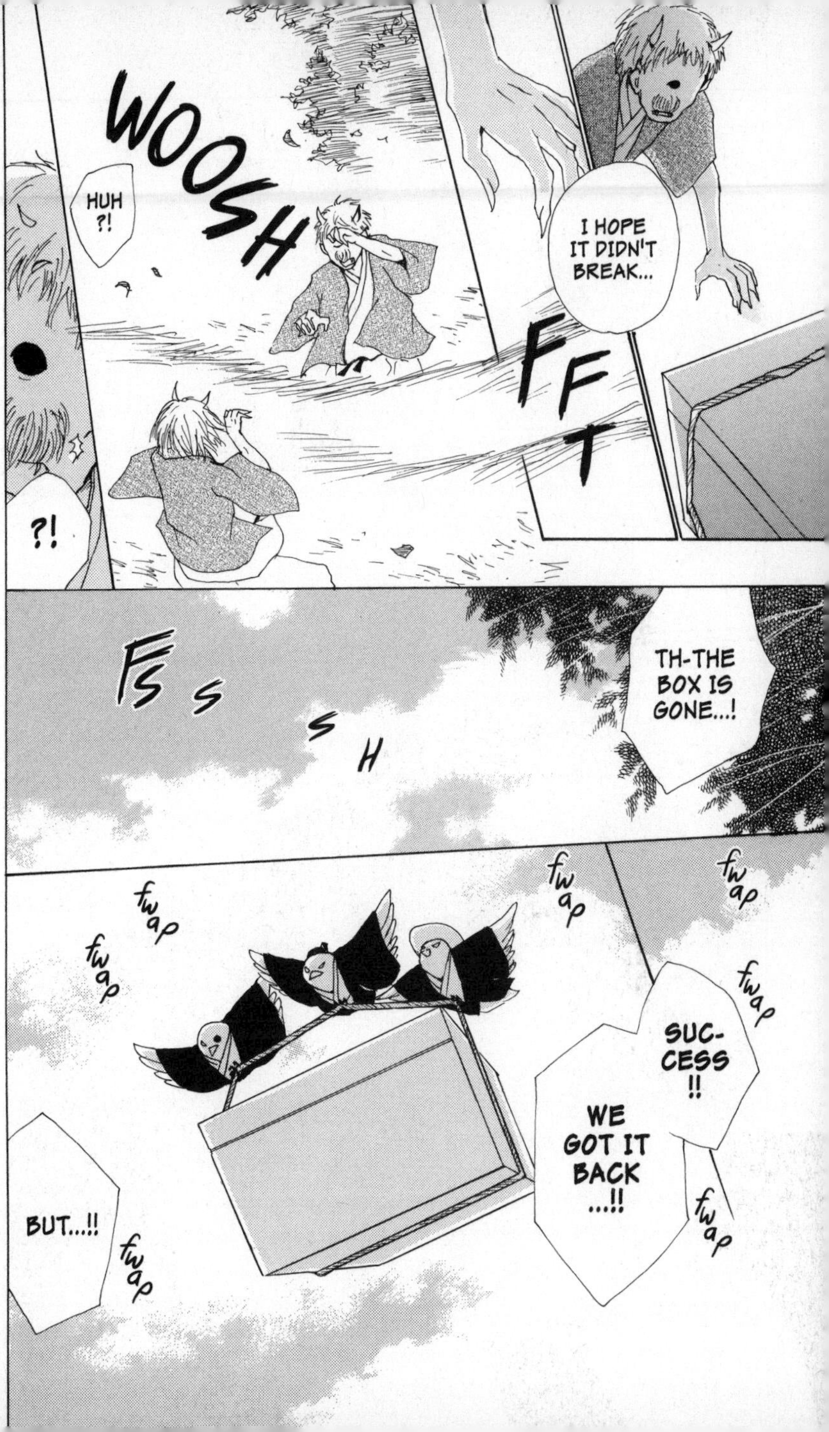

I HOPE IT DIDN'T BREAK...
WOOSH
HUH ?!
FFT
?!
TH-THE BOX IS GONE...!
FSSSH
fwap
fwap
fwap
SUC-CESS!!
WE GOT IT BACK...!!
fwap
fwap
fwap
BUT...!!
fwap

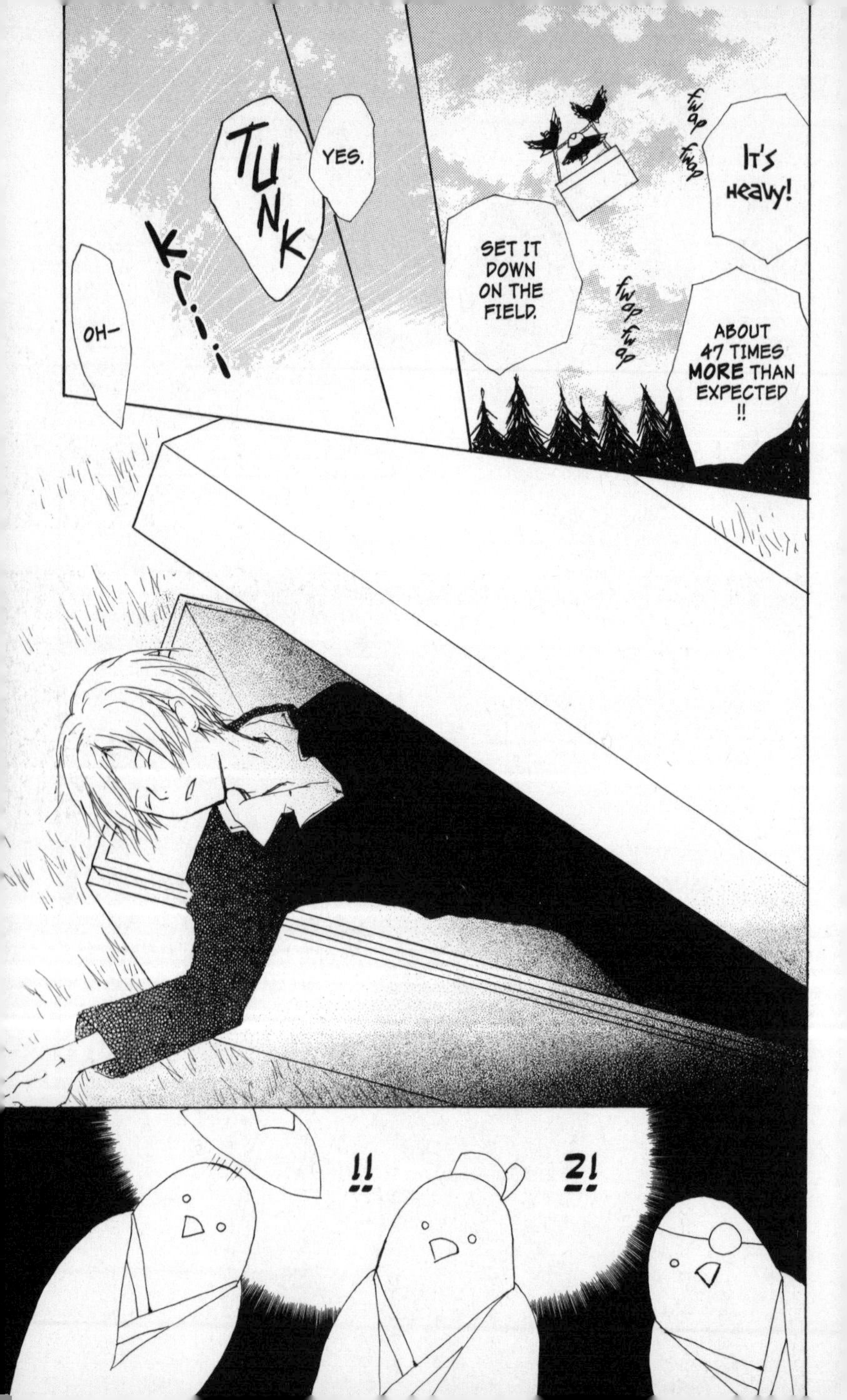
IT'S HEAVY!
fwap fwap
ABOUT 47 TIMES MORE THAN EXPECTED !!
SET IT DOWN ON THE FIELD.
fwap fwap
YES.
TUNK
Kr...i
OH-
?!
!!

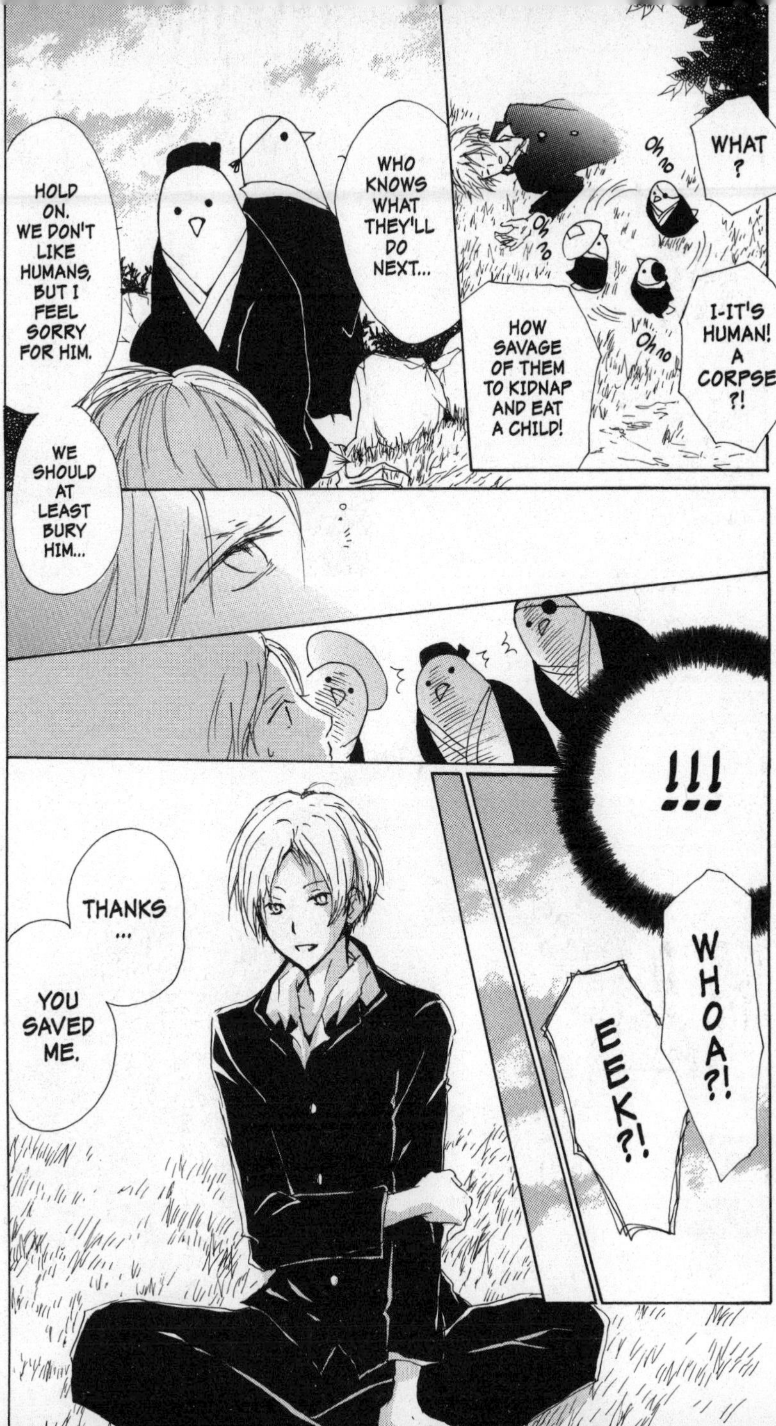
WHAT?
Oh no
Oh no
Oh no
I-IT'S HUMAN! A CORPSE?!
HOW SAVAGE OF THEM TO KIDNAP AND EAT A CHILD!
WHO KNOWS WHAT THEY'LL DO NEXT...
HOLD ON. WE DON'T LIKE HUMANS, BUT I FEEL SORRY FOR HIM.
WE SHOULD AT LEAST BURY HIM...
!!!
WHOA?!
EEK?!
THANKS...
YOU SAVED ME.

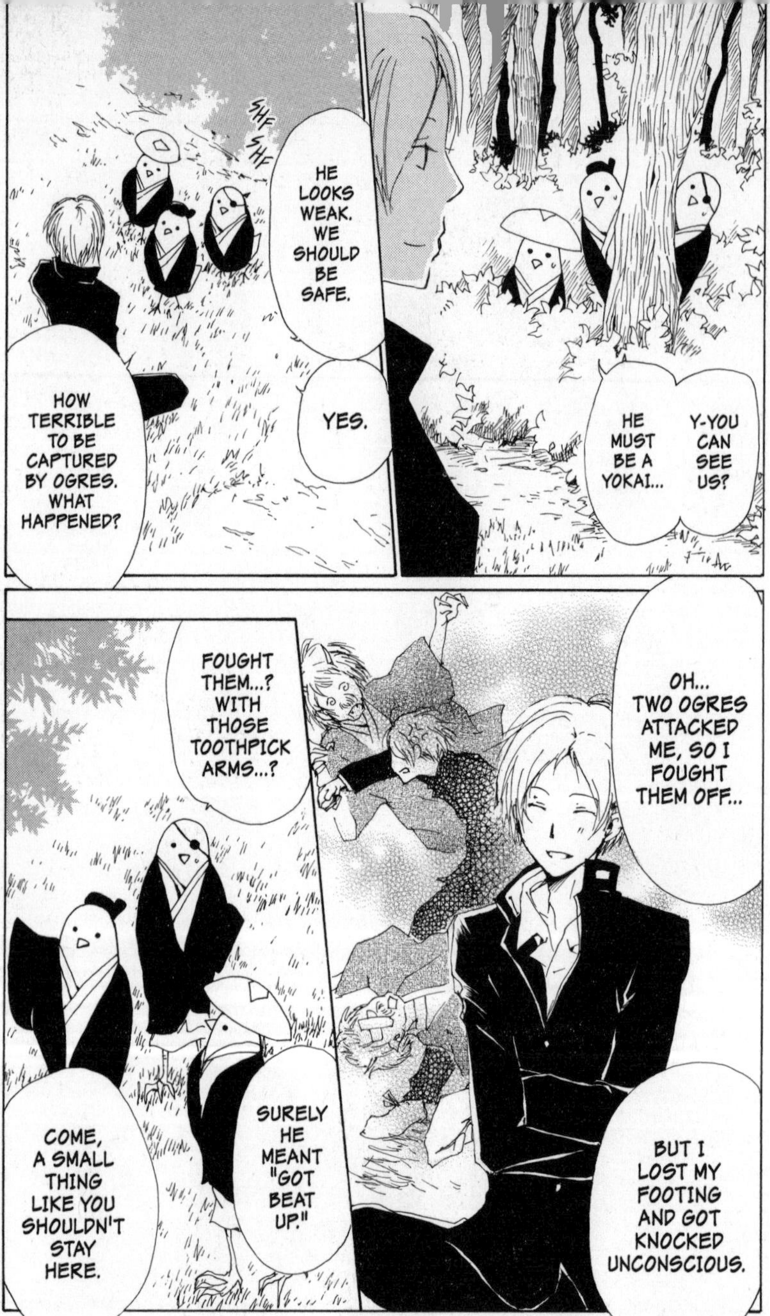
Y-YOU CAN SEE US?
HE MUST BE A YOKAI...
HE LOOKS WEAK. WE SHOULD BE SAFE.
YES.
SHF SHF
HOW TERRIBLE TO BE CAPTURED BY OGRES. WHAT HAPPENED?
OH... TWO OGRES ATTACKED ME, SO I FOUGHT THEM OFF...
BUT I LOST MY FOOTING AND GOT KNOCKED UNCONSCIOUS.
FOUGHT THEM...? WITH THOSE TOOTHPICK ARMS...?
SURELY HE MEANT "GOT BEAT UP."
COME, A SMALL THING LIKE YOU SHOULDN'T STAY HERE.

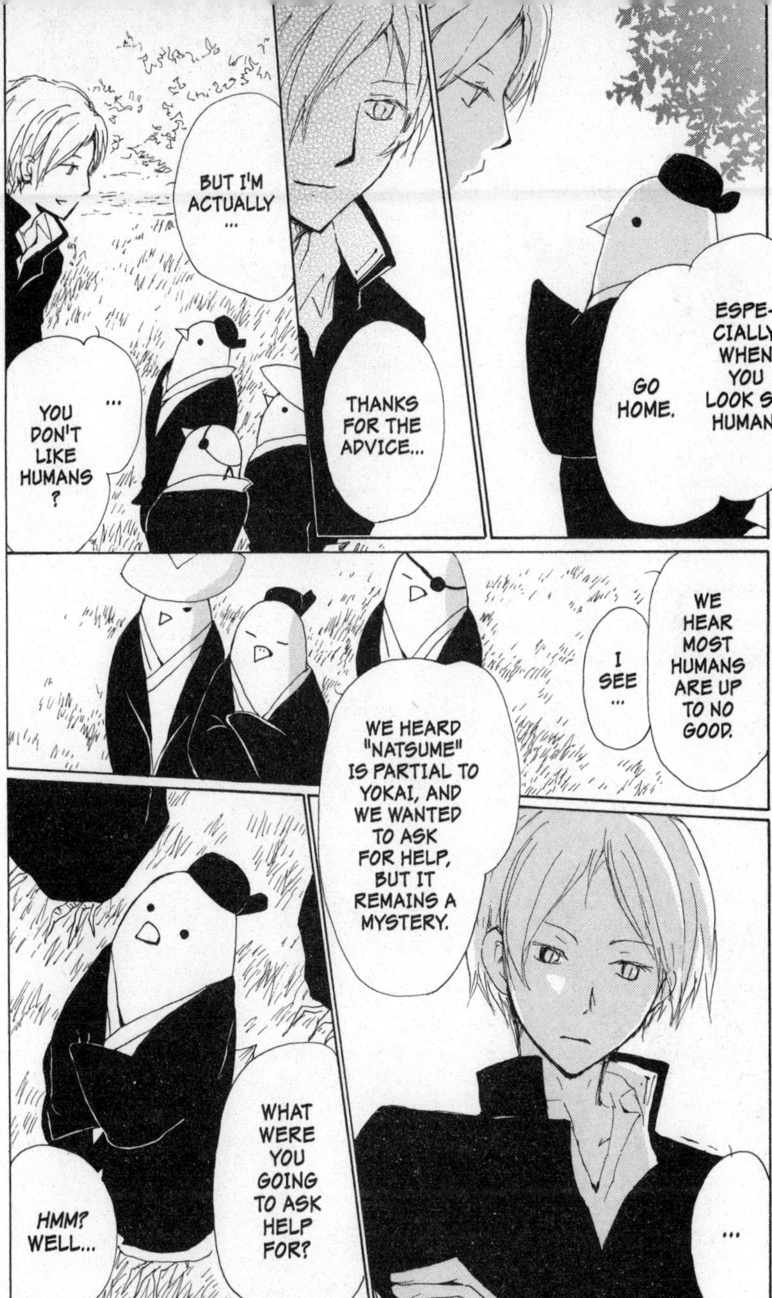

GO HOME. ESPECIALLY WHEN YOU LOOK SO HUMAN.
THANKS FOR THE ADVICE...
BUT I'M ACTUALLY ...
... YOU DON'T LIKE HUMANS ?
WE HEAR MOST HUMANS ARE UP TO NO GOOD.
I SEE ...
WE HEARD "NATSUME" IS PARTIAL TO YOKAI, AND WE WANTED TO ASK FOR HELP, BUT IT REMAINS A MYSTERY.
...
WHAT WERE YOU GOING TO ASK HELP FOR?
HMM? WELL...

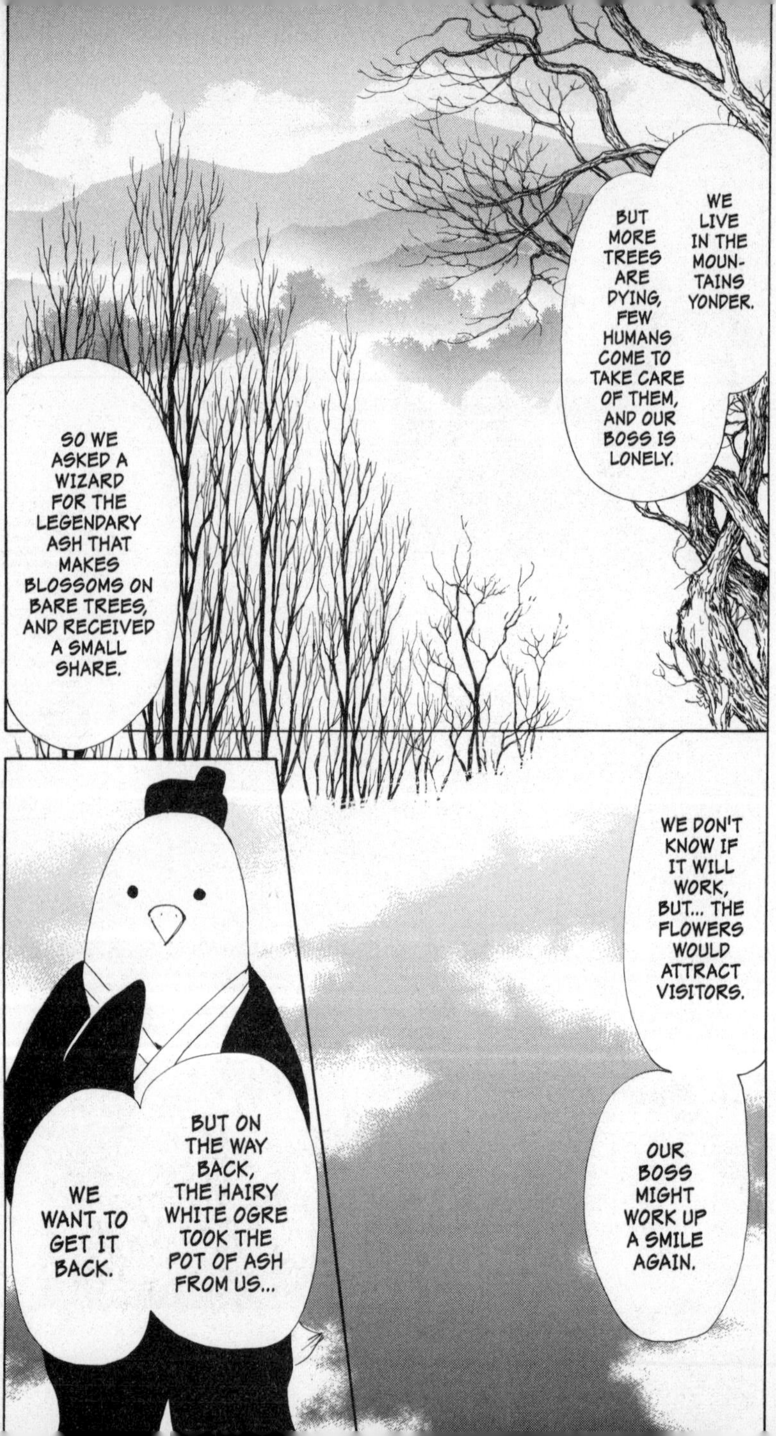
WE LIVE IN THE MOUN- TAINS YONDER.
BUT MORE TREES ARE DYING, FEW HUMANS COME TO TAKE CARE OF THEM, AND OUR BOSS IS LONELY.
SO WE ASKED A WIZARD FOR THE LEGENDARY ASH THAT MAKES BLOSSOMS ON BARE TREES, AND RECEIVED A SMALL SHARE.
WE DON'T KNOW IF IT WILL WORK, BUT... THE FLOWERS WOULD ATTRACT VISITORS.
OUR BOSS MIGHT WORK UP A SMILE AGAIN.
BUT ON THE WAY BACK, THE HAIRY WHITE OGRE TOOK THE POT OF ASH FROM US...
WE WANT TO GET IT BACK.

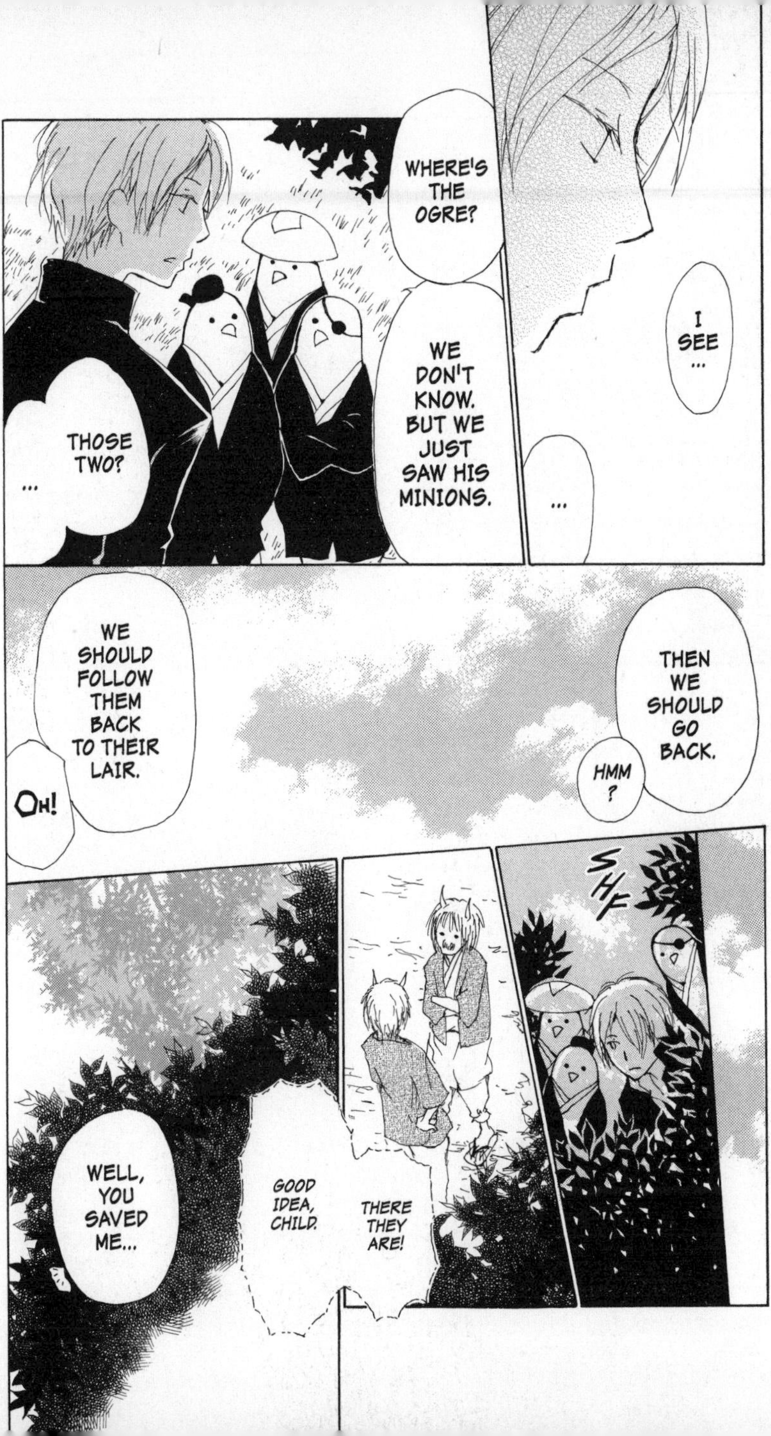
I SEE...
...
WHERE'S THE OGRE?
WE DON'T KNOW. BUT WE JUST SAW HIS MINIONS.
THOSE TWO?
...
THEN WE SHOULD GO BACK.
HMM?
WE SHOULD FOLLOW THEM BACK TO THEIR LAIR.
OH!
SHF
THERE THEY ARE!
GOOD IDEA, CHILD.
WELL, YOU SAVED ME...

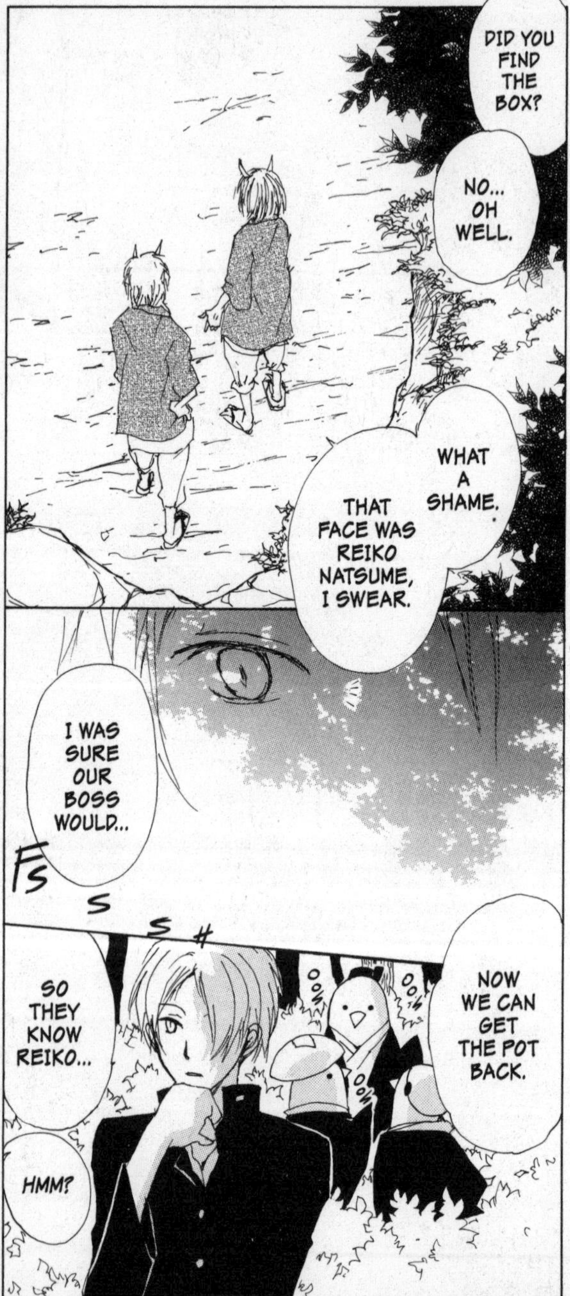
DID YOU FIND THE BOX?
NO... OH WELL.
WHAT A SHAME.
THAT FACE WAS REIKO NATSUME, I SWEAR.
I WAS SURE OUR BOSS WOULD...
FSSSH
NOW WE CAN GET THE POT BACK.
SO THEY KNOW REIKO...
HMM?
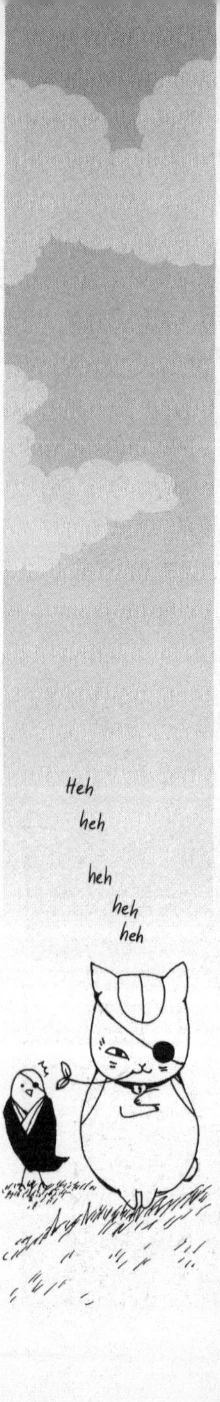
Heh heh heh heh heh

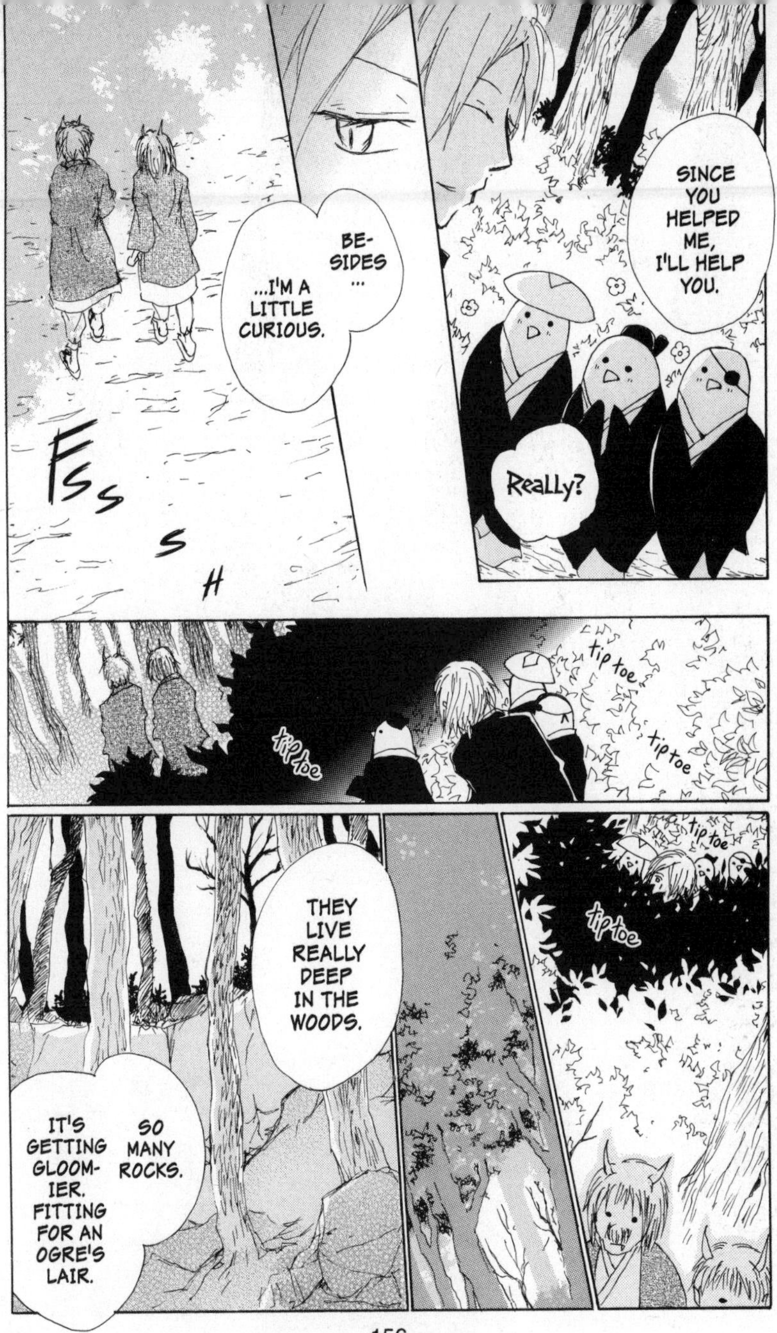
SINCE YOU HELPED ME, I'LL HELP YOU.
Really?
BE-SIDES...
...I'M A LITTLE CURIOUS.
FSSSH
tip toe
tip toe
tip toe
tip toe
tip toe
THEY LIVE REALLY DEEP IN THE WOODS.
SO MANY ROCKS.
IT'S GETTING GLOOM-IER. FITTING FOR AN OGRE'S LAIR.

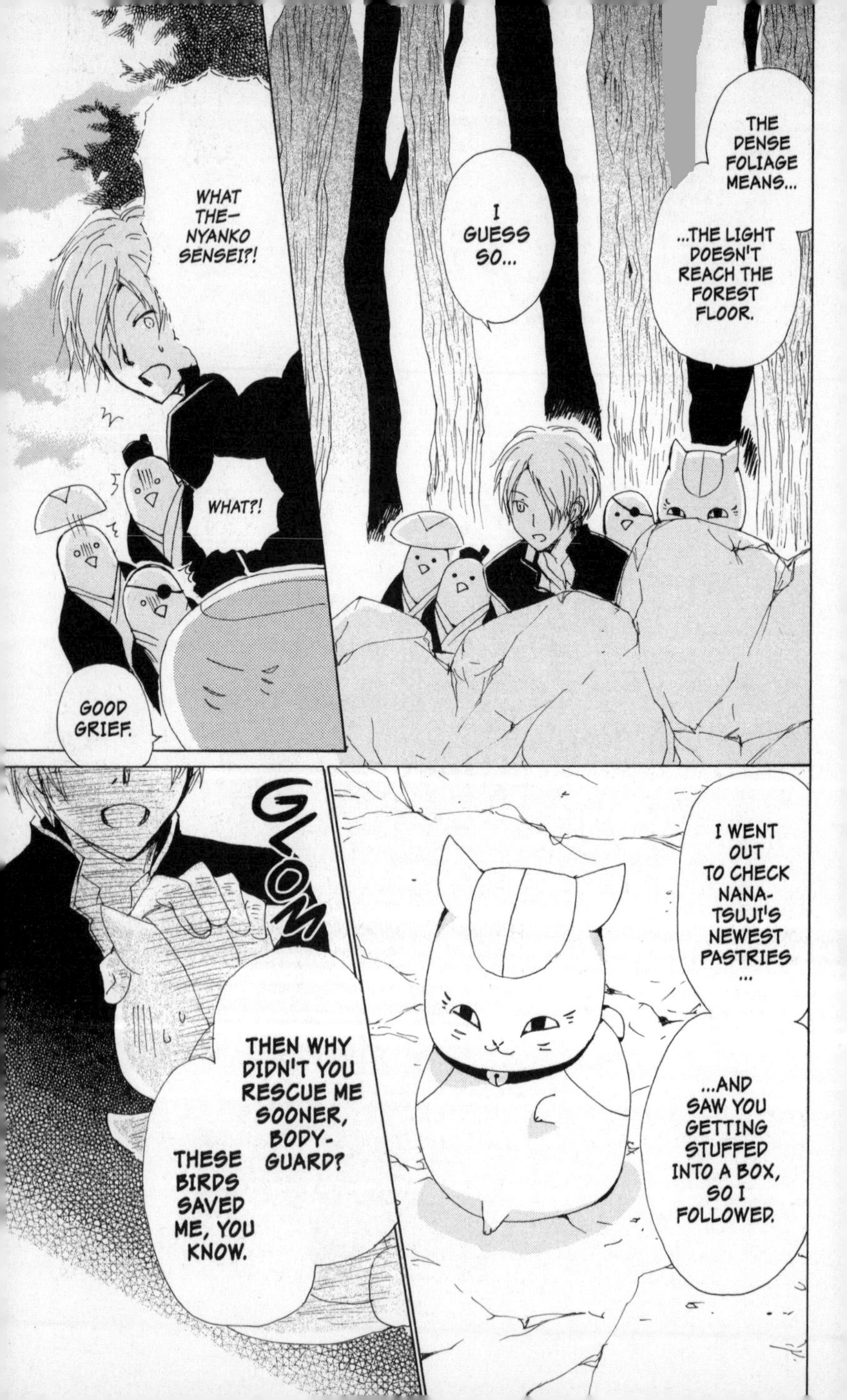

THE DENSE FOLIAGE MEANS...
...THE LIGHT DOESN'T REACH THE FOREST FLOOR.
I GUESS SO...
WHAT THE— NYANKO SENSEI?!
WHAT?!
GOOD GRIEF.
I WENT OUT TO CHECK NANA-TSUJI'S NEWEST PASTRIES ...
...AND SAW YOU GETTING STUFFED INTO A BOX, SO I FOLLOWED.
GLOM
THEN WHY DIDN'T YOU RESCUE ME SOONER, BODY-GUARD?
THESE BIRDS SAVED ME, YOU KNOW.

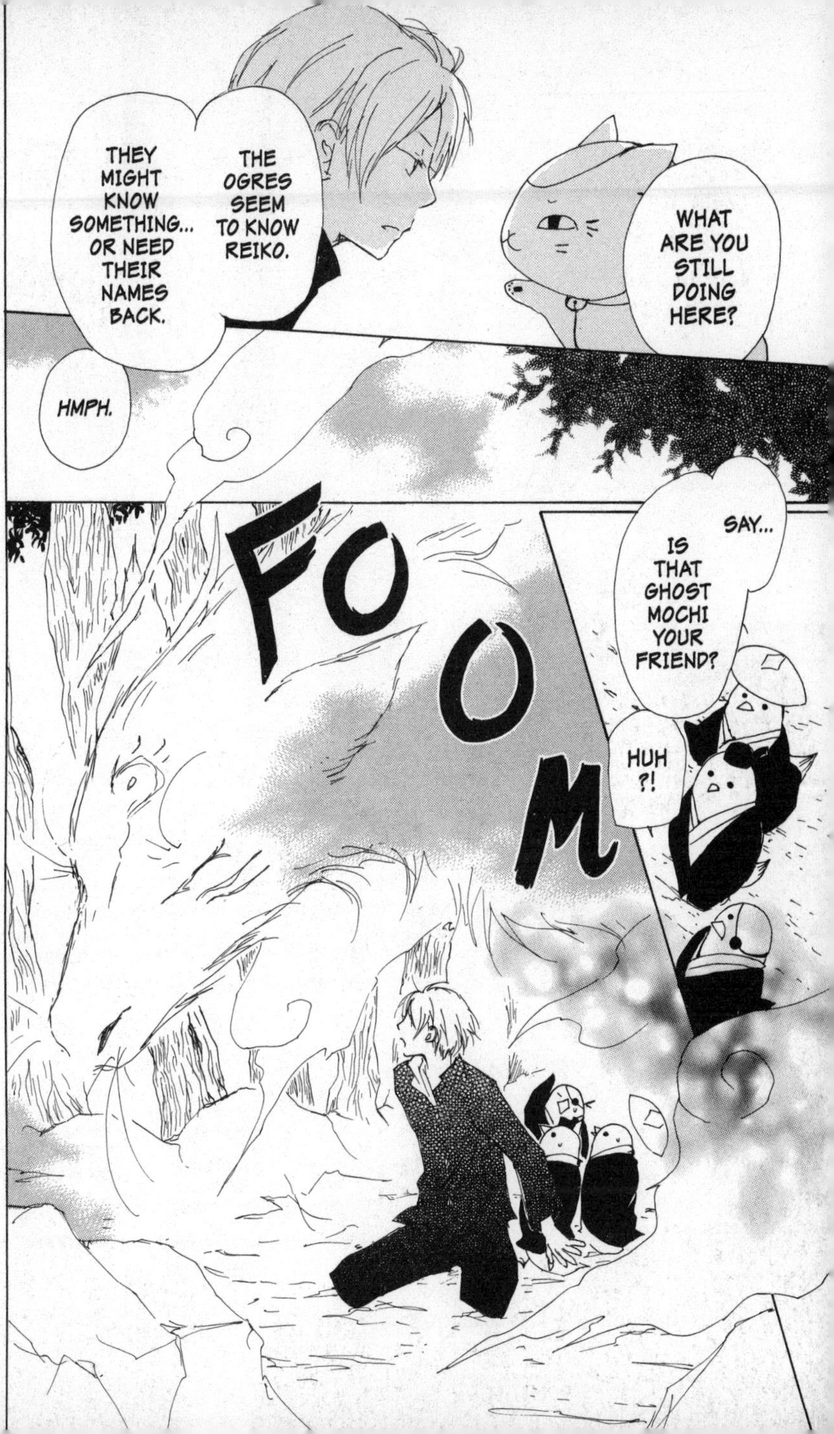
WHAT ARE YOU STILL DOING HERE?
THE OGRES SEEM TO KNOW REIKO.
THEY MIGHT KNOW SOMETHING... OR NEED THEIR NAMES BACK.
HMPH.
SAY... IS THAT GHOST MOCHI YOUR FRIEND?
HUH ?!
FOOOM

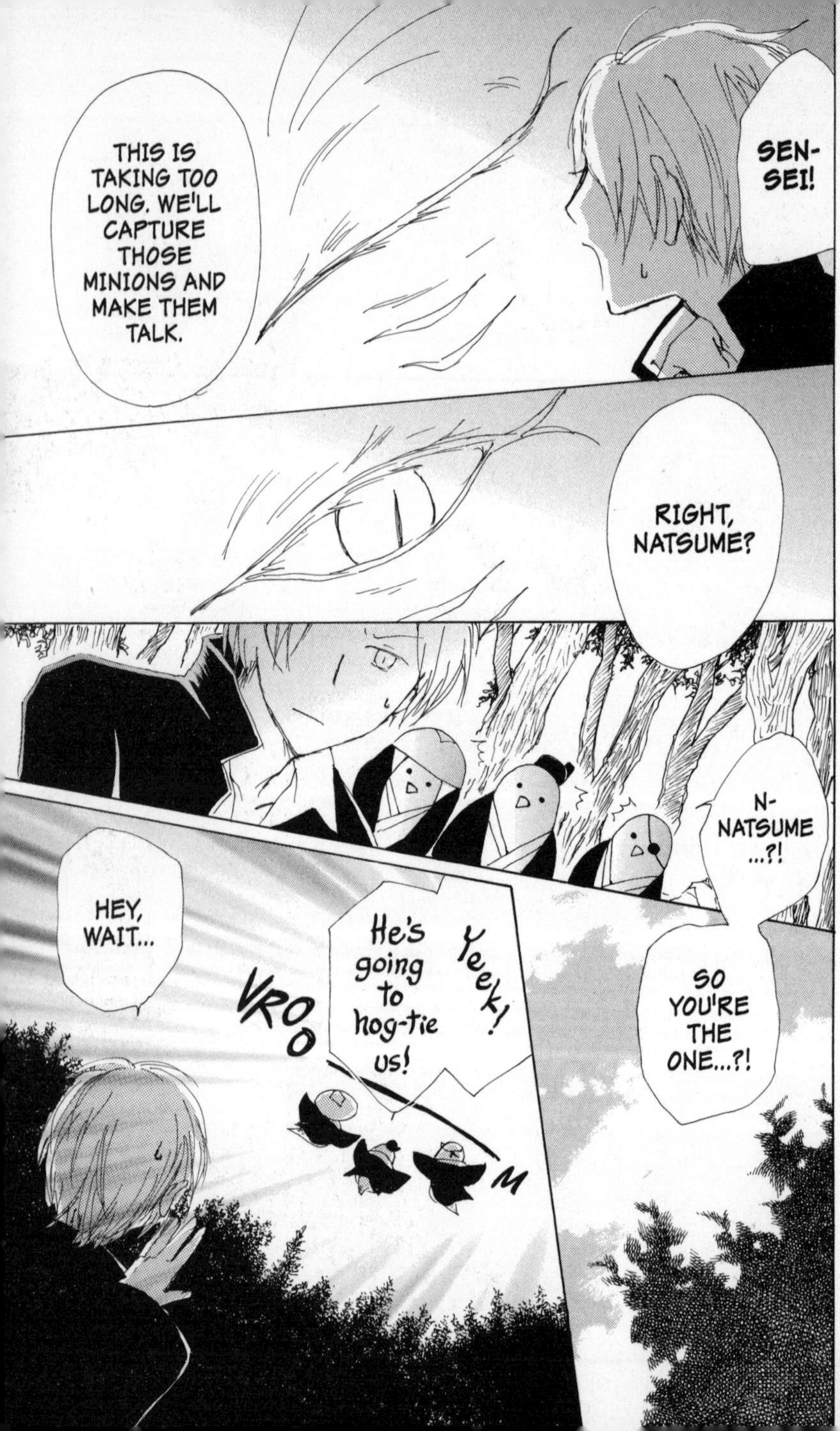
SEN-SEI!
THIS IS TAKING TOO LONG. WE'LL CAPTURE THOSE MINIONS AND MAKE THEM TALK.
RIGHT, NATSUME?
N-NATSUME ...?!
SO YOU'RE THE ONE...?!
Yeeek!
He's going to hog-tie us!
VROOM
HEY, WAIT...

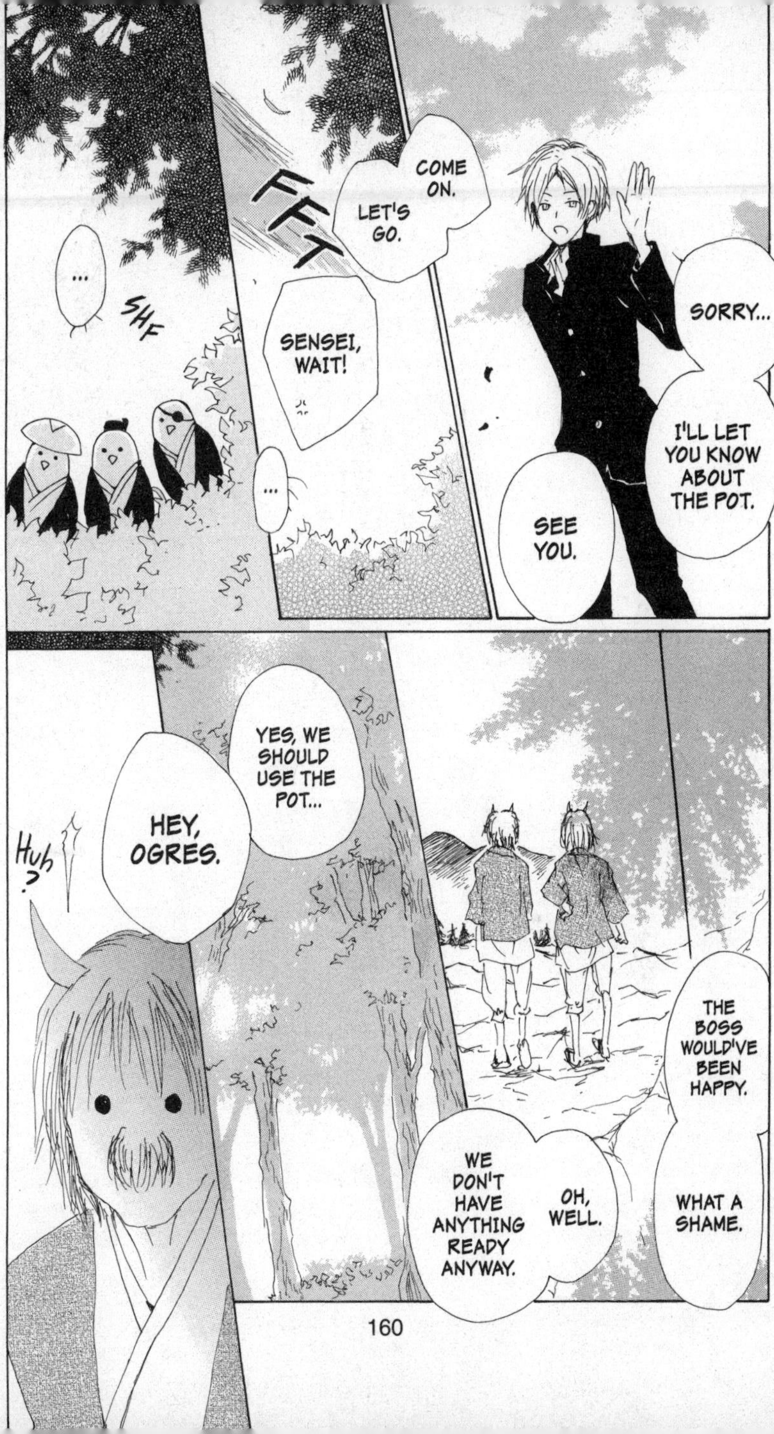
SORRY...
I'LL LET YOU KNOW ABOUT THE POT.
SEE YOU.
COME ON.
LET'S GO.
FFT
SENSEI, WAIT!
...
...
SHF
THE BOSS WOULD'VE BEEN HAPPY.
WHAT A SHAME.
OH, WELL.
WE DON'T HAVE ANYTHING READY ANYWAY.
YES, WE SHOULD USE THE POT...
HEY, OGRES.
Huh?

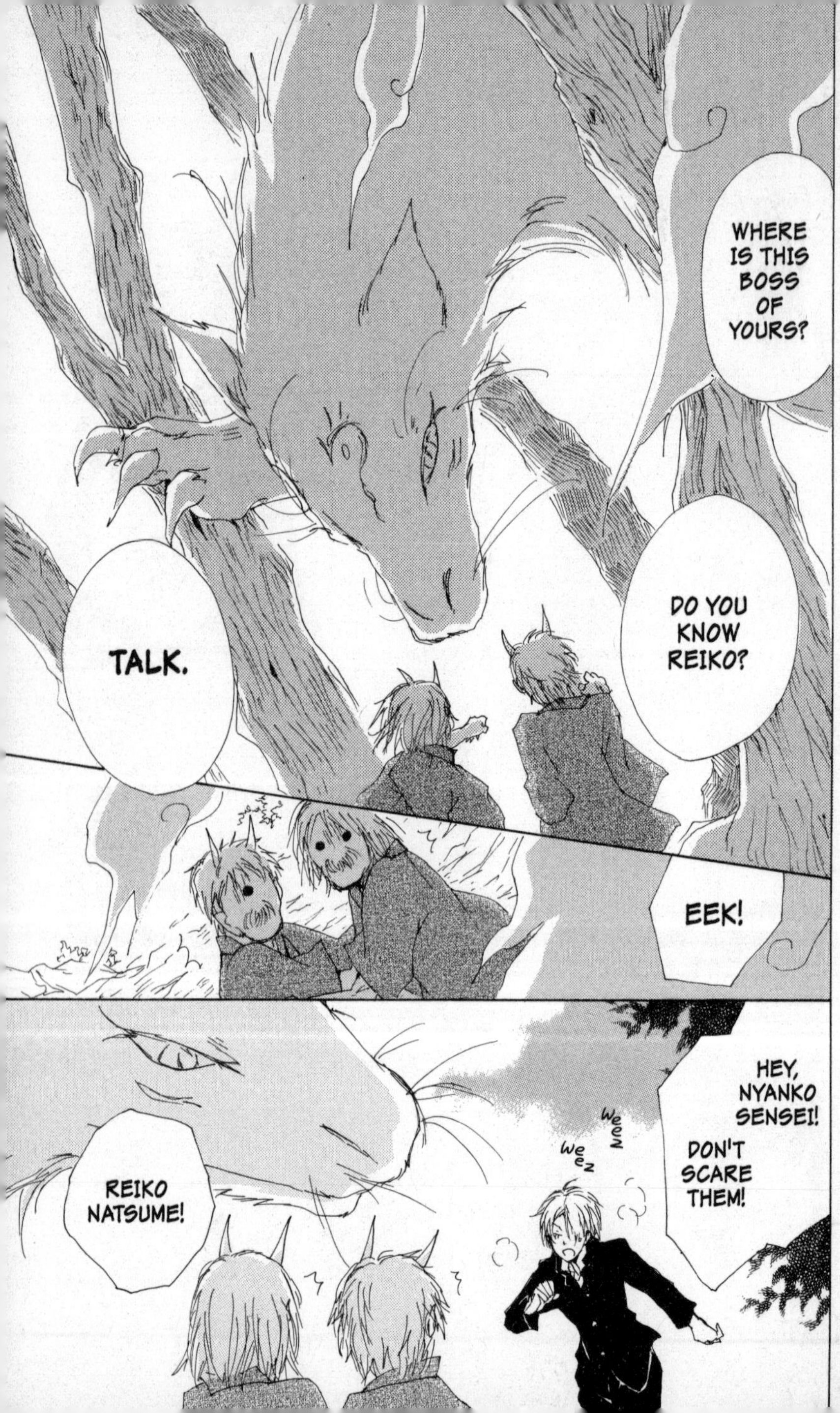
WHERE IS THIS BOSS OF YOURS?
DO YOU KNOW REIKO?
TALK.
EEK!
HEY, NYANKO SENSEI!
DON'T SCARE THEM!
Ween
REIKO NATSUME!

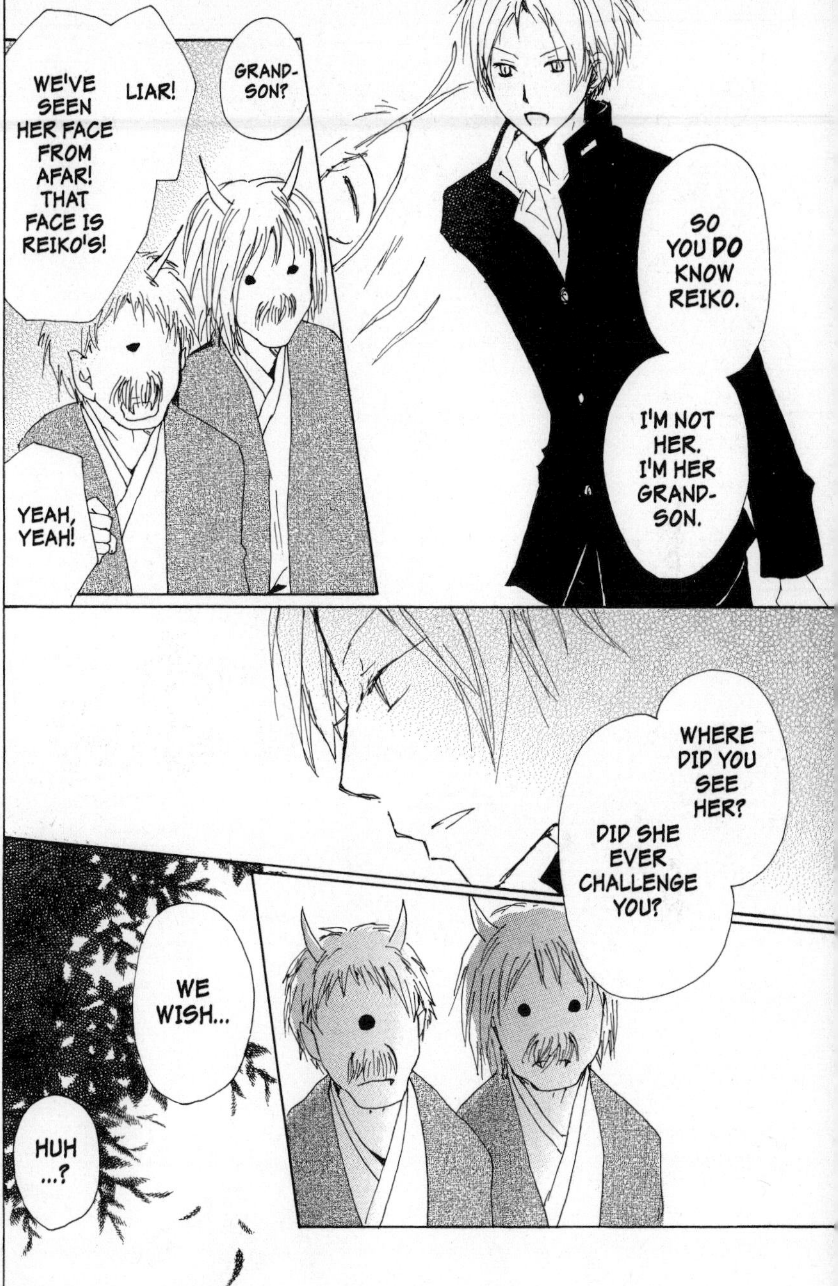
SO YOU DO KNOW REIKO.
I'M NOT HER. I'M HER GRAND-SON.
GRAND-SON?
LIAR!
WE'VE SEEN HER FACE FROM AFAR! THAT FACE IS REIKO'S!
YEAH, YEAH!
WHERE DID YOU SEE HER?
DID SHE EVER CHALLENGE YOU?
WE WISH...
HUH ...?

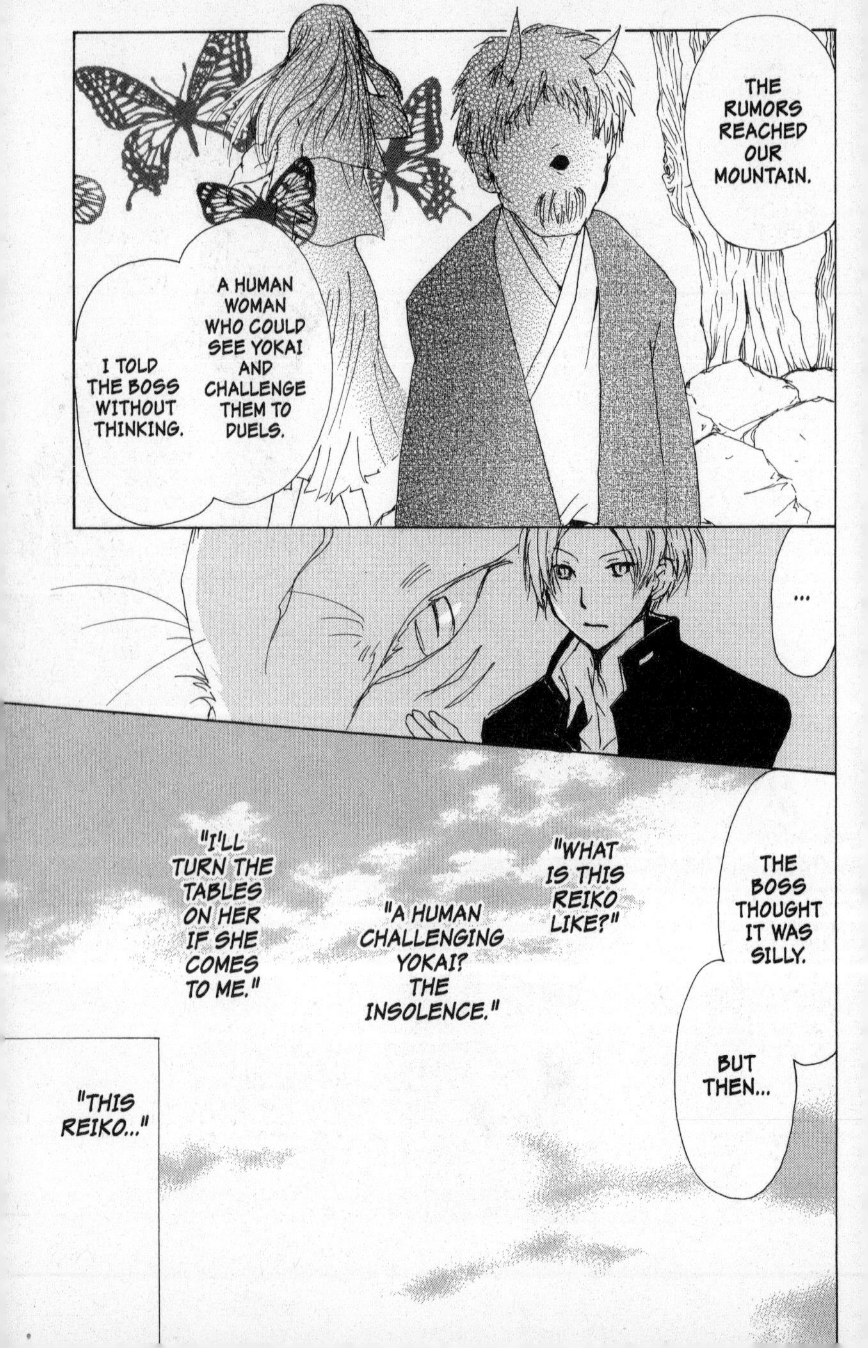
THE RUMORS REACHED OUR MOUNTAIN.
A HUMAN WOMAN WHO COULD SEE YOKAI AND CHALLENGE THEM TO DUELS.
I TOLD THE BOSS WITHOUT THINKING.
...
THE BOSS THOUGHT IT WAS SILLY.
BUT THEN...
"WHAT IS THIS REIKO LIKE?"
"A HUMAN CHALLENGING YOKAI? THE INSOLENCE."
"I'LL TURN THE TABLES ON HER IF SHE COMES TO ME."
"THIS REIKO..."

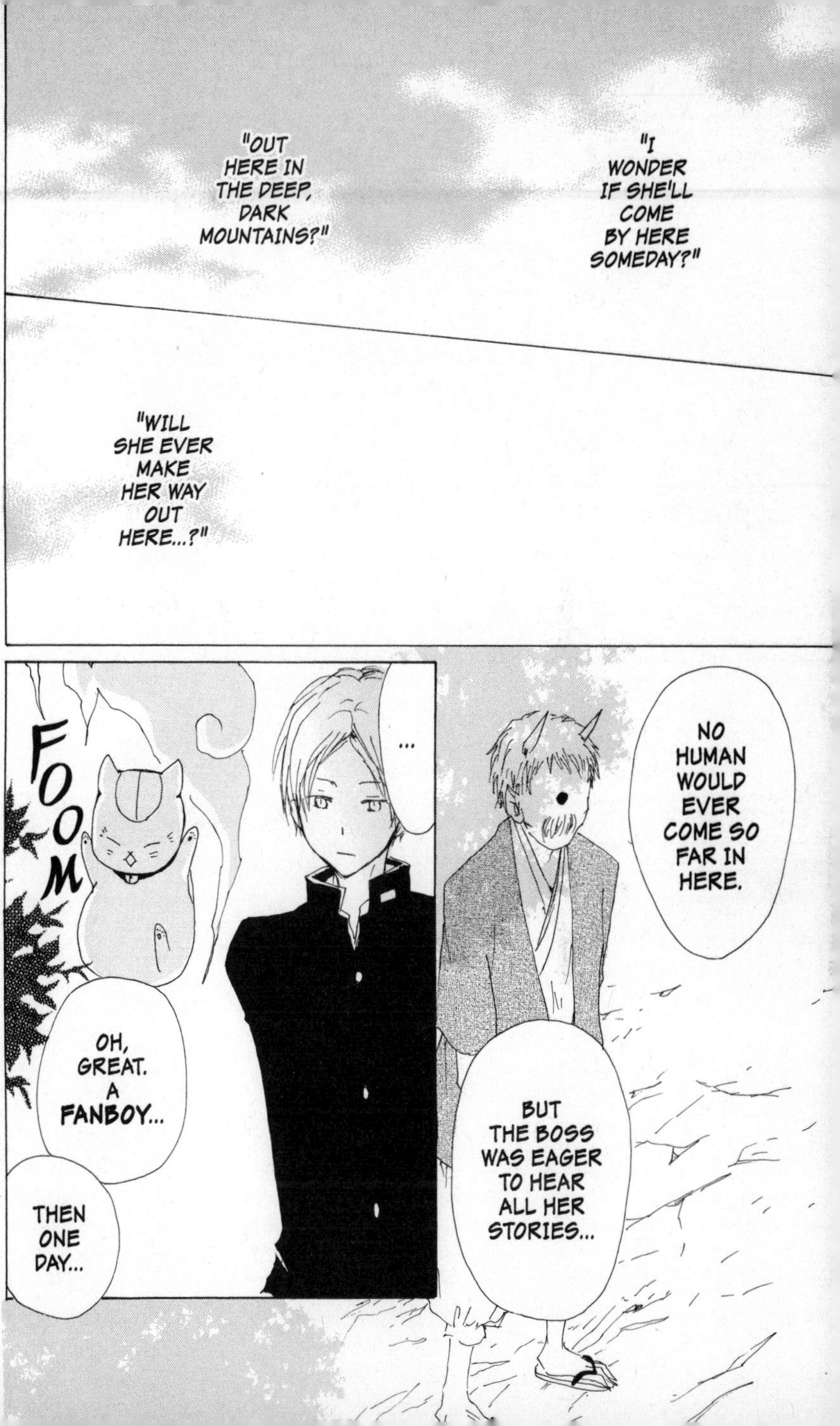
"I WONDER IF SHE'LL COME BY HERE SOMEDAY?"
"OUT HERE IN THE DEEP, DARK MOUNTAINS?"
"WILL SHE EVER MAKE HER WAY OUT HERE...?"
NO HUMAN WOULD EVER COME SO FAR IN HERE.
BUT THE BOSS WAS EAGER TO HEAR ALL HER STORIES...
...
FOOM
OH, GREAT. A FANBOY...
THEN ONE DAY...

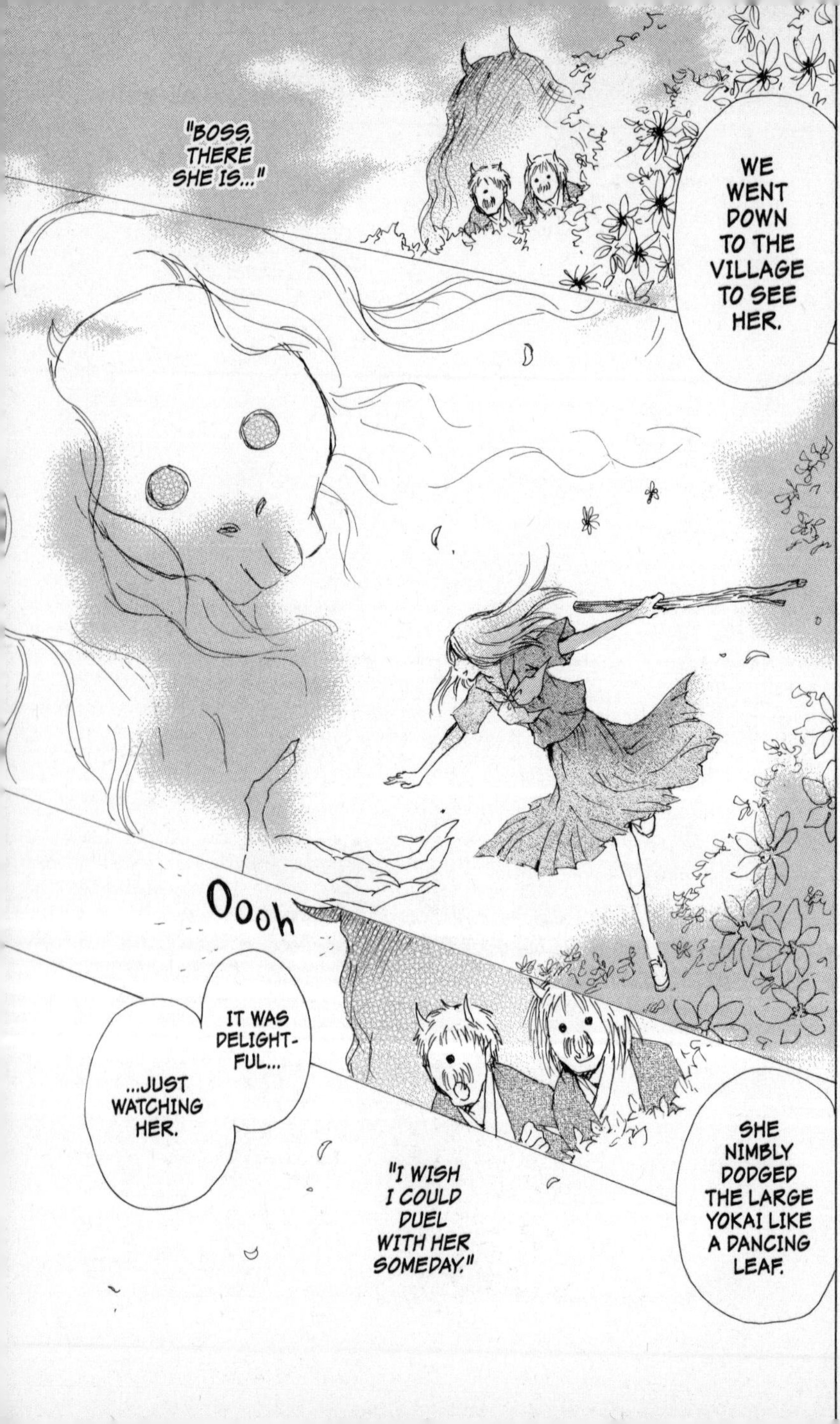
WE WENT DOWN TO THE VILLAGE TO SEE HER.
"BOSS, THERE SHE IS..."
Oooh
SHE NIMBLY DODGED THE LARGE YOKAI LIKE A DANCING LEAF.
"I WISH I COULD DUEL WITH HER SOMEDAY."
IT WAS DELIGHTFUL...
...JUST WATCHING HER.

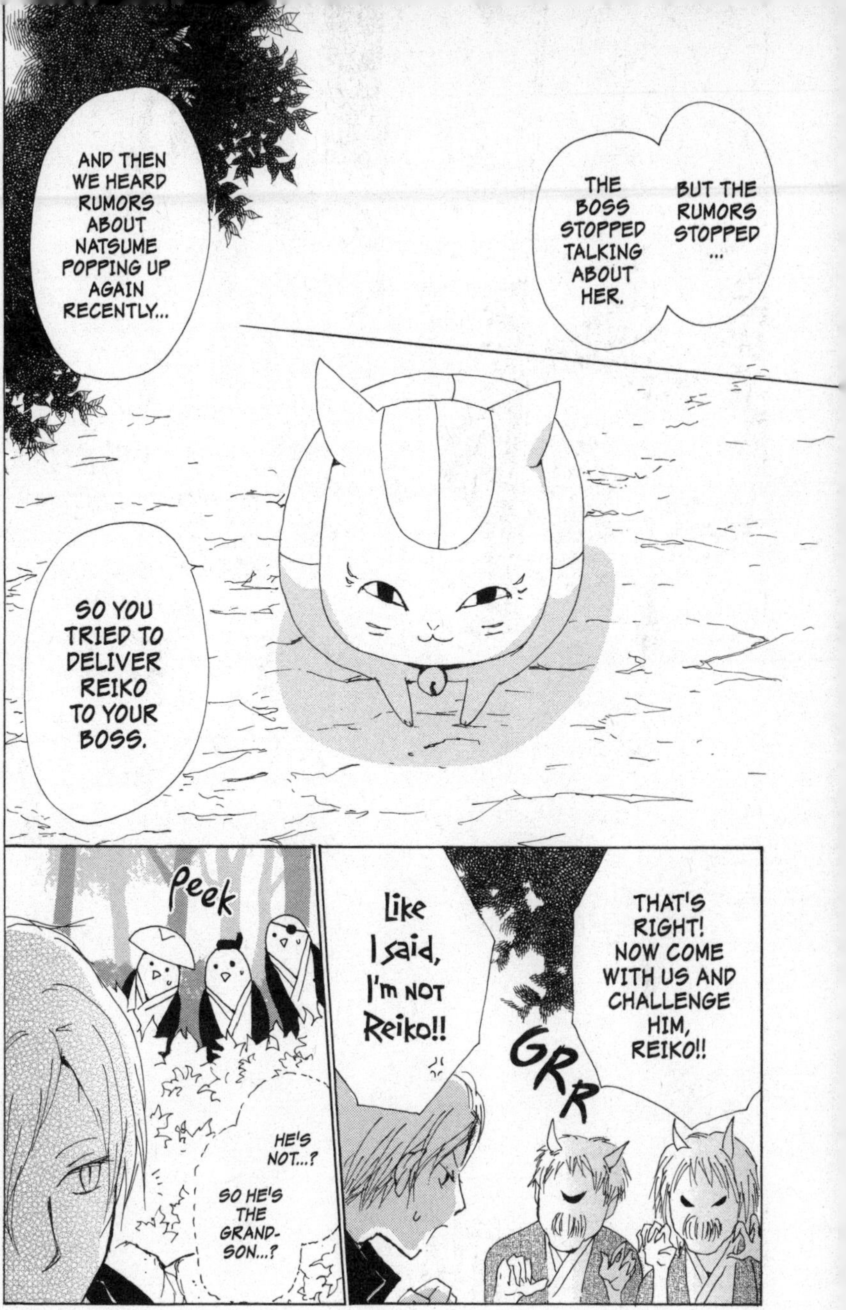
BUT THE RUMORS STOPPED ...
THE BOSS STOPPED TALKING ABOUT HER.
AND THEN WE HEARD RUMORS ABOUT NATSUME POPPING UP AGAIN RECENTLY...
SO YOU TRIED TO DELIVER REIKO TO YOUR BOSS.
THAT'S RIGHT! NOW COME WITH US AND CHALLENGE HIM, REIKO!!
GRR
Like I said, I'm NOT Reiko!!
Peek
HE'S NOT...?
SO HE'S THE GRAND-SON...?

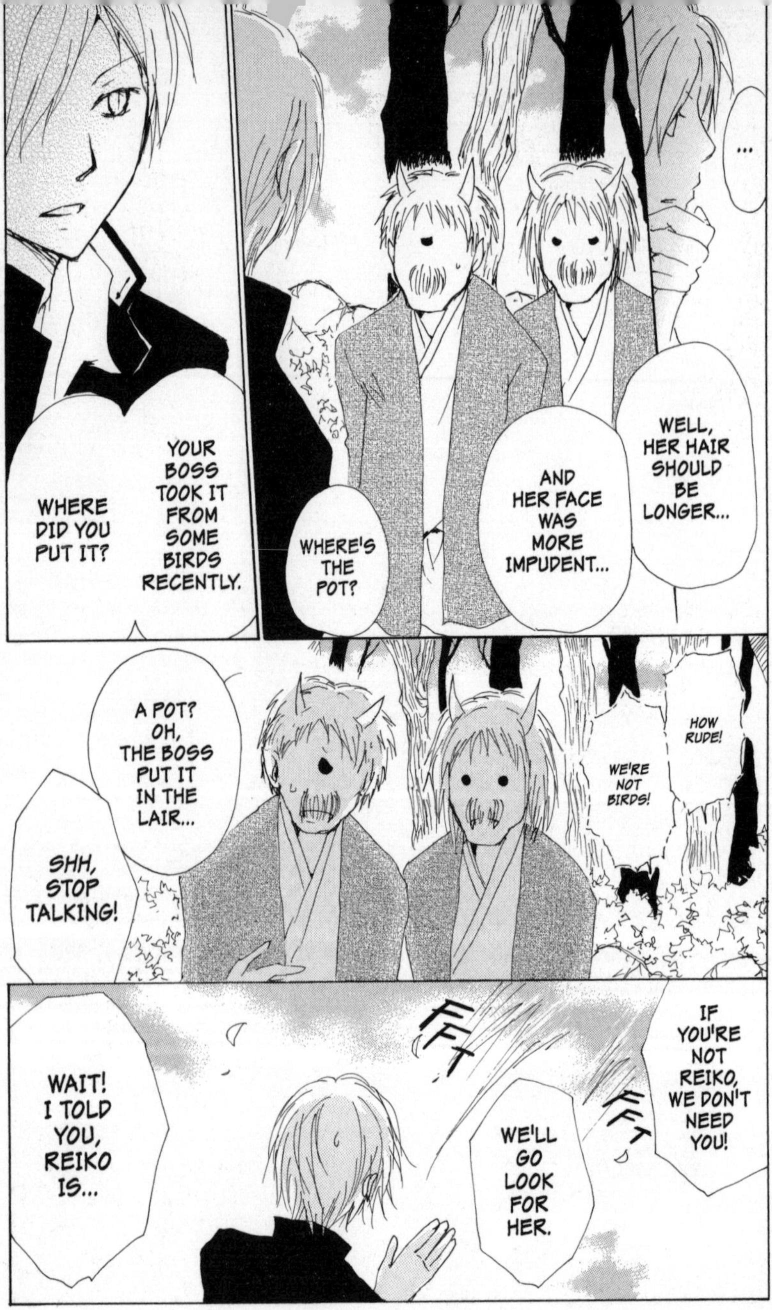
...
WELL, HER HAIR SHOULD BE LONGER...
AND HER FACE WAS MORE IMPUDENT...
WHERE'S THE POT?
YOUR BOSS TOOK IT FROM SOME BIRDS RECENTLY.
WHERE DID YOU PUT IT?
HOW RUDE!
WE'RE NOT BIRDS!
A POT? OH, THE BOSS PUT IT IN THE LAIR...
SHH, STOP TALKING!
IF YOU'RE NOT REIKO, WE DON'T NEED YOU!
FFT
FFT
WE'LL GO LOOK FOR HER.
WAIT! I TOLD YOU, REIKO IS...

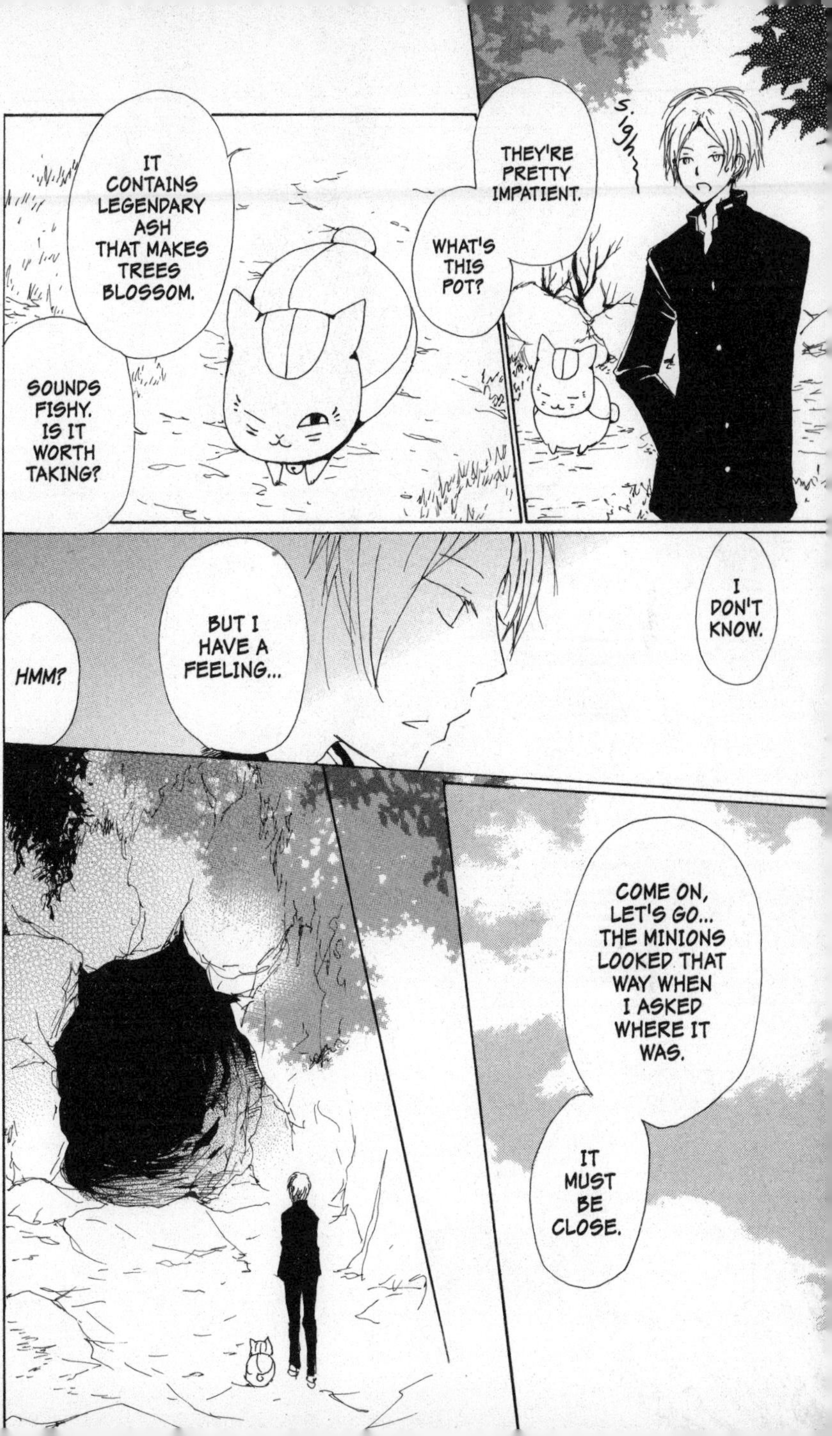
sigh
THEY'RE PRETTY IMPATIENT.
WHAT'S THIS POT?
IT CONTAINS LEGENDARY ASH THAT MAKES TREES BLOSSOM.
SOUNDS FISHY. IS IT WORTH TAKING?
I DON'T KNOW.
BUT I HAVE A FEELING...
HMM?
COME ON, LET'S GO... THE MINIONS LOOKED THAT WAY WHEN I ASKED WHERE IT WAS.
IT MUST BE CLOSE.

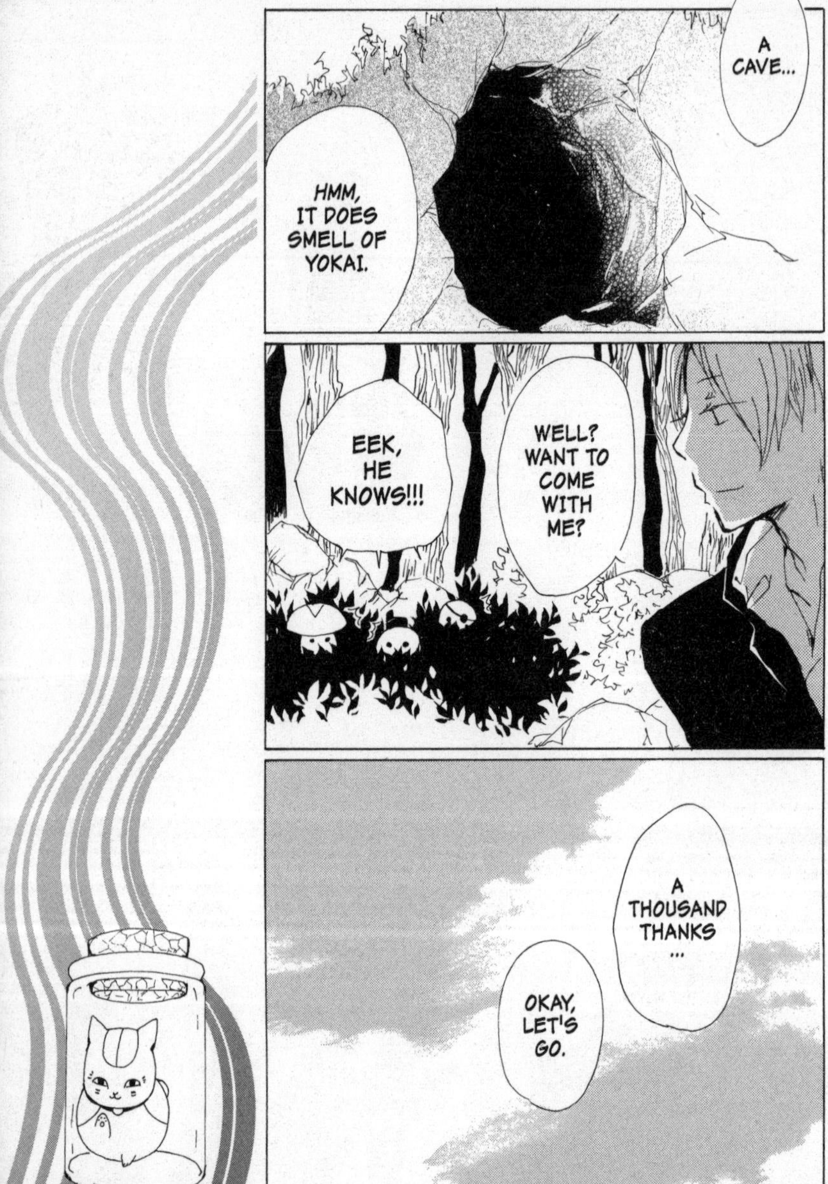
A CAVE...
HMM, IT DOES SMELL OF YOKAI.
WELL? WANT TO COME WITH ME?
EEK, HE KNOWS!!!
A THOUSAND THANKS ...
OKAY, LET'S GO.

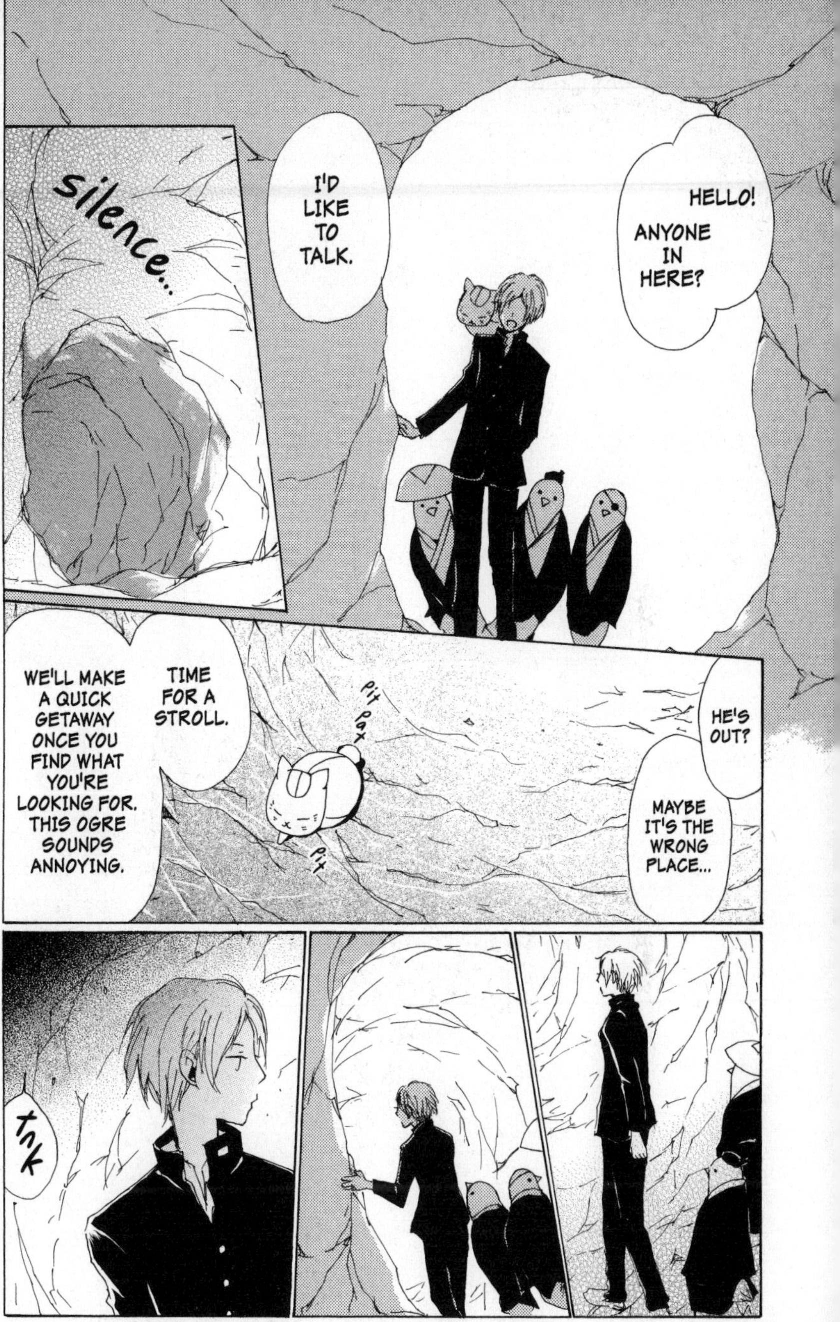
HELLO!
ANYONE IN HERE?
I'D LIKE TO TALK.
silence...
HE'S OUT?
MAYBE IT'S THE WRONG PLACE...
pit pat
pit
TIME FOR A STROLL.
WE'LL MAKE A QUICK GETAWAY ONCE YOU FIND WHAT YOU'RE LOOKING FOR. THIS OGRE SOUNDS ANNOYING.
tnk

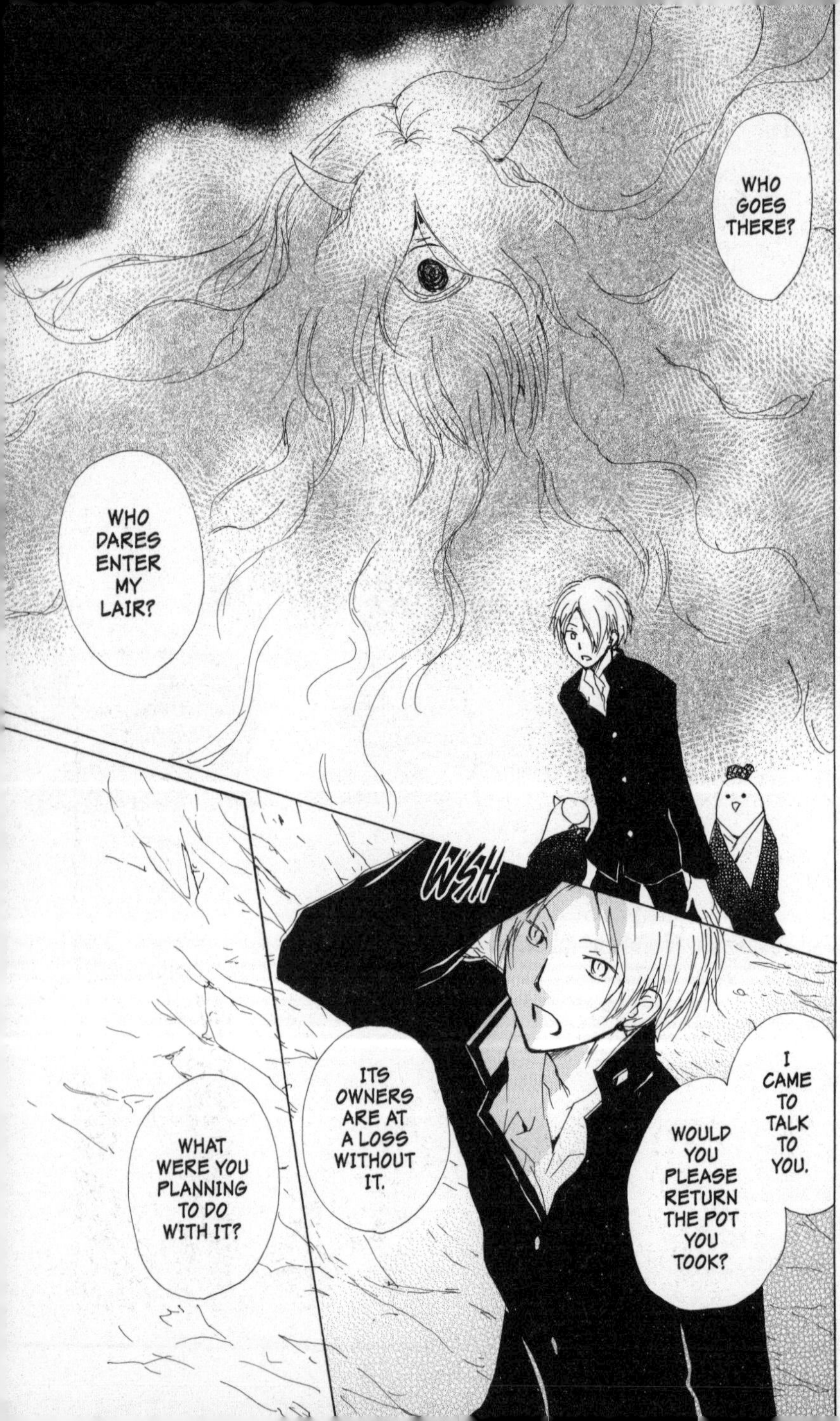
WHO GOES THERE?
WHO DARES ENTER MY LAIR?
WSH
I CAME TO TALK TO YOU.
WOULD YOU PLEASE RETURN THE POT YOU TOOK?
ITS OWNERS ARE AT A LOSS WITHOUT IT.
WHAT WERE YOU PLANNING TO DO WITH IT?

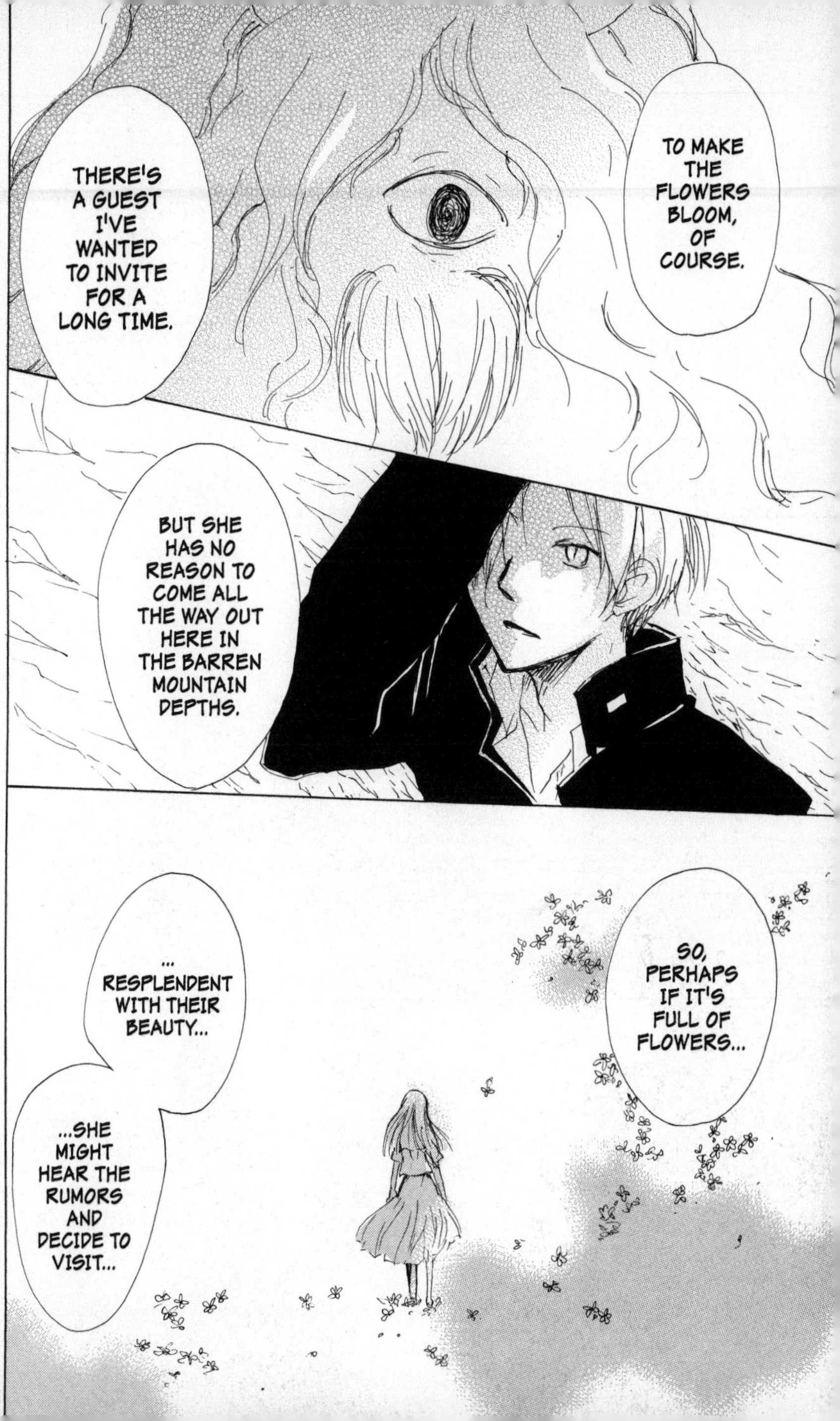
TO MAKE THE FLOWERS BLOOM, OF COURSE.
THERE'S A GUEST I'VE WANTED TO INVITE FOR A LONG TIME.
BUT SHE HAS NO REASON TO COME ALL THE WAY OUT HERE IN THE BARREN MOUNTAIN DEPTHS.
SO, PERHAPS IF IT'S FULL OF FLOWERS...
... RESPLENDENT WITH THEIR BEAUTY...
...SHE MIGHT HEAR THE RUMORS AND DECIDE TO VISIT...

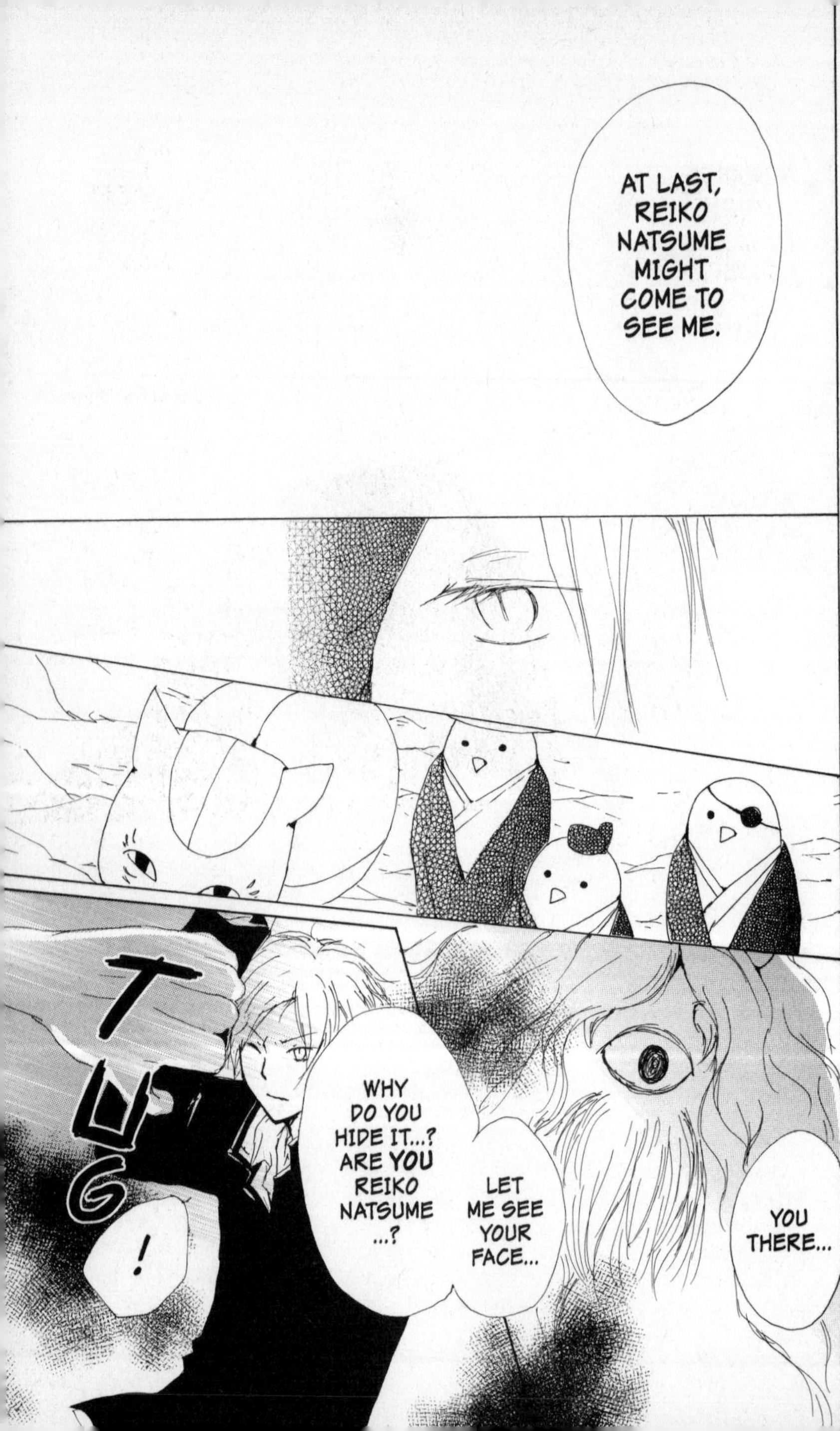
AT LAST, REIKO NATSUME MIGHT COME TO SEE ME.
YOU THERE...
LET ME SEE YOUR FACE...
WHY DO YOU HIDE IT...? ARE YOU REIKO NATSUME ...?
TUG
!

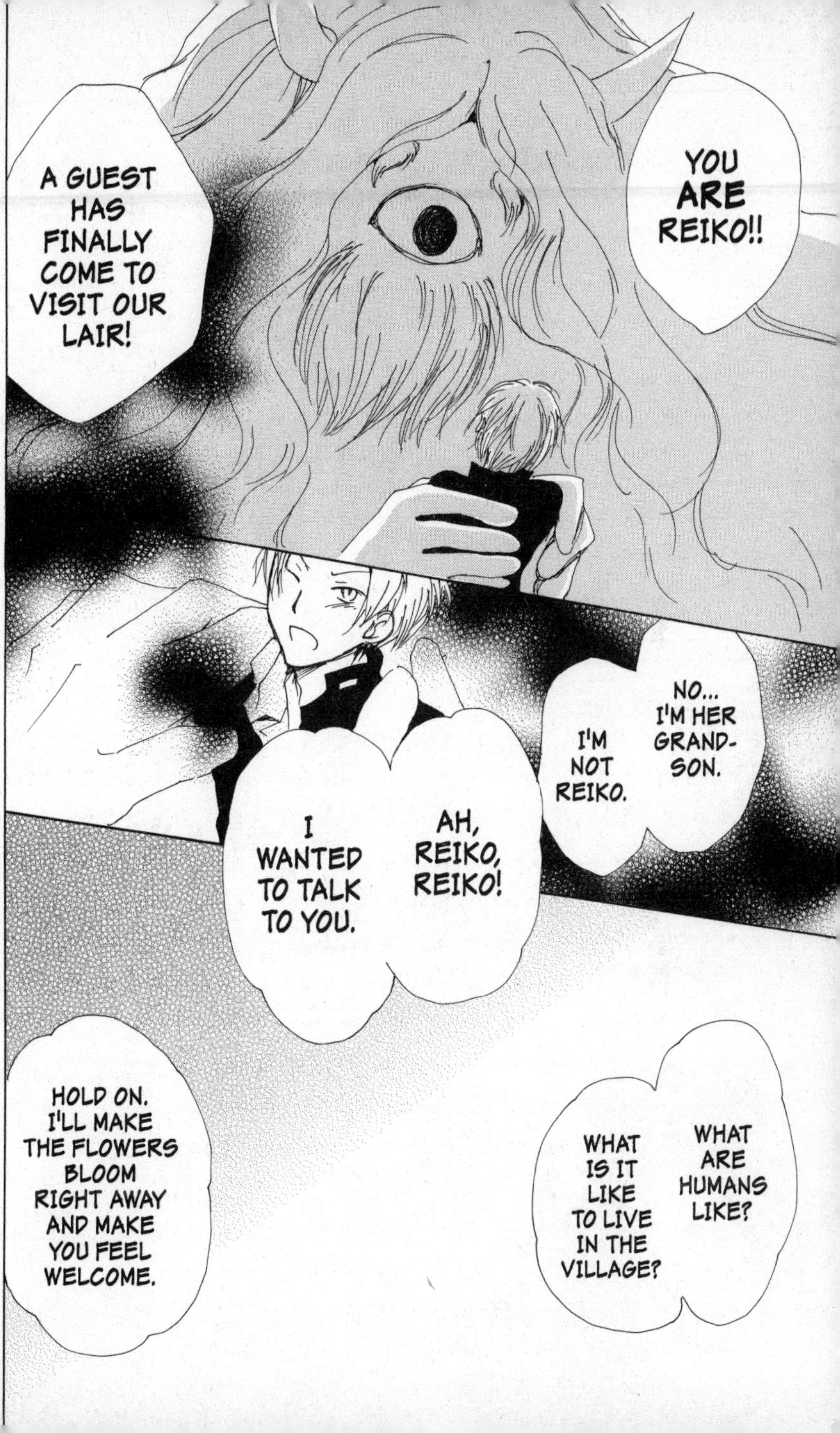
YOU ARE REIKO!!
A GUEST HAS FINALLY COME TO VISIT OUR LAIR!
NO... I'M HER GRAND-SON.
I'M NOT REIKO.
AH, REIKO, REIKO!
I WANTED TO TALK TO YOU.
WHAT ARE HUMANS LIKE?
WHAT IS IT LIKE TO LIVE IN THE VILLAGE?
HOLD ON. I'LL MAKE THE FLOWERS BLOOM RIGHT AWAY AND MAKE YOU FEEL WELCOME.

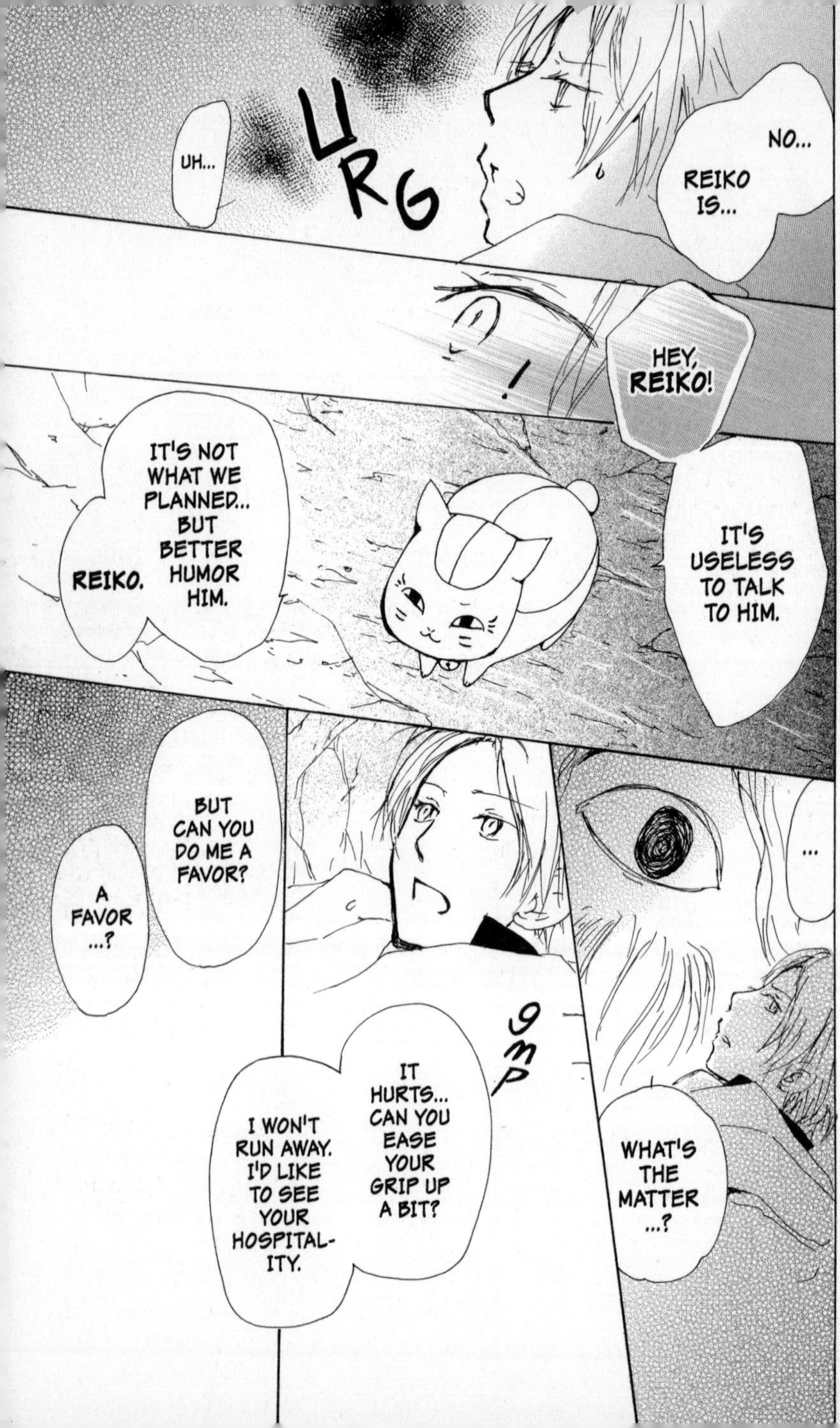
NO... REIKO IS...
URG
UH...
HEY, REIKO!
!
IT'S USELESS TO TALK TO HIM.
IT'S NOT WHAT WE PLANNED... BUT BETTER HUMOR HIM.
REIKO.
...
WHAT'S THE MATTER...?
IT HURTS... CAN YOU EASE YOUR GRIP UP A BIT?
I WON'T RUN AWAY. I'D LIKE TO SEE YOUR HOSPITALITY.
BUT CAN YOU DO ME A FAVOR?
A FAVOR...?

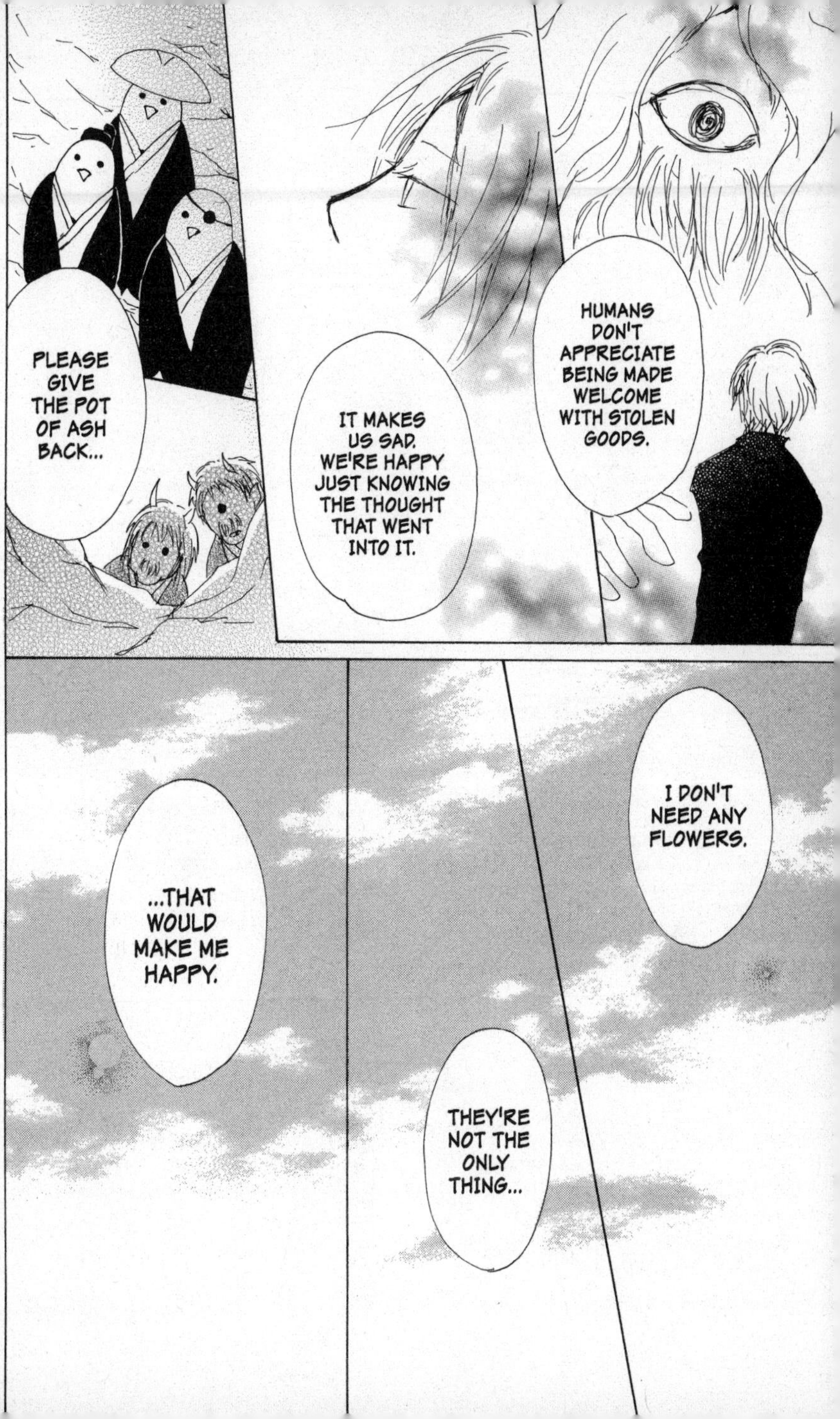
HUMANS DON'T APPRECIATE BEING MADE WELCOME WITH STOLEN GOODS.
IT MAKES US SAD. WE'RE HAPPY JUST KNOWING THE THOUGHT THAT WENT INTO IT.
PLEASE GIVE THE POT OF ASH BACK...
I DON'T NEED ANY FLOWERS.
THEY'RE NOT THE ONLY THING...
...THAT WOULD MAKE ME HAPPY.

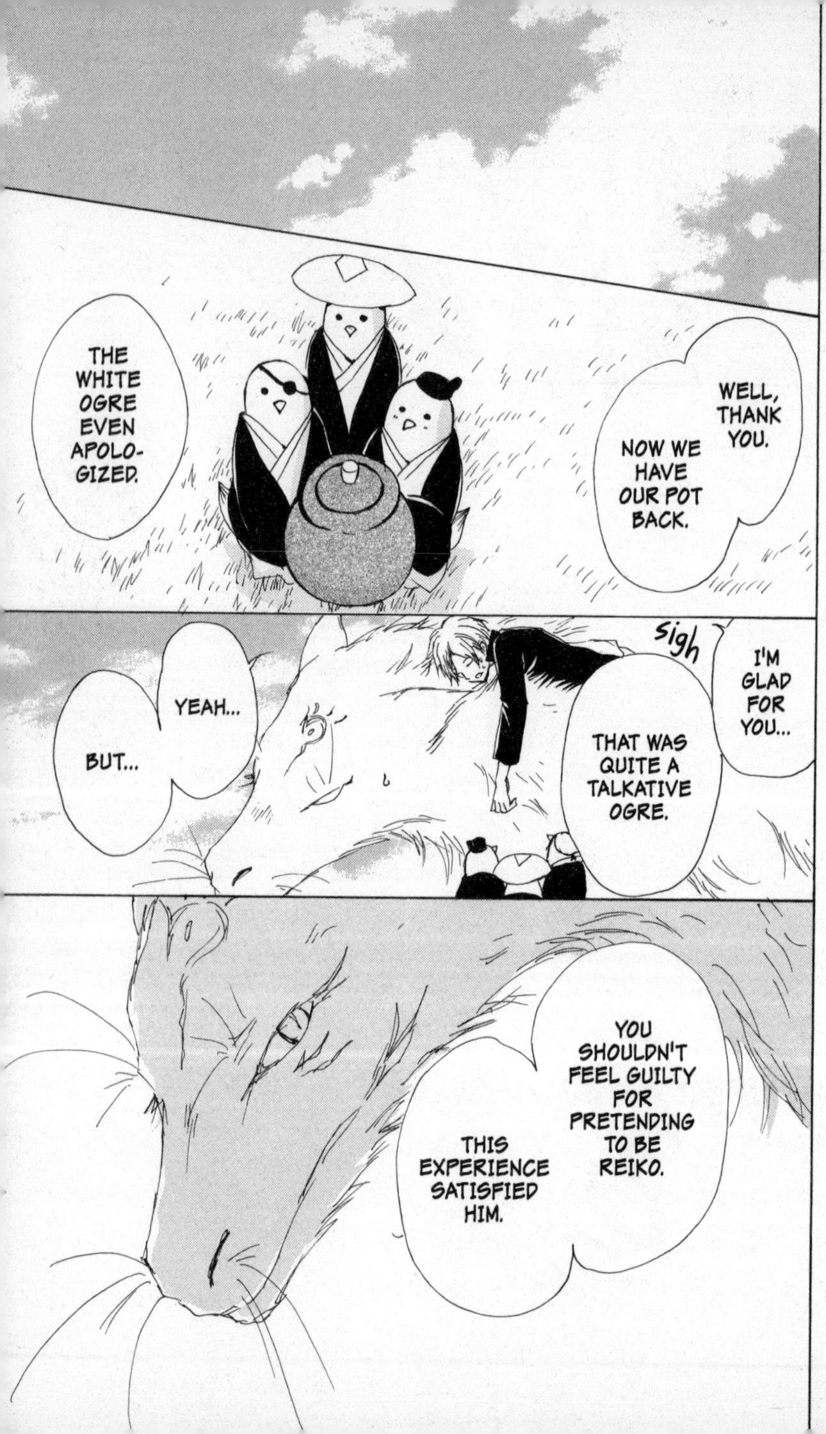
WELL, THANK YOU.
NOW WE HAVE OUR POT BACK.
THE WHITE OGRE EVEN APOLO-GIZED.
I'M GLAD FOR YOU...
Sigh
THAT WAS QUITE A TALKATIVE OGRE.
YEAH...
BUT...
YOU SHOULDN'T FEEL GUILTY FOR PRETENDING TO BE REIKO.
THIS EXPERIENCE SATISFIED HIM.

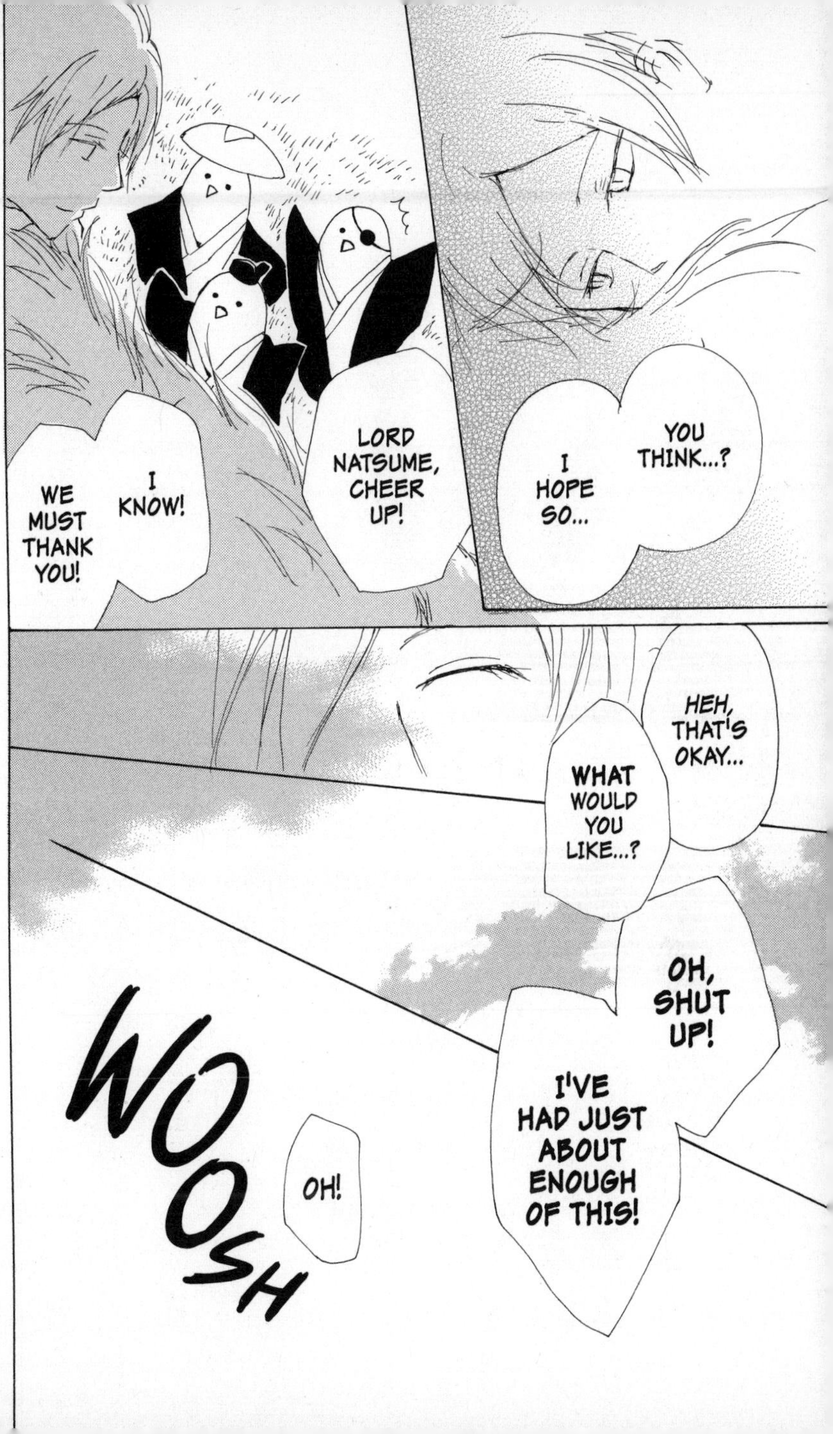
YOU THINK...?
I HOPE SO...
LORD NATSUME, CHEER UP!
I KNOW!
WE MUST THANK YOU!
HEH, THAT'S OKAY...
WHAT WOULD YOU LIKE...?
OH, SHUT UP!
I'VE HAD JUST ABOUT ENOUGH OF THIS!
OH!
WOOSH

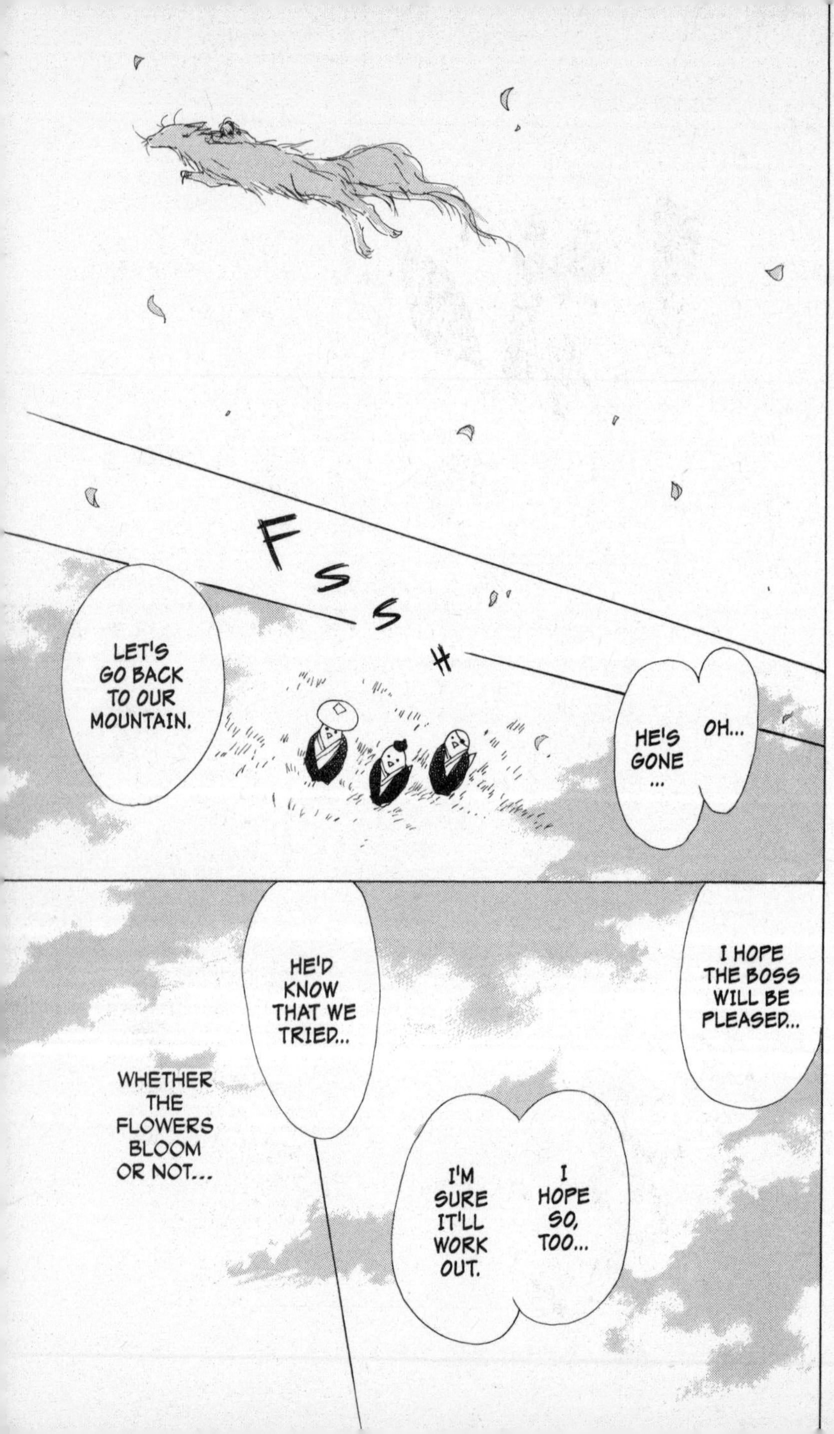
OH...
HE'S GONE...
FSSH
LET'S GO BACK TO OUR MOUNTAIN.
I HOPE THE BOSS WILL BE PLEASED...
HE'D KNOW THAT WE TRIED...
WHETHER THE FLOWERS BLOOM OR NOT...
I HOPE SO, TOO...
I'M SURE IT'LL WORK OUT.

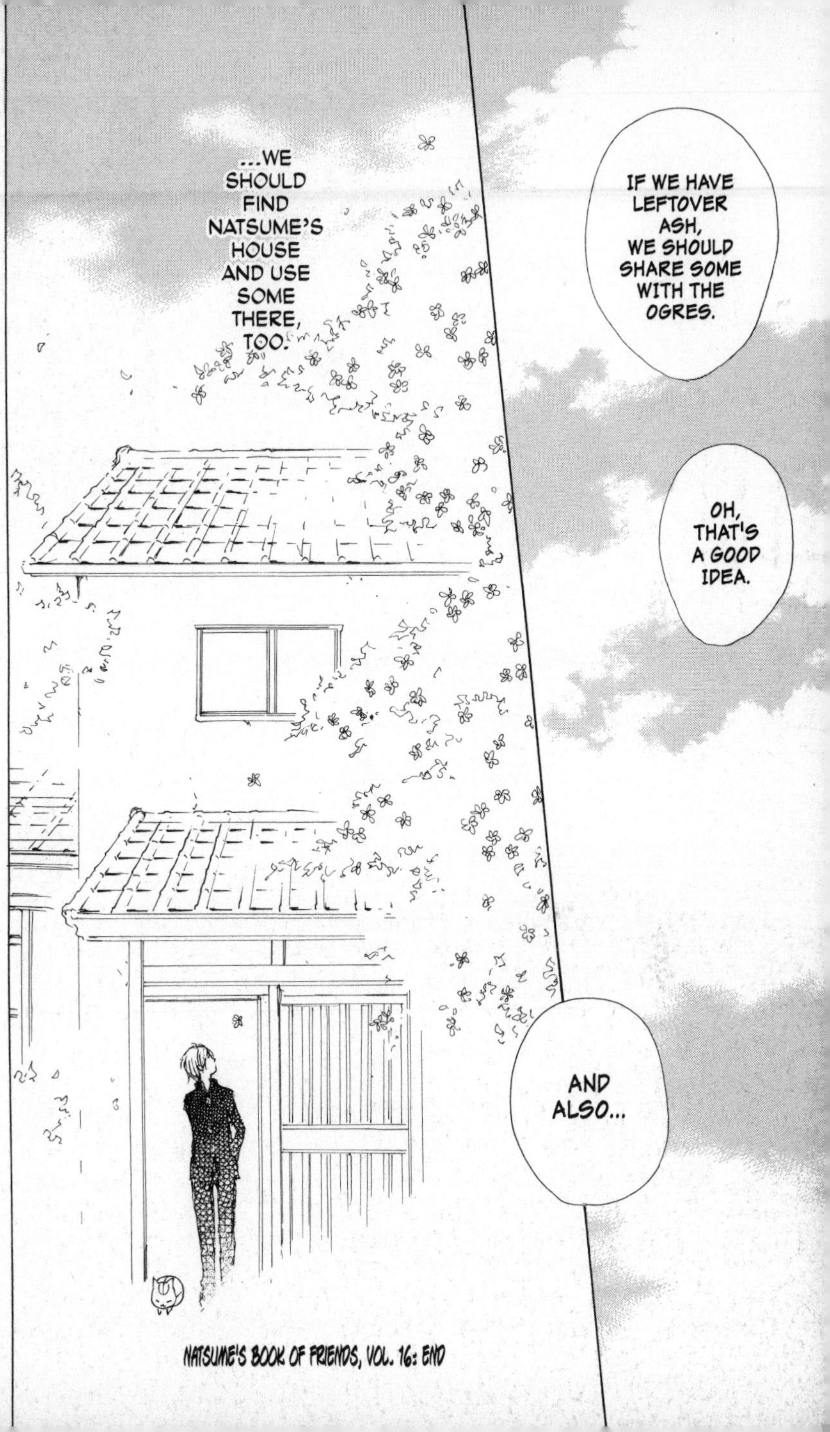
IF WE HAVE LEFTOVER ASH, WE SHOULD SHARE SOME WITH THE OGRES.
OH, THAT'S A GOOD IDEA.
AND ALSO...
...WE SHOULD FIND NATSUME'S HOUSE AND USE SOME THERE, TOO.

NATSUME'S BOOK OF FRIENDS, VOL. 16: END

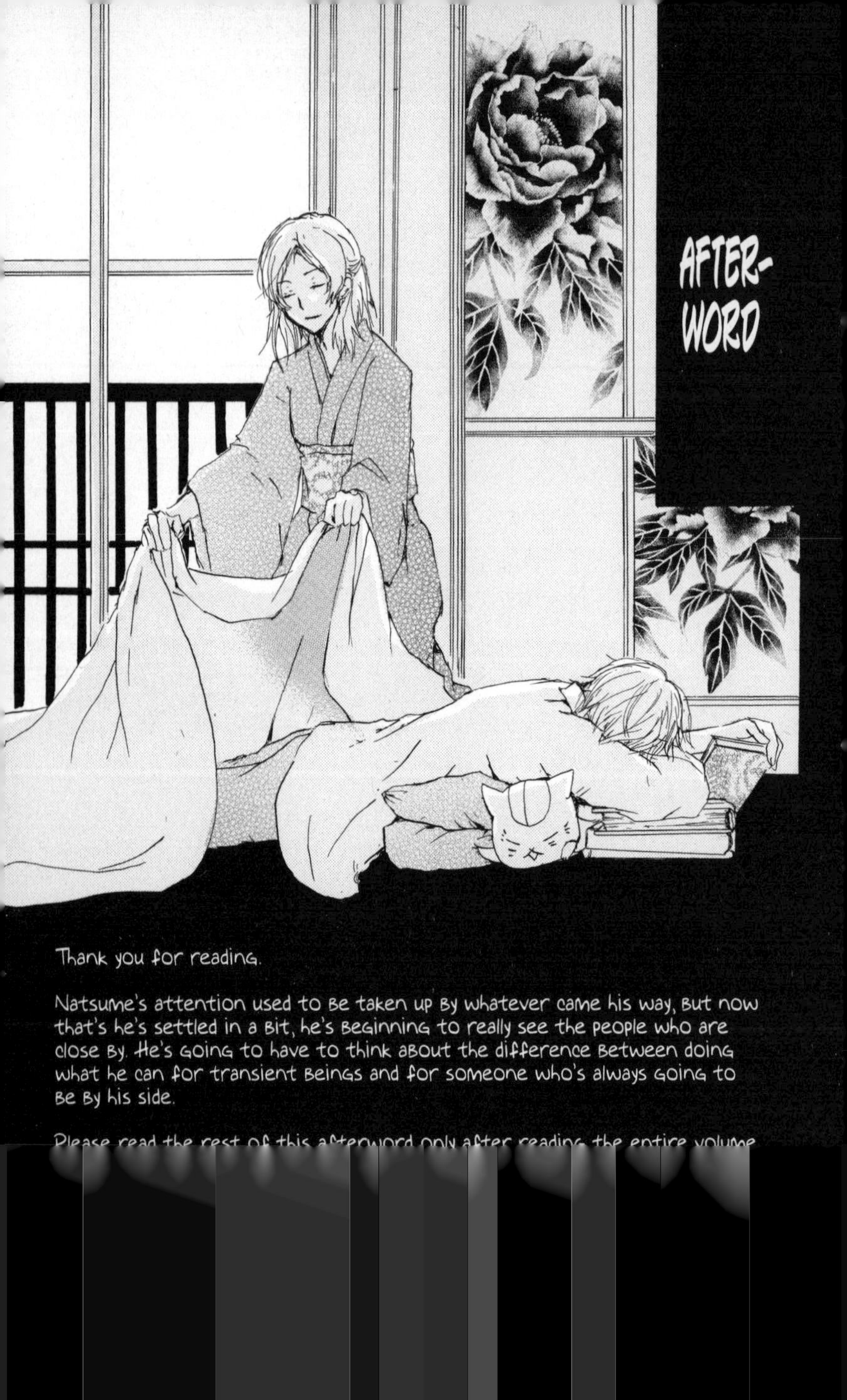

AFTER-WORD

Thank you for reading.

Natsume's attention used to be taken up by whatever came his way, but now that's he's settled in a bit, he's beginning to really see the people who are close by. He's going to have to think about the difference between doing what he can for transient beings and for someone who's always going to be by his side.

[redacted]

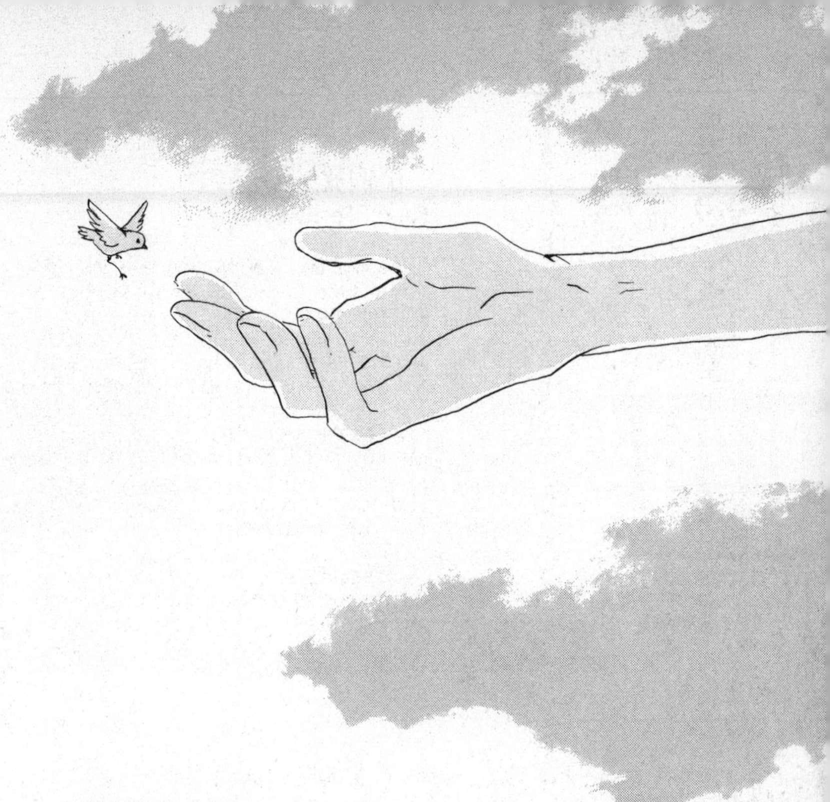

CHAPTERS 64-65

Do Not Get Involved

I hadn't drawn Taki in a while, so it was a lot of fun. She's a very important character to me, so I keep holding her back until I can use her carefully. When I draw girls, I want to feature their expressions or words even if I have to pause the rhythm of the story. I'm weirdly conflicted that it might make her upstage Natsume, the main character who's a little bit dense. That's the difficulty and fun about drawing Taki, too.

Since Natsume has been mostly involved with yokai whose gender isn't very important, he's been desensitized a bit. I hope this was an episode that reminded him that love is a bit more delicate.

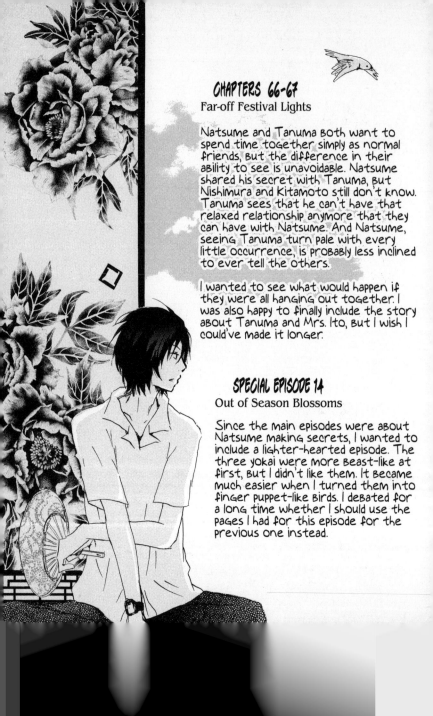

CHAPTERS 66-67
Far-off Festival Lights

Natsume and Tanuma both want to spend time together simply as normal friends, but the difference in their ability to see is unavoidable. Natsume shared his secret with Tanuma, but Nishimura and Kitamoto still don't know. Tanuma sees that he can't have that relaxed relationship anymore that they can have with Natsume. And Natsume, seeing Tanuma turn pale with every little occurrence, is probably less inclined to ever tell the others.

I wanted to see what would happen if they were all hanging out together. I was also happy to finally include the story about Tanuma and Mrs. Ito, but I wish I could've made it longer.

SPECIAL EPISODE 14
Out of Season Blossoms

Since the main episodes were about Natsume making secrets, I wanted to include a lighter-hearted episode. The three yokai were more beast-like at first, but I didn't like them. It became much easier when I turned them into finger puppet-like birds. I debated for a long time whether I should use the pages I had for this episode for the previous one instead.

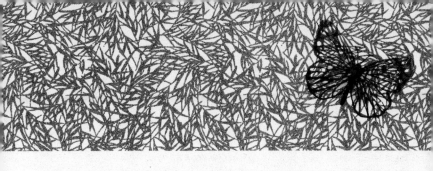

Like last volume, this one was also published during my 10th anniversary year of working on *Natsume's Book of Friends*, so a variety of projects were planned. It was a year full of happiness and gratitude, and I almost felt like I didn't deserve everything that everyone did for me. I know it's cliché, but I'll pull myself together and work hard to deliver books that my readers can enjoy.

Thank you so much for following me through all these years and 16 volumes. I'll work hard so you'll keep reading. Thank you.

Thanks to:

Tamao Ohki
Chika
Mika
Mr. Fujita
Hinata
My sister
Mr. Sato
Hoen Kikaku, Ltd.
Thank you.

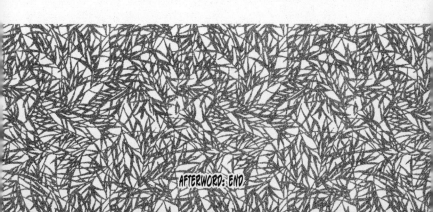

AFTERWORD: END

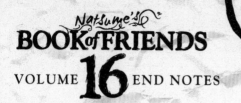

Natsume's
BOOK of FRIENDS
VOLUME 16 END NOTES

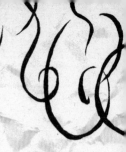

PAGE 24, PANEL 3: Sweet red bean soup

Called *shiruko* or *oshiruko* in Japanese, this is a porridge made from red beans and often served with *mochi* (chewy rice flour cakes).

PAGE 153, PANEL 1: Legendary ash

The legendary ash is from a Japanese folktale in which an old couple adopt a dog they love and cherish. One day, the dog indicates a spot in the field where they should dig, and out pours a pile of gold. The greedy neighbors kidnap the dog and try to make him repeat the feat, but all they dig up are nasty things, so they kill the dog. The kind old couple buries the dog and plants a tree in his memory. The dog later appears in their dreams and instructs them to cut down the tree to make a mortar. When they pound mochi with this mortar, out pours a pile of gold. The evil neighbors "borrow" the mortar, but all they get is rubbish, so they burn the mortar. The kind old couple takes the ash home, and the dog instructs them once again to scatter it on a bare cherry tree. It blooms, and a passing feudal lord is so impressed by the miracle that he gives them a handsome reward.

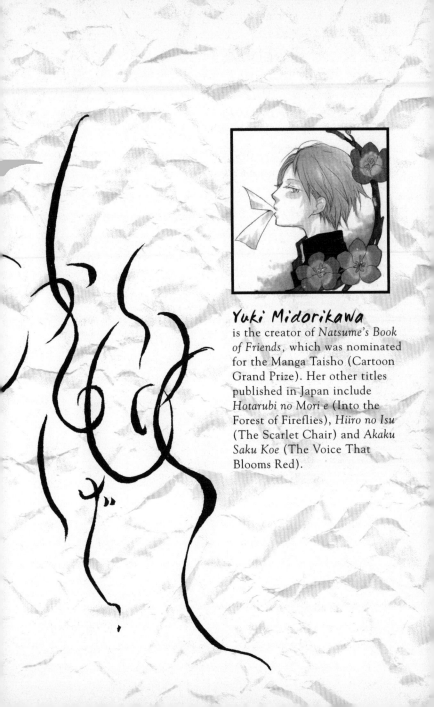

Yuki Midorikawa
is the creator of *Natsume's Book of Friends*, which was nominated for the Manga Taisho (Cartoon Grand Prize). Her other titles published in Japan include *Hotarubi no Mori e* (Into the Forest of Fireflies), *Hiiro no Isu* (The Scarlet Chair) and *Akaku Saku Koe* (The Voice That Blooms Red).

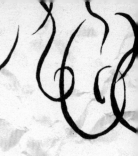

NATSUME'S BOOK OF FRIENDS
Vol. 16
Shojo Beat Edition

STORY AND ART BY *Yuki Midorikawa*

Translation & Adaptation *Lillian Olsen*
Touch-up Art & Lettering *Sabrina Heep*
Design *Fawn Lau*
Editor *Pancha Diaz*

Natsume Yujincho by Yuki Midorikawa
© Yuki Midorikawa 2013
All rights reserved.
First published in Japan in 2013 by HAKUSENSHA, Inc., Tokyo.
English language translation rights arranged with HAKUSENSHA, Inc., Tokyo.

The stories, characters and incidents mentioned in this publication are entirely fictional.

Printed in Canada

Published by VIZ Media, LLC
P.O. Box 77010
San Francisco, CA 94107

10 9 8 7 6 5 4 3 2 1
First printing, June 2014

www.viz.com

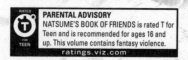
RATED **T** **FOR TEEN**
PARENTAL ADVISORY
NATSUME'S BOOK OF FRIENDS is rated T for Teen and is recommended for ages 16 and up. This volume contains fantasy violence.
ratings.viz.com

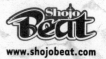
www.shojobeat.com

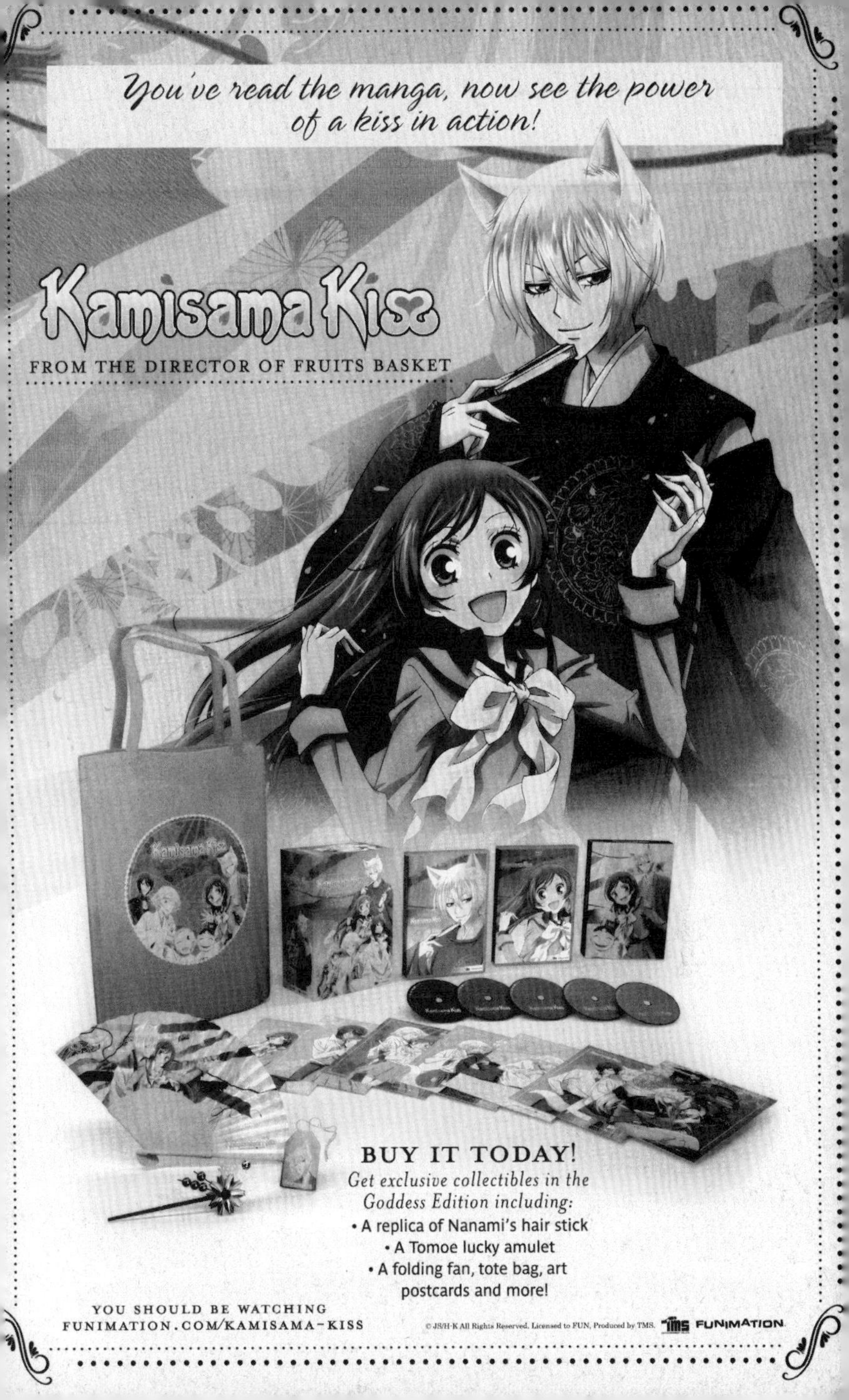
You've read the manga, now see the power of a kiss in action!
Kamisama Kiss
FROM THE DIRECTOR OF FRUITS BASKET
BUY IT TODAY!
Get exclusive collectibles in the Goddess Edition including:
• A replica of Nanami's hair stick
• A Tomoe lucky amulet
• A folding fan, tote bag, art postcards and more!
YOU SHOULD BE WATCHING
FUNIMATION.COM/KAMISAMA-KISS
© JS/H-K All Rights Reserved. Licensed to FUN, Produced by TMS.
TMS
FUNIMATION

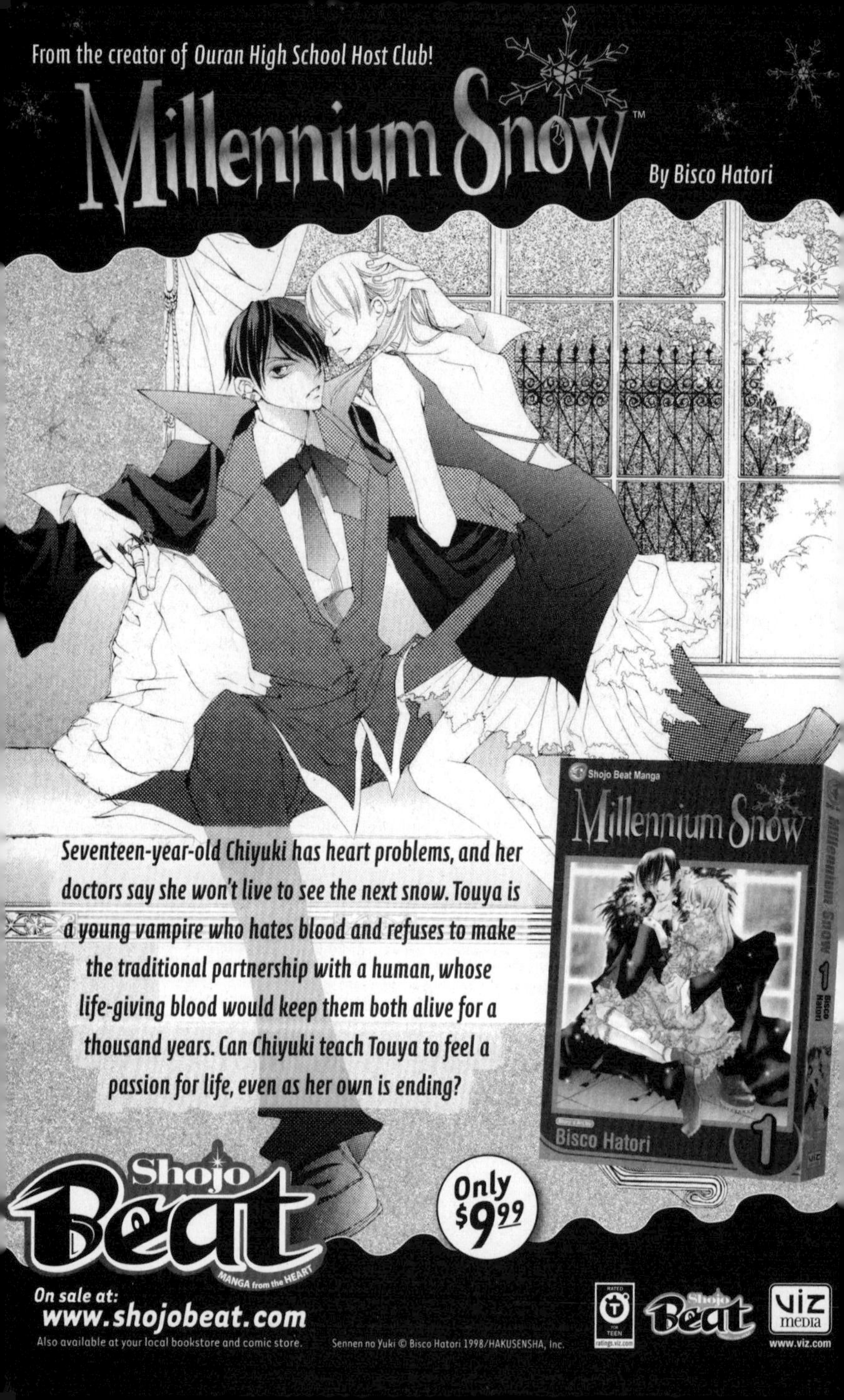
From the creator of Ouran High School Host Club!
Millennium Snow™
By Bisco Hatori
Seventeen-year-old Chiyuki has heart problems, and her doctors say she won't live to see the next snow. Touya is a young vampire who hates blood and refuses to make the traditional partnership with a human, whose life-giving blood would keep them both alive for a thousand years. Can Chiyuki teach Touya to feel a passion for life, even as her own is ending?
Shojo Beat Manga
Millennium Snow
1
Bisco Hatori
Only $9.99
Shojo Beat
MANGA from the HEART
On sale at:
www.shojobeat.com
Also available at your local bookstore and comic store.
Sennen no Yuki © Bisco Hatori 1998/HAKUSENSHA, Inc.
RATED T TEEN
ratings.viz.com
Shojo Beat
VIZ media
www.viz.com

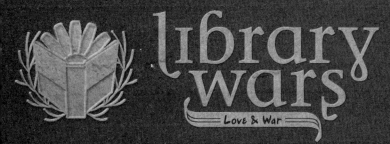

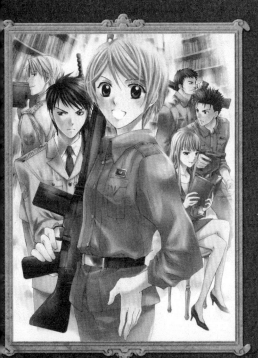
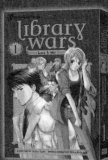

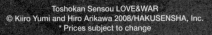

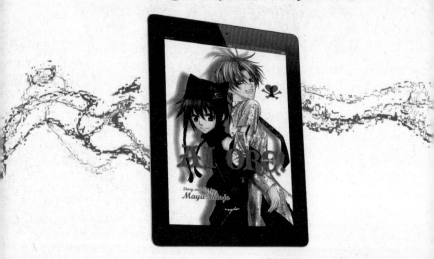
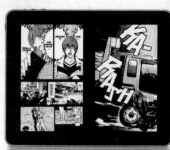
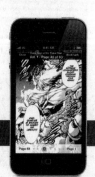

SURPRISE!

You may be reading the wrong way!

It's true: In keeping with the original Japanese comic format, this book reads from right to left— so action, sound effects, and word balloons are completely reversed. This preserves the orientation of the original artwork—plus, it's fun! Check out the diagram shown here to get the hang of things, and then turn to the other side of the book to get started!

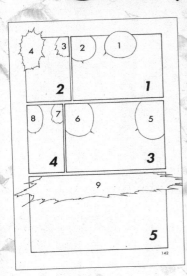

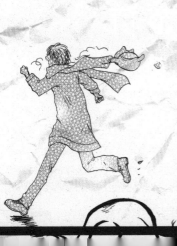

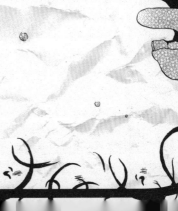

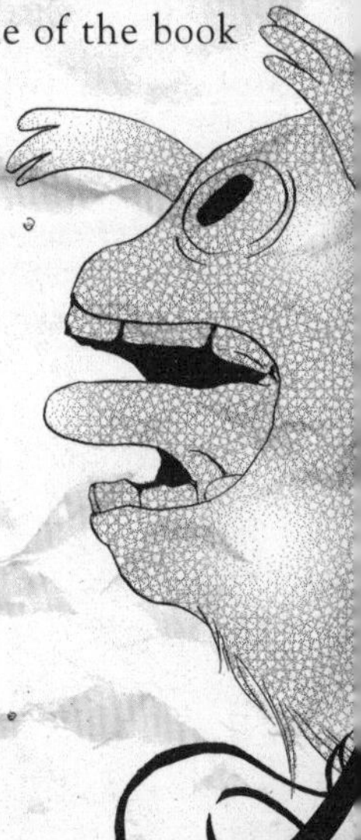